PROPHET OF BLOOD

PROPHET OF BLOOD

*The Untold Story of Ervil LeBaron
and the Lambs of God*

By
Ben Bradlee, Jr.
and Dale Van Atta

G. P. PUTNAM'S SONS
NEW YORK

Library of Congress Cataloging in Publication Data

Bradlee, Ben.
  Prophet of blood.

   1. LeBaron, Ervil.   2. Church of the Firstborn of the Fulness of Times—
Biography.   I. Van Atta, Dale, joint author.   II. Title.
BX8680.L48L422   1981   289.3'3   [B]   80-39864

ISBN 0-399-12371-7

PRINTED IN THE UNITED STATES OF AMERICA

For Martha and Lynne

CONTENTS

Section of photographs follows page 160

PROPHET OF BLOOD

1.

MORMONS, MOUNTAINS...
AND MURDER

Exodus.

Images immediately spring to mind at the word: drums pounding out a theme, fire, cries of death and exultation, arms raised with sling, bow or rifle in hand and, finally—breaking through the curtain of upheaval—a mass of people leaving for a place from which they swear they will not be moved again. A Supreme Being is generally credited as the moving force when a people develop within them that kind of indefinable, passionate yearning for a home safe from outside oppression, where a man is free to work out his own circumstances based on the sweat of his brow and the occasional blisters on his character.

The Jews can twice testify of the power—and sanctity—of exodus. The first Mosaic journey has been indelibly written on the world's consciousness, and the consequences of their European exodus following the ignominies of World War II are still being written about. Such experiences have defined Jews as a distinctive people, a race apart, and gives rise to their most stirring songs and tales.

So it has been with the Mormons of America.

Their prophet, Joseph Smith, taught them that the United States is the Promised Land of the Western Hemisphere. In fortifying this assertion, Smith wrote in documents which have been canonized and considered fact by Mormons that: God began mankind in Missouri, where Adam and Eve dwelt; Jesus Christ Himself, who spoke of feeding his "other sheep," visited the American continent following His crucifixion and Missouri is a planned stop for his second coming; Columbus was inspired to find America, and the Pilgrims to seek sanctuary here; and God had a hand in writing the Constitution—help which overrode the faults and moral failings of its human authors and deified it as a sacred document.

11

Because of such unusual revelations from their leader, Mormons clung to Missouri soil as if it were hallowed ground, which to them it was. They futilely invoked Constitutional protection when their neighbors vilified them in print and stole their land—all measures calculated to rid the midwest of the Church of Jesus Christ of Latter-day Saints, as Mormons were officially named. When Smith appealed for relief to the governor, he issued an "Order of Extermination" to the State Militia which said, "The Mormons must be treated as enemies and *must be exterminated* from the state, if necessary for the public good." Smith then petitioned the United States Congress, which turned a deaf ear. Finally, he personally pleaded with President Martin Van Buren— whom Mormons regard as a modern-day Pontius Pilate after uttering a classic hand-washing statement to Smith and his companions: "Gentlemen, your cause is just, but I can do nothing for you."

The ultimate conclusion of such coexistence in Missouri, presaging the events of World War II, was based on the blind rage of one segment of humanity against a smaller, but thriving religious group. The Mormons were tarred and feathered, flogged publicly and burned out of their homes by nightriders. So great was the animosity for—and fear of—Mormons that when a mob of 240 Missourians killed nineteen of them in one community, they refused to spare a ten-year-old boy who begged for his life. After one man in the mob shot the youngster, he observed, in words foreshadowing Hitlerian rhetoric, "Nits make lice." Finally, in Carthage, Illinois, another mob murdered the imprisoned Mormon prophet.

The resilience of the Mormon religion was tested in the months that followed. If a people are to survive, a leader must emerge whose determination and wisdom exceed the hopelessness of such a group, and Brigham Young, the Mormon Moses, was more than equal to the task. He led his pioneers in a grueling journey across country until finally, on July 24, 1847, he looked down on the then-desolate and arid Salt Lake valley, dotted only by an occasional shrub. Here, for a while, the Kingdom of God would go unchallenged. And, with His help, the Saints could make the desert blossom as a rose. Fortifying his vision, Young saw in the distance the fulfillment of the ancient prophecy of Israel: "And it shall come to pass in the last days, that . . . the Lord's House shall be established in the tops of the mountains." Imbued, then, with the kind of heroic resolution needed for empire-building, Brigham Young declared on that summer day in 1847: "This is the place."

One hundred and thirty years later Brigham Young's dream had long since been realized, and a monument erected to his visionary words. He could not have selected a spot more geographically suited to the Mormon need for isolation. The valley is more a bowl, a kind of great chalice in which the City of Saints has been built.

The western edge is rimmed by the low-lying Oquirrh mountain range whose northern tips run into the colossal Great Salt Lake. But both the inland sea and Oquirrhs are eclipsed by the mighty Wasatch

Range, an outrider of the Rockies whose craggy granite peaks shoot up to 11,000-foot heights without much warning. It is in the northeastern jut of this range that Salt Lake City is cradled, a metropolis of 500,000 which, because of its Mormon heritage and presence, is like no other. Urban ills like street crime and drugs are subdued; its slums can best be described as modest. Perhaps this is because the heart of the city is a religious center, the ten-acre Temple Square.

On the square sits the Tabernacle, a large domed building which looks like the upper half of a dirigible. From inside its doors, the Mormons have built a reputation as singing Saints since the world-famous Mormon Tabernacle Choir, backed by a 10,000-pipe organ, broadcasts a religious program each Sunday. Near the Tabernacle is the huge Mormon Temple, which took forty years to build. The Square's position as the soul of the city was fortified by Brigham Young's decision to lay out all streets according to the cardinal points of the compass, and number them according to the distance and direction they lie from the square. And atop the tallest of the Temple's six spires he ordered emplacement of the hammered-bronze, gold leaf statue of the Angel Moroni. The wingless being, with a trumpet raised high, overlooks Salt Lake, and symbolizes Mormonism; Moroni was the last of a long line of prophets, the son of Mormon, whom the Latter-day Saints believe lived and preached on the American continent around the time of Christ. His familiar figure adorns all Books of Mormon, found more frequently in area motels than Gideon's Bible.

About two-thirds of Salt Lake's population are Mormons. They provide the moral and political leadership of the state—so much so that the U.S. president, when coming to Utah, acts as if it were Rome, and visits first with the Mormon Church president and then with the state governor.

An abstemious people, the Saints generally don't drink liquor, coffee and tea; even Coca-Cola is a borderline taboo. This diet code gives rise to a proliferation of chocolate and ice cream stores, where the Mormons make up for abstaining from forbidden alcohol by overindulging in sweets. The LDS also don't smoke—gum wrappers fill their car ashtrays, family pictures their desks, and no-smoking sections the local businesses and restaurants.

Certainly the most pervasive examples of Mormon dominance are the hundreds of square, red-brick ward (a small territorial unit presided over by a bishopric) chapels, usually topped by a steeple without a cross. Some non-Mormons who live in the Salt Lake valley feel overwhelmed by the church. Wrote one California transplant to the morning newspaper: "After living in . . . the extremely one-religion city of Salt Lake for the past eight months, I've heard enough about the Mormons to last eight lifetimes. I'm tired of hearing the latest Mormon issue on the six o'clock news or seeing it draped across the front page of the paper. I could care less. I counted three Mormon churches on a seven-block trip to the grocery store. They are everywhere. . . ."

Non-Mormons are particularly irritated at being dubbed Gentiles, a categorization the Mormons even apply to Jews. And some flinch when they hear citizens refer to each other as "Brother Jones" or "Sister Smith." But most of all, non-Mormons complain about the lack of excitement in Utah where, they feel, nothing ever happens. After all, it's almost bereft of night life and, because of the dominance of a religion, robbed of the daily titillations of Los Angeles or nearby Las Vegas.

Utah is, indeed, a separate universe resting upon the twin pillars of the Mormons and their mountains. Both are bulwarks against the *outside*. Together they define the state: isolate it: identify this American Zion as a foreign mecca replete with its own mores and rites. Utah's geography and its people exude a certain hardy strength, an ambiance that is—at the same time—absolute, serene and peculiar.

In Murray, a prosperous suburb south of Salt Lake, an industrious, kindly country doctor practiced his trade in a one-story red brick building, as unassuming as the doctor himself. Dr. Rulon C. Allred was a naturopath, someone who believes in a system of therapy that relies almost exclusively on natural remedies, such as sunlight, supplemented with diet and massage. That Allred wasn't an MD hardly mattered to his patients.

A youthful seventy-one in the spring of 1977, the doctor struck most patients at once as a man of integrity: his profile was patrician, and a sense of nobility surrounded him. He was not a somber man, as the smile wrinkles which radiated from his eyes indicated and, were it not for the fact that he was slender, his zest for life might have led those he knew to describe him as robust. The corn-colored hair which had refined into a thinning full gray gave him the look of a man not so much slowed by time as enhanced by it. The doctor saw about thirty patients a day. He called all the ladies "dear" and he was not afraid to hug the men. Allred dispensed as much advice in his little offices as he did medicine, but those who felt the naturopath's hand during a massage treatment said he had the master's touch.

Though he enriched the lives of those around him, this doctor's life would not have merited mention in a book had he not also been married to eleven wives or so. Being a modern-day polygamist, he might still have avoided the public spotlight, if not for the fact that at least 2,000 of his compatriot polygamists in Salt Lake, Montana and Mexico, called Rulon C. Allred their prophet, viewing him as a religious Caesar. Only this latter role suggested he might not expect a quiet demise.

Rulon Allred may well have been trapped by his polygamist heritage. His father, Byron Harvey Allred, at one time Speaker of the Idaho House of Representatives, was a quiet rebel, and a powerful one. He clung to the principle of polygamy after Mormon renunciation of it, and took a second wife in 1903, fleeing to Mexico to raise his family in peace. Rulon was born in 1906 in Chihuahua, the first of ten children, to one of Byron's wives. Father Allred ordered the siblings born after Rulon to look up to their older brother and follow his lead.

It was only after Rulon's graduation from the Los Angeles Naturo-pathic College in 1930, that he and his father, for the first time, were at odds. Byron Allred met an old Mormon missionary companion claiming to be head of the Mormon Church and wishing to re-establish divinely granted polygamy. Byron wrote a virtual Bible for the polygamist leader in 1933, *A Leaf in Review*, which supported his friend and the religious continuation of plural marriage. This prompted the discon-certed Rulon, an active Mormon, to write a number of earnest letters he expected would seriously challenge his father's beliefs. But oddly enough, instead of son convincing father, the reverse began to occur and Rulon's wife, threatened to leave him if he did not get the absurd notion of additional wives out of his head. But Rulon could not, and she left him.

Rulon's medical practice drastically dwindled when fellow Mormons learned of his imminent excommunication. Alone during some of the rougher years of the Depression, Rulon turned to menial work in the oil fields of Long Beach. When his father died in 1937, Rulon moved to Salt Lake City where he enjoyed some of his brightest years—particu-larly since, despite his religious beliefs, many patients came to the doctor's downtown office after Utah granted him a license to practice in 1939.

He bought a three-story house on a twenty-acre farm that was a children's paradise. The suburban residence also became a gathering place for Salt Lake valley polygamists and it was not unusual to have fifty persons seated at the doctor's feet on a Sunday.

The Allred family's rosy existence came to an abrupt halt in 1944 when a three-state police raid netted forty-six polygamists, including Dr. Allred. They were charged with a variety of crimes: "unlawful cohabitation," a conspiracy to "advocate, promote and teach, encourage and advise polygamous marriages," violation of the Mann Act (a kidnapping law) and even a federal obscenity charge—which was dropped when it was revealed the "obscene" literature included Mor-mon scriptures used by all LDS members.

In May 1945, Dr. Allred was one of fifteen sentenced to serve up to five years in the Utah State Prison. He and ten others were freed the following December after they promised neither to promote nor live polygamy again. Unable to abide by such an agreement, the doctor fled to Mexico. When he returned to Utah in 1948, he voluntarily turned himself in for jumping parole, but jailers were reluctant to incarcerate Rulon again, and he was released within a month. He thereupon became extremely cautious and secretive about his movements. Letters and phone calls included code words, and locations of family members were never spoken of openly. When, in the early 1950s, an even larger polygamist raid occurred, Allred was nowhere to be found.

In 1960, Rulon Allred hit his full stride as a religious leader. Starting with a small split-off polygamist sect which first met in a brother's garage, Rulon built a congregation of more than 2,000. He was as wily as he was kind, and his winning gentility was only occasionally broken by a stern but loving rebuke of one of his followers.

Rulon Allred was never more at home than when he offered a discourse on polygamy, which he called the "most holy pearl" God ever gave man. "There are more righteous women in the world than there are righteous men," Allred explained to a newsman. "And every righteous woman deserves a righteous man. Plural marriage has nothing to do with lustfulness and sensuality. It is a deeply spiritual matter." As could be expected, the sacred principle was sometimes terribly abused, Allred acknowledged. "Many men who are living plural marriage are unkind and inconsiderate of their wives while pursuing their own desires," he tactfully put it. His brother Owen, who is tearful when he speaks of abusers, said he and Rulon deplored the existence of some polygamists who had become the "worst scum of the streets." Both sensed it was from these spotted practitioners that their trouble would always come.

It was difficult for Rulon Allred to discuss polygamy without criticizing the large, world-recognized Mormon Church, which had abandoned the practice. Comparing himself to Martin Luther, Allred said he could show ninety-five areas in which the Mormons had changed their doctrines, proving the need for a reformation. Each time the church officially denounced the practice of polygamy in a statement, Allred would tell his faithful the Mormon Church "is walking in darkness at noonday." For the moment, Rulon said, "we are not able to get into [their] temples, brothers and sisters, because they have us locked out. We're not welcome in their churches; we're a bunch of scalawags because we believe in the fullness of the gospel. And that's a terrible sin today."

Rulon Allred was not particularly afraid of death. He once began a sermon, "I do not know how long God will permit you or me or any of the rest of us to live," and advised his faithful to make the best of life while they had it. Because of a bleeding ulcer, he had already faced death three times, and been miraculously healed, according to his wives. The last restoration, in 1965, had been aided by a physician's knife.

But friends and family worried more that Rulon would die an unnatural death—the victim of a religious fanatic's whims. He had been threatened by some rival polygamists and, after one of his wives dreamed that someone had walked into his office and shot him, he was guarded by an armed relative for a short time. Though a peaceful man, Rulon once kept a gun under the seat of his car for self-defense.

In 1976, Rulon Allred started dropping hints that he would not be around much longer. Along with these, he stepped up his sermons and talked about the urgency of accomplishing the Lord's work. Some of his loyal flock, who took comfort in his gentle and serene ministrations, became alarmed in the spring of 1977 when he began telling them with uncharacteristic foreboding that "something was going to happen" which would thrust their group, and polygamy in general, back into the limelight. "I plead with you," he urged, "to get your lives in order, because if you don't, your iniquities will be exposed to the world." Allred was recorded on tape making essentially the same statement on three different occasions that spring, each time before an audience of 250 to 500 people. Pressed to be more specific, Allred replied he could not. He was just sure "something" would happen.

His last major sermon, on April 3, 1977, focused on the wickedness of the world. "There is so much to say that one hardly knows where he should start, or whether it should be left unsaid," Allred began. The Lord's people must be prepared for ill times. Already, he said, "we cannot pray in our schools, we cannot salute the flag . . . we cannot own our own land and our own water. If you think that isn't true, you will see it is true. The tribulations that are coming upon the U.S. will surpass your and my vision to realize. The fire of the Lord will go through this land in revolution and in trouble until it is purged." He concluded that the faithful must expect to be martyrs. "In the past forty years, thirty-two million people have been cruelly murdered for political reasons. *The principal reason was that they believed in God.* [We] must be a godless people to live."

On May 7, Rulon attended a wedding and—unusual for him—he embraced most of those there, expressing personal appreciation for each, as if it were his final word of parting. Sunday the eighth was Mother's Day, and he took each of his wives aside and lavished praise on her, promising his continual devotion. He held his regular Monday-evening meeting with the family, during which they discussed religion and enjoyed activities. Wife Mabel was darning socks. It was a comfortable evening, primarily because Rulon Allred exuded an air of tranquillity—the kind of serenity that often invited comparison to a poem about a family doctor who was always there: "Half the people had the notion that the doctor could not die."

Tuesday was always the heaviest work day for Rulon Allred—and May 10 was no different. At least there were no indications that it would be "a day of infamy for this nation, for this state, for this city," as his brother Marvin Allred would later say. Rulon saw patients in his office every weekday except Thursday until 3:30 P.M., but on Tuesday he permitted late scheduling.

By 4:30 P.M., Dr. Allred had already seen thirty-eight patients, and three sisters from Heber City, ninety minutes distance, were receiving treatment in back rooms of the modest five-room brick building. Two elderly patients sat on a west wall couch in the twelve-seat waiting room. Next to them, on another couch, a forty-three-year-old millionaire businessman, Richard Bunker, waited nervously, thumbing through a *Reader's Digest*. Bunker had no appointment, but was allowed to drop in on the doctor for business discussions. He had invented a new printing process but was edged out of the company which utilized it. He leaned toward Allred and his group. Bunker had donated a large western Utah ranch to Allred, whom he'd known for twenty-four years. But Bunker still ran the ranch, and was in this day to discuss some personnel problems and policy changes. Allred had noticed Bunker once during his forty-minute wait, and nodded, indicating he would see him soon.

Melba Allred, one of Rulon's wives for more than forty years and his personal receptionist/secretary/nurse for seventeen years, scurried around the office handling patients and calls. The latest call had come from Rulon's close brother Owen, who was second behind Rulon in the religious leadership. Owen had asked Rulon if he had time to talk to Bunker, who had come to Owen about the business matter. Rulon said there were patients waiting, but he could probably squeeze Bunker in for a few moments.

"I love you, dear brother," Owen said, delivering his customary emotional send-off.

"I love you, too, Owen," answered Rulon, "and you're going to have to take the responsibility from here on." Owen Allred would think nothing of the apparent non sequitur until twenty minutes had passed.

Fifteen minutes later, at 4:45 P.M., two young women strolled into Rulon Allred's office.

Both were of medium height, between five feet five and five feet seven inches, of medium build, and in their early twenties. One, whom Bunker thought attractive, sat next to him on the couch. She wore a ribbed red T shirt and faded Levi's; a purse was draped from her shoulder to the opposite hip, which was as distinctively curvaceous as her chest. He discounted the girl's companion, who strode over to the open door which separated the waiting room from the office. She also wore Levi's and had a purse draped over her shoulder. But she had donned a blue ski parka which partially covered her white T shirt where her bustline made barely a wrinkle. That, taken with her rough face, made her decidedly less attractive, Bunker thought. But he'd be polite, if introduced, because she seemed to be a relative who was familiar with the office and expected to see Rulon unannounced.

Through the plate glass window above her desk, Melba saw the two girls walk into the office. But she was busy, only glancing up for a moment and seeing the girl standing in the doorway. Melba stepped into a back room. "I thought she was there to pick something up," the receptionist later recounted.

Rulon gave his wife a weary smile when she stepped into the back room where he was treating one of the Heber City sisters. "I'll take over," she offered, mindful that he had only lately rallied from a winter bout with the flu.

"Thank you, dear," he said, drawing a sample of blood from the woman's finger. He took the vial into the hall outside, while Melba plugged in a vibrator and began massaging the patient.

Rulon saw the lone girl standing near the doorway and brushed past her, entering the laboratory diagnosis room to the girl's left. He only reached a few steps before he heard a noise behind him and started to turn around.

Before he was fully turned, Rulon saw a small black gun the girl was pointing at him—only an instant before she fired two shots which ripped through his body.

"Oh my God! My God!" he yelled, pushing his hands out in front of him, trying to block the bullets. His expressionless assailant pumped five more shots into him as he fell, and turned around to walk casually away.

Hearing shots and her husband's scream, Melba came running into the hallway in time to see the girl departing. The girl sitting next to Bunker calmly stood up when her companion came in view. Bunker saw that she, too, now had a gun in her right hand. The pair strode out the front door and shut it behind them.

Rulon's eyes and mouth were half open, his face white, when Melba reached him. He was sprawled out on the laboratory floor, hands and forearms raised, his elbows still quivering from the impact of hitting the floor. Blood was pulsating from his chest, and she saw bullet holes in his neck and head. "He's been shot!" she cried out. "Oh, what shall I do?" After a few seconds she managed to get up and hurry to her desk to call the police. As she began to dial 411—the information number, which was all she could remember—she looked through the glass window and saw Bunker open the front door to a sight that horrified her.

Hoping to see the getaway car and perhaps write down the license number, Bunker was surprised to find the door opening against him. The same two girls were coming back in. His first instinct was to grapple with one of them. "I'm not brave, I was just in trouble with nowhere to go," he recalls. While he managed an armlock with his left arm around one girl's neck, pinning her gun against the wall at the same time, the other girl pointed the small weapon three inches from his face.

"Please don't kill me!" he pleaded. "I'm a father with a lot of children." At this point, the assailant may have pulled the trigger only to find the gun empty.

After a few tense seconds, Bunker released his neck grip on the girl, gave both of them a hefty push out the door and slammed it. Jamming the door with his foot, he looked for a lock. There was only a key-operated latch and, knowing he could be shot through the wooden door, he spied a bathroom at the end of the waiting room and hoped he could make it there.

When he moved away from the door, both girls shoved it open in time to see Bunker back-pedaling the eighteen-foot length of the waiting room. One stopped, holding her gun with both hands in a police grip, and fired. The shot went high, but speeded Bunker's flight to the restroom where he shut and locked the door.

While one girl covered the waiting room, the other walked through the waiting room where Melba blocked her way, standing between the girl and her prone husband. With almost surreal desperation, the two confronted each other, until Melba finally moved away, thinking her husband was dead already—and that he would want her to live.

The girl, who had apparently obtained the loaded .38 from her companion, now aimed it a few inches from Allred's head and missed, causing powder burns on the doctor's face. The bullet crashed through the wall, ricocheted in the waiting room before it tore through a floorboard near the restroom, where Bunker heard the wood splinter and thought he was still being shot at. It was the last shot fired.

This final burst startled a fifth eyewitness, Mary Swigart, fifty, who had just entered the office. The two killers, grimly emotionless, brushed past her, one of them holding a dark curly wig in her hand.

For a moment, Mary stood there, dumbfounded. "What's the matter with you?" she blurted out a second later, reaching for one of them. "Are you nuts?"

Apparently oblivious to her presence, one of the girls said to the other, "Hurry, let's get out of here!" Those were the only words spoken by the two during the entire sequence of events, which lasted less than five minutes. Melba knelt beside her husband after the second assault, and kissed him. "Sweetheart, speak to me," she begged, but knew she'd hear nothing. She went back to the phone and, seeing Mary Swigart, said, "They've just shot the doctor."

"Oh, no." Mary was stunned for a moment. "Can I help?"

"Do you know what the number for emergency is?"

"911," Mary responded, and stepped outside quickly to tell another arriving patient, Natalie Kimball, "Those two girls just shot the doctor." They had walked rapidly by, one of them swinging a wig in one of her hands. Half a block away, Boyd Hansen had finished the day's work and was waiting for a bus when he heard "a couple of pops." He saw the two girls step out of the office, go back in and return to the street, finally disappearing north up an alley next to the corner gas station.

About the same time, the Heber City sisters were emerging from the back rooms. One had hidden behind a bed and another was too paralyzed to move. "I stayed back in the room because I was afraid to come out for fear I would get shot," she later told one policeman.

A half-dozen Murray City police officers led by Detective Sergeant Paul Forbes converged on the scene at 133 East 4800 South within two or three minutes of the emergency call.

Forbes opened the door and saw Bunker on the phone, relating the event to someone. The eyewitness was in a state of panic. In the struggle, he'd lost a fountain pen, sunglasses and a calculator with a pouch that had contained one of his business cards, fully identifying him to the assailants who had presumably taken these possessions. Melba was slumped in a chair, apparently in shock. Forbes strode to the doctor's prone body and felt for a pulse beneath the reddened white smock. He could see gunshot wounds in the doctor's head, throat and chest. The paramedics arrived and, though they knew Allred was dead, worked on the victim. By law they were required to continue until Forbes had called Dr. Clifford N. Cutler, who could officially pronounce him dead, from across the street. Dr. Cutler looked at Allred's fixed and dilated pupils, found no respiration and observed four gunshot wounds—one in the front of Allred's neck, one in his right shoulder, another in his lower left chest and another in front of his right ear. Allred was quite dead.

Forbes detailed his men to interview the witnesses, sketch and photograph the murder scene, mark the body's position and bag the shell casings scattered around the floor. A brief description of the assailants was obtained from Bunker and broadcast over the police radio. Among those who heard it was Paul Forbes' brother, Dick, an investigator for the Salt Lake County Attorney's Office, with a background in polygamy investigations. Dick headed for the scene immediately. He knew that Rulon Allred was the influential leader of thousands of polygamists, which immediately gave the murder investigation an odd tinge. Arriving on the scene, he excitedly blurted out to his brother, "Do you realize this will probably be the biggest case Utah will ever have?"

News of the murder flashed quickly through the Salt Lake valley. Allred's followers lined the streets outside the office, many of them weeping. Owen sped to his brother's office in a truck and begged to see him. After forty-five minutes, police allowed him in. He knelt over his brother's body and tried to touch him. "What am I going to do without you, Rulon?" Owen implored, and wept.

The police had a few immediate theories. The girls might have shot the doctor in hopes of stealing some drugs; they could have been disgruntled patients or relatives of unhappy patients who wanted the doctor dead; or it could have been a religious assassination—the least likely possibility in the normally humdrum Utah world of crime.

The phone rang constantly in the office with offers of help and questions from disbelieving associates. About 5:20 P.M. came the strangest call of all. When Dick Forbes picked up the phone, a female voice laughed and then hung up.

The first suspect in the case was Alex Joseph, probably the most famous polygamist in the Western Hemisphere. An ex-policeman himself, Joseph agreed without hesitation to meet with Paul and Dick Forbes, and another detective.

Alex had become Allred's greatest nemesis. Once they had been close—particularly after Joseph was drummed out of the Mormon Church for expressing an interest in Allred's sect. Joseph brought converts and $72,000 with him to an Allred commune in Montana's Bitterroot Valley. Joseph cultivated Allred's friendship, and even offered to take the responsibility for some financial transactions Rulon had bungled. But he began to see chinks in Rulon's religious armor, and grew disenchanted. At one point, Alex recalled, he was surprised to hear the self-proclaimed pacifist Allred say that "he had a right to assassinate anyone he wants to."

Rulon and Alex had a falling out in 1970 and Alex left the group. Given Alex's outspoken views, Allred knew he would never remain quiet about their private activities if he ever left. Alex had often debated the necessity for secrecy among polygamist practitioners, maintaining it created an image of shame about their beliefs. Rulon was right about his fears; his low-profile group was slowly "exposed" by Alex's antics— from a land fight in federal court to a movie he had made of himself.

Alex told journalists that donations of Allred's thousands of followers had made the doctor a millionaire. In fact, in 1977, Allred had control over millions of dollars in property as the Presiding Elder of the Apostolic United Brethren (AUB—within the group sometimes called "All Us Boys"). His own estimates showed an annual receipt of tithing amounting to at least $125,000.

Alex didn't stop there. He told of Rulon's wives and as many other secrets as newsmen were interested in. He labeled Rulon and his ilk the "dour-faced" polygamists who gave the marital style a bad name, pawning off a viable life-style as an excuse for religion. The media and talk-show hosts loved Alex's brand of polygamy, his candor, his humor and the machismo of the pistol-packing ex-Marine. With a dozen beautiful wives arrayed behind him, Joseph could make the practice seem almost desirable to the most monogamous newsman. Once those very wives had told reporters they'd do anything for Alex, including murder, which statements had invited headline comparisons to Charles Manson. Within minutes of the Allred murder, one of Alex's ex-associates called the doctor's office and informed police that Joseph must have ordered the hit.

When Paul and Dick Forbes came to call, Alex immediately put his cards up front. He would not act as a witness in the case, but he would help the police investigation as much as he could. First of all, he stated, neither he nor any of his group had committed the murder. He then proceeded to offer background information on various polygamist groups, and pointed the finger at one rival leader, Ervil LeBaron.

According to the official police report:

"Alex stated that for a number of years there has been an ongoing feud between the various different organized colonies of polygamists throughout the western states and it is common knowledge among all of them that Ervil LeBaron had made threats toward leaders in all organizations indicating that he would take their lives at one time or another."

The detectives were well aware of LeBaron, since a man who had investigated him, Salt Lake County sheriff's sergeant John Llewellyn, had brought his immense files to the murder scene. But they were surprised that Alex was so sure it was LeBaron, not dopers or upset patients, who had killed Allred.

Little more than a week later, Alex Joseph was quite willing to charge Ervil LeBaron with the murder publicly. He agreed to a May 22 local television interview with KTVX reporter Phil Riesen. The hour show captivated Utahans, who began to realize this was a very unusual murder. (Few of them even knew that polygamy was still practiced in their Utah towns.) Riesen quickly zeroed in on the Allred murder. "Do you know who killed Rulon Allred?"

"Yes, I do," Alex replied.

"Who?"

"Ervil LeBaron's group."

"Where are they?"

"They're on the underground," Alex surmised. "They're hiding and they themselves, the LeBarons, from what I can understand—and I've had [little] personal contact with them—but, they brag—and you hear this bravado—of having killed seventeen people. The law enforcement agencies of the United States are aware of nine. . . . I'm surprised they haven't already come out to claim [the Allred murder], and they will pretty shortly."

Riesen was well aware that most viewers had never heard of Ervil LeBaron, or of the polygamist subculture that existed in the Salt Lake valley and parts of the west and Mexico. So he asked Alex, "Explain to me why a rival polygamist group would want to assassinate the head of another polygamist group. What is the reasoning behind that?"

"The Pope syndrome," Alex began. "Your religious leaders are always invincible and infallible. Now, if you can blow one full of .38 caliber holes, you prove that he's not infallible and that he's not invincible. . . . Once he's buried, then all these people who believe . . . wander off."

"Who would have ordered the assassination in the [LeBaron] group?" Riesen asked.

"That one wonderful, mighty and strong, invincible, infallible Ervil LeBaron!"

"Where is he now?"

"Hiding. He's probably hiding up in Ogden. He might be your next door neighbor. . . ."

2.

FUNDAMENTALISM

The murder of Rulon Allred—along with a spate of renewed publicity directed at the mysterious, underground world of polygamy—set skeletons to rattling in the Mormon closet. Though church officials hastened to point out that both Allred and the man police quickly concluded was responsible for his murder, Ervil LeBaron, had been excommunicated from Mormondom years ago, they feared that all the commotion would nevertheless prompt an anti-LDS backlash from a Gentile majority which harbored suspicions that most Mormons were polygamists anyway.

The fact is they are not, but plural marriage—illegal in the United States since 1862 and banned by the Mormons in 1890—continues to flourish in the west. Estimates of the number of people still practicing what the government once called "lewd and lascivious cohabitation" vary widely, but 30,000 is a commonly accepted figure.

Joseph Smith made polygamy a sacred commandment of the church in 1843, citing the Biblical charge to "multiply and replenish the Earth," as well as the fact that previous prophets had had several wives. Despite this holy precedent, some believe that it was the handsome Smith's known appreciation for a well-turned ankle ("Whenever I see a pretty woman I have to pray for grace," he once said) that prompted him to have a "revelation" on polygamy as a way of institutionalizing sexual variety. Even Smith's first wife, Emma, doubted that her husband was promulgating the word of God, and in a jealous rage once threw one of his plural wives out in the snow.

Despite the word of Joseph, many of his followers, who came from puritanical New England backgrounds, balked at the command to polygamize. In fact, scholars believe that less than 20 percent of Mor-

24

mondom actually practiced plural marriage. Even Brigham Young commented that he "desired the grave" upon learning of Smith's revelation. However, Brigham gamely resolved that "we must gird up our loins and fulfill this, just as we would any other duty." He eventually overcame his reservations, did his duty with twenty-seven wives, and concluded that polygamy was a noble practice that kept women chaste and helped rid society of prostitution.

"Our government says that a man may ruin and destroy as many of the daughters of Eve as he pleases, but he is forbidden to acknowledge but one as his wife," Brigham complained.

The Saints developed rationales for polygamy as the times dictated. Since the church had many enemies, it is felt that plural marriage was an excellent way to increase membership as quickly as possible. Another more benevolent purpose of plural marriage was to provide companionship and financial security for even the homeliest of spinsters. No woman, it was thought, should have to suffer through life alone.

But if polygamy was becoming more and more acceptable inside the Utah Territory, it was bitterly controversial almost everywhere else, and in the late nineteenth century one of the hottest debates in the nation was whether Salt Lake City was a place of God or a den of iniquity. Congress banned plural marriage in 1862, the U.S. Supreme Court determined in 1875 that the practice was "odious throughout Anglo-American culture" and efforts to convince the Saints to abandon their sacred "principle" were stepped up. These led to the disinfranchisement of polygamists, the disincorporation of the Mormon Church, the confiscation of church property and money and the fining or jailing of leading Mormons.

The turn-of-the-century antipolygamy crusade trumpeted out of Washington and elsewhere produced some of the most colorful and virulent rhetoric in the country's political annals. Polygamy itself was referred to as a "foul conspiracy" perpetrated by the "vile infernal Mormons . . . those sallow skinned devils with their swollen genitals." In such a climate there developed a deep split within Mormondom over the wisdom of continuing to practice plural marriage. Finally, in 1890, church officials decided to cut their losses. In a proclamation known as "the Manifesto," issued as part of a deal for Utah statehood, then-Mormon president Wilford Woodruff decreed that polygamy would be outlawed, and that any church member caught continuing to practice it would be excommunicated. Woodruff said the Lord had shown him a vision of what terrible persecution the church would yet undergo if plural marriages continued.

Most Mormons, anxious to join the mainstream of society, greeted this news thankfully and accepted it as a revelation from God. A rather vocal minority, however, viewed the decision as a sellout of one of the church's most sacred religious principles. Now held anathema by their own church as well as by Gentile society, polygamists were driven underground where, according to popular myth, they lived in a taboo-ridden netherworld. Scattering to avoid newly coordinated attempts by the government and LDS officials to stamp out their lifestyle, they settled throughout the west. Many took refuge across the border in Canada and Mexico.

Within the Mormon Church itself, however, some officials secretly continued to perform plural marriages. In 1906, Mathias Cowley and John W. Taylor, two members of the Quorum of the Twelve (the church's governing body), were stripped of their positions for still practicing polygamy.

Several small plural marriage groups formed and coexisted quietly during the early 1900s. But it was not until 1929 that a group later called the Fundamentalists emerged as a united polygamous front, of sorts, under the leadership of Lorin Woolley. Woolley was a charismatic who, along with his father, John, had served as a bodyguard to the third president of Mormondom, John Taylor—a polygamous fugitive who died while still on the run from federal lawmen.

According to Woolley, a few leaders of the church met with President Taylor on September 26, 1886, and presented him with a document which advocated the banning of plural marriage so that persecution against Mormons could stop. A consensus on what to do could not be reached, so it was agreed that Taylor would "take the matter up with the Lord." That night, as he was standing guard outside the president's room, Woolley said he saw a light under the door and heard the voices of three men talking inside, despite the fact he had allowed no one to enter. The next morning, Woolley claimed, Taylor told him he had been visited by Joseph Smith and Jesus Christ.

In another meeting that same day, Taylor told twelve persons they were each obligated to continue the principle of plural marriage whether or not the church renounced it in the future. During this eight-hour meeting, Woolley wrote that Taylor "frequently arose and stood above the floor, and his countenance and being were so enveloped by light and glory that it was difficult . . . to look upon him."

After this session, Woolley claimed that President Taylor called still another meeting in which he "set apart" five men—including the two Woolleys—and conferred upon them the highest priesthood authority on earth. A sixth man was allegedly set apart later.

Though a version of these claims were published in 1912, it wasn't until 1929—when every supposed witness except Lorin Woolley was dead—that Woolley first asserted the right to govern for the Lord on earth.

Predictably, the LDS hierarchy dismissed all this as delusions of grandeur from an excommunicated fringe element. But despite the church disavowal, Woolley began garnering a substantial number of excommunicated Mormons upset over the 1890 abolishment of polygamy. He established a "Council of Friends"—seven men he claimed held authority over the Mormon Church. Named to the council besides Woolley himself (the senior and presiding member) were: J. Leslie

Broadbent, John Y. Barlow, Joseph W. Musser, Charles Zitting, Legrand Woolley and Louis Kelsch. Broadbent inherited leadership of the growing polygamous faction when Woolley died in 1934, but when Broadbent also died a short time later, he was succeeded by John Barlow. Barlow added two new members to the council—LeRoy Johnson and Marion Hammon—even though Woolley had decreed that Kelsch would be the last man ever "called."

Fundamentalists revere the memory of Barlow, for it was he who started the famous polygamist colony in Short Creek, Arizona—an unpoliced, wild and lonely strip of virtually uninhabited gorge-cut desert north of the Grand Canyon, straddling the Utah-Arizona state line. In this inaccessible setting, Barlow hoped to nurture the principle of plural marriage and build the cornerstone of a polygamous movement that he and his followers believed would eventually sweep the earth and bring the Mormon Church and other critics to their knees.

Authorities tried to stamp out Short Creek before it could get started by conducting a raid in 1935 in which three men and two women were arrested. But the colony kept growing and by 1942 it had formally organized as the United Order, a traditional Mormon concept of communal living in which all money, property and food are pooled for the common good. The Short Creek population reached thirty-six men, eighty-six women and 263 children.

In the early years of Short Creek, before the substantial population increase, there was an occasional raid, and gossip about goings-on in the colony was rife in parts of Arizona and Utah. But the situation was generally tolerated. When a group of people were that isolated and bothered no one else, few seemed to want to make an issue out of their religious quirks. This was, after all, a land of rugged individualism where people believed in "live and let live."

However, in the early fifties welfare eligibility workers in Kingman, Arizona, the seat of government for Mohave County—some 400 road miles southwest of Short Creek—noticed an ever-increasing stream of applicants for welfare from women who listed the same man as their husband. As the requests mounted, there were more children and more wives per man. It was also noticed that the age of the wives was sometimes only thirteen to fifteen. The age of consent in Arizona was eighteen, and no girl could marry below the age of sixteen, even with the approval of her parents. If she did, and became pregnant, her husband was liable for statutory rape. Under such circumstances, there was mounting pressure among Arizona state and local officials to do something about the Short Creek "problem" once and for all. Governor Howard Pyle assumed jurisdiction over the case and it soon became his cause célèbre.

A raid was planned for more than a year. Pyle got the Arizona state legislature to appropriate $50,000 to be used in the investigation and lawmen set about gathering evidence. Undercover agents, some disguised as Hollywood movie scouts, passed through Short Creek. Warrants charging 122 adults with conspiracy to commit polygamy, rape, bigamy and other crimes were secured. To ensure maximum publicity, Pyle had reporters around the country tipped off to the operation weeks before it was to occur.

The press dubbed it "The Great Love-Nest Raid," and when it finally occurred on July 26, 1953, Pyle went on the radio and explained to the citizens of Arizona that a "state of insurrection" existed at Short Creek which required swift and sure action, lest the polygamists expand their number by "thousands" within the next ten years.

In sharp contrast to Pyle, Utah's governor, J. Bracken Lee, refused to support the raid. "If we're going to wink about a guy fooling around with several women, we shouldn't persecute these people who are taking good care of their families," he said.

Moving under cover of darkness heightened by an eclipse of the moon, more than 100 Arizona law-enforcement officers swept into Short Creek in a two-pronged attack from the north and east. The great bust was to have been a big surprise, but as it turned out the Short Creekers knew all about it and had stationed boys outside of town to shoot off firecrackers as the police approached. So it was the raiders who were surprised when they arrived to find the entire colony out waiting for them, dressed in their Sunday best and singing "America."

The men were arrested and hauled away to the county jail in Kingman, while most of the women and children were taken to Phoenix. Trials were started for the men and convictions secured, but most sentences were suspended as the costs of keeping the families soared to more than $1,000 a day. It wasn't long before the men, women and children returned to Short Creek, where they remain to this day—the only change being that they have renamed their community Colorado City.

The patriarch of Short Creek, John Barlow, died in 1951, two years before the raid. He was succeeded as leader of the Council of Friends by white-haired Joseph Musser, who, during Barlow's tenure, had gained considerable influence among polygamists through the publication of *Truth* magazine, a monthly that preached the Fundamentalist gospel. Musser had been in ill health since 1949 when he suffered a paralytic stroke, and some members of the council opposed his leadership because they doubted he could function properly. This friction reached the point of an outright schism when Musser named Rulon Allred to the council and made him his special counselor. Allred had been treating the ailing Musser for months, and rebellious council members charged that the appointment was simply Musser's way of thanking Allred.

Fundamentalist Elders on the council were also angered by Musser's surprise choice of a Mexican Indian named Margarito Bautista to be an Apostle of the Council. Bautista was an intellectual from a town named Ozumba, south of Mexico City. He had come to the Mormon colonies in

Chihuahua at an early age to learn English and LDS doctrine. From there he went to Salt Lake City where he became a dedicated Temple worker and rose quickly within the LDS establishment. He finally left Salt Lake in his fifties to bring the gospel back to Mexico, but he gradually concluded that the church was straying too far from the teachings of Joseph Smith, and he turned to Fundamentalism.

When the Elders refused to endorse either Allred or Bautista, Musser retaliated by dissolving the old council and forming a new one with Allred as his heir apparent. Musser's move effectively split the Fundamentalist movement, and most of the members elected to stay with the old council, comprising what remains to this day as the Short Creek faction. Musser was able to convince about 1,000 polygamists to follow him.

Musser died in 1954, creating a problem as to which group could legitimately claim to be his successor. Allred assumed the presidency of the new council. The old council's nominee to replace Musser, Charles Zitting, died a month after assuming his post, and the two men next in line declined to accept leadership roles. Finally, LeRoy Johnson agreed to head up the group, after claiming to have had a confirming visitation from Christ. Johnson remains the head of the Short Creekers to this day—a crusty and reclusive octogenarian who rules over his five to ten thousand followers from a palatial house in a canyon above Salt Lake City, and another house in Short Creek itself. The temperate faithful who pay their 10 percent tithes to the Short Creek establishment don't seem to begrudge Johnson this bit of intemperance.

Around the time of the Fundamentalist split, a third group of independents emerged which held that neither the Allred nor Short Creek factions had proper authority. No centralized independent leadership has ever developed, but the number of independent polygamists existing as unaligned small family groups is substantial. Of the estimated 30,000 polygamists in the U.S., today, half are divided between the Allred and Short Creek groups, and the other half are independent.

Clusters of independents—all following different beliefs—are found in parts of Idaho, Montana, Utah, California, Wyoming, Arizona, Colorado, Oregon and Washington. Some even live in New York and other eastern states.

Though there are some notable differences between the practices of the Allred and Short Creek factions, philosophically, most polygamists today differ little from the Fundamentalists of the Lorin Woolley era, or the Mormon pioneers before that.

Most are "the salt of the earth"—farmers, carpenters, factory workers, tradespeople or machinists; others are professionals—business executives, lawyers, insurance salesmen or computer programmers. They practice their religion with Bible Belt, faith-healing ardor and believe that they, and only they, possess the "fullness of the gospel" which they say makes them scripturally "a peculiar people."

Though many Americans still hold to the myth that polygamists are a bunch of oversexed crazies, the reality is that the vast majority are sober, frugal, hardworking and highly moral. Excommunicated by their church, ostracized by society and once persecuted by government, polygamists tend to view themselves as modern martyrs whose sexual practice has been sanctioned by God. They like to point out that the average polygamous family is a bedrock of stability, especially when compared to a monogamous society riddled with divorce, infidelity and single-parent families.

Far from being promiscuous, the strictest Fundamentalists such as the Short Creekers have sex only to reproduce, abstain during pregnancy and also while a mother is breast-feeding. The more liberal Allred group and other independent polygamists, however, admit that such self-denial is too much to expect today.

Since the polygamist man has the luxury of having more than one wife, theoretically his wives "control the marriage bed" and summon him when they want, or whenever they think they are the most fertile. Practically, however, it is the man who is Lord of the Manor in every respect. Women are conditioned to be sweet and submissive and to bear all the children a man wants. To not submit to a husband's request is to risk damnation in the afterlife.

Many polygamist women admit that, all other things being equal, they would rather have their husbands to themselves. But they believe the principle of plural marriage has been divinely ordained, and adhere to the Mormon doctrine that there are an infinite number of "spirit children" in the preexistence waiting to be born, which makes it mankind's fundamental obligation to create as many earthly bodies as possible for them to inhabit. Thus there is a definite relationship between the carnal, cosmic and spiritual realms. Polygamists enter into "celestial marriage" for this life and the hereafter, where, they are told, the finest men assume the status of gods and rule over their own dominions. For those women who can overcome jealously and greed, God's promises are great: her husband will come to her in heaven, lift the veil from her eyes and be her savior. This life is only a primer for the next.

Still, a polygamist wife must trust and rely on the man in most all respects, for once she enters into plural marriage and has children, her options are often limited if she grows unhappy and wants to get out. Only one of the polygamist's marriages is legal and duly recorded civilly. All other marriages are performed secretly with no documentation, the better to preserve deniability should a legal confrontation later arise. And since polygamous children are usually conceived extralegally (delivered by midwives or sympathetic doctors like Rulon Allred) they often end up without birth certificates, Social Security numbers or death certificates—virtual nonpersons legally.

Thus, when it comes to sharing things like insurance, inheritances, Social Security or other forms of public assistance, plural wives are subjected to the whims of their husband and his first wife. This makes some of them feel trapped.

"Once I had a child, how could I leave him?" asks one disenchanted wife. "And after eight, I was virtually under lock and key . . . if I said we were never married, that would mean I was a concubine and my children illegitimate."

Such complaints are probably in the minority, for polygamy continues to grow. Though liberalization in the Allred group has attracted a variety of converts, polygamy is increasing primarily because most of the many children it produces choose to live the principle themselves. And when they decide to marry (or others decide for them), they usually do so while still in their teens.

Men usually marry in their early twenties, and the first wife is about the same age. Longtime polygamists average three wives, and leaders generally have at least seven. A few have had as many as twelve. There is more heated competition for wives who grew up in polygamous families as children (as opposed to a family converted from monogamy) since it is felt they are more likely to be harmonious "sister wives." Men often also seek actual sisters as wives on the theory that a woman might be more willing to share her husband with her sister than a strange woman.

Wives are usually involved with selecting each other, according to the "Law of Sarah"—which dictates that honorable plural wives must pray with their husband and help him find additional wives to add to the glory of the family. Rather than make the initial overture themselves, polygamist husbands often send one of their other wives out on scouting missions to sound out a prospect on her interest in joining the family.

Once a wife joins the family she usually has four children. That is an average, but some have had as many as fourteen to seventeen. Wives often take jobs—usually as teachers or nurses—to help support all these children, while one wife stays home to babysit.

Children are raised to conform to a rigid set of do's and don'ts, and the extent of their contact with the outside world—be it through school, television or other media—is restricted. Such "pagan" holidays as Halloween and Christmas are ignored, while July 4 and Joseph Smith's birthday (December 23) are observed. Intemperate, worldly influences, it is thought, serve only to undermine a child's spiritual strength and edge him or her away from the foundation: the family. A closeness and allegiance to family—both immediate and extended—is deemed essential, and by all indications, this message gets through. One polygamist Utah teenager, for example, is able to count (like an African *griot*) about 120 living brothers, sisters, cousins and "mothers." He says he knows and loves them all.

Schoolteachers—particularly around Salt Lake City and southern Utah—have become accustomed to having brothers and sisters in their classes that are only a few months apart in age. But the "polygs" are easy to spot, and when other students begin calling them names and tell them to go back to their own people, they usually do. They are generally tutored in the private homes of Fundamentalists who condemn the permissiveness and debunking of heroes and religion in contemporary education. Only a few of these polygamous schools are accredited.

Tutored in someone else's home or their own, polygamist children generally find that they and their parents live in spartan environments. With so many mouths to feed, wages don't go as far.

To offset this problem, Short Creekers turn over all their property, wages and food to the "United Effort" and then they are doled out whatever the powers-that-be consider they need. About 150 families in the Allred group operate a number of optional communal groupings. Tithing paid to leaders usually goes to pay for the poor, sick or widows.

If an Allreder decides he wants to leave the group, he can generally make some sort of amiable settlement with the leaders and take all or most of his money with him. But those who leave Short Creek can take nothing with them. They have long since signed deeds of property to the fully incorporated United Effort. And if a polygamist feels he has been cheated, he rarely has standing to take his complaint to authorities, since polygamy itself is illegal.

Despite Mormon ostracism of polygamists, they still consider themselves the truest of the true Mormons, and believe that one day they will be welcomed back into the church with open arms when the LDS hierarchy awakens to its apostacy. In the meantime, most polygamists still hold the Mormon Church to be the only divinely recognized church in the world today.

Though it is the Mormons' 1890 ban on polygamy that has kept the church and Fundamentalists apart to this day, there are lesser issues dividing the groups, including the polygamists' belief that the Word of Wisdom—calling for abstinence from alcohol, tobacco, coffee and tea—is not a commandment but advice; that special and sacred Mormon underclothing (garments) has been changed and shouldn't have been; that Adam was God, making Adam the literal father of Jesus Christ; that the United Order communal living situation should never have been abolished by the Mormon Church and that missionaries should undertake their missions "without purse or scrip."

One of the most interesting controversies is linked to a section of the sacred Mormon scripture, Doctrine and Covenants, which says there will be a "one mighty and strong" who will set the House of God in order one day.

Fundamentalists, for the most part, believe that the scripture refers to a resurrected Joseph Smith, who would return to reunite the polygamists with the Mormon Church. Many polygamists, however, have emerged to claim that they are the "one mighty and strong" that they are "enough to form a splinter sect of their own," according to one historian.

All these issues can be reduced to one word: authority. Who really holds legitimate claim to the priesthood? Mormons revere the president of their church, Spencer Kimball, and consider him a prophet—God's representative on earth. Polygamists respect Kimball, but maintain that their seven "High Priest Apostles" hold higher authority than he does—with the top man being LeRoy Johnson or, now, Owen Allred, depending on the group.

Mormon leaders avoid commenting on polygamy whenever possible because they are admittedly sensitive about speaking out against one of the sacred revelations of Joseph Smith. As one church writer has observed: "Either polygamy was revealed by God, or the entire fabric of our faith is false." Fundamentalists are nothing if not keen students of Mormon history, and in carrying on the polygamous legacy of Joseph Smith, they have emerged as ideological purists oblivious to secular pressure. In trying to convert Mormons back to polygamy, the Fundamentalists realize that their best ally is in Smith—the foundation of the church itself—and they argue convincingly that the church's 1890 decision to abandon one of its most sacred tenets was crass political opportunism.

For Joseph Smith's revelation on polygamy was not an invitation—it was a command to leading Mormons, and they resisted it only at the peril of losing their places in the celestial kingdom. It is evident that Smith's revelation was a bitter pill.

The late Fawn Brodie—UCLA professor, writer and author of the critically acclaimed biography on Joseph Smith entitled *No Man Knows My History*—suggested one reason for this:

"Actually," she writes, "what they [the Mormons] could not bear—though few of them ever recognized it—was the ever-accumulating unconscious burden of guilt which polygamy inflicted upon them. For the Mormons were in most respects even more Puritanical than their neighbors—they abhorred tobacco, alcohol, and even the milder stimulants of tea and coffee. Their fanatical punishment of adultery was only one expression of their sensitivity to the gentile accusation of libertinism and licentiousness. Like most other middle-class Americans they longed for respectability. There was too much of New England in their consciousness to permit them to continue in polygamy without being perpetually on the defensive and uneasy at heart."*

Mormons contend that plural marriage was never stressed by Joseph Smith as one of his most important teachings. They also note that the church has never renounced the "principle" of plural marriage and still expects it to be lived in the hereafter; it has only been suspended in this life because it runs contrary to the laws of the land. The implication is that God—though maybe not a political animal like man—is nevertheless not unaware of changing times and social mores, and occasionally

*Fawn Brodie, *The American Mercury*, April 1946, p. 401.

sees fit to modify doctrine accordingly. Witness the changes between the Old and New Testaments.

Thus, to a great extent, Mormons have sanitized the legacy of Joseph Smith and allowed some facts of history to be replaced by legend. Today's Mormons are told of the prophet's visions, prophecies and martyrdom, but the fact that he was a polygamist is rarely noted.

If modern-day Mormons have a certain degree of ambivalence toward plural marriage, so do today's law enforcement authorities: they simply no longer enforce the law banning polygamy. No one in the United States has been prosecuted for polygamy in years, despite the efforts of several plural marriage activists to get themselves arrested in an effort to test the constitutionality of the statute.

In 1878, the U.S. Supreme Court ruled in *Reynolds vs. the United States* that polygamy did not fall under the blanket protection of the First Amendment's freedom of religion clause. ". . . It is impossible to believe," the court wrote at the time, "that the constitutional guarantee of religious freedom was intended to prohibit legislation in respect to this most important feature of social life [marriage] . . . To permit this would be to make the professed doctrines of religious belief superior to the law of the land, and in effect to permit every citizen to become a law unto himself. Government could exist only in name under such circumstances."

But nearly a century later, in 1972, the Supreme Court backed away from the Reynolds decision when it upheld the right of the Amish religious sect to remove its children from public schools after the eighth grade. The court concluded in *Wisconsin vs. Yoder* that the state's interest in its system of compulsory education was not so compelling that the religious freedom of the Amish could be abridged. In a dissenting opinion Justice William Douglas warned that the court was laying the groundwork for polygamy to be legalized: "What we do today," he wrote, ". . . opens the way to give organized religion a broader base than it has ever enjoyed; and it even promises that in time Reynolds will be overruled."

Thus, given the strong chance that any polygamy conviction might be overturned on appeal—and the practice thereby declared legal—prosecutors are not anxious to enforce a law they fear is anachronistic. Besides, asks one Salt Lake City deputy district attorney: "Why tie up the courts to prosecute people who are as moral as hell?" In addition, authorities are reluctant to break up families by putting polygamous husbands in jail, their wives on welfare and their children in foster homes.

Said Abraham Lincoln once, comparing his problems with Mormons and polygamy to a big log: "It was too heavy to move, too hard to chop, too green to burn—so we just plowed around it." Despite cyclical bursts of moral outrage and prosecutorial fervor, Lincoln's quote still seems to reflect official policy on polygamy today, a century later.

3.

THE LeBARONS

The roar of the Twenties was naturally muted crossing desert country into Utah. What heel-kicking there was in the little southern town of La Verkin was more likely over the dirt clod that defied field plows or clogged precious canal waters. Like all of Utah's small farming communities, its citizenry were abstemious Mormons who wouldn't think to try the Charleston, considering they frowned even on waltzing. The town's temptations were limited, focusing La Verkin gossip only on eccentric personalities or the occasional off-color statement, rather than on any titillating actions of the townsfolk. At least, that was the case until 1924.

On one spring night of that year, the town's temporal and spiritual leader, Bishop Morris Wilson, hurried over to the home of Alma Dayer LeBaron on a secret mission.

LeBaron's wife, Maud, thirty-one, answered the door, as Wilson blurted out, "You must hurry."

"It's finally come?" Maud asked.

The bishop wheezed a little. "You must get out of town. I've never seen the men like this. They're madder than hornets. I don't know what they'll do. You've got to go, Maud."

Maud's husband was in Salt Lake City but she realized she must start immediately. She assured the bishop, who offered money to aid in the flight, that she and the children would leave as soon as possible.

While she stepped up preparations to leave La Verkin, she counted their blessings. One of the biggest had been their sojourn in La Verkin. She and her husband, who went by his middle name, Dayer, had arrived a little more than a year before, and he had quickly established a reputation as an industrious handyman particularly adept at painting houses.

Bishop Wilson had welcomed them to the community. After all, Dayer had a proud ancestral Mormon heritage. His grandfather, Benjamin F. Johnson, a close friend of prophet Joseph Smith, had been particularly attentive to Dayer before he died in 1905. And Dayer had married one of the well-respected McDonalds of Arizona. In their fourteen years together, the couple had been active Mormons and parents—four girls and three boys comprised their brood. An eighth child, Joel, as healthy as the rest, had been born in peaceful La Verkin in 1923, accentuating their joy with the area.

But the nagging Mormon serpent, polygamy, had plagued Dayer and Maud. Recurring visions about a second wife, shored up by advice from an excommunicated Apostle that the Lord still blessed such unions, had troubled the pair. Maud, whose job it was to select a second mate, had settled on one of the town's fairest daughers, Prudence Smith (not her real name) who, at eighteen, was some twenty years Dayer's junior. In secret, Maud and Dayer whittled down the girl's resistance to a marriage outside the auspices of the church, and persuaded her to go to Salt Lake in December 1923 where the deed was done.

Rumors began in La Verkin when Prudence threw over a boyfriend whom the town had assumed would marry her, and she began being seen with Maud. When she disappeared before Christmas, the wildest tales were concocted. Somehow the truth was learned, and Prudence's uncle, Bishop Wilson, who had blessed her when she was born, found it his sad task to excommunicate her January 30 for "unlawful conduct and entering into Plural Marriage." Prudence did not return from Salt Lake until March.

Church trials for Dayer and Maud followed in rapid succession, and both were excommunicated February 17 for "violative conduct." Following such religious expatriation, which meant virtual ostracism in a small Mormon town of the 1920s, the mood of La Verkin grew ugly toward the LeBarons. Dayer's older sons overheard several men talking about killing their father, and one identified a mob leader who was counting on a LeBaron lynching. Such talk, however idle, prompted Bishop Wilson's final warning and a hasty departure.

Dayer, tipped off by a high Mormon official in Salt Lake that there was a warrant for his arrest, traveled his own way to a border rendezvous. In El Paso, a gray-haired gentleman met the two wives with horse and buggy, converting the back into a covered wagon under which most of the family hid. He drove them across the border, unmolested. Dayer had already arrived separately—and safely. He had been waiting by the roadside in Juarez looking for his family among the incoming buggies, not knowing for sure they would come.

None of the family knew what awaited them in Mexico, and in the fear of that forlorn trek, a ninth child was conceived, Ervil, who was destined to make the LeBaron name infamous.

Dayer had been to Mexico before as a teenager with his parents. He was the son of Benjamin Franklin LeBaron (known as Franklin) and

Sara Jane (Jennie) Johnson, who were first cousins. The key man in Franklin's life was his polygamist uncle and father-in-law, Benjamin F. Johnson, and Franklin had spent many of his early years visiting Uncle Ben's ranch in Spring Lake. Johnson had seven wives and children, many of whom were perfect playmates for Franklin. At age twenty, he married his cousin Jennie, daughter of Uncle Ben's seventh wife. Dayer was born to Franklin and Jennie after their move to Tempe, Arizona, in 1886, their fourth child and third son.

Franklin and Jennie subsequently found a woman suitable to be his second wife and the three, with son Dayer and the other children, left for Mexico in February 1902.

When fifteen-year-old Dayer and his family reached the remote western Sierra Madre mountains in the state of Chihuahua, some 3,500 Mormons were already thriving in the area. Most had settled there to avoid harsh federal prosecution of polygamy. In 1886, the first envoy had purchased 50,000 acres on the Piedras Verdes River, obviously delighted with the smooth, flat land and easily tilled soil. The town was named Colonia Juarez, after the great Mexican libertarian, Benito Juarez, who was both a Lincoln and Washington to his people. Juarez flourished for a year—until the Mexicans pointed out that the Mormons had settled on privately owned land, the wrong plot.

Undaunted, the colonists moved upstream to the land they actually owned—a desolate, uneven parcel at the mouth of a canyon where the soil was so sandy and the stream so small that some abandoned the project and returned to Utah. But the same pioneer stock that had tamed the Salt Lake desert was determined to do the same here.

It was not long before a fortuitous calamity occurred which the Mormons called a miracle, and took as a sign that their venture was blessed of the Lord. An earthquake transformed their stream into a sizable river; and unearthed a hot springs twenty miles upstream which now fed into Juarez. In that semiarid colony, water was more valued than gold, and more than one neighbor whispered the morning after the quake to another: "God moves in mysterious ways . . ."

The Mormons eventually settled six colonies in Chihuahua and two in Sonora. Located about 150 miles southwest of El Paso, Colonia Juarez served as headquarters for the area. The nearest Mexican town, Nueva Casas Grandes, was and is fifteen miles east of the town.

By the turn of the century, the most prosperous colony, Colonia Dublan, had become a commercial center in Chihuahua. It was the only colony served by a railroad, situated, as it was, only a few miles from Casas Grandes. It was to this busy hamlet that Dayer and his family had arrived in 1902. His father, Franklin, had already purchased a cozy brick home to which he later added two bedrooms and a kitchen. The LeBarons covered their two lots with fruit orchards—the beginning of the nursery business that became the LeBaron livelihood.

But Franklin's natural proclivity to be a polygamist like his Uncle Ben was thwarted—and, in fact, never realized. The unknown fiancée who had traveled to Mexico to live the Lord's law stood him up at the altar, where he waited at the appointed hour with Jennie and a secret preacher.

Dayer, however, was destined to achieve his father's dream. By the time he was eighteen, he had moved to Colonia Juarez, became an Elder in the church and married Cynthia Barbara Bailey. The two had a boy in 1905, the same year that Uncle Ben died.

Johnson's death was pivotal. All the considerable LeBaron claims to Lordship over the earth emanate from an authority they believe Johnson had, but which Johnson himself never alluded to in his extensive autobiography or numerous conversations with his own family. The LeBarons counter that this was a deliberately hidden authority given Johnson secretly by his good friend Joseph Smith. When Dayer was ten, his brother Conway said, grandfather Ben had given him "special charge" over the Johnson family. Some LeBarons maintain Johnson came to Dayer as an angel in the 1920s and tapped him out with power over the world. Certainly the LeBarons themselves admit that Dayer did nothing with his power except to pass it on as if he were a minor runner in a 440 relay.

This claim, that he had an invisible "mantle" from Joseph Smith, was to be as divisive among Dayer's seven sons as the birthright was to Jacob and Esau. In fact, a chronicle of their lives reads like a rewrite of the Old Testament. Three of the boys claimed they were prophets as great as Moses, and started their own churches. The character of one of them was often compared to the purity and kindness of Jesus Christ, while another's cultist practices have been likened to the Biblical account of Sodom and Gomorrah. Following in-family doctrinal disputes, one son would be shot and killed, and another son implicated in the murder. All were aftereffects of this hidden mantle with which Dayer claimed to have been blessed.

Within a few years after Uncle Ben's death, Dayer left Mexico for Mesa, Arizona. His wife Barbara, during a visit to her mother in Salt Lake, had been persuaded to leave Dayer. "My father was so broken-hearted that he went into the mines in Arizona and stayed for four years," said one of his daughters. "He hardly ever saw society again— just reading the scriptures and working in the mines. He didn't want to look at a woman again." Eventually Dayer surfaced and married Maud Lucinda McDonald on October 25, 1910. The following year, Dayer had a vision which he described to his son Alma:

"It was his 100-year vision about the future of Mexico. He saw himself walking alone in the desert near the border. He came upon a house, and a voice told him to go upstairs, from which point he could see Mexico from coast to coast. He saw dark clouds overhead representing ignorance, then the sunshine came and progress was made. He turned to look at America and saw rampant destruction."

At the time, Dayer was an active Mormon. It must be noted that Mormons believe that prior to the "end of the world," the U.S. Constitution will "hang by a thread," and the government will fall. So Dayer's vision of a gathering in Mexico for protection was not altogether out of line with Mormon philosophy. At least not until he added that church headquarters would be there, as would the Lord's Anointed.

He didn't make such thoughts and visions known while he regularly attended the LDS wards in Arizona. His first child by Maud, Irene, was born in 1912; she was to be the only one of his children to stay in the Mormon Church. Benjamin Teasdale, no doubt named with grandfather Johnson in mind, was born in 1913; next came Ross Wesley, in 1914. Lucinda came in 1916; Alma Dayer, Jr., in 1918. Jennie, born in 1919, died at the age of six. Esther, the future family historian who would portray herself as an immensely talented and popular siren, was born in 1921.

After World War I, Dayer acquired large land holdings in Colonia Pacheco, a mountain Mormon colony about thirty-five miles west of Colonia Juarez. Though he enjoyed prosperity in Pacheco, Dayer was a driven man, haunted by this or that vision. "He said he had a monitor within his bosom that told him what to do and what not to do," recalls son Alma. "This monitor told him to sell out and go to Utah. He didn't want to do it, but he knew the prompting had come from God." He sold all his holdings at a great loss, accepting IOUs he knew he'd never be able to collect.

Dayer felt his vision was fulfilled when, stepping off the train in Salt Lake, he encountered excommunicated Apostle John W. Taylor, Jr., at whose house he stayed. Taylor urged Dayer to take a second wife, citing alleged revelations his father had received while president of the church, which were never told the body of Saints. Under such pressure, Dayer married Prudence Smith of La Verkin. It was shortly thereafter that the LeBarons had to flee to Mexico.

When Dayer returned to Juarez in 1924, the colonies of his youth were not the same. The entire peak population of 6,000 Mormons had been driven back to the United States in the summer of 1912 by incessant revolution. When the troubles in Mexico died down, less than a third of the colonists trickled back to reclaim their land and homes. These were Mormon stalwarts, who would not be likely to be sympathetic to Dayer's recent expulsion from the church. In fact, W. Ernest Young, bishop of the Juarez Ward from 1922 to 1933, said as much. "They came to my house first and thought we would receive them just like they had in the old days of plural marriage. He soon found out that we didn't because I was indoctrinated against the Fundamental stuff—I called it fake polygamy." Despite the immediate opposition of Bishop Young, who also acted as mayor and police chief, Dayer felt he had been led by God to Mexico and was determined to stay until he died, which he did.

Dayer purchased a nearly valueless red brick house in the northeast portion of Juarez for Maud and the children. This home, as well as a nearby one he bought for Prudence, had been abandoned during the Exodus of 1912, and badly needed a general fixup, Dayer's specialty. Dayer also obtained a dry farm in Colonia Garcia, which he leased out. The LeBarons were indigent according to next-door neighbors, the Martineaus, who described the area as the "poor part of town."

Dayer was regarded in town as a crackpot. The local children would sometimes follow him down one of the town's tree-lined dirt streets, shouting and bleating, "B-a-a-a-a-h, b-a-a-a-h, billy goat Dayer," a reference to the fact he, like the billy goats he owned, had more than one mate. The townsfolk, some of whom were still living polygamy them-selves, did not discourage such open ridicule. Dayer apparently antago-nized them because he preached polygamy to anyone who would listen, including LeRoy Hatch, a close LeBaron associate, future bishop and town doctor.

Hatch says the older children, particularly Ben and Alma, belittled their father, sometimes calling him "the old hound dog." Such disre-spect was probably the natural mimicry of children who heard similar comments from playmates—and parents—with whom they associated at school and church. Too, Dayer was not in Juarez long enough to instill orderly discipline; he often was in the United States on protracted house-painting expeditions.

Maud, their mother, earned the children's deepest love, and the respect of the townsfolk. She was a fine piano teacher; many neighbors said most of the children of Juarez, some of whom went on to profes-sional careers, first learned music under her able tutelage.

Little is remembered about Prudence and her children. She was a modest woman, not given to easy friendship with neighbors, and had six children by Dayer before she left him in 1937. She later remarried and now lives in Utah, hoping she will not be discovered for any past association with the LeBarons.

The last four of Maud's thirteen children were born after her arrival in Colonia Juarez. The first to come—her ninth child—was Ervil, born on February 22 (Washington's Birthday), 1925; Floren arrived in 1927; Verlan in 1930; twins born in 1932 died within a day. The wide spectrum of ages among the LeBarons virtually formed two families. Esther said she, Joel and Ervil "were like triplets growing up, always together. We were about the same age." Since the oldest daughter left while Esther was young, and the second was incarcerated in an asylum, Esther was essentially the only girl raised among seven brothers.

Early life was difficult for the children because of the family's outcast status. They weren't totally alone in that; other excommunicants for polygamy in Juarez were Thomas Jones, a 1925 arrival, and Uncle Cleve (Dayer's younger brother Grover Cleveland) who'd come to Juarez in 1928 with two wives.

The Jones family, who had befriended the LeBarons immediately, were fond of having parties. The Mormon brethren worried that Jones was propagandizing polygamy at the get-togethers—and the Juarez

High Council absolutely did not want good members trying to keep up with the Joneses. An edict was issued from the pulpit banning all Mormons from visiting the Jones and LeBaron homes—except to conduct business.

The no-visit fiat was quickly translated to a practice of total disassociation from the LeBarons; no invitations came to them from other homes to playmates' birthday parties or adult socials. It was not long before, inevitably, the ugliest transmutation occurred: inactive isolation developed into active aggression. The LeBaron boys and girls, and Joneses, were taunted and bullied.

One who suffered bloody noses along with the LeBarons, Ossmen Jones, vividly recalls those days. "The Mormons wanted to make a public case out of the LeBarons and my family to scare the hell out of anyone else who might want to live the principle. I mean, it was rough. I was beaten up many times. I dreaded going to school; I hated to, in fact." A contemporary of the children admitted the treatment was horrendous. "Kids can be cruel, very mean and ornery. They pounded on the LeBarons, threw rocks at them and chased them home after school." The bullies were seldom discovered, and even more rarely punished. It was open season on the LeBarons.

Added to the LeBarons' isolation was the incomprehensibility of their harassment. Most of their antagonists had been born to polygamist wives; some of the town's leaders still had extra wives—at least until 1939. In that year, Bishop Young recorded the death of one resident, noting "at the time of his death he was the last polygamist with more than one living wife in the Juarez state. The wives of the others had died." In the private journal entry, this bishop, who presided during the LeBarons' roughest years, stoutly defended polygamy: "Why does the so-called Christian world fight and downgrade what is in the Bible? From cover to cover the Bible is the history of polygamy. Jesus Himself is through that progeny, and called the son of David." The apparent duplicity of the LeBaron persecutors was explained away because Dayer's plural marriage was not approved by the church as their marriages, some of them post-Manifesto, had been. But the LeBaron children couldn't comprehend such fine distinctions.

As a final blow—and insult—the LeBaron boys and girls were required to deny their parents if they wished to be nurtured at the Mormon bosom. So each of them dutifully promised to ignore their parents' teachings, and were successful to the extent that "we were good Mormons and actually hated the thought of ever living the principle ourselves," said Esther.

The late teenage years are personality-molding. Children generally leave home for college or other ventures during this time and out of the parental garage, they test germinating thoughts, determine which talents to develop and begin serious interaction with their peers. Perhaps there is no more demanding testing-ground than a Mormon mission, where "finding yourself" can become a daily ordeal. The teenage missionary must find an apartment, budget his meager funds, cook for himself and think for himself. He must daily meet strangers, and often rejection, in his attempt to sell—not an encyclopedia set or Tupperware bowl—but a church that will radically change the buyer's life. In doing so, the missionary must offer stirring testimonials that it has worked for him. The mission becomes an intensive search for an often-illusive truth which may be found by equating natural occurrences as signs from above, or receiving what they felt were unexplainable manifestations from God, be it an overwhelming feeling, an actual voice or vision.

Alma, Joel and Ervil went on their Mormon missions during the early 1940s when proselytizing in Mexico was particularly difficult. The Mexican government had banished all non-Mexican ministers beginning in 1925, so the Mormons had to rely on local talent, much of it from the northern Mormon colonies. But many of the colony boys were fighting in World War II. Leadership was short and the hours were long.

To add to the boys' difficulties, the Mexican government passed a law against door-to-door tracting, which meant the missionaries only preached by invitation. Too, converts came at a snail's pace, not easily lured from the ruling religion, Catholicism. Thus, the LeBarons had to contend with the routine missionary difficulties, plus a hostile government, a strong opposing church, a large body of recent Mormon apostates and, most important, their own background. The latter was the battle each eventually lost.

Alma's first assignment as a new missionary in July 1940 was to Ozumba, near Mexico City. A month later, a second LeBaron, Joel, was injected into the mission field. Ervil, always close to Joel, quit school at the same time and, after numerous entreaties, persuaded the Mormon colony's leaders to send him on a mission as well. He was commissioned to an area near Mexico City, Joel many miles to the south in Vera Cruz.

Without Joel, Ervil was more interested in basketball than baptizing. Dean Farnsworth, a one-time missionary companion, recalls that Ervil would break appointments with potential converts "to stay outside and practice basketball." Farnsworth complained to the mission president, who transferred Ervil to Puebla where it was assumed his older brother Joel would stimulate his interest. To the dismay of mission leaders, however, Joel's effect on Ervil was anything but momentous. He rarely rebuked his younger brother, adopting a laissez-faire attitude which would later prove to be fatal for him.

Brother Alma, feeling a momentary jingoistic desire to serve his native country at war, left for Arizona in December 1943 to register for the U.S. draft. He was interrupted en route by older brother Benjamin, who'd been claiming divine revelation since 1935. Under Ben's tutelage, and seeing a vision of his own, Alma embraced the principle of polygamy and went hunting for a second Mexican wife back in San Marcos, in the state of Hidalgo—where he had previously wed a female Mormon missionary. Alma's search caused a local scandal, similar to the uproar Dayer caused years before in La Verkin. Ever quelling brush fires, Arwell L. Pierce, president of the Mormon mission to Mexico, traveled by train to San Marcos to investigate at the urgent request of Alma's father-in-law. Pierce found Alma was "in the state of apostasy" and left before Benjamin LeBaron arrived.

President Pierce was worried that now Joel and Ervil might cast their lot with their brothers in San Marcos. Too, Pierce had noted that Ross, still another brother, had also been skirting the area in the curious role of a tie salesman to the Mormon missionaries. But Joel and Ervil responded to a concerned missive from Pierce with a letter categorically denying any interaction or sympathy with Ben. Temporarily assuaged, Pierce took the letter at face value and traveled to the semiannual Mormon General Conference, April 1944, in Salt Lake City. But while the mission leader was away, the San Marcos congregation apparently grew hostile toward Alma's polygamy harangues. Reportedly fearing for his life, Alma begged Joel and Ervil's help, causing them to abandon their Puebla mission for San Marcos, never to return.

Rebelling against the mother church was not difficult for Ervil. According to his contemporaries, he'd never really been interested in Mormonism or the scriptures. With Joel, it was a far different matter. Theresa Martineau, who visited them both during those troubled times, relates: "When I first saw Joel after he'd decided to leave the church, his face was very, very ashen. For him, it was a real struggle, but for Ervil it was nothing." On Friday, April 28, almost immediately on Pierce's return, Joel met him for a private talk. He explained that he had fasted and prayed, and could no longer support church leaders. "I know the church doesn't want men like me, with my beliefs in it," he stated, openly and honestly. Rather than call a religious tribunal that day, Pierce allowed Joel the chance to bring Ervil to the mission home for a similar admission. He returned Monday without Ervil, who refused to come. With Joel present, a court was held Tuesday, May 2, and he was dishonorably released from his mission and excommunicated from the church for disloyalty and advocating polygamy.

Joel emerges from the mission records as a particularly amiable and well-loved missionary. "Joel remarked to President Pierce that he was grateful for the courtesy and kindness extended to him before, during and after the trial," the records show. The day after his excommunication, he went sightseeing with other missionaries. Pierce lent him the eighty-peso railroad fare to Colonia Juarez. Joel was noticeably relieved to leave Ben, Ervil and Alma to their own shenanigans.

Various Juarez associates tried reasoning with the rest of the clan, who'd moved near Ozumba. One of those sent to reconvert the LeBarons was Harold Brown, an influential native Mormon. Brown's appraisal of the situation years later is noteworthy: "Those boys grew up under a conflict with an excommunicated father and mother, while living in a little Mormon community where their whole life was in the church. They seemed to get along fine until they reached nineteen, twenty, twenty-one years of age. And then this would begin to be an emotional, traumatic thing for them."

Next, a six-man diplomatic corps met the LeBarons in Ozumba May 30. They were led by Anson B. Call, Juarez bishop for thirty-seven years, who thought a personal appeal might work. Alma directed the delegation to the edge of an impoverished farm, then went to get his two brothers, who were living in a tiny willow-limb lean-to nearby. One of the group recalled Ben, Ervil and Alma marching across the field abreast, "their clothes filthy and torn, each pair of pants held up by one rope suspender crossing their shoulder from one side to the other. They were sandy complected, and all had matted red beards." Apparently they'd been eating wild choke cherries that had stained their hair. The brief meeting was punctuated by cursing and shouting by the LeBaron brothers.

Periodically, the LeBaron trio wrote abusive letters to Pierce, ridiculing and threatening him. Finally, Alma and Ervil published an open letter stating an angel of the Lord told them Ben was the only anointed prophet on earth.

Such actions were an inevitable catalyst to excommunication. In consecutive trials at the Mexican mission home, Ervil and Ben were excommunicated June 6; Alma was severed from the church after a mission home trial June 9.

Ironically, at the same time the LeBaron sons were leaving the church, father Dayer, the root cause of their disaffection, was trying to get back in. He and Maud wrote numerous letters to the Salt Lake hierarchy, and even to Pierce, in their efforts to be reinstated. But they were an unpredictable couple—one day blessing Pierce for excommunicating their sons and cursing him for it the next. The Mormons decided they would be unstable members, and the two were never allowed back into the church.

Nineteen forty-four was also a year which saw a very interesting meeting take place.

That year, a man who had grown up with Maud LeBaron in Thatcher, Arizona, visited her in Mesa. He and Maud's brother had been best friends. His name was Spencer Woolley Kimball, a relative of Fundamentalism's father, Lorin Woolley, and a proud descendant of one of the church's most respected polygamists, Heber C. Kimball. The first Apostle to be appointed from outside Utah (October 1943), Kimball had accepted an invitation from Maud to visit her and to discuss her and Dayer's possible reinstatement. In his private journal, Kimball recorded of this visit:

"She seemed to have a good spirit and attitude and began telling me of her problems when her three tall apostate sons came uninvited into the room. They had also been excommunicated for apostasy and they were very belligerent, cold, haughty, defiant. They demanded of their mother what she was telling me. She gave them little satisfaction, but said since she knew me she had asked for some help from me. The one boy had his shirt off with his [specially designed and marked Mormon Temple] garments prominently displayed. I am sure it was intended to impress me. I told her and later them that if they wished to see me further I would be at the hotel and that I would do anything I could for them. They followed me to the door. *Never before have I come in such close contact with Lucifer and his devils.*"

Kimball's son, Edward, who included the anecdote in a book on his father, said that throughout Spencer's journals, comprising more than thirty volumes, he never again connected individuals or a family to Satanic influence. The information is significant in light of the fact that Kimball eventually rose to become the twelfth president of the Mormon Church in 1973. He would later receive threats from Ervil LeBaron, which caused security around him to multiply following the Allred murder. That Kimball identified a potential deadly enemy some thirty years before the fact reinforces for the Mormon faithful his stature as a prophet.

Benjamin Teasdale LeBaron had been the family's brightest hope. He was the firstborn son, an able athlete, intelligent, charming and capable of inspiring the confidence of others. It may be that no single flaw felled him, but rather a combination of circumstances which crowded up and overcame him. He felt a singular responsibility, as the first son, to win the brass ring—the mantle—which his father held in trust for the most worthy son. While yearning for that imaginary gift, he had a need to please Mormons who were his friends, but who would have blanched had they known that Benjamin *presumed* he might lead the Lord's world someday. No doubt their demeaning attitude toward him and his family must have been painfully evident, and this probably only intensified Ben's desire to impress his peers.

Benjamin LeBaron may have long fought a battle he could not win—a battle against genes, against a hereditary insanity which offered no cure. That conclusion comes from Dr. Hatch, for years the LeBaron family doctor. He first reached it at the time he attended Brigham Young University in Provo, Utah. Ben had been confined in the Utah State Hospital for the insane in the same town. At Maud's insistence, Hatch agreed to give Ben a blessing. (The Mormon Church believes in a literal "laying on of hands" for blessings and ordinations. A member of the higher Melchizedek priesthood places both hands on the head, usually with the help of another priesthood member and after anointing the person with a dab of oil, he pronounces a blessing intended to reassure the sick person, heal him or cast out evil spirits.) When Hatch entered the hospital on a Sunday to perform the blessing to which he'd reluctantly agreed, he was told that Ben was in solitary confinement after exhibiting "aggressive and physically abusive" behavior. His disease had been diagnosed as *dementia praecox,* literally an irreversible mental deterioration in a young person. Hatch explains the disease is hereditary and symptoms include delusions of grandeur. A dictionary notes it is a form of schizophrenia usually beginning at puberty and characterized by introversion, disassociation and odd, distorted behavior.

At the age of nine, Ben himself later declared, extraterrestrial spirits started instructing him. During his saner moments, he blamed the various asylums in which he was incarcerated for worsening his illusions. Attendants made fun of him, treated him like he was "not all there," and sometimes whipped him which, he said, naturally caused his mind to wander. Referring to himself, Ben noted in one treatise that, at twenty-two, he was sent to an insane asylum "for further examination and scientific research. They were completely baffled. They could not cure him of thinking faster than they did or of working miracles, so after nine weeks of violent abuse he was falsely accused and sent away branded as insane." The afflictions, he added, were prerequisites to his declaration that he was the One Mighty and Strong, purportedly God's greatest prophet before the end of the world. Scriptures predicted the man would be "marred," and Ben felt he fulfilled that requirement, mentally and physically.

In one of a dozen pamphlets, beginning in 1935, Ben explained that one day when he heard a scripture about the prophet read, "it struck my mind with such unusual force that I soon afterward retired to the hill nearby to inquire of the Lord further concerning the matter, and as I asked who the messenger would be, was told that *I was that person."*

Naturally, he could hardly keep such a pronouncement quiet. Among the first to be informed that Ben was "The Man" were the leaders of the Mormon Church. Ben corresponded with them regularly, more fervently after a being from his netherworld spoke to him July 4, 1942. After picking up his two very willing apostles, Ervil and Alma, in Mexico in 1944, Ben traveled to Salt Lake for his "Hiawatha Whitefeather" period, penning his epistles under that new name. He soon added many other names to his diatribes against the Mormons like Bull Catcher, World Champion, Eighth Priest, Elephant Strangler and Wolf Skinner.

Personalities like Ben's are commonplace in asylums across the country, but the elder LeBaron deserves mention because he succeeded in converting Ervil. He also persuaded a third follower, Sydney (not his real name), who had married two women, Charlene and Sybil (not their real names), and was on the run from the law for his polygamy.

From Charlene comes a picture of early life under this patriarchal group—Ben, Ervil, Alma, and Sydney—in the summer of 1946. "We were not to put our noses into any of the men's business and when they were talking, we were to be quiet and stay right out of it," Charlene says. "We were to follow our husbands in anything they said—it didn't make any difference what it was, whether we knew it was right or not."

If the women didn't obey, the men would threaten to punish their children or take them away. Recalcitrant mothers were cursed, reviled as "filthy old sows" and other more perverse creatures; the children were also railed against, called brats, bastards, etc. "It made no difference what filthy name he could call us. Many times I was told I was not worth any more than to be a rug on the floor for Sydney to wipe his feet on."

Sydney and Alma willingly imitated Ben's "inspired" language after Ben argued it was necessary "to get people over their prejudiced ideas, so they wouldn't feel embarrassed or ashamed if somebody used 'ass' or something like that. He said it wouldn't bother people if everybody used that kind of language," Charlene says.

When Charlene's father visited the Mexican colony, he was nearly heartbroken by the sight of his daughter and her children "in rags, cast off and even afraid to speak." Ben told him that there was no such thing as sin, that any deviant practice was acceptable unless the perpetrator's conscience bothered him. "I've never, in all my experiences—and I will say that I've worked among the roughest type of people on the face of the earth—run into any people like these," the father would say later. "You could not hold them to any kind of conversation that did not include sex." But his daughter wouldn't leave; she was too afraid.

When Dr. Hatch buttonholed Ben at the time for "carrying on lewd practices" with the fifteen-year-old daughter of one of his adherents, Ben retorted that man could not sin, and that his indecent advances toward the girl were by way of testing her resistance to evil. Since he found her "too passionate," Ben was trying to "correct the situation" in his own way.

In the late 1940s, buoyed by his four obedient followers, Ben announced that the House of God was about to be straightened out. Taking Sydney with him, Ben traveled to Salt Lake where his antics were legion—and became legend among the polygamist subculture. After practicing a peculiar shout for years, Ben would often roar in a frightening manner. Then he would explain that the sound was issued because he was the "Lion of Israel."

As another quirk, Ben habitually "had a way of putting his heel up on a chair or whatever he happened to be sitting on—the other leg hanging down—claiming he was 'putting his heel upon the serpent,' " relates Owen Allred, adding that "twice because of public actions among those acquainted with his seemingly harmless idiosyncrasies, he was confined to mental institutions." One of those public actions began when Ben started shouting he was the One Mighty and Strong in a Salt Lake County courtroom, after which he yanked a policeman out of the middle of a nearby busy intersection and held up traffic for half an hour while he did 200 pushups (the figure varies). "See," he said, "nobody else can do that many. That proves I'm the One Mighty and Strong."

A Salt Lake City hospital accepted the proselyting pair in April 1953, releasing Sydney after a few days and transferring Ben to the state hospital in Provo. Ben was released briefly, but then readmitted to the mental hospital from June 1953 to 1958. Ironically, Verlan, studying at Brigham Young University, worked nights as a hospital attendant during the time his brother was a patient there.

Sydney returned to the LeBaron family ranch in Mexico without Ben and ordained Ervil and Alma to the "Apostleship of the 144,000 for Ben LeBaron." Acting on behalf of his imprisoned leader, Sydney instituted nudism and free love more than a decade before it became an American fad. "Sydney was acting like the cock of the walk. He began getting revelations as fast as you could talk, and I was drinking it all in," Alma admits. Quickly fed up, Ervil vowed he'd never follow Ben—or Sydney—again, which he didn't. But Ben had taught him some writing skills—an inflammatory style which he later copied—as well as a few tricks about getting and keeping power.

There followed a colorful one-week period which has caused continued embarrassment to the LeBaron family, though they certainly didn't inspire it and did all they could to prevent it.

Sydney's primary revelation was that a flying saucer would soon arrive to collect passengers good enough to live with the people of Enoch, whose city, because of the people's righteousness, had been relocated on the North Star. Sydney told Alma that they'd all have to go nude to get a deep suntan for the Enoch excursion, or get burned en route. Alma conveyed the news to Charlene. "He told me that if we didn't take our clothes off, that Sydney would rip them off. Sydney ripped six or seven dresses off me, and I don't know how many off Sybil. Even the children went naked." Alma said Sydney guaranteed them each would "get" the Holy Spirit of God if they went nude.

A day after the nudity edict, Alma saw Sydney and his family naked on the roof of their house, screaming and yelling. Joel and Ervil ordered Alma to get them down, threatening to call the civil authorities. When Alma communicated this to Sydney, he called Joel a criminal, and Alma a coward for refusing to join them. Alma retreated to observe things from behind a mesquite bush. Sydney shouted about Joel for a while, before the family clambered off the roof to vociferously pray that God would send the much-needed flying saucer before they were arrested. Predicting their transport vehicle would land near the road, Sydney and family walked barefoot and naked through the thorny mesquite bushes until they were out of earshot. According to Charlene, Sybil had become so badly sunburned that she had blisters on her back. The heat caused a fever which Charlene described as "some kind of a spell, her body was trembling and her joints were all out of place, and she just looked horrible." When she emerged from her trance, both Sydney and Sybil agreed she'd had intercourse with a higher extraterrestrial being. Ben had previously preached "that a woman should go with any man that wanted her, whether he was Chinese or Negro, because resurrection came through intercourse." Sydney apparently surmised after Sybil's fever that she was now resurrected, and could pass that resurrection on to others. So she made love to Sydney, and he made love to Charlene. Each wife was then instructed to spread this resurrection around and "give it to any man that wanted it."

The morning after the rooftop episode, Alma visited Sydney's house and found it "a filthy stinking mess—worse than any hippie mess." As he climbed a nearby hill in search of Sydney, he realized he'd been duped. "I felt a deep disgrace come over me," Alma recalls. "I thought of going to South America so as to never face friends and relatives again."

He found Sydney and family sitting around the ashes of a fire under a peach tree in Dayer's fruit orchard. Alma says Sydney and Sybil were "totally insane." They'd been eating tree bark, and their children's faces were blackened from chewing on charcoal. Joel and Ervil decided to notify Sydney's father in Canada and the local authorities, after clothing and feeding the family. A local investigator from nearby Galeana gave Alma custody of Sydney until the relatives arrived, and allowed Alma to shackle Sydney to a cottonwood pole in a goat shed for restraint. The chain had six to eight feet of slack, enough to lie down in a bed on the dirt floor.

Alma advised Sydney's wives to leave their husband until he could prove he was sane. But during one of his more lucid periods, Sydney managed to extricate the pole from the ground and escape. He dragged it more than a mile to the house of a second cousin, who sawed the chain off and returned Sydney to the ranch, where Sybil and Charlene greeted him with open arms. When the family decided to stay, Alma announced he washed his hands of them.

Several days passed before Sydney's oldest son was spotted riding a bicycle through town—nude. Joel, Ervil and Alma immediately called Sydney to an impromptu hearing, where a decision ordering Sydney's expulsion from the community within the hour was rendered. In reply, Sydney simply marched his children through the desert toward the mountains, which naturally alarmed the LeBarons, who feared that they would all starve to death.

Rounding up three teenagers, Alma followed the family, packing a .32 automatic. About a half mile from the ranch, Sydney spotted them 200 yards behind him and began cursing. Alma was a criminal who deserved "fixing up," Sydney yelled, and raced toward Alma, who drew his gun and shouted back, "Don't you come any closer or I'll blast your guts out." Sydney halted. Alma then drew a line on the ground, telling Sydney and his family that if they crossed it, he'd shoot them.

Alma held them there, in an effort to protect the children, until the civil authorities arrived.

Local officials took Sydney to the Galeana Mayor's office. A hearing ensued, after which the mayor told Sydney to leave the valley or go to jail. He left.

Sydney has now been incarcerated in various institutions across the United States and Canada for the last twenty years, as has Ben. Ben sometimes stays in Geronimo, Arizona, where he lives in a house he built while apparently enjoying occasional periods of sanity. Periodically, he will send shockingly obscene letters to past friends. One of his cleanest went to Rulon C. Allred in September 1957. Ben told Rulon he was presently confined in Utah State Hospital. "They don't think that I am sick mentally. They are holding me for believing in Polygamy." He concluded, in what serves as a tragic summation of his life: "You may think I am kidding but I always hear the voice of the Lord all the time. I never make any mistakes. I am infallible and perfect in all my ways, as a little child is. I don't think so. I know so. The Lord has told me."

Dayer LeBaron seemed to have visions for all seasons. While his children were growing up in Colonia Juarez, Dayer had been greatly troubled. Burdened with family problems, he told daughter Esther years afterward that he asked the Lord "if he couldn't go get lost in some big city where he could make a good living and let the children grow up in happiness." But, said Esther, her father was commanded to stay in Juarez "suffering the persecution silently." The family needed Job-like testing, for it was only natural that Satan would harass Dayer's bound-for-glory progeny, he was told. By the time most of the children were grown and gone, and the youngest, Verlan, was fourteen, the vision aparently expired.

The means for a place Dayer could call his own arrived with Esther's husband, Floyd Spencer, in early 1944. Dayer prevailed on him to sell his home and Arizona business, and buy several fifty-acre *parcelas* located about forty miles south of Casas Grandes. In December, another revelation led Dayer to a mesquite jungle six miles north which he declared was, finally, *the place*. This was to be Colonia LeBaron.

Uncle Cleve, the only brother to follow Dayer in polygamy, and others arrived to prepare the area for farming and living. At the time, the only son there to aid him was Joel. Ben, Alma and Ervil were preaching in Mexico City; Verlan was studying at Juarez Academy; Ross was in Salt Lake and Floren was traveling.

Life in early Colonia LeBaron was difficult and primitive. Fruit orchards were planted, which expanded as Dayer's children gathered and claimed their own *parcelas* under an agrarian reform program the Mexican government sponsored. A few cows lingered around adobe huts, which had no electricity or water. The almost constant daily fare was beans and a tough bread which an early resident called "2,000 percent whole wheat. It was cracked wheat with nothing else in it." Mice ran up and down the walls at night, but the worst blight was the bedbugs, which infested adobe walls, but favored nesting and laying eggs in mattresses.

Despite its failings, Colonia LeBaron was a refuge. One of its inhabitants, Rulon C. Allred, came running there in 1947, jumping parole on his polygamy conviction in Utah so he could live with his wives in

Mexico. Welcomed by Dayer, Allred built the community's largest and finest house.

Few details about his sojourn are available. Associates said the Allreds and LeBarons were compatible, unless religion or authority were discussed. Both Ross and Alma LeBaron claim Allred made demands on Dayer. Dayer was asked to relinquish his property and goods to the United Order of John Barlow, the man to whom the Allreds, and most Utah Fundamentalists, had then sworn allegiance. Naturally, Dayer didn't give in. So Allred abandoned his house and returned to Utah in May of 1948 where he served only four more weeks in jail before winning his unconditional release.

One of the most dismal aspects of early life in the colony was the presence of Dayer's daughter, Lucinda, who apparently went mad at about age sixteen. The LeBaron family, including Dayer, originally thought her ravings were the result of possession by evil spirits. Though not certain that was the case, the Juarez church leaders agreed to administer a blessing to her. Dayer, who couldn't participate because he'd been excommunicated, begged and received permission to kneel at his daughter's feet during one blessing. Dr. Hatch, who suggests Lucinda suffered from *dementia praecox,* said the church leaders' only effect on Lucinda was to calm her down. "But when her father would appear in the room she would become extremely violent again."

For a time Lucinda overcame her problems. She graduated from Juarez Academy in 1935 and left for Utah. Described as a lovely girl, she became a regular pianist for various Fundamentalist meetings there. In 1940, Dayer arrived and bargained with one of their leaders, who agreed to take the twenty-four-year-old Lucinda as a plural wife, a decision he soon regretted. Though she had a son, and twins by him, Lucinda too often exhibited bouts of rage and, once, was picked up on Salt Lake's Main Street totally nude. The husband, who felt Dayer had duped him by not mentioning Lucinda's early illness before the marriage, wrote father LeBaron to come and get her. Dutifully, Dayer took her back to Colonia LeBaron where she proceeded to get worse. Finally, Joel and Verlan decided to commit her in a state institution. While Maud was away teaching piano in Las Vegas, Verlan and Alma spirited Lucinda off to Arizona, where she presently resides in a rest home.

As Dayer grew older, his sons began badgering him for whatever it was he had been promising them all these years. No one was really sure. His own wife, Maud, said Dayer never talked about carrying any mantle, or at least "I never paid much attention to it." Ben was a regular petitioner, as was Ross Wesley.

Ross had been living in Salt Lake City for years, before he came to Colonia LeBaron in 1950. Amid normal society, Ross had difficulty adjusting. "It's a fact that the LeBarons have a tendency to be high-strung," he said. "We're highly sensitive, highly nervous and prone to crack up because of some family problems." Ross claims that on March 8, 1950, Dayer conferred on him all the "keys that he had been given as an heir to Joseph Smith." Other family members have maintained that Ross simply received a father's blessing on that date. Esther says that after Ross returned to Salt Lake that May, she asked Dayer who was going to get the mantle. "He said he didn't know."

In January 1951, Dayer was nearly sixty-five, and obviously approaching death. Lucinda's nine-year-old daughter helped take care of him, cleaning his false teeth, spoon-feeding him and emptying the bedpan. Perhaps because of lead paint poisoning, Dayer had lost control of his muscles, and was partially paralyzed. The events of the next several weeks are somewhat hazy, and contradicted by different sources. However, in a written testimony she signed, Maud declared:

"He looked at his feet one morning. He had become very thin, and his feet larger by contrast. He began to cry aloud. I asked, 'What are you crying for?'

" 'I know that I am going to die.'

"I replied, 'Crying will not help you any. Are you afraid to die?'

"He answered, 'No, I am not, but I have not finished my work.' "

Repeating the same story at the age of eighty-six, Maud, who, in an interview with the authors, was frequently coached by children Alma and Esther, said Dayer sent for Joel. Joel was most fond of taking care of his father, and willingly came down from the nearby mountains where he had been working. Maud said she and Ervil, who held Dayer's paralyzed hands over Joel, both witnessed the passing of the mantle. Ervil later wrote in a pamphlet:

"[Joel's] father called him to his bedside and gave him a very strict and solemn charge. He there put all his earthly affairs in Joel's hands. He put him under a covenant and promise to carry on the work he had commenced, and to build on the foundation that he had laid, and said unto him:

" 'When I die my mantle will fall upon you, even as the mantle of Elijah fell upon Elisha, and even as the mantle of my grandfather [Benjamin F. Johnson] fell upon me; and you will have to round up your shoulders and bear it, because there is no one else qualified. I have tried to qualify your older brothers, but have only met with rebellion and opposition.'

"After having said these things . . . he told Joel that great things would be required at his hands, and said that the Lord would uphold him and strengthen him and give him wisdom to solve the many problems that would come before him in carrying out his life's work. He also gave him the promise at that time that he would not fail."

Joel returned to the mountains, about the same time brother Floren received a letter from Owen Allred, saying Dayer had no authority and never would. Floren asked his father about it and was supposedly told, "I want you to understand that I do have some authority through the mantle my grandfather conferred upon me. The day will come when we will take the lead over the Allreds and everyone else."

After a long and tumultuous life, Alma Dayer LeBaron died January 19, 1951.

The esoteric reality of his life was surely one of sorrow. If spirits seemed to speak to him, and a wild imagination conjured visions of awesome and wonderful things, then they were sadly inconsistent. His vacillation successfully hindered his best moments. Dayer's spirits, if judged by their servant's actions, were misguided or, at least, their subject was inadequate to the calling. He had clung to one single principle despite the humiliation from scoffers, and insults borne by his children: plural marriage. But for all his energy and desire, he could never successfully live it. His second wife disowned him, and buried him years before he was dead. Certainly Dayer had progeny, one or two children who must have made him proud. But before he died, they most resembled King Lear's brood, scrapping for the crown, however invisible, he might offer them. Ultimately, for him, the final creation of his life, Colonia LeBaron, was a failure too. This was no "place of peace, the shelter, not only from all injury, but from all terror, doubt and division," as John Ruskin has defined the home. The ranch shielded its residents from none of those misfortunes.

Dayer was buried up the road from Colonia LeBaron near the town of Galeana. After a drive on a dirt road beyond the town, crossing several small rivulets, the visitor reaches a cluttered one-acre Catholic graveyard hidden by mesquite bushes. The crosses are close together, decorated by paper flowers whose colors have run and faded in the elements. This particular day, Dayer's daughter-in-law, who had not been there for a while, could not find his unmarked site. She pointed to the graveyard's northeast corner, and said it is somewhere *there*.

4.

A NEW CHURCH

Following the death of their father, the LeBaron boys seemed to flounder. Margarito Bautista, the crafty Mexican, was first to win their fealty. His attempt at building a breakaway, all-Mexican, Mormon sect had come to naught in 1948 when most of his constituency, including his own nephew, rejoined the Salt Lake Church.

Undaunted, Bautista had proceeded to win his way into the heart of Fundamentalist leader Joseph Musser, partly by pledging support from several Mexican communities. Musser rewarded Bautista with a place on his high-ranking Council of Seven in May of 1951, only a few months after Dayer's death. Also elevated at the same time was Musser's personal physician, Dr. Rulon Allred, who became Musser's "special counselor" on the council.

Emboldened by his new authority, Bautista traveled to Colonia LeBaron that August. He had been fond of Dayer and had often discussed religion with him into the wee hours of the morning. He quickly ordained Dayer's sons, Joel and Ervil, as elders in the new Fundamentalist branch he formed at the LeBaron ranch. But the loyalty of the LeBaron brothers fluctuated greatly, much to the irritation of the Fundamentalist Elders who, nevertheless, always seemed to "forgive" them. In 1953, Bautista dissolved the Fundamentalist branch he had created around Colonia LeBaron, and established a United Order cooperative instead—something the LeBarons had dreamed of for years. Joel was named to head the new movement.

In June of 1955, a group of twenty-eight Fundamentalist Elders on their way to Mexico City stopped for still another confrontation with the aberrant brothers. At this meeting, five of the seven LeBarons were

54

present—only Ross and Ben were not—and again they were said to have contritely confessed their sins.

"In the presence of eleven men," remembers Owen Allred, "they solemnly promised that they would never again assume unauthorized authority, or seek to step beyond or above the priesthood that presided over them, and whom they claimed to uphold. Of their own choice, they made covenant that if they ever turned to their former ways, they would know that they could not be forgiven, and would be delivered to the buffetings of Satan. Every brother was a party to that promise. Every visitor present can testify to it."

In August of 1955, two months after the Fundamentalist gathering at Colonia LeBaron, brothers Joel and Floren left the homestead and went to Salt Lake City. The LeBaron family thought there was nothing unusual about the thirty-two-year-old Joel wanting to see the United States after seventeen years away from it.

Shortly after arriving in Salt Lake, Joel addressed a group of about thirty Fundamentalist Elders and, according to Owen Allred, "gave them to understand that he and his brothers were keeping their promise and would uphold those who presided over them."

However, Floren would later assert that Joel had come to Salt Lake with quite a different purpose in mind: to start a new church in accordance with the mantle he believed had been bestowed upon him by his dying father.

By September, Joel had dropped his bombshell: he, Floren and brother Ross—who had been living in Salt Lake for years—would indeed start a new church. It was to be named the Church of the Firstborn of the Fulness [sic] of Time. When Joel had first mentioned that he had received a revelation from God to carry on with the mantle given him by his father and start a new church, Floren, at least, was shaken. Fearing that his brother was being led astray by the devil, he urged Joel to seek some sort of confirmation from the Lord that the revelation was true.

Joel hiked up to a canyon above Salt Lake City and prayed, asking for a sign that he was worthy of the mantle. After a time he returned to tell Floren he'd gotten his confirmation—in the form of personal visitations from no less than nineteen prophets, including Abraham, Moses, Christ and Joseph Smith. "I put them to the acid test, and I know I was not deceived," Joel assured Floren. The acid test, according to Joseph Smith, constituted actually grabbing the hand of a resurrected prophet during a vision.

Ross was bound to be a little put off by all this. While he'd been living in Salt Lake, he had grown bolder and bolder in his own claims to Dayer's mantle. Somehow, Ross and Joel resolved their differences over the mantle and were able, along with Floren, to unite sufficiently to organize the new church. On September 21, 1955, Ross and Floren ordained Joel as president. He, in turn, ordained them to lesser positions; the three brothers together comprised a "trinity." After the ordinations, they went to the Utah State Capitol building where they filed notarized copies of articles of incorporation with the Secretary of State's office.

Once the euphoria wore off, it wasn't long before Joel and Ross were at loggerheads about how the fledgling church was to be run and who was in fact to run it. These issues stemmed from the more basic question of who had the right to Dayer LeBaron's mantle. Each brother claimed the right to preside over the other, and since neither would back down, a split was inevitable. Finally, one night, Ross angrily ordered Joel out of his house, and the two brothers were to have little or no contact with each other again. Floren sided with Joel, but Ross, undaunted, formed his own church a few months later—a church he still presides over today in Salt Lake City, his only followers a herd of sixty goats. Ross spends his spare time building toy flying saucers, modeled after the ones which he insists Christ will use as transportation for the Second Coming.

Joel now set about the decidedly uphill task of trying to get the Fundamentalist Elders he had nominally followed just a few months before, to now follow *him* and accept him as the Lord's prophet. He made public the text of a revelation he said he'd received, aimed at none other than Rulon C. Allred. The revelation called on "my servant Rulon" (who had become president of the Fundamentalist Council of Seven following the death of Musser) to gather his followers in Colonia LeBaron, a ranch referred to as the "Land of Zion." It ordered Rulon to serve as Joel's counselor and have him consecrate all his followers' tithing to the Firstborn Church so that it could be used for the Lord's work.

The revelation concluded by warning: "And again I say unto you: the time has fully come spoken of by the mouths of mine holy prophets, when I have set my hand again the second time to gather my people to Zion, and this sign I give unto you that you may know, that all those who reject these words and do not speedily repent shall be turned over to the buffetings of Satan and shall be cut off from among my people, and Satan shall have power over his and I will have power over mine, and I will be even in the midst of them, that the sheep might be divided from the goats, and that the wheat might be divided from the tares, that my people might be prepared to be caught up unto the clouds while fire and brimstone are rained upon the face of the whole earth, to the utter destruction of the wicked and ungodly. Even so, amen."

The Allreds, when they learned of Joel's "revelation," considered it heresy of the first order. Rulon staked out a position above the fray, as if not to dignify the new sect by giving it too much attention. "I have not felt justified in contending with persons so evidently misled by teachings contrary to the teachings and principles of the gospel as restored by the prophet Joseph Smith," he commented to one interviewer, castigating the LeBarons for "giving revelations to those they once acknowledged as qualified to administer the gospel on their behalf. . . . We consider that the Church of the Firstborn is a particular abomination, being founded by false prophets and upon false doctrines and perversions of the word of God."

As Joel set about the task of trying to win converts to his movement in and around Salt Lake City, brother Floren returned to Mexico and broke the news to the folks back at the ranch, who were understandably shocked.

"We were horrified," remembers Alma. "We figured Joel had gone off the deep end." Ervil said it was like learning all his brothers and sisters had been killed. "He loved Joel so much, and felt so close to him, that to think he had become a false prophet, Ervil felt terrible," adds Alma.

The matriarch of the family, Maud, wept as if Joel had been injured or killed. "To think so many things have happened to my children, and now to have this happen to Joel," she sobbed to her son Verlan. Amidst her anger and despair, Maud also told several witnesses something that cast doubt on the legitimacy of Joel's holy claims.

Irene Kunz LeBaron, Verlan's second wife, recalls: "Mother LeBaron said, 'Why, he [Joel] never held anything. Father LeBaron never gave it to him.' I heard this with my own ears. She said Joel had flipped his lid. When Father LeBaron died he was paralyzed. For weeks before, he could not even raise his hands. They had to raise him up and feed him by spoon. No way could he ever have called Joel unto him. No way could he ever have used his hands [to bless him]. But later, all of a sudden here Maud comes up and says she was a witness when Dayer gave the mantle to Joel. I couldn't believe it. I went to her and asked her about it. And she said: 'Well, I just didn't understand, I got mixed up. The passing of the mantle was supposed to be hid from the world, like they were keeping it a secret.' She was my mother-in-law, but she was a storyteller."

Joel was now under fire not only in Utah but among the people of his own home as well. Floren LeBaron nevertheless urged the leaders of the United Order in Colonia LeBaron to convene a meeting so that he could explain more about Joel's new church. Given the colony's already tarnished reputation and the LeBaron brothers' vacillation in following Fundamentalist authority, many at the meeting angrily rejected the claims of Joel and Floren out of hand.

Floren made little or no headway with his family until he reached into his pocket, pulled out a rumpled piece of paper and read aloud Joel's revelation to Rulon Allred. At this, Ervil turned thoughtfully quiet and took notice. Verlan—heretofore incredulous at Joel's claims and worried that they would further blacken the family name—was sufficiently moved by the revelation to rush home, wake up his wives at 2 A.M. and read it aloud to them. Irene started sobbing and said it couldn't be true, but Verlan thought no one could simply come up with something like this unless it had been divinely inspired, and he suggested they all at least think more about Joel's possible prophecy.

Alma, for his part, listened to what Floren read and remembers feeling ". . . a thrilling, burning feeling within my bosom. It made me feel real good. It made me feel like that was a true revelation. It felt like it was the spirit of God inspiring me, not a bad spirit." The oscillating Alma was soon baptized as the third member of the Church of the Firstborn of the Fulness of Times.

However, almost everyone else in Colonia LeBaron still had serious doubts about Joel and his new church. They longed to question him in person about his revelation, beliefs and experiences, but he remained in Utah. It was decided to raise some money and send Verlan to Salt Lake City for a talk with Joel. Verlan returned with a very negative report, telling the curious it was his opinion that Joel was a "false prophet." At this, Floren—who had been elated after seeing how Joel's revelation had at least stemmed the colony's strongly negative reaction—grew deeply depressed, and Alma wavered in his newfound faith. They both got more and more anxious to see Joel.

Finally, in early 1956, Joel left Salt Lake—a prophet with no disciples—and returned home to Colonia LeBaron, where he learned he had only two followers. Far from a heroic homecoming, people greeted Joel, at arm's length, skeptically and as an object of curiosity. Many of them were waiting to size Joel up and speak with him.

One of the first was Ervil. Though Joel's revelation to Allred had given him pause, Ervil still told intimates he thought that with his superior knowledge of the scriptures, he would riddle Joel's position with so many holes that the new prophet would soon have to abandon his claims. But after the two closeted themselves together for several hours, Ervil found, much to his surprise, that every argument he raised turned in favor of Joel. Since this had never happened before Joel's trip to Salt Lake, Ervil concluded he was now dealing with a genuine prophet. He became the church's fourth member, and after he joined, Maud LeBaron became the fifth to be baptized, reasoning that if it was good enough for Ervil, maybe Joel had something after all. Others in the colony applied the same logic and the conversions began to increase.

Another who had been waiting his turn with Joel was Margarito Bautista, the aging Fundamentalist leader from Ozumba. Bautista was furious at this sudden change in a man he had named head of the United Order in Colonia LeBaron. He raged at Joel, dismissed his grandiose claims out of hand and interrupted every time Joel tried to speak on his own behalf. Bautista tried to get Ervil, whom he considered the most intelligent of the LeBaron brothers, to renounce his new faith and label Joel a pretender. But it was to no avail. Finally, realizing he was waging a losing battle, Bautista told Ervil and the rest of the LeBarons he would give them five years. If they could set up a "valid consecration order" within that time, then he would "bow the knee," and assume there was some merit to Joel's claims.

Having made this somewhat idle and face-saving statement, a despondent Bautista left Colonia LeBaron and returned home to Ozumba. He remained bitter toward the LeBarons till he died in 1961, and some think his clash with Joel undermined his own faith. Pressed on his deathbed to appoint a successor to himself, Bautista wearily asked to be left alone, explaining that he had "lost the spirit."

Bitterness toward the LeBarons remained strong in the Allred camp as well, but in early 1956, Rulon Allred, by now the head of his own Fundamentalist split-off group, decided to make one final effort to "straighten the LeBaron boys out." He sent two of his trusted disciples—John Butchereit and a companion—to Mexico with instructions to pick apart Joel's position point by point. Joel calmly rebutted each point on the list, and the Allred group suffered a severe blow to its prestige when the two emissaries announced that not only did they find merit in Joel's claims, but that they were renouncing their positions in the Allred faction to be baptized into the Church of the Firstborn.

Butchereit, especially, quickly immersed himself in his new faith and became a missionary. It was not long before he could find it within himself to write: "I wish to say here to all men and especially to my former associates among the Fundamentalists that any man [other than Joel LeBaron] who tampers with and professes to [be prophet] is playing with fire. . . . If these men do not repent, come to the waters of baptism and be cleansed, they are in open rebellion against God's legitimate authority. . . . When the folly of these individuals who so profusely spread propaganda against the LeBarons is uncovered, their accusations vanish into thin air as did similar propaganda against Joseph Smith and Christ . . . and I am a firsthand witness that the charges are false."*

That Rulon Allred and Fundamentalists of other stripes were "playing with fire" if they did not rally to Joel's banner, was one of the first of several veiled threats to come out of the LeBaron camp during the early years of the church. Another tract, published in 1962, would specifically take Allred and his brother Owen to task for engaging in "character assassination" against the LeBarons, and note that the penalty for such behavior under Civil Law as practiced in the days of Moses . . . was death. Enforcement of Moses' Civil Law—the Ten Commandments— was to become one of the primary tenets of the Church of the Firstborn.

Though Joel had incorporated the church in the fall of 1955, it was not until April 3, 1956, that he formally "called the church to order" in Colonia LeBaron. There was some significance to this early spring date. It was 120 years to the day—according to Mormon scripture—after the "dispensation of the gospel" was committed to Joseph Smith by Elias at the Kirtland Temple in Ohio. Joel called members to be rebaptized. He

Ensign, Vol. 3, Nos. 9 and 10. Nov.–Dec. 1963., pp. 21 and 22.

named his brother Alma presiding bishop—or head of the church's economic affairs—and Ervil, the scriptorian, was tapped to lead a missionary program.

If this missionary effort were to be at all successful, Joel deemed it necessary to commit his doctrine and his claims to writing, so that the world could know what he stood for. He assigned Ervil the task of writing the Firstborn Bible, as it were, which they decided to call *Priesthood Expounded.*

The two brothers spent nearly a year composing the fifty-six-page booklet. Joel would do the "revelations" while Ervil would dig out scriptural justification for the divine disclosures and do the actual writing. Ervil often toiled for hours over the wording of a single sentence. When Ervil finally completed his writing, the finished product was neither conciliatory in its approach nor tolerant of other paths to truth and spiritual enlightenment.

"If we LeBaron brothers," Ervil wrote, "are so fortunate as to be able to explain [the principles of priesthood authority] correctly in this time of confusion and turmoil, when all others of our time have utterly failed to do it, then let every man and woman sit in silence and put their hands on their mouths, recognize where the authority is, and cease to speak evil of the servants of God."

Priesthood Expounded went on to set forth the LeBaron concept of how priesthood authority—the right of the Firstborn—must follow the lineage of a chosen family and be passed by the holder to a successor he designates. For the LeBarons, this principle relied on the tenuous and disputed connection between Joseph Smith and Benjamin F. Johnson— the man Ervil called "the bosom friend and companion of the prophet. . . . He became to the prophet what John the Beloved was to the Saviour."

Ervil wrote that Smith adopted Johnson as his son and appointed him to "stand at the head of the prophet's posterity." This conferral of authority, he continued, was "kept secret by command of God, for this is the priesthood that was to be hid from the world" until the last days. The secret was now being revealed because Joel LeBaron had been called to set the House of God in order, he explained.

Ervil concluded by warning that those who did not now follow Joel ". . . will find no inheritance among the people of God, and ere they are aware, the judgments of the Almighty will overtake them."

Rooted in Mormon doctrine is the concept of gathering. Since the inception of the church, the Saints have been taught to gather, and they have done so—first in Ohio; then "Zion" in Jackson County, Missouri; Nauvoo, Illinois; and finally the Great Basin in the Rocky Mountains. Although such concentrations of Mormons often invited persecution, gathering also promoted unity of spirit, lifestyle and culture.

True to their Mormon ancestry, Joel and Ervil determined in 1958 that there should be a gathering of the Lamanites (Indians) in Colonia

LeBaron. Ervil had established a Firstborn mission many miles to the south in Mexico and attracted a number of people to join the church. The LeBarons invited all their converts (by 1961 they would claim a total of 500 church members, though no evidence of that has ever been produced) to help them build up Colonia LeBaron, promising that as part of the United Order system of communal living, everyone would be fed, clothed and sheltered.

In a February 1, 1958, bulletin announcing a general church conference for that April, Ervil grandly envisioned that the Lamanites, who he said would flock to the colony "by the hundreds and thousands," would help the LeBarons clear the land, build houses, shops, a textile mill, a sawmill, an electric power plant, a radio station and a printing establishment. Ervil ordered Alma, the presiding bishop, to provide for the Mexicans' "temporal welfare" in return for the services they rendered.

Though the converts never materialized in anywhere near the numbers foretold by Ervil, enough did come to constitute a serious financial burden on the colony in general, and Alma in particular, who sank into heavy personal debt during this period. It soon became apparent that the "Lamanites" cared little, if at all, about the LeBaron gospel. They were simply dirt-poor Mexicans looking for a free meal. Since the colony had virtually no means of generating capital other than farming, and since tithing from the few existing church members was committed mostly to missionary work, Alma eventually announced that the freeloading would have to end and 90 percent of the colony's population would have to move on. The Mexicans were understandably bitter when the LeBaron promises were not fulfilled, and Ervil's Lamanite Gathering was chalked up as an experiment which produced something less than a shot in the arm for the Firstborn missionary program.

Ervil was now second in importance only to Joel, and despite the setback with the Lamanites, his influence within the fledgling Firstborn Church continued to grow. Joel, his stature as a prophet notwithstanding, did not cut much of a divine figure, remaining a simple, down-home agrarian. He still toiled in the fields around the colony and spent much of his time caught up in the nitty-gritty of day-to-day life. Ervil, on the other hand, rarely, if ever, stooped to manual labor. When not out in the missionary field, he would spend his time reading or writing, and charting overall goals and directions for the church. As Joel opted more and more to maintain a low profile, Ervil subtly moved to fill the power vacuum.

This maneuvering was not lost on all the other LeBarons and early converts living in the colony. The first to take note of it publicly was Noel Billingsley Pratt—who was born and raised in Colonia Dublan, one of the nearby Mexican Mormon colonies. In 1956, he became the first non-LeBaron to convert to the Firstborn Church.

In 1957, Pratt began mimeographing and editing a monthly semiofficial Firstborn publication called *The Rolling Stone*. In the December

1958 issue, Pratt attacked Joel and the young church in an article entitled "Self-Criticism or the Case of the Ugly Duckling." Calling the church "a woman" that lacked organizational muscle and a well-defined program, Pratt blamed mainly Joel, saying that the new prophet had not represented the Lord "in much of anything." He called on Joel to assert his authority more, but warned: "Beware that you do not mistake the arm of your brother Ervil for that of the Lord."

And in early 1959, Pratt published another tract in which he warned directly of Ervil's mounting influence: "The root of the whole trouble," he wrote, "is Ervil. We do not belong to Joel's church. We belong to Ervil's church."

5

A FRENCH LEGION

The struggling Church of the Firstborn in Mexico was soon to acquire new disciples from a most unexpected source: a group of Mormon missionaries in France, led astray from LDS gospel by Bill Tucker, a stocky, five-foot-sixish charismatic from southern California.

Tucker came from a mixed Protestant-Catholic religious background, but neither faith seemed to offer the fervor and passion he thought a religion should. So at age fifteen, Tucker became a Mormon convert and quickly immersed himself in the world of the Latter-day Saints, despite a busy high school schedule in Pasadena where he was a star football player and gymnast.

Tucker went on to UCLA where he pursued an intensive course in biology and was graduated early, accumulating enough credits to bypass a master's degree and enter directly into a PhD program. His involvement in science did not affect his devotion to his religion, but being a scholar, Tucker had gradually come to read about and investigate earlier phases of Mormon history, including polygamy and Fundamentalism.

When he discovered that the early Mormons had practiced plural marriage, Tucker began a thorough study of the principle, and he also became acquainted with Fundamentalist tenets and arguments. Some impressed Tucker, and for the first time, he began to entertain doubts about the Mormons' abandoning principles they once held so sacred. But at the time, these doubts weren't strong enough to shake his basic faith in the church.

In 1956, Bill Tucker decided to postpone the pursuit of his PhD at UCLA and accept a call to be a Mormon missionary in France—

thereby setting into motion a series of strange events that would dramatically change his life and those of dozens of others.

In Paris, Tucker plunged into his work with such boundless energy and enthusiasm that other missionaries felt like they were standing still by comparison. He was intense, self-disciplined and he led by example. Because of these personal qualities, and his apparent dedication to advancing the work of the church, Tucker was chosen as counselor to French mission president Milton L. Christensen—the number-two position in the country and the highest honor for any missionary. He learned to speak fluent French, traveled extensively throughout the country and was credited with "setting the French mission on fire"—elevating it from one of the least successful Mormon outposts in Europe to one of the most successful.

However, Tucker's scripture-reading was leading him increasingly away from the gospel according to Salt Lake, and toward the gospel as practiced by the Fundamentalist rebels. He found himself more and more intrigued by the "mysteries" that rank-and-file Mormons were warned not to become exposed to. He considered such warnings stifled curiosity and were an insult to a member's intelligence. Gradually, he came to suspect the church of hiding something.

Tucker began sharing his concerns with others in the mission field and discussing Fundamentalist concepts. He used the strategic access afforded him by his job to reach many of the missionaries scattered throughout France. Soon, secret "study groups" were organized.

"Bill began instilling Fundamentalism in those sessions," remembers Marilyn Lamborn, an early participant, "but always with the idea of making us more spiritual. We were seeking truth. If the principles of Joseph Smith, Brigham Young and John Taylor had been cast aside, it was our obligation to go back and find out about it. We did not preach fundamentalism to others. We had many intellectual discussions about it. We were 'delving into the mysteries'—something which we'd been taught not to do all our lives."

Mysteries were concepts or elements of early Mormon doctrine such as plural marriage, The Creation (and disbelief in evolution), signs of the end of the world, and the proper lineage of priesthood authority. The church believed that if its members began to investigate these issues—for which there was not enough accepted doctrine available to draw conclusive answers—they might apostatize, and spin off into another, perhaps unhappy, religious life. Mysteries were red herrings which diverted attention from the basics of the gospel: obedience to commandments, faith, repentance and the most important elements of Christ's atonement, salvation and exaltation.

Tucker spoke to perhaps a third of the French missionaries about Fundamentalism. Initially this did not appear to be a calculated attempt to subvert Mormon doctrine: Tucker merely seemed anxious to share his questions with others to try and provoke a healthy spiritual skepticism. But as more questions were raised, as more investigations were conducted by more people into theretofore forbidden areas, and as more cathartic secret meetings were held, a feeling evolved among a dozen or more leading missionaries that they had come up against a wall of taboos erected by the LDS establishment—and had broken through to discover the truth. If the beginnings of Tucker's movement were innocent, the results were, in fact, Mormon heresy.

They were even more heretic because Tucker had succeeded in enlisting the elite of the missionary field, including three district presidents: John Stephens, Donald Cannon and Daniel Jordan.

Some of the dissident missionaries claim they didn't realize where Tucker was leading them at first. One of them was Marilyn Lamborn: "At the time, I didn't even know Fundamentalism was taboo. I was just thrilled with my new knowledge. I'd write home and say these beautiful doors were being opened to me. I guess my letters must have sounded crazy. I really didn't think I would ever have to give up my beloved church. I didn't know I was headed in that direction. I thought I was just blessed with extra knowledge.

But gradually we came to think that the church members were just a bunch of sheep who'd believe anything their leaders would tell them. They were being fed a watered-down diet of nothing. There was nothing really strong in the Mormon Church to make you fervent, like the original believers. Nothing to really turn you on, or give your life purpose. All the Mormons had to do was get up and talk about the Word of Wisdom—don't drink and don't smoke. That's about as strong as the sermons ever got."

Inevitably, the activities of Tucker and his followers created a split within the French mission. The mere decision by some missionaries to investigate Fundamentalism further provoked bitter opposition and outraged reactions among others remaining true to the Salt Lake line. Men and women who once had jointly sung the praises of Mormondom and vowed to take that gospel to all of France, now began to divide. Tensions increased.

In January of 1958, David Shore—a missionary who had grown close to Bill Tucker—completed his two-year stint in France and returned to the U.S. By this time, Shore and Tucker had reached the firm conclusion that the present-day LDS establishment was "out of line" and only a shell of a church. They had decided that hidden somewhere on earth was a "One Mighty and Strong"—a prophet who held true priesthood authority. The time was right for him to emerge. Recalls Marilyn Lamborn, "David promised Bill before he left that he would go looking for the One Mighty and Strong when he returned home, and investigate the Fundamentalists further. First, he went to the Deseret Bookstore in Salt Lake City."

There Shore picked up reams of Fundamentalist literature, including Ervil LeBaron's *Priesthood Expounded*, and sent it all back to Tucker in France. Tucker read all the tracts but was most impressed by

Priesthood Expounded. He had Marilyn Lamborn type up copies of some of the literature and pass it around to the other dissident missionaries.

Walter Jennings, for one, was sufficiently impressed by *Priesthood Expounded* to write Ervil in Mexico asking for additional information about the Church of the Firstborn. When he received this, he concluded that the claims of the LeBarons were "perfectly just" and superseded those of the Mormon Church. Under these circumstances, Jennings and another missionary, Harvey Harper, decided to leave France and return home, rather than continue to preach what they no longer believed to be true.

Jennings and Harper explained their positions to French mission president Milton Christensen during two meetings held in August of 1958. Bill Tucker attended the second meeting, and in this session, Christensen picked up a hint of where Tucker himself stood. It was then that Christensen realized the full dimensions of the problem: the likelihood that more than a dozen of his leading missionaries would renounce their church for an apostate group. Such a mass defection in the mission field was unheard of in all of Mormondom.

News of the revolt spread quickly to other LDS missions in Europe and to the highest levels of church authority in Salt Lake City, including then-president David O. McKay. It was determined that leading church officials—scheduled to be in London in September for the dedication of a new Mormon temple—should closely question the dissident French missionaries and, if necessary, launch excommunication proceedings. On September 8, 1958, Tucker, Donald Cannon and John Stephens—the three men deemed responsible for infecting the French mission—were taken to the British Mission Home in London where church authorities interviewed them separately until three in the morning.

In their line of questioning, the church authorities seemed to treat as fact many of the rumors they had heard about the French missionaries. Tucker was portrayed as the devil incarnate who was casting some sort of spell over the others. He was written off as beyond salvation, but the officials endeavored to save Cannon, Stephens and the others from Tucker's clutches. The church wanted to avoid excommunication, at least partly because that would only call undue attention to an already embarrassing situation.

The questioners appealed to Cannon and Stephens not to forsake their church and bring disgrace upon themselves, their families and Milton Christensen, the French mission president. They would be allowed to spend the rest of their time in France doing nothing, if only they would complete their mission honorably.

Questions of doctrine and priesthood authority were never discussed. The president of the LDS British mission lectured the three men on the evils of polygamy as if that subject were the sole issue in question. He refused to allow the dissidents to address what they considered to be the primary issue: priesthood authority. Finally the three men were able to make it plain that they no longer wished to stay on as missionaries and asked to be excommunicated.

The next morning, all the rest of the French missionaries were interviewed to separate the faithful from the apostates. Each was asked whether he or she supported McKay as a prophet of God. Ten said they did not. At least three others who didn't had already left Europe for home.

The ten dissident missionaries were ordered to report to the British Mission Home at nine o'clock the following morning. Before the meeting, Don Cannon received a long-distance call. Jesse Curtis had phoned Cannon's parents after all, and the shaken parents were now on the line to speak with their wayward son. Wrote Cannon in his journal: "Those few moments were by far the most difficult I spent in this whole experience. I would have done anything to have been able to spare them the grief and pain they felt, short of denying my beliefs; but I knew what had to be done."

The meeting was called to order by Henry D. Moyle—a member of the Quorum of the Twelve, who had been personally dispatched from Salt Lake City by McKay to restore the French missionaries to their senses. Moyle allegedly began by announcing that McKay had received a divine revelation that the missionaries had a secret pact among them. If they would admit to this, and deny allegiance to it, they would be forgiven and welcomed back to the mission.

The missionaries could only smile. The charge was absurd enough on its face, but to link it to divine inspiration only reinforced the missionaries' convictions that they were right.

At a second meeting, when the authorities saw their words were having no effect, they became furious. Milton Christensen, the French mission president whose prestige had suffered such a severe blow, was beside himself with rage. According to Cannon, he walked in front of all the ten missionaries and, shouting, condemned each one of them to hell.

After this meeting, the excommunication trial followed. Henry Moyle presided over a court made up of seven other persons: Hugh B. Brown (another member of the Quorum of the Twelve), Isaacson, Christensen, and four other faithful French Missionaries. The trial itself was short. One official named to defend the missionaries asserted only that some of them should not be excommunicated because they had been brainwashed. That was the extent of the defense. After a brief recess, the decision was handed down: nine of the ten were excommunicated.

The nine were: Bill Tucker, Donald Cannon, John Stephens, Daniel Jordan, Niel Poulsen, Loftin Harvey, Jane Alda, Marilyn Lamborn and Nancy Fulk (who went by her middle name of Eunice). Marlene

Wessel, who initially had said she did not support David O. McKay as a prophet, was not excommunicated, but she decided to go home with the other nine anyway.

"Such a thing had never happened before in the Mormon Church, nor has anything like it happened since," remembers Wayne Owens, a French missionary at the time who served on the excommunication court.* "It was astonishing, and the impact on the church was electric. All the leaders were in a state of shock, and it was regarded as a family tragedy."

Aboard an inexpensive ocean liner—the TSS *New York*, Greek Lines—sailing from Le Havre to New York—eight of the excommunicated plus Marlene Wessel (Loftin Harvey returned home by other means) were still on a spiritual high. It was the headiest period of their lives. They had never felt so free, so sure of the righteousness of their cause and their faith in God. "It was a marvelous trip," recalls Marilyn Lamborn. "I was happy as a lark. Thrilled to death with everything."

Bill Tucker—who for two years had immersed himself in religion and lived an ascetic life—finally allowed his mind to drift to more temporal concerns. He developed something more than just a spiritual interest in "sisters" Lamborn and Fulk, talking to them both at length and, on alternate nights, taking each on romantic moonlit strolls along the ship's deck.

Despite the romantic interludes, Tucker still found plenty of time to lead intense spiritual discussions on board ship. Much of what he talked about centered around *Priesthood Expounded*, which, Tucker said, he had read cover-to-cover six times. He had pitted it against other scriptures and found it doctrinally sound. He said he was going to Colonia LeBaron, in the desert of northern Mexico, to investigate the Church of the Firstborn for himself.

It was evident that Tucker's endorsement carried immense weight. Most of the others announced that they would go to Mexico too, and as the ship prepared to land in New York, the French missionaries were enraptured by the prospect of undertaking their journey to Zion.

"As I finish this account, we have been to sea five days," Donald Cannon concluded in his journal of the period. "I am determined to go to Mexico. All of our studies have led us there. God's authority is still on this earth, for it was promised to remain. We shall find it."†

---

*In 1972, Owens was elected to Congress from Utah as a Democrat. He served on the House Judiciary Committee during its 1974 hearings on the impeachment of Richard Nixon, and he voted to impeach. Owens ran for the Senate that same year and was defeated.

†*Ensign*, Vol. 1, No. 6. August 1961, p. 8.

6.

THE MEXICAN ZION

In Ogden, Utah, Marilyn Lamborn's parents sadly climbed into the Cadillac parked in front of their modest home and began driving east toward New York for a reunion with their apostate daughter.

The Lamborns were good, faithful Mormons, and the news from the French mission field had crushed them. "This was worse than a death in the family," remembers Marilyn's older sister, Carol. "Neighbors and friends gathered at my parents' house to grieve for Marilyn just as if she had died."

Then too, the Elders of the Mormon Church had made matters even worse. A member of the Quorum of the Twelve had called to report that Marilyn had come under the influence of the devil-ridden Bill Tucker. He warned the Lamborns never to allow their daughter into their home again lest they too become afflicted with the same dark spirit. But LaVerne and Willard Lamborn had rebelled at that: Marilyn was their daughter and would always be welcome in their home.

The unhappy parents had decided to reserve judgment on Marilyn until they could see her in person. Perhaps it was still possible to bring her back to her senses.

Marilyn's brother-in-law (her sister Carol's husband) Earl Jensen was even prepared to go to James Bondian lengths to save Marilyn. Jensen was a former agent of both the FBI and CIA, well versed in electronics and skulduggery. He had recently returned home from a stint as head "security attaché" for the American Embassy in Tel Aviv. As devout Mormons, the Jensens found that the cocktail party circuit in the foreign service was not for them; it was an empty life without any redeeming spiritual values.

"We decided the best thing for us to do was to move back to a place like Sacramento, California, which we did, buy a little home on the corner, establish ourselves in the ward and become good, card-holding, simple Elm Street Mormons," remembers Carol. "That was the greatest happiness we could ever hope for."

Thus when Marilyn was excommunicated, the Jensens were as upset as anyone else. Earl was suddenly inspired: he would do a black-bag job on Bill Tucker. He would ride out on one of the tugboats escorting the Greek liner carrying the French missionaries into New York harbor, climb aboard and plant some Communist literature in Bill Tucker's luggage. The right customs men would be tipped off and Tucker could be arrested as a subversive. As Bill was being questioned and detained, friends, family or church officials could whisk the other missionaries away and attempt to deprogram them.

Earl and Carol determined that they needed to get the blessings of the Lamborns before carrying out the scheme. But the parents had already left Ogden on their long drive to New York. Earl left messages en route and in New York, but he could never make connections before the boat docked, so the bag-job idea was abandoned.

Most of the people waiting to greet the missionaries expected them to walk off the ship and leave for Mexico en masse. But they didn't. Their new beliefs hadn't colored their feelings for family and friends, and those who were met, willingly left New York and allowed themselves to be taken home to various parts of the country. Those who weren't met—Bill Tucker, Dan Jordan and Neil Poulsen—did leave immediately for Colonia LeBaron, having told the others they would contact them as soon as they "found out."

Tucker had made no attempt to keep the missionaries together, but the Lamborns, at least, took no chances. They immediately separated Marilyn from the suspected devil and refused to speak with him.

The novelty of being home in Ogden again wore off quickly for Marilyn—a thin, intense woman with searching eyes and a birdlike face. She missed Bill. She missed the spiritual exhilaration of being with the other missionaries, along with their comraderie and common sense of purpose. She felt isolated in a Mormon wasteland—thousands of miles away from where Zion was unfolding in northern Mexico.

Finally, she and Donald Cannon, who was in nearby Salt Lake City, decided to set out for Mexico. They took a bus to El Paso, and from there another bus south toward Colonia LeBaron. The colony was miles from a main highway at the time, so the bus left them off at the intersection of a dirt access road. They were in the middle of the Mexican desert and it was after midnight.

Just as they were getting ready to spend the rest of the night by the side of the road, one of the Romneys from Colonia Juarez happened by in a pickup truck and offered to drive them to their destination. Marilyn remembers thinking at the time that the fortuitous appearance of the pickup was a "major miracle"—and further evidence that God was looking out for them on the road to Zion.

They arrived at 4 A.M. Everyone was asleep, so they lay down beside a woodpile. When they awoke after sleeping a few hours, the first person they encountered was Charlotte LeBaron, Verlan's wife. She was boiling water over an open fire, preparing to wash a load of laundry, when she noticed the two strangers. They introduced themselves as French missionaries, and that was enough for Charlotte to greet them with open arms. For Bill Tucker and his two companions who had just left the colony had impressed the LeBarons greatly—as well they might have, given the talent then available down at the ranch—and the fledgling church was fairly giddy at the prospect of having attracted a bright and young new wave of converts. Things were looking up.

When Charlotte told Marilyn and Donald that Bill and the others had left the day before, Marilyn's heart sank, only to rise again when Charlotte quickly added that they all planned to return within a week for the church's conference. Marilyn hoped that when Bill returned, they would be married in the midst of true priesthood authority. In the meantime, Marilyn and Steve met the LeBarons.

Ervil LeBaron fancied himself quite a ladies' man, and others who lived in the colony during the early days generally attest that he was. He was tall, dark and handsome, and his recent appointment as Patriarch—the number-two man behind prophet Joel and the spiritual leader of God's kingdom on earth—entrusted him with the power to bless others and assure their "calling and election" in the afterlife. This was no small point of attraction to Colonia LeBaron women, who generally were treated like chattel and needed the promise of a hereafter to make this life—wherein they were doomed to pay for Eve's transgressions—the least bit palatable.

Ervil already had two Mexican wives. Although father Dayer had always taught his sons to spread their seeds liberally among the Lamanites so as to uplift Mexican stock, Ervil now badly wanted to add a white, American wife to his stable. The first such woman that he'd had a chance to meet for a long time was Marilyn Lamborn. While Bill Tucker was still away, Ervil devised various ways of getting Marilyn alone, and missed no opportunity of flattering her.

"I had been without male attention for three years," Marilyn recalls. "Before that I'd been a very average American girl. I had a lot of boyfriends and dates. Ervil was a very attractive man, though he didn't appeal to me—honest to gosh—because I was in love with Bill. But Ervil certainly thought he was attractive. Very tall, kind of gangling, strong looking. He'd been waiting for an American wife to save him from all his problems with his two Mexican wives. They were fighting all the time.

"His philosophy was you had to have at least three wives. At least three. One was an abomination before God. Two, you brought on more troubles than you could ever hope for. . . . He said he needed an English-speaking wife to bring up the standards of the Mexican women."

One day Ervil took out a snapshot Tucker had given him of the French missionaries posing aboard the ocean liner on their way home from France. "You know, Marilyn," he said, "they showed me this picture, and I knew immediately that you were to be my wife. It was a revelation just straight out of heaven."

Though Ervil would use this same line with numerous women over the next several years, Marilyn—feeling that she was now surrounded by holy men—had no reason to doubt his sincerity at the time. On the way home, the missionaries had decided that if they went to Mexico and joined the LeBaron church, they each would be faced with a test: the willingness to give up the one thing in life that they held most dear. Marilyn felt Ervil was her test. Should she accept his offer or wait for Bill, the man she really loved?

Beside herself, Marilyn took Donald Cannon aside and asked for advice. He reminded her that she had initially received what she considered to be divinely inspired feelings that she was to marry Bill. So she put Ervil off and waited anxiously for Bill to return. Finally, she actually went up to the cutoff road and waited for his car to appear. When it did, they embraced, and both blurted out they had come to the realization that they should be married. Bill said she'd be his first wife.

Most of the French missionaries showed up at Colonia LeBaron for the Firstborn conference in October of 1958. There were a total of about fifty people in attendance and the session was a "spiritual feast." The discussions were rich, the fervor intense and the mood upbeat. The conference netted dozens of new baptisms for the church, and it was the missionaries who were the stars of the show, who would bring in still more converts. The normally stoic LeBarons could not suppress their delight.

"You could tell by the expressions on their faces that they thought we were Christ Himself come to save them all," remembers Marilyn.

Shortly after midnight on the last day of conference, October 19, Marilyn and several other French missionaries were baptized into the church at a natural spring not far from the colony. Then, dripping wet, Marilyn emerged from the pool and was married to Bill Tucker, along with two other French missionaries—John Stephens and Jane Alda—in a double ceremony. Joel officiated and read from the scriptures illuminated by car headlights. Ervil also attended the ceremony—perhaps somewhat reluctantly, since Marilyn had eluded him.

The Tuckers left for California. Bill had been appointed by Ervil the Firstborn Church's "mission president of the western states." They were still missionaries, but for a different cause.

Rather than face the music with Marilyn's parents immediately in Ogden, the Tuckers decided to first reveal their new life, and lifestyle, to Marilyn's sister Carol and her husband Earl Jensen in Sacramento.

Though Carol was apprehensive about her sister's visit, family was family, and her door would always be open for Marilyn—even if she was married to the devil's agent.

"So here comes this Bill Tucker," recalls Carol, "and I will never forget walking out on the front porch and seeing him walk down that driveway. He was in a pin-stripe suit that was ill-fitting, a white shirt which wasn't all that white, a tie that really didn't match. He was very short! But he had an absolutely marvelous smile and eyes that gleamed. I asked myself if that was the kind of smile Satan would have."

Earl Jensen, no mean scriptorian himself, had been waiting to confront the infamous Bill Tucker for some time. The two men virtually abandoned Carol and Marilyn and closeted themselves for several days discussing Mormon scriptures.

"This was a life and death struggle," continues Carol. "I heard things that I had never heard before. And I saw looks on Earl's face that I had never seen before. It was frightening, but also very exhilarating. They met head-on, but there was this tremendous mutual respect."

The Jensens agreed to set up another confrontation between a group of the dissident French missionaries and Mormon leaders in Sacramento. Both sides treated each other with detached courtesy, but according to Carol Jensen, the Mormons were "humiliated." They were unable, or unwilling to answer, specific questions on the evolution of Mormon doctrine. They were embarrassed and we were embarrassed for them. It was a very awkward evening."

Now seriously questioning the Mormon faith which had been the bedrock of his life, Earl Jensen was sufficiently moved to travel to Salt Lake City and get responses from as many of the Quorum of the Twelve as he could get in to see. Finally, he concluded that someone in the LDS Church was wrong and he told Carol he was going to Mexico to investigate the LeBaron movement. He returned baptized.

This was no small turn of events in the life of a once-staunch Mormon who had led the effort to deprogram Marilyn and proposed a black bag job to dispose of Bill. While Earl did not insist that Carol also convert, she must have felt considerable pressure to do so. She should make up her own mind, Earl told her, but he himself was moving down to Mexico lock, stock and barrel.

So for the record, Carol went down to Colonia LeBaron in the spring of 1959 on an investigative mission and attended the church's semiannual conference. Unprepared for the colony's austerity and dusty primitiveness, she turned up in a silk dress with matching high heels, heavy makeup and perfectly coiffed dyed-blond hair. Among a group of religious pioneers whose tastes in fashion tended toward Mexican Gothic, she stood out like a sore thumb.

Carol was greeted by the French missionary, Eunice Fulk, who, mistaking her for Marilyn, rushed to hug her with such enthusiasm that they both toppled over and fell into a ditch. Carol had to walk into the conference meeting in the churchhouse with dirt spots on her silk dress and mud stains on her spit-polished high heels. It was stifling hot and there were flies everywhere. Of the approximately 100 people in attendance, she recognized a handful of the French missionaries, who pointed out the LeBarons to her.

Carol wasn't immediately sure if she could leave her life of leisure and plenty for such asceticism and starkness, but she was attracted by the "marvelous simplicity" of the LeBaron gospel, and she thought, surrounded by her family, that she could adapt to life at the colony. She met Ervil and the two talked "for a long, long time," she remembers. He showed her around and preached the virtues of plural marriage.

After spending six weeks at home in North Carolina painting her mother's house and working part-time at a hosiery mill, Eunice Fulk had been unable to stand it any longer. She hadn't heard anything from Bill Tucker but, like Marilyn, she just left for the colony anyway. She hitchhiked to El Paso by herself—carrying $40, a sleeping bag and a small round night case—then took a bus to the colony, where she was greeted with open arms. Joel and Ervil spent the first day talking doctrine with her, but she remembers being most impressed by their mother, Maud, who seemed to epitomize the pioneer woman.

In short order, Ervil also found time to take Eunice aside and confide that it had been revealed to him that they should marry. Eunice wasn't torn as Marilyn had been. She merely countered that it had been revealed to her she was to marry Bill Tucker.

While Eunice was hoping Bill would ask her to marry him, she wasn't sure he would. She hadn't exactly been thrilled to learn that he had already wed Marilyn and she wondered why he had never called her in North Carolina. Bill and Marilyn were due to return shortly, so she settled down to wait, anxiously. When they finally arrived, Eunice was baptized a member of the Firstborn Church and married to Bill immediately afterward. But the joy of that occasion was tarnished soon enough when Bill and Marilyn left the colony the very next day to go back to the States—leaving Eunice behind without a honeymoon and feeling every bit the second wife.

Characteristically, Eunice chose not to dwell on the setback. Work would take her mind off her troubles, so she plunged into fixing up a room in the tattered adobe house where she was staying with Verlan's wife, Irene. The room had been used for storage and was covered with an inch-thick layer of dust. She cleaned it out, painted it and put in a ceiling. Later the room became the "bridal suite" for all the colony's newlyweds.

When her room became livable, Eunice began work on another construction project: her own house, where she proposed to live with Bill and Marilyn. The couple were in El Paso for the time being where Bill had a job teaching biology at Texas Western University. He sent Eunice money and promised that they would all be together in the colony soon. Meanwhile, with the help of some others, Eunice set about digging a foundation and dragging down rocks from the mountains. As she grew tan and strong working outside in the hot sun, she worried about how she would compare with the thinner, bonier Marilyn, who had enviable, long, slender hands.

* * *

Finally, Bill and Marilyn moved back and helped to finish the house they would live in for the next eight years. Marilyn was pregnant, and in August of 1959, she gave birth to a son—the first of ten children to be born to her and Bill in Colonia LeBaron.

Although Eunice helped Marilyn in the delivery of Aaron, as would any good "sister wife," she soon began to find plural marriage "hard as hell." It had sounded like a wonderful principle when Bill explained it to her, but the day-to-day reality of sharing a man with another woman was hard to bear. It grew still harder after several months when Bill decided to add a third wife to hie brood: Rhonita Stubbs, the daughter of a prominent family in polygamous Short Creek who had recently converted to the LeBaron movement.

Eunice's jealously persisted until Bill finally announced he wanted a divorce. He ordered her to leave the house. She refused at first, but after a time, she complied.

In 1961 Eunice married a Mexican named Mauro Guttierez, who had been converted to the Firstborn Church by Maud LeBaron. Mauro lived in the mountain village of Babicora—south of Colonia LeBaron— a community of a few thousand people where Joel was trying to establish a satellite colony for the Firstborn Church.

Mauro had three other wives besides Eunice, and he acquired several abandoned shacks a few miles outside of Babicora for his families to live in. The shacks had crumbling walls, dirt floors, no windows and foot-long rats. Eunice moved in.

The Tuckers and the Jensens, the rest of the French missionaries and other Americans had left comfortable homes, respectability and often-promising careers behind, and had started from scratch in a valley tucked away in the barren wilderness of the northern Mexican desert, surrounded by the Sierra Madre mountain range. Amidst the cactus and mesquite bushes, they must have felt like the pioneer Mormons who settled the Salt Lake valley in the 1800s. There was no electricity, no running water, no gas, no toilet facilities, no medical help within forty miles and no farm machinery. The climate was harsh. There was pitiless heat, bitter cold, relentless, dusty winds and driving, heavy rains. In such weather, crop failure was almost chronic and most residents of the colony eked out a threadbare existence on a diet of eggs, beans, tortillas and potatoes.

When savings ran out, most of the men were forced to seek work in the States and send the money home to support their families. At least 10 percent of their incomes was earmarked for the church. Other men, like Bill Tucker, Earl Jensen, Dan Jordan and Ervil—served as missionaries much of the time, often going "without purse or scrip." Outsiders viewed the residents of Colonia LeBaron as a religiously fanatic fringe element. But the Firstborn members saw themselves as a determined and industrious group bound together by strong religious convictions.

"We all lived in this euphoria," remembers Marilyn Tucker. "We felt all this suffering, sackcloth-and-ashes and humility was part of a big plan. We were all going to be greatly rewarded for it. Every day we were imbued with the feeling that what we were doing was spiritually important. We were the chosen people of God having our mettle tested."

The high spirits ebbed occasionally, however, when Firstborners grew tired and depressed over their poor and austere lives, and they wondered why the Lord didn't smile upon them a little more if they were, in fact, the chosen.

The Tuckers and the Jensens, however, were able to build houses which allowed them to approach the lifestyle they had become accustomed to in the United States. The Jensen house even became the showpiece of the colony. In time, Earl installed the community's first flush toilet. Later, Earl imported a generator and supplied his house with electricity for two hours a day.

The Tuckers launched a chicken packing and egg business which serviced the colony and surrounding communities. Besides their other domestic responsibilities, Marilyn and her sister wives became butchers. They killed the chickens, cleaned them, packaged them and marketed them. Hundreds of hens were relied upon to produce eggs.

Alma LeBaron ran a communal garden for residents of the colony. As for basic supplies, the Firstborners initially had to rely on an old man from a neighboring village who would come through town periodically on a wagon pulled by two horses. Everyone would gather round, and buy flour, sugar, bread and other staples. Later, the Jensens started a store for the colony.

There were a "community washeteria" where girls would do family laundry using scrubboards and water heated in tubs over an open fire. Boys would hoe gardens, build houses or help perform other heavy physical labor. "We lived to survive," remembers Marilyn Tucker. "Every meal had to be cooked from scratch, and it was a big project just to get three meals on the table. Plus we had the chicken business. I would get up very early in the morning and fall asleep just dead tired at night. Every day was a hard, hard workday."

As more people moved down to Colonia LeBaron, a need for schools evolved. There was a nursery, kindergarten and an elementary school. There was no schoolhouse, as such; those responsible for teaching would do so out of their own homes.

The school was basically run by Ervil, who, as Patriarch, considered himself head of the "political and civil kingdom of God" as well as spiritual leader. This was in keeping with having Joel maintain a head-in-the-clouds posture removed from day-to-day decision making which might compromise his image as a prophet. Ervil's power was enhanced by the fact that in the early sixties Joel was away much of the time in Babicora, trying to solidify that community as a mountain outpost for the church.

Ervil was a great believer in militaristic discipline, and this atmosphere permeated the school. The colony children would assemble at seven every morning in front of the churchhouse, and then go marching off to their classes in tight formation. Ervil installed a rigid disciplinary demerit system at the school enforceable by a "people's court" made up of other students. When a pupil had accumulated enough demerits, he was hauled before the court and the rest of the student body. Though each offense carried with it a prescribed penalty, the court would formally mete it out anyway. The penalties were spankings, usually carried out by parents, who almost always abided by the will of the court.

As part of an effort to establish a United Order, Ervil also decreed that a communal kitchen be set up at which all the residents of the colony would eat breakfast and lunch. Women were rotated through the kitchen on a regular basis, and those who weren't cooking usually stayed home and tended the ever-increasing number of babies that were being born. Besides an effort to economize, Ervil hoped to create a one-big-happy-family spirit in the colony with his communal kitchen, but many were unhappy eating most of their meals away from home and viewed it as an attempt to abolish family life altogether.

In addition to the communal kitchen, women of the colony found themselves on the front lines of virtually all other menial and physical labor that needed to be done. Children and Mexican peasants paid 10 pesos (50 cents) a day helped out, but it was the women who were the driving forces. The key male leaders of the colony were unavailable for such daily chores since they were charged with "matters of the mind"—be it missionary work or writing new tracts and doctrines.

Ervil, especially, deigned not to soil his hands. He was sickly, always seemed to have the flu, and used this as an excuse to avoid strenuous work. When he wasn't away trying to win converts for the Church of the Firstborn, or writing doctrine, he might be seen walking around the dusty streets of Colonia LeBaron, head down deep in thought, clutching the worn, dogeared Bible he always carried with him.

The church was in its heyday in the early sixties. Ervil and the leading French missionaries launched an aggressive missionary campaign throughout most of the western states, and in the heart of Mormondom—Salt Lake City itself. They were bold and highly visible—establishing an office in Salt Lake, challenging all comers to debates, buttonholing faithful Saints at general LDS conferences or as they came out of their local wards. Though the Firstborners made some inroads and were able to convert a number of Mormons, there is no evidence that they ever represented a serious threat to the church.

The LDS establishment, however, was alarmed by the activities of the LeBarons and perceived them as a serious menace. Leading church officials felt impelled to publish indictments of the group, security personnel were ordered to monitor Firstborn activities closely and Leroy Hatch—the genial country doctor in Colonia Juarez—was encouraged to spy on the doings at Colonia LeBaron from his home base fifty miles to the north. Hatch willingly did so, using his professional visits with many of the colony's women—and some of its men as well—to catch up on all the latest gossip. The men and women of the colony were fully aware of what Hatch was doing, but they liked the old man and didn't seem to mind.

Among other things, Hatch reported to Mormon authorities that he foresaw violence associated with the LeBaron movement. As foreigners in a foreign land, the Mormons had to exhibit a respect and basic courtesy for their "hosts"—the Mexicans. The Saints did so, and were tolerated—if not liked—by the natives, as a result. But Hatch thought many of the Firstborners—as possessors of what they thought was the world's only path to truth and enlightenment—displayed a decided intolerance toward the Mexicans bordering on contemptuous racism which would not serve them in good stead in the long run.

Then there was polygamy. The practice was a basic part of the Church of the Firstborn, and though it was tolerated by official Mexico, most of the Catholic citizenry were offended by it—especially women, who did not want their men to get any such wild ideas.

And finally, besides a potential for violence from the surrounding community, Hatch saw the likelihood of violence from within the LeBaron family itself. The family claimed to be the rightful heir to the holy tradition of Joseph Smith, and there had been considerable contention among Dayer LeBaron's seven sons to see who would become the prophet himself. Now, despite the apparent ascension of Joel—the claims of brothers Ben and Ross notwithstanding—Hatch could see at least Ervil getting restless beneath the surface calm. The doctor turned out to be right on all counts.

Early the morning of January 1, 1966, Mauro Guttierez, the affable Mexican Firstborner, was drinking in the New Year with his Firstborn comrade Ossmen Jones at a bar in Babicora, where Joel LeBaron had wanted to establish a foothold.

Mauro, forty-two, had been living in Babicora for several years with his four wives—including Eunice Fulk. Mauro was well known in town, and generally well liked, but he did have his enemies—those who bitterly resented him for propounding what they viewed as adultery in a bastion of traditional Catholicism.

The New Year's revelry was interrupted by a brawl outside the Babicora bar involving one of Maruo's friends. He and Jones decided to break up the fight. According to Jones, Mauro was carrying two .45 automatics in the waistband of his pants. Mindful of his enemies, Guttierez drew one of the weapons. As he did so, he was hit by at least fifteen bullets fired by three different assailants who had been waiting in ambush. Mauro fell to the ground, dead.

The murder was never officially solved. It did, however, generate considerable publicity—most of it unfavorable to the LeBarons. *Time* magazine was moved to dispatch a reporter to Colonia LeBaron to do a violence-and-cultist-intrigue-type piece on the small band of American zealots who claimed to have found Nirvana in a desert of northern Mexico. The reporter, Nelson Wadsworth, hired a Mexican journalist to look into the Guttierez murder. Wrote the journalist in a memo to Wadsworth:

"The people who live [in Babicora], about 2,000 persons, say that M. Guttierez was doing great harm as minister of the LeBaron sect. He lived with four wives, which among Mexican families of the Catholic faith is condemned, even though the authorities tolerate it. Many are sure this crime was committed or ordered done by someone who was offended by this way of living."

However, Bill Tucker had a different viewpoint. He charged in an interview with Wadsworth that "hired assassins" had gunned down Guttierez because he had been too successful in converting the people of Babicora to the Church of the Firstborn.

"Mauro is the first martyr of our church," Tucker said, "and he won't be the last."

Nine months later, in October of 1966, Colonia LeBaron was shaken by another murder—this one in the colony itself.

John Butchereit—the former Allred Fundamentalist who had once been dispatched to Mexico by Rulon "to straighten the LeBaron boys out"—was living in the colony and helping run the poultry plant. He was also a scriptorian and a leading Firstborner who, of late, had been growing increasingly disenchanted with the direction, or lack of direction, of the church. Butchereit had publicly criticized Joel and Ervil for mismanagement, in particular citing sloppy accounting procedures in the collection of church tithing.

Butchereit, sixty, lived for a time with the Jensens, but feeling unwelcome, he had soon moved to the outskirts of the colony to a shack near one of the chicken coops. Friends urged him to move back. Since Butchereit was openly contemptuous of Mexicans and refused to learn Spanish, some thought it was unsafe for him to be apart from the other gringos.

One October night, two of three men walked into Butchereit's shack and shot him dead. One theory about the reason for the murder was that the Mexican fiancé of a colony schoolteacher whom Butchereit had hired as a secretary had done it in a jealous rage. A more likely scenario was that the fiancé and two drunken friends seen carousing near Butchereit's quarters shot him out of spite after he refused to let them borrow his car.

The fiancé was never seen again, but the following day, his two friends were arrested and charged with the murder. The pair spent some time in jail, but were eventually released without explanation. There were allegations that bribes had been tendered, but no one could probe the mysterious intricacies of Mexican justice sufficiently to establish any proof.

For many of the French missionaries, the Guttierez and Butchereit killings served as testimony that they were living among a people who were less than sympathetic to the Church of the Firstborn. The murders also prompted a resurfacing of prejudices they had tried to bury during their time in Colonia LeBaron: that they were living in a wild and lawless society where life was cheap and justice was bought and sold with regularity.

Some residents of the colony, interviewed years later, suspected Ervil was responsible, but those conclusions were probably reached in light of the infamy LeBaron had by then attained. There is no evidence linking Ervil to either killing.

The two murders were setbacks in the growth of the Firstborn Church, but both together did not hurt the LeBaron movement as much as the decision of Bill Tucker—later that same year of 1966—to leave the church.

Tucker—leader of the French missionaries who had given such a vital boost to a fledgling cult—had come to a parting of the ways with Ervil. It became apparent to Bill that Ervil was traveling off on his own doctrinal tangent more and more, and undermining Tucker's work in the California mission field. After winning converts for the Firstborn Church, Bill would learn that Ervil had visited the new members and given them an Old Testament harangue about a wrathful and vengeful God—which contradicted what Tucker had preached.

Rather than continue working at cross-purposes with Ervil, Bill arranged for a summit meeting with Ervil and Joel to try to iron out their doctrinal differences and present a united front. They couldn't, and Joel, in a rare show of strength, sharply berated Ervil for straying from the fold.

But Ervil persevered, and continued with an increasingly unsubtle undermining of his brother's word. And about this time, Ervil apparently perceived Tucker as a threat, for, while in California, Bill wrote to his wife Marilyn—in French—and said he'd been told Ervil planned to kill him.

Seeing that Joel either lacked the inclination or the ability to control his brother, the Tuckers left Colonia LeBaron in early 1967 and moved to southern California where Bill took a job as a chemist with Lever Bros. Marilyn remembers this period as excruciating—much harder than leaving the Mormon Church. They had spent seven years of their lives in a pitiless Mexican desert for a principle they now were renouncing. They began a slow evolution away from religious fanaticism until they reached a point where they believed in no God at all. Late in 1967, Bill died suddenly of a ruptured appendix. He was only thirty-one.

In hindsight, Marilyn feels that she and other residents of the colony in the early sixties were lulled into a sense of complacency as to the direction Ervil was actually heading.

"We hadn't taken Ervil's fiery ramblings seriously before the threat to Bill," she recalls. "But we suddenly realized that when Ervil casually talked about 'wiping someone out' or 'doing away with him' if he stood in his way, he was serious! He really began to feel that he had God's power to go and take lives if he so desired. . . . There was a lot of talk about 'put to death, put to death.' "

7

ERVIL ON HIS OWN

On a day when the air stood still in the small wooden chapel and the sweltering temperatures wilted spirits, he sat before them smothered by his own importance. Sweat coursed down his high forehead, but he ignored it. His perspiration was visible proof he worked for the people even while he sat in front of and above them. Not until the droplets looped over his Gibraltar eyebrows to disappear into those eyes—his mesmerizing elements—did he wipe the salty sweat away. He briefly looked out at the congregation, taking in their listlessness as his brother Joel droned on at the pulpit. If he were speaking . . . It was an idle thought, no more active than the fly which caught his attention. A quick flick of his hand and he had it, crushing and mashing the greasy speck between his fingers. The people would be proud to shake his hand afterward.

The exact year in which Ervil Morrel LeBaron developed an awesome aura of self is unclear. Certainly Ervil had been denied his hallmark air of consequence when he was younger. He'd fought to achieve it, but the Mormon discrimination had obliterated his efforts at companionship. His father, who had promised the LeBaron boys everything and given them next to nothing, had passed on. Ervil had jumped too quickly in proclaiming brother Ben the prophet. He realized the folly of Ben's claims as they became clearly intertwined with his insanity. Worse than Ervil's foolish but willing discipleship, it was not out of the question for him to claim he was duped and proceed to crown himself. He had now been cast into a lesser role.

Joel had no such blots on his record. While the sputterings of Ben and brother Ross Wesley may have demeaned claims to godliness, he had remained aloof from all his brothers. Naturally when Joel proclaimed himself the One Mighty and Strong, this was the LeBarons' last stand. It was the third strike—a fortunate one for Ervil, who no doubt immediately saw the advantage of having his meek and gentle brother as the front man for his own machinations.

Now it was 1960. Ervil was thirty-five, and primarily responsible for the meteoric rise of Joel's Church of the Firstborn. His pride was evident when he began to address the congregation after Joel. The topic was vintage blood-and-thunder.

"The Holy One of Israel has again set His hand to gather His people," he intoned, and the gathered members, now mindful of their high and holy calling, sat up. "The signs of the times declare that the coming of the Son of Man is drawing near. It is now expedient to make preparations for this great event before Babylon is laid waste in one general ruin."

He began to warm to his subject, and call up vocal pictures not seen in the world since Rome laid waste to Carthage, razing the entire city and salting the fields so they would never produce again.

"The Almighty has decreed," and his hands rose in an expansive gesture to signify the super being's actions, "that the overflowing scourges and terrible destructions which shall shortly come upon the land shall commence upon the Mormon people who fail to heed the voice of warning. . . ." Now he knew he had them. Many in the audience had left Mormondom and considered its members insufferable do-nothings who had fallen away from the true gospel.

Ervil, the Patriarch, began to detail the future, quoting scriptures from memory while hitting one hand into the palm of the other.

This land of Mexico, he explained, was the place for the gathering of the Lord's army before the final showdown. His commanding, masculine movements and booming voice conveyed the forbidding details of things to come. "I the Lord God will send forth flies upon the face of the earth," he recited, "which shall take hold of the inhabitants thereof, and shall eat their flesh, and shall cause maggots to come in upon them; and their tongues shall be stayed that they shall not utter against me; and their flesh shall fall from off their bones, and their eyes from the sockets." A few in the congregation were shuffling, queasy at such thoughts, but they were uniformly riveted to the Patriarch's doomsaying.

"There is a state of gross wickedness in high places," he proclaimed, which would eventually bring down the wrath of God. After an hour of this demagoguery, he issued the final warning. "Let those who love the Lord God take heed, call upon Him while He is near, and harden not their hearts against the work of God, neither turn a deaf ear to the message of His servants." Absolute quiet accompanied his last words. Ervil LeBaron's narcissistic vision was finally fully confirmed in the pool of faces who looked up to him.

Ervil had come a long way in just a few years. When Irene Kunz first saw him in 1953 working in a corral at Colonia LeBaron, he seemed a typical country bumpkin, clad in a well-used white, going on gray, shirt whose sleeves were rolled up to cover the fact they barely passed his elbow. His Levi's were five inches too small and split in the crotch, an embarrassment because he wore no undershorts. Baling wire served him for shoelaces, and he totally ignored the discomfort which came from wearing no socks compounded by the holes in his shoes. "I'll never forget that scene," she recalls. "He was just a strikingly good-looking guy who reminded me of those pictures you see of Abraham Lincoln. Long legs and big raw-boned hands."

Ervil was equally impressed by the sixteen-year-old Irene and lost no time. "I've had a revelation," he pronounced to Verlan as they walked together. "She will be my next wife."

Verlan stopped dead in his tracks. He revealed she was already married—to him. Ervil quickly shuffled off his revelation with a slap on his brother's back, "Ahhh, I was just joking."

It was not long before Ervil's brothers were wise to his mammoth polygamous ambition—to rope in all the wives he could—and his concomitant charm which would aid him to do just that. Alma explained years later that Ervil's passion for wives was characteristic of strong men. "The stronger a man is physically, the stronger his desire for women. If he is weak, he usually don't have as much sex drive." Ervil was "crazy about women," he added. "He used to dream about having twenty-five or thirty wives so he could multiply and replenish the earth. At least he did in those days. He wanted to govern them, and provide for their physical, social and economic needs. He wanted to be like Brigham Young, a great man. . . . And he had a way with women, I'll tell you."

Father Dayer had personally encouraged all the boys to marry Mexican women to upgrade conditions for the Mexican people, by raising sons through them. He assured them their own bloodline would remain pure when they married white wives. Dayer himself, immediately upon arriving in Mexico after being ousted from Utah, had nearly proposed to a Mexican servant girl who worked in the first house in which he stayed. Maud protested. She did not want her husband—or any of her sons or grandchildren, for that matter—marrying the heathen and taking on the "curse of the skin." That all her sons ultimately took Mexican spouses was attributable more to the lack of white women willing to marry any of the LeBarons than either parent's advice.

Ervil first wooed Maria de la Luz Vega (Americans called her Mary Lou), the reigning beauty queen during a celebration, in Saragosa, Chihuahua. Though he and the demure girl became engaged, she didn't want to marry him right away. No problem, this son of a polygamist decided. He could pick her up later after he'd married other women. So he opted, for the moment, to court another Mexican woman, Delfina Salido, whom he'd met in Chihuahua while visiting a friend. She fell in love with him and readily agreed to marry him in 1950.

Delfina would have been better off marrying a Mexican. Life in Colonia LeBaron was even more indigent than in most native towns and, though Delfina was young and pretty despite some chubbiness, Ervil was rarely solicitous of her following their marriage. The two lived in a single room which had no other furniture besides the bed, requiring her to stack used and unused clothes and diapers in a Number 3 tub shoved under the bed. Even when she became pregnant with their first child, Ervil remained indifferent to her. The day of the child's birth, the expectant father was enraged when Delfina moaned during every contraction and told her to "shut up." The midwife reprimanded Ervil several times before sending him from the room. His response: "That doesn't hurt any more than if she got her fingers smashed."

About 1955, before the Church of the Firstborn was founded, Ervil told Delfina that he was "going to the mountains," to visit a "friend." Actually he'd finally persuaded Mary Lou, the stocky beauty with thick black hair, to become his second wife. After a short honeymoon in Ozumba, he brought her back on the bus to Colonia LeBaron.

Verlan intercepted the pair cutting through the mesquite bushes toward Delfina's house.

"Where are you taking her?" he asked Ervil, pointing to Mary Lou.

"To my house," said Ervil, without emotion.

"That'd be terrible," Verlan responded. "You can't surprise Delfina like that." So Ervil agreed to let Mary Lou spend the night at Verlan's while he explained the new marriage to Delfina.

Irene, who was sleeping with Verlan that night, vividly recalls what happened next:

"All I remember is hearing somebody screaming. I woke up and I could hear those screams. At first you thought it was an animal. And Verlan said, 'Oh my God, it's Delfina.' And I said, 'What happened?' He said, 'I think she's cracked up.' So we got on our clothes and went over there quickly. When we got there she was just out of her head, crying."

Stable until that night, Delfina tipped into a derangement that would institutionalize her intermittently over the years to come. The children were generally farmed out to other families when Delfina had dish-throwing fits or other manifestations of "the nerves," as it was politely called. Others thought it was evil spirits driving her and cast them out, but they were never cast very far. Ervil was often gone on long missionary tours, and the children seldom lived with Delfina longer than six months.

Most early colonists expound on the marked difference between Anglo and Mexican wives. The native wives "are very jealous and hotheaded. They don't understand plural marriage," said one. A husband with several mistresses is not uncommon in Mexico, but no decent Catholic girl puts up with it if she knows it's happening. The native women at Colonia LeBaron were, indeed, unable to stomach this strange doctrine of polygamy and were further enraged by the obvious preference among the men toward Anglo wives. One child of a Mexican mother and American father said the men couldn't help but favor the white women. "My mother may have been more intelligent than his American wives, but she wasn't as educated or adept. Mexican people don't have modern culture. They don't know how to dress or decorate—or seduce a man."

The net result of such preference was a lack of harmony in their polygamous relationships—and wife beatings. Dr. LeRoy Hatch, the Colonia Juarez general practitioner who treated the colony's women, said only the Mexican wives were beaten. According to several contemporaries, Ervil, indeed, beat both his Mexican wives, but never raised a hand to their American counterparts. One Mexican woman said Mary Lou, considered an amicable and easygoing woman, once displayed black and blue stripes down her back which Ervil had inflicted with his belt. She was seven months pregnant at the time.

Delfina's mistreatment was a sore spot for the Salido family, and more than once, her brothers threatened Ervil. Certain that they were coming one evening, Ervil persuaded a friend to sit on his door stoop with a rifle all night. Word of his in-law difficulties reached all the way to Mexico City where Fundamentalist leader Margarito Bautista wrote in 1958: "The worst is Delfina's people want to kill Ervil Morrel and they may do it if he is not careful."

At the time, Bautista was angry with Ervil for persuading Fundamentalist followers into abandoning Bautista's cause and heading for Colonia LeBaron. Ervil offered them sugar plum visions of conditions at the ranch, promising free transportation to Chihuahua, good food, good homes and good times once they got there. To some groups, he offered $100 for every adult who came, and $50 for every child. Ervil never made good on the promises. Those who were hauled to the ranch were surprised by the deplorable plight of those already there. Most of them, with intensely bitter feelings, had to pay their own way back to southern Mexico.

Still, it wasn't all a failure for Ervil. He had netted two powerful converts, Fernando Castro, easily the most potent Mexican leader the Firstborn Church ever had, and Aurelio Rios. The latter was most important to Ervil's future, since his family contributed three fanatical bodyguards and two wives to Ervil.

Like all Mormons, Ervil believed that all the Indians of the Americas would someday make up a faithful and formidable army for the Lord when He chooses to come again. But Ervil's attempts to win many of them over were no doubt more directly related to the colony's need for laborers, and his own desire for wives, money and the adoration of others. He had little concern for their feelings or rights. He once bribed officials in nearby Galeana to let him build a dam which eventually obliterated a number of Mexican landholdings. The ranches received no compensation, and all the reservoir's water went to Colonia LeBaron. On another occasion, Ervil advised brother Alma to end a land dispute with a local Mexican who had left their church by turning a herd of cows loose in the man's prize garden.

A further example of Ervil's attitude is offered by Rhea Kunz. With money from the sale of a Utah home, Fundamentalist Rhea was hoping to homestead a *parcela* in Mexico. She found one to her liking and asked Ervil to act as translator during the negotiations. She instructed him that the poor Mexican family should be as pleased with the deal as she. He upbraided her for being too straitlaced. "They're just a bunch of Mexicans, anyway."

Ervil's white supremacist attitude was easily conveyed—despite the language barrier. And Ervil's designation of the Mexicans as second-class citizens, a cursed people who might someday be blessed with a white skin, enraged the locals a number of times—constituting, occasionally, a very real danger to his life.

Daniel Ben Jordan, one of the French missionaries, was a full head shorter than Ervil, but capable of whispering in his ear. Both brother Alma and sister Esther blame this cold man with the coal-black eyes for infecting Ervil with a Satanic cancer. "Ervil was directed by what sort of advice and encouragement he got," Alma observed. "Dan influenced him negatively." From a great man of God, Dan brought him down "under a spell of the devil." Esther sounds the same knell: "Dan was pushing him. If Ervil hadn't had Dan with him . . ."

Dan was a strange man, generally friendless. His intelligence had won him a position as a district president in the French mission, but he had not acquired many comrades along the way. Though he was drummed out with the rest, he had little affinity with his fellow excommunicants. Almost immediately, he latched on to Ervil, idolizing him, looking up to him and seeing the qualities he wished to emulate: keen perception, with a bent towards subtle manipulation. Ervil welcomed his shadow, despite his strange little quirks, like habitually raising an imaginary gun at people and saying, "Pow." Delfina couldn't stomach him, particularly since Ervil would spend hours in their bedroom with Jordan, plotting and scheming. She began to call him Ervil's wife, and no one disagreed.

When Ervil planned to acquire converts in Mexico City in 1959, the twenty-five-year-old Dan was a natural to play Castor to his Pollux. What really happened during the three months they were there may never be known. The pair exploded out of the area as if the fiends of hell were on their heels. Their hasty explanation to residents of Colonia LeBaron, where they made a quick stop, was that the Mafia, Catholics and Knights of Columbus were trying to "stop the great mission we have to perform" through whatever means were necessary. They had suffered persecution and their very lives were threatened, they said. Ervil told one confidant about the "miraculous ways they were preserved down there, their hair-raising escapes."

The fleeing duo checked into a YMCA in El Paso for a night's respite, but Dan's gun accidentally went off and shot a large hole in the mattress. Both men ran out and down the street, temporarily separating. They finally met at their car, got in, and didn't stop driving until they were in Utah.

Their first stop was at a friend's house where Irene happened to be visiting. Once inside, Ervil and Dan closed all the curtains in the house and, in hushed tones, described the danger which faced them. Their story added some excitement to dinner, which was interrupted by a knock on the door. Ervil and Dan both jumped up so fast "they almost turned the whole table over. Everything went flying," Irene remembers, "chairs and everything else. They went running—you could hear them go thomp, thomp down the wooden stairs into the basement."

The couple who owned the home answered the door to find two local Mormon leaders checking on their welfare. After they left, the embarrassed hostess cried. Ervil and Dan, guns drawn, were cowering and pacing in the basement. Irene called husband Verlan to tell him Ervil had lost his mind, just like Ben. Whatever the cause, the change was permanent. All his associates couldn't help but notice the paranoia which had overtaken their patriarch.

Ervil depicted a massive conspiracy among the numerous branches of the Knights of Columbus in Mexico against him and the Church of the Firstborn. He thought the combined weight of Catholic clout in Mexican political circles was sure to crush him unless he won strong allies. The tactic he and Dan had decided upon was to befriend the Masons of Mexico, who were strongly anti-Catholic and were competitive with the Knights. Though Ervil's analysis was mistaken—neither organization was very powerful in the country—he persisted in trying to gain friends among the Masons, and in hiding.

One of his favorite hideouts was Esther's house. It was typical for him to slip into Colonia LeBaron and stay with her, never notifying any of his wives when he came and went. One of Esther's daughters noted his visits in her journal. January 6, 1962: "Uncle Ervil is hiding out because the Catholic officers are trying to find him dead or alive." January 20: "In about every room there is one of the Uncles who have to hide out because some Mexicans are after their lives." January 8, 1963: "Uncle Ervil has been hiding out here all day." August 24: "Uncle Ervil hid out here today." And so on.

Ervil's children became used to his furtive stops at their home. "He always carried a gun, and kind of sneaked around in the middle of the night," one said. "If someone knocked, he ran and hid—even when nothing was going on!" He wrote one wife in 1963 that he'd purchased another gun and wanted all family members to own firearms and know how to use them. To his list of persecutors and deadly enemies he now added the Mormon Church which, he wrote, was mounting "a vicious campaign of muscle men to stop us from passing literature."

Constantly seeking to protect himself, Ervil even groomed a hardened convict, Billy Randell, to act as his bodyguard and killer-avenger, if necessary. Randell had made headlines in Utah as the ringleader in a 1957 state prison riot. First, he faced a charge of assaulting a prison guard, which was dropped, and then was accused of helping murder a fellow inmate. Known as King Con at the prison, Randell testified in a surprisingly effeminate voice that he thought it was a bad idea to carve the convict up. "I suggested we throw him off the fourth tier of A-block to the concrete floor below," he stated at the trial, according to a *Desert News* account. He coolly related how, after the murder, he had helped clean bloody knives, tear up bloody clothes and flush them down a toilet. Randell was acquitted when it was determined he had helped authorities during the riot, acting as a go-between. After he was released in 1962, he headed for Colonia LeBaron to see if the nice things a one-time Firstborn cellmate had said about it were true. At first the paranoid Ervil thought Randell was there to kill him. When he got over that, he wanted Billy to be his private bodyguard, packing a .38 and following Ervil everywhere. Ervil told one confidant that Billy was "just the type of a guy he needed for a bodyguard and a guy that could kill people IF NECESSARY." Randell played along with the paranoid Patriarch for several months but he finally blew up at Ervil and left the community.

Analyzing Ervil's skittishness, an early intimate, Marilyn Tucker, is most eloquent: "He kept us constantly hyped on the idea that people were out to get us, that our work was so important in the eyes of God that naturally the forces of evil were going to try to kill us." The dramatic irony of Ervil's paranoia, Mrs. Tucker notes, "is that Ervil later formed the very group that he had us living in fear of. Maybe in the back of his mind he was planning the assassination of big government figures, for all I know. And maybe, out of his own conscience, he had reason to be fearful for acts not yet done." Certainly more than a decade of hiding served him in good stead when the combined forces of a dozen state and county police departments, the FBI, Secret Service and Mexican *federales* attempted to locate the elusive LeBaron.

Ervil LeBaron remained respected by the Colonia LeBaron flock until he courted his friend Nephi Marston's wife.

Nephi was a Church of the Firstborn stalwart converted by Ervil, and intimately acquainted with the LeBaron family since the late 1940s. His father had been a follower and financial backer of Benjamin LeBaron's shenanigans.

For a time, Nephi left the LeBarons, but after the Church of the Firstborn was formed, he came drifting back. His alignment with the Firstborn Church annoyed, in fact infuriated, his wife, Anna Mae, who was an intractable Mormon, a studious scriptorian who knew the rightness of her church. Her comely figure and owlish face could be seen leading the ward choir having, as she did, a lovely voice. Friendly, outgoing and totally committed, she stuck with Nephi after his apostasy no doubt because of their three children, Eddie, Ramona and Fay. She screamed at him every time he mentioned the Firstborn Church, forcing him to practically sneak out to drive down to Colonia LeBaron for conference—never being sure that the door wouldn't be locked against him when he came back. When this situation began to be too much for him, Nephi asked Ervil to return with him and convert this woman.

Anna Mae later related that when she opened the door to the object of her spite, Ervil, she fell in love with him immediately. No doubt sensing the instantaneous conversion, Ervil whipped out one of his many handy revelations and said he had been given the word that she should move to Mexico at once. Anna Mae packed up and left with him, leaving Nephi to arrange their affairs for a total move.

Though Ervil may have been reluctant to engage in a liaison which would make a cuckold out of his friend Nephi, Anna Mae was apparently determined to entice him to do just that. The first to suspect was Anna Mae's friend Sally (not her real name), who had once been told she would marry Ervil, but did not particularly like Ervil since the days he and the others would lock her in a barn when Ben had commanded them to. Living in the Colonia LeBaron house at the time with Anna Mae, Sally realized that Ervil was spending far too much time with her friend. However, Anna Mae's confession to one community member that she was completely in love with Ervil, and the subsequent discovery by another member who walked in on Ervil passionately kissing Anna Mae on her bed, made the inevitable conclusion hard to ignore. Gossip spread through the colony, but no one could say for sure that the two were sleeping together.

Then arrived the naive Nephi, a plodding, trusting soul, who had no suspicion that anything had changed. He was delighted his wife had joined the church until he began to hear some of the community rumors. "He was just frantic when he came to me," said one friend, "actually crying about it. 'Has Anna Mae been living with Ervil?' he asked." The friend related incidents in which they'd been caught by several people and added that, while Ervil no doubt had never slept with her, the pair were certainly close.

Nephi marched straight to Ervil. Ervil laughed, "You're just imagining things." Meanwhile, he was telling Anna Mae that Nephi did not deserve her because he was destined for a lesser glory in the next life. Whereas if she married Ervil, she would be hitting the jackpot. Anna Mae needed no encouragement and, in a town where there were few legal marriages or divorces, she secretly wed Ervil. Delfina knew nothing about it until Anna Mae threw up several mornings in a row, pregnant with her first child by Ervil. Nephi was beside himself with grief and rage, but the persuasive Ervil managed to placate him. However, the community was shocked at their Patriarch's behavior, at his ignoring the six-month grace period church rules required when one spouse left another. No one thought the act more odious than the church prophet, Joel, and this created the first tangible wedge between the two brothers.

Like an aftershock following a major earthquake, Ervil took Sally as his fourth wife. "She was high-pressured into it," a friend said. "He told her he'd had a revelation that she should marry him; she'd grown up with this thought anyway [the prophet Ben had foretold such a union]. And, she was lonesome—let's face it." Sally had previously been married to a Utah man, but they had divorced when their only child was about eight. However, Sally's second marriage to Ervil LeBaron was of little consequence, lasting only a few months.

But that of her friend Anna Mae to Ervil was of great consequence. For a man who subscribed totally to the credo that the end justifies the means, Ervil was lastingly justified in the hasty action that led to this marriage, in spite of community disgruntlement over it. Anna Mae was to prove the one unwavering rod and staff that would comfort him as he walked, sword drawn, through the valley of his own shadows of death.

Complaints about Ervil's general laziness when it came to physical labor were abundant. "If there is an idler in the church, it is Ervil M. LeBaron, and everyone knows it," an early convert wrote. Another noted that the other LeBaron brothers were hard workers but "about all I've ever seen Ervil do is sit around and read books." This apparently infuriated several associates, like the one who recalls: "He wanted to lie around all day in a sort of reverie with his fantasies and dreams and revelations which he called hard work. Physical labor was way beneath him."

Ervil's immediate family rarely criticized him for this. Verlan, the long-suffering victim of Ervil's languor, shared thirty-five cows with his brother during the pre-church days at the ranch. Early each morning, the two would go out to milk them, but somehow Ervil never quite got around to tugging at his cows' teats. He'd stand and preach, waving his arms and stool as if he would sit down momentarily once he'd made his point. The sermon ended when Verlan finished milking the cows, after which Ervil mooched breakfast from his brother.

Ervil had a natural excuse for not dirtying his hands with humdrum menial activity: his failing health. Shortly after returning from his Mormon mission in 1945, he contracted a malaria which stayed with him almost five years. Ben tried numerous "miraculous ministrations" to cure him, since Ervil didn't believe in doctors, but the disease was tenacious and permanently damaged his ability to resist a number of other afflictions. He bundled up in large tweed coats and scarves, huddled next to stoves and swallowed a number of awful-tasting remedies like castor oil. Sometimes concern for his health reached ridiculous extremes: he would not kiss wives who had symptoms of any disease, and insisted on wearing a red wool sweater at all times, even in bed. His mother even sewed patches of wool inside his undergarments to keep him warm. A close friend said Ervil's energy shortage was legitimate. He often appeared sapped of strength, looking tired as he shuffled around the colony.

Some Firstborners thought his ill health was more show than reality, since it allowed him to spend many days in bed, propped up by pillows, launching into discourse after discourse. One pointed to the similarity between Ervil and the great Apostle Paul, who was also afflicted with a "thorn in the flesh" which several scholars have deduced was a recurring attack of malaria. Yet, members told Ervil, it didn't slow Paul down from managing to earn his own living by the "toil and drudgery" of tentmaking. Firstborners as a whole accepted Ervil's no-work intellectual role then, willingly doing their own share of labor to keep him free for his headier pursuits.

Ervil also was apparently oblivious to the plight of others, particularly when it came to food. Once when eggs at the ranch were very scarce, Ervil was invited over to his brother's house for a small meal. A plate of five eggs was placed on the table for the family of seven and Ervil scooped four on his plate and gulped them down. He exhibited even more callousness when he would go from house to house having meals with his Firstborn Church followers. For them, it was generally a privilege to have the Patriarch dine there. But his prodigious and aggressive appetite offended many.

Just as he was an unenviable dinner companion, Ervil was also an unrewarding conversationalist. Casual small talk was foreign to him. The same dynamic qualities that made him a powerful speaker alienated many people when it came to ordinary social intercourse. Anyone who hailed him as he walked the colony deep in thought, sometimes talking to himself and tugging at his eyebrows, might be the recipient of a lengthy discourse. He was known for marathon—eight or more hours—priesthood meetings. One person remembers a nonstop, seventeen-hour filibuster from Ervil on religion, while a woman recalls one which lasted four days. "There were eighteen people in my kitchen who sat there from seven in the morning until two the next morning," she said. "I'd feed them breakfast, lunch and supper and clear the table in between."

An additional irritant to some listeners was Ervil's scripture juggling. "He can quote scripture until you get sick of him, and he'd twist everything to what he wanted to say, making everything applicable to his own peculiar line of thought," says one contemporary. Ervil employed the same device—selective use of Biblical quotations out of their original context—when he was writing. Certainly one of Ervil's most peculiar quirks was to ghost-write articles for the *Ensign*, the Firstborn monthly, and place another person's name on it. The next time he penned an article, he'd "quote" the previous article, citing the person by name, to reinforce another theme. On and on this would go until he'd wind up quoting four or five different persons, in actuality repeating all his own scribblings.

Often LeBaron would fall asleep during writing projects. He'd recline in a chair, meditating, and doze off. Carol Jensen, because she spent several months alone with him in a trailer, vividly recalls the somnolent side of Ervil's writing. "He'd sit and think until he was almost morose and then he would write, just scrawl things and scrawl things. I just felt so bad that he couldn't say it straight. He would get tired and weary and grab his forehead and rub his eyebrows—be so mentally weary that he would just go to sleep. Then all of a sudden he would wake up, not say anything and go over and start writing. He'd say, 'The Lord has just revealed this to me, that it's got to be this way.' Sometimes I could see it, and sometimes it was just absolutely ridiculous."

If the sign of a religious leader was the number of otherworldly disclosures he professed to have, Ervil easily bested Isaiah, Moses, *and* Jesus Christ combined. Perhaps he was trying to live up to his mother's evaluation that he was the most religious of her sons. More than likely, he thought it was the sign of a prophet.

One of Ervil's wives complained he used self-serving "words from above" to justify his own actions and reduce the obstacles in his way. The frequency—and sometimes stupidity—of Ervil's revelations was illustrated by her in a single anecdote. Once when they were driving between San Diego and Los Angeles Ervil stopped for gas at a Mobil station. About five miles out of the station, Ervil intently said, "You know, it was told to me what kind of oil to use in this car."

His wife, who felt free to tease him now and again, said, mockingly, "Oh, really?"

"Yeah, I was told. It was revealed to me that I should only put Mobil oil in this car."

"I'd like to know more about that," she said, "who revealed it to you." She kept at him until he finally admitted the gas station attendant had advised him. If she hadn't pressed him on it, she was expected to believe he'd got it from God.

Harold Blackmore, a polygamist independent, expounds on such purportedly divine utterances which, however false, can go a long way toward winning friends and influencing people: "Ervil was very prone to get personal, put his arm around you, cuddle up in a confidential manner. He had mysterious and secret things to impart to you if you'll just give him your ear. When he told some people that God had told him something about that person, they weren't capable of coping with it. They'd think, 'My heavens, God singled me out especially by one of his prophets with a vision from heaven. I'd better do what he says.' "

Not so with Blackmore. Once, Ervil was staying at his house in southern Utah along with Joel and Verlan. One morning at the breakfast table, Ervil told Harold, "I've got something very confidential to tell you, Brother Blackmore."

"Oh?" Blackmore replied, skepticism apparent in the rise in his eyebrows and voice. "Is that so?"

"Yeah. Let's go outside."

"Come on," Blackmore chided him, "it can't be that confidential. If it's worth telling, you can say it right here in front of these other people."

"Well," Ervil said, a little hesitant. "A messenger from heaven came to me last night and told me to tell you you're supposed to get in line to follow us, put your work and strength behind this great cause [the Firstborn Church]."

Those at the table turned to Harold, in great awe and surprise. Surely he would now fall in, since the Lord had called him. Blackmore weighed his words, and looked Ervil in the eye. "Well, Ervil, if that messenger from heaven was so damn crippled he couldn't come into the next room and tell me, I don't want to hear anything about him."

Ervil's jaw dropped.

A family destined to have a great impact on Ervil, providing him two wives and unparalleled loyalty, was the Leland Chynoweth (Sha-noth) clan. Leland, called Bud by his friends, had been the son of a smalltown Mormon farmer and bishop, one of nine children. He worked for twenty-eight years as a chief aircraft inspector for Utah's largest employer, Hill Air Force Base in Ogden. His wife, Thelma Ray, was very active in the Mormon women's association, Relief Society. She was a forceful and capable woman, eventually turning her family into a matriarchal, rather than patriarchal, unit.

Their first child, a boy, died at the age of seven. Glen came next, eventually one of the west's numerous self-employed truckers, and always an active Mormon. Third in line was Lorna, born in 1944 and pampered with dancing and modeling lessons. Two years after, Victor arrived. He was the family politician, a thinker and a salesman. He was to acquire part ownership in several auto dealerships where younger brothers Mark and Duane would work.

Mark, born in 1952, was a natural musician. Duane came in 1956 and, as the youngest of the boys, had very little self-confidence. By the time he was ten, Thelma decided what he needed was a little positive thinking and concentrated attention from his mother, which apparently did the trick. Rena, the baby of the family, was born in 1958. The Chynoweths were a very close family, a typical Mormon household— but then association with Ervil LeBaron was to change all that.

Urged by a brother to check out the LeBaron church in 1961, Thelma, always open to new ideas, prodded her family to make a two-week visit to Colonia LeBaron. Only Glen stayed home. Thelma returned to Utah bubbling over with Firstborn beliefs, but Glen rebutted some of his mother's new beliefs so forcefully that she burst into tears. Thelma wavered until the death of her own mother; after that a visit from Joel LeBaron clinched her conversion. Thelma, Lorna and Mark were baptized; husband Bud and sons Victor and Glen were not.

Upon meeting Ervil for the first time, Thelma was overwhelmed. He was without doubt the greatest man she had ever encountered, the best catch possible for eighteen-year-old daughter Lorna, who became Ervil's fifth wife in 1962 on Thelma's insistence. (Rena would later become his thirteenth wife.) When the couple married quietly in Utah, Lorna's father, Bud, was not even told about it. As Ervil and Lorna left for Las Vegas to honeymoon in Verlan's trailer (while he checked into a motel), Thelma informed Bud that their daughter had decided to teach school in Mexico—at Colonia LeBaron. Lorna had been attending modeling school in Ogden, and she was a pretty 105 pounds. Her liberal ideas apparently changed some of Ervil's rigid beliefs, such as the edict that intercourse was only for procreation. She was probably the first wife to whom Ervil was truly romantically attracted. Lorna moved to the colony with him, where she became the epitome of American teenage beauty—her hair was teased, makeup was effectively applied and she rapidly came to exemplify savoir-faire to the unrefined colony girls. Her relationship with Ervil was rocky, and she left him several times. But she bore him at least eight children and would remain loyal to him when the police of two countries were hunting for him.

The same year he married his most desirable wife, Ervil also took his least desirable, and sixth mate, Sue Jones (not her real name).

Utah born and raised, Sue was sweet but grossly overweight, a condition she accentuated by wearing a short boy's haircut. She was visiting a girlfriend, when she met Ervil for the first time and, like several others, fell in love with the handsome Patriarch. Her girlfriend, after hearing from Sue she'd "like to marry that guy," promptly told Ervil, who called the embarrassed Sue upstairs in the Salt Lake home. "I've had a revelation that you should marry me," he predictably notified her. She did, almost on the spot.

Ervil tolerated her at best and ignored her most of the time. Wanting to please him any way she could, the servile Sue dutifully took jobs in Las Vegas and other American cities and sent most of her money to Ervil. She incurred substantial debt by buying him a large new wardrobe, thus updating his nineteenth-century fashion-consciousness. Still, he was never very nice to her. Once, when he came to Nevada with another wife, he spent only a few hours with her and then departed with his traveling companion to a motel. Sue sobbed uncontrollably through the night.

Another time, according to a friend, she visited a doctor, to find out why it was so difficult for her to get pregnant. He started asking her questions, ending with, "When did you last have intercourse with your husband?" Sue answered, "Oh, it's been about nine months." The doctor's look was incredulous. Yet no matter how badly Ervil treated her, she continued to be subservient to him.

Ervil went on to acquire yet another wife. One of his most curious beliefs was that the Virgin Mary had become the mother of Christ at the age of fourteen. Therefore, he concluded, there were a small number of girls in Colonia LeBaron who would be selected by revelation and found worthy to have the privilege of marriage to him at that same age.

Carol Jensen, a strong Ervil adherent, avers that it was theoretically wise to marry one's daughters at such an early age. She explains:

"If you're going to raise up a generation in plural marriage, it is very important to not let the young girls get romanticized in the worldly sense. To get very close to the childbearing age of puberty and marry them off to older men—I know it sounds horrible—rather than younger men their age is the goal. If you accept the premise that a woman's mission in this world is to grow in the household of her parents to childbearing age, and to learn all the homely arts, why should there be any postponement before she begins what she was born into the world for?"

Such thoughts were perfect in theory for Carol, but she says "it was the greatest test I ever had" when Ervil asked for her thirteen-year-old daughter, Kristina. Despite her total infatuation with Ervil, Carol thought Kris was too young to marry a thirty-eight-year-old. For her part, Kris disliked Ervil, and Carol had to apply heavy doses of persuasion to get the girl to agree to become his seventh wife.

Ervil's initial approach to Kris had been odd. He had asked to walk her home after church, saying that when they passed Delfina's house she would see them and vent her jealous rage on Kris rather than his other wives. He seemed sincere and she had nothing to lose, so she walked with him. But it wasn't long before Kris realized his true intentions, and was repulsed, partly because she was attached to someone else. But then her mother spoke to her at length about Ervil's great mission and also about how difficult it had become for him to acquire wives in competition with younger men. Meanwhile, Kris had also become fast friends with Lorna, who also urged her to wed Ervil. A respect for her elders, the desire to "fit in," obedience to her mother, affection for Lorna and pity for Ervil finally combined to win the young girl's acquiescence. The wedding ceremony was restricted, and those attending it, probably in April 1963, were told to keep it confidential.

Ervil was perfectly satisfied marrying a girl who didn't love him. He was sure he could command her affection in time. For the moment, he said it was most important that she was on his "ball team," a common Ervil expression. He could use her talents and abilities now and she, in turn, was guaranteed heaven's top spot. But he was soon complaining that she was frigid, and resisted his charm for too long. She became an obsession to him, and, ultimately, the only wife he really loved, according to a number of Ervil's close friends.

Ervil divorced Delfina and legally married Kris in 1966 in Arizona— the only wife ever accorded that privilege. He took her on many of his trips, while his other wives had to remain behind, often complaining that they did not receive a tenth the attention he gave to Kris. Yet it was only natural that Ervil's ego would rise to the challenge of a wife whose affections were unattainable.

Kris begged Ervil, at the age of seventeen, to let her move to Las Vegas. Ervil demurred, thinking it dangerous to send her into such an atmosphere. But she persisted, and Ervil finally consented.

His initial fears for the apple of his eye were soon realized. Kris fell in love with a musician, and her feelings for her husband slowly turned to bitter disenchantment. "Ervil tells me that if I stick with him no matter what happens he'll get me in the celestial kingdom," she would tell friends. "And he also tells me the hereafter is merely an extension of this life. Well, I'm perfectly miserable in *this* life. I don't want to be miserable up there too. So what good is it even if I do have salvation?" The marriage finally came to an end when Kris broke her neck in a 1971 car accident and Ervil neither visited her nor paid the hospital bill. She officially divorced him in 1974, gaining custody of their two daughters.

A shy, petite lady, Kris now lives in seclusion, avoiding public attention and her former husband, who threatened to kill her in 1976 if she didn't give up their children. She rarely talks about her past life with LeBaron and becomes upset when she does. In a lengthy conversation with a friend, she summed up that relationship:

"He never fully felt my acceptance, and I think probably that was always a challenge to him, something that he was bound and determined to get one way or the other sometime." She paused, visibly shaken. "There was always the romantic factor missing from my life. Not that he wasn't romantic. He was, and he longed to have me fall in love with him, but that was the thing I couldn't do." Her attitude changes from pity to a kind of deep quiet strength. "*He had me*," she said slowly, "*but he never had me.*"

From 1960 to 1965, Ervil was compelled to seek wife after wife. Using words from God as if they were confetti showered upon easily influenced females, he proposed to a wide range of women, marrying two of them: one, the thirty-ish, dowdy daughter of a Utah family that had been converted to the Firstborn Church, and the other, an attractive fifteen-year-old from California, whose parents had also joined the LeBaron movement.

In a polygamist community, control of the women confers power, and Ervil understood that. Influencing them was tantamount to having a crony in every home. And where fathers sometimes have more than fifty children and five wives, the mothers carry incontrovertible sway over their own offspring, including their marriageable daughters, a very valuable commodity in the polygamy subculture. The Short Creek group managed to subvert female power by promoting a religio-sexual council of seven elderly men who were accorded the right to appoint brides and grooms, and had been known to swap daughters among themselves. Joel LeBaron deplored the practice, and told his followers they would have freedom of choice—a doctrinal concept called "free agency"—in matters of the heart. But the prophet's Richelieu, Ervil, deliberately attempted to set up a subtle power base among the women and a marriage brokerage service that, though undetected for a short time, challenged Joel's magnanimity toward his brother.

Ervil's office became the equivalent of a fortune-teller's tent as the young ladies of the community trooped into it for marriage counsel. Sometimes he would immediately tell them whom to marry; at other times he was more subtle, offering a list on which his name usually held the most prominent position and included, usually, his brothers or Dan Jordan. He was effective at twisting arms by noting that rejection of divinely suggested unions, which were pleasing in the sight of God, would seriously jeopardize their eternal blessings. His most frequent refrain to the young ladies who didn't relish the thought of going to bed with old Mr. So-and-So was: "Marry for principle, let love come later."

To understand Ervil's interest, one must look through the glass more darkly. Close friends say he actually conducted a bartering business with the females of the community. When Earl Jensen gave up daughter Kristina to Ervil, he was promised one of Ervil's nieces. Ervil was instrumental in obtaining another niece for Bill Tucker, whose friendship he actively sought. A third niece went to Dan Jordan.

He crossed his promises, sometimes offering the same girl to several different men in an effort to secure their conversion to the church, their alliance to him or, more often than not, their dollar donations to himself as a bonafide church representative.

A former mayor of North Salt Lake, whom Ervil was propagandizing for one of his schemes, said, "Part of the bait was that he could get some wives for me. It made me sick that he would deal that way." One witness to the offer, a close LeBaron relative, said she was shocked and furious to hear it. "He told this man, 'You get on our ball team and you can have your pick of any girl you want in the church because I can get any girl I want for you.' " She surmised, then, that it was a typical Ervil pitch, but it was rarely heard of because there were usually no witnesses around.

Naturally, LeBaron's own daughters were the prize gems he had to offer. As a father, he was tyrannical about the boys with whom each associated, asserting, as did other church leaders, that the younger men should "go out to Babylon" to get their wives, and leave those at home to the Elders. The attitude gives some substance to his hatred for Kim Jensen, Kristina's brother. The boy and Ervil's daughter Lillian saw each other regularly. When Ervil found out, he wrote Kim a letter warning him to stop it, but Kim continued. Finally, Ervil arranged a church trial presided over by Dan Jordan. The outcome was that if Kim persisted in "dating" Lillian, he'd be expelled from the church. Obviously, she was slated for someone else. But Kim continued to see Lillian secretly until one day Ervil caught them. "Listen," Ervil glowered, "if I catch you in my yard again, I'm going to kill you." Jensen was terrified. "I was all of fifteen at the time," he recalls, "and that just scared the hell out of me. He was dead serious. I could see it in his eyes. He just looked right through me." Despite his fear, he did continue seeing Lillian through a fence, Romeo-and-Juliet style. But "I sure never went into the yard anymore."

Most of the girls in the community were disgusted by plural marriage, according to Alice LeBaron, another of Ervil's daughters. "I had every man down there propose to me at one time or another. They'd come to you and they'd say, 'Oh, we've had a revelation that you marry so and so.' Let me tell you the way us girls put it. It was kind of a joke, kind of vulgar. We called them 'revelations . . . right between the legs'!" Even though the teenage girls laughed about it, Alice said most of them later wound up marrying into it. She condemns them for lacking the strength to change their lives and "settling for less. They don't have drive. I've always had a drive for the best, and I knew I didn't want polygamy when I was young." She even defied her father, who tried to marry her to a number of older men from the time she was thirteen. Concluding a lengthy tirade against plural marriage, she stated that "polygamy is simply a big scheme to control people."

Inspired by the aphrodisiac of influence, Ervil formulated an organization exclusively for women, United Women of Zion (1961–1964). At its core were his three favorite henchwomen: Carol Jensen, Anna Mae Marston and, as president, his sister, Esther Spencer. The single most important group rule was secrecy. Initiation was simply the extraction of a pledge that each would tell not a living soul what went on at the meeting. Husbands weren't to know; Ervil asked those who kept journals at the time to cease and desist. He scheduled the meetings. Runners—usually Esther's daughters—were sent out with a roll to check those who would be at the meeting that night. Those who declined to come received a personal visit from the Patriarch. Active resistance to the group was rare, but the few that opposed it were labeled "hellions" and "witches" by Ervil, according to a friend.

The purpose of the organization was not immediately evident. Ervil began unfolding his great expectations for the women by belittling their husbands. Wives were so much better and stronger than their spouses, that he was depending upon them to carry forth the work. At a time when John F. Kennedy was heralding the New Frontier, LeBaron was borrowing liberal doses and declaring the United Women of Zion would be "educators of the new world." They must develop the entire platform for this visionary society, and attention would be required for all of its details. Colonia LeBaron would be the testing ground.

Ervil lectured for hours and hours on the minutest aspects of orderly life, outlining the preferred style of dress and eating habits, and rearing children.

The frequency of the meetings varied according to his whims. This naturally grated on women who worked all day, and would rather be home tending their children at night. Even so, surprisingly little bickering existed over the group, which averaged about thirty in attendance. One of those whom the meetings did rub the wrong way preferred a home study group with her husband and his other wives. She viewed United Women as Ervil's "attempt to get authority over women, have a good hold on them." At one UWZ gathering, she stood up and argued with Ervil over a point. The reaction was swift. Women crowded around her after Ervil left. "How *dare* you talk to him like that in in front of all those people!" one said. Another chimed, "How can you be so disrespectful?" She was told the devil must have inspired her, and they "considered me to be a more darkened person after that because of what I said." Her husband supported her display of courage, unafraid of Ervil's disfavor.

A flurry of rules for the new society were laid down in mid-July 1963 through the United Women. They passed a law against going to "wicked shows," or all movies at Casas Grandes. Ervil also told them it was wrong to kiss while courting. Then, the new dress code was served up. Shirts must be below the elbow and skirts six inches below the knee while sitting. On July 17, Ervil reiterated the importance of UWZ secrecy, giving a lengthy lesson on how they could keep things quiet from outsiders like their husbands. Behind this move was the open discussion about murdering enemies.

"Ervil's prime subject that we weren't supposed to talk about was always our enemies," says one participant. "I remember one meeting in particular when he went into the gory details of how we'd kill our enemies—kill them on the street and then drag them into the house. He was just full of that killing stuff all the time. We never named any individual enemies but talked about groups, mostly this murderous group of the Catholic Church, the Knights of Columbus. They were always after his life."

He approached individual women about heading up a secret female military unit. After one UWZ meeting, in which he'd declared that the enemies would "be pushing up carrots in our gardens and nobody will ever find them," he asked one lady, "Do you think you could ever kill anybody?"

"What do you mean?" the woman countered, shocked.

"Now don't get excited," Ervil motioned. "We have to defend our lives. We have to defend our country. Why not? Do you think you could ever kill somebody?" She might, she quietly agreed, in self-defense.

Another woman recalls being taken aside and talked to about a female militia. He explained to her there were "certain individuals" who didn't live up to the Ten Commandments and deserved the death penalty. Growing agitated, Ervil grabbed her arm and said if anybody got in his way, "They will be crushed!" After a short silence, she asked him, "You mean, put to death?" Suddenly realizing she might not be sympathetic to him, he backed off and scoffingly concluded, "Where did you ever get *that* idea?"

At one particular UMZ meeting, Ervil explained just why women, whom he'd asked to gain proficiency in the use of firearms, might be selected to protect the church—or him. "He said the women were going to do the killing because people weren't suspicious of women," a participant recalls. "We would have to protect the men of the church. And that if we were all of a sudden called on and told to go kill so and so that we weren't to question it, we were just to go do it. It wouldn't be held against us."

Another UMZ member went straight to Joel and detailed what Ervil had been saying, but he didn't believe her. "He was just joking if he said it," was Joel's frequent response to such reports.

Meanwhile, Ervil continued to act out his paranoid fantasies. In one home, he leaped around the kitchen, pointing to all the items which could be used as weapons. "He got so wound up about how to fight the enemy," the hostess remembers. "He was saying how you should keep all kinds of weapons in your home like a hammer in the kitchen drawer. Telling me how you use a chair as a weapon, just anything. How you really have to be quick at the draw. He gave me the spooks that day."

Ervil took an eleventh wife, Vonda White, a woman as callous as she was intractably loyal. Vonda's mother, reflecting on the oldest of her six children, said recently, "She used to be beautiful . . . before. Sometimes I wonder if it isn't the devil [influencing her]." Vonda's "before" took place in Stockton, California, where parents Herbert and Mildred White proudly saw her earn a straight-A average in high school. "She always helped people then," Mrs. White says. "She always was for the underdog." A sister reported that Vonda was well liked in Stockton, and recalled that Vonda would sit up late at night reading her to sleep.

Vonda was an avid reader of religious material—primarily Mormon. Since her mother was an active Mormon, Vonda followed suit enthusiastically, participating in many Mormon meetings and activities. But, says her sister, the fact that their father was not a Mormon caused a split in the family. "Our parents weren't united," she stated. This, as well as the fact that "she was very sheltered," may have influenced Vonda later. "These kinds of things [cults] appealed to her intellectually."

Dependable and ambitious, Vonda attended a full two years of junior college in Stockton—a level of education rare among LeBaron's wives. While in school, she met and married a local CPA who came from a wealthy Filipino family. Mrs. White points to her son-in-law's immaturity as a reason for the couple's breakup after two children. "He joined the Mormon Church, but he expected Vonda to wait on him hand and foot so it didn't work out. He said he didn't want the responsibility of a family."

Before separating, the couple moved to San Francisco where, in 1966, Vonda joined the Church of the Firstborn. She stopped to visit her parents on the way to Mexico and was "very secretive" about the trip's purpose. She called them from El Paso and said she'd never return, which she didn't. Typically, matchmaker Ervil tied her to another Firstborn member to hold her in Chihuahua. That marriage began inauspiciously: the hapless husband had diarrhea so badly the day of the ceremony that he fainted. Since Vonda was simply too much for him, they were not together very long. Ervil whisked her out of the relationship and secretly married her himself.

Little is known about Ervil's tenth and twelfth wives, sisters of a

Mexican whom Ervil had converted at their home, Huetepec, Puebla, where they'd been members of Margarito Bautista's Fundamentalist group. Both girls were described as backward and shy. One of the few persons who knew her, a man who stayed at their home a number of times, said the older girl was "very hospitable and attentive to a person's wants and needs." He observed that she and Ervil "lived in different worlds. Because of that, she was very obedient; she would never question Ervil. She was very solicitous. Ervil told me that of all his wives, she gave him the least problems. She never complained." Her younger sister was "remarkably intelligent," he added, "and extremely sweet."

Ervil continued on the prowl for women, flattering here, promising there and generally saying whatever was expedient to enhance his case. His wives and children were dim constellations around the central sun—himself. No one felt it more than his nine children by Delfina: Sylvia Esther, Sarah Jane, Alicia, Lillian, Arturo (Morrel), Rebecca, Isaac, Pablo and Delia. They were with him during years of supreme poverty, when there was never enough to eat. When money did come in, it was Papa who ate the best. His children as well as several family friends testify that Ervil ate steak, vegetables and his beloved fried potatoes while his offspring subsisted on three meals of wheat mush a day. Their clamor for a bite of his food usually sent him to the bedroom to eat most of his meals in peace. He developed and enforced a rule that it was disrespectful for women and children to speak louder than a man. The children whispered in his presence, no matter what they had to say.

His idea of discipline was antiquated and uneven. Growing up in a LeBaron home was doubly difficult because each of his wives had authority to take the switch to any of his children, though only Lorna was known to lose her temper and inflict unnecessary pain such as a bloody nose. Because Ervil distrusted his Mexican wives, he asked others to rear Delfina's children, and the two oldest by Mary Lou. His two favorites, Sylvia Esther and Arturo, had the rosiest existence since their grandmother, Maud, raised them. But the others were well treated. "We were the elite of the colony," says one of those children. "[After the period of poverty] we always had a maid, someone to do everything for us. The houses I lived in always had running water."

One daughter, Alice, seemed to have a continuously hard time—no doubt because she openly rebelled against her father.

"My dad is absolutely repulsive to me," she says, frankly. "I mean, I can't even stand him as a father. As a human being I couldn't stand to be around him. He grossed me out. I thought he was fat, and I always remember him having garlic breath and body odor. I couldn't understand those women at all because I couldn't stand to have him touch me." Once when he slapped her, she slapped him back. Generally, her independence kept Ervil trying to win her love. But he'd run out of patience, like the day he and Alice fought when she was fourteen.

Having promised her to another man, Ervil was chagrined to learn that Alice was dating a Mexican boy at school, so he finally told her she was not to go to school anymore. As a rule, he was against his children attending public schools because they would be out of his reach, hearing things which might cause dissatisfaction. During his lecture to Alice, he touched her and she said, with venom, "Get your hands off me." Ervil lost control and beat her severely, only stopping because of fatigue. She ran away to her boyfriend's house and stayed for more than a week. She left for good after she was sent to stay at Esther's house. While Alice was there, Esther suffered a nervous breakdown. Much of the housework fell to Alice, who finally packed her things and flagged down a bus to Chihuahua. The driver, who sympathized with her reasons for leaving, allowed her to ride free.

Life with Ervil had its lighter moments, too. He did occasionally take his children to movies, at least once to Disneyland, and loved to go to boat shows in San Diego—once promising one of his sons to buy him a fleet of ships someday. He was a fair dancer, and a good canasta and pinochle player. The games were usually interrupted by his lessons on how to play—which sometimes got tedious. But it was amazing, also, to watch him win. "He always wanted to take the trump," recalls one player. "Even if he had the worst damn hand in the world, he'd go for broke."

Wives and friends say that Ervil was "a very moral man within the bonds of matrimony" in the pioneer days of the Firstborn Church. But the standards he originally set up fell one by one—literally to suit his own pleasure. He told friends he would only marry virgins; then he married Anna Mae. He preached it was wrong to wed sisters as Joel and Verlan had done; then he married the Mexican sisters. And he believed sex was a God-given act for procreation only. But that went by the boards too.

One woman, who married a LeBaron, says the family generally embraced the Fundamentalist concept of intercourse. "You marry a LeBaron and it's quite a thing. Sex is only for reproduction, amen! I was really very surprised. They believe you wait and if you get pregnant, fine. If not, maybe they'll try again in a month. I had three kids, and I had sex with my husband seven times—in three kids." Ervil adhered to the same principle, undoubtedly aided by the fact he'd married a strict Catholic girl, Delfina, who held the same view and was prudish to the point she would never let him see her naked.

The demands of such younger wives forced Ervil to re-evaluate his attitude, and he embraced the new wife-style wholeheartedly. According to a friend, "He would send for them [his younger wives] over at Anna Mae's and have a little 'afternoon delight,' shall we say. And these were girls who married him for religion only."

But Ervil had his limitations. He refused to make love close to Conference time, feeling it was a spiritual drain. One wife, unhappy because she wasn't pregnant, begged Ervil to drop the rule since she was at the height of her fertile period. He acquiesced and she conceived.

*   *   *

Generally, those who came to the Church of the Firstborn looking for an earth-shaking leader found Ervil's powerful declarations far preferable to Joel's pitch for free agency and self-determination. The difference between them was basic: Joel made suggestions; Ervil made decisions.

Obviously, Ervil was a mildly successful charlatan. To recount anecdotes and quotes which tend to expose his questionable intentions is to remove the incidents from the context in which they were originally seen. He employed a sleight-of-mind which distracted listeners from what he might really be saying. By convincing them of his superiority, he deprived them of the warning signals common sense would normally have produced. "I think the main thing that put people off was that [physically and mentally] his size was not their size," says one intelligent man who should normally not have been cowed working at LeBaron's side. "He was head and shoulders above most of the rest of society. So he wasn't really liked by anyone. He was an enigma. He was the Patriarch. People feared him. They knew they were no match for him. They resented him like hell!"

One way to gain such standing is to offer unwavering criticism of others' opinions and actions. Ervil did just that. He berated the community time and again for what they were, compared to what they should be. He would make disparaging comments about his own wives, and their natural response was to try harder to please him. By employing criticism so frequently, he implied that he was the single arbiter of good and bad. His decisiveness became the community standard, so much so that many sought his imprimatur on both complicated and simple matters.

LeBaron also succeeded in depriving Firstborners of outside food for thought. Ervil saw to it that the community had no library and, using the United Women of Zion to his own ends, actively discouraged novel-reading and other contacts with outside stimuli. He was planning to win the people for the long term. Knowing that time away from Colonia LeBaron's isolation might rekindle some independence, Ervil portrayed the United States as a blood-red Babylon to be avoided at all costs. Any who ventured among relatives or friends there were placed on the alert to beware any changes in their own character, and thus were made suspicious of some possibly healthy input that could improve their cognitive abilities.

Deprived of any comparative capability, the colony considered Ervil LeBaron their Shakespeare, their Kant, their Kennedy—he was the most stimulating person in residence. He had vision. When one Firstborner would talk about money, Ervil would speak of the day when they would all be millionaires. When another discussed the possibility of running for local political office, he prophesied that one among them would be in the White House someday. He spoke of a reachable heaven in which the miseries of this life would magnify into a thousand glories.

His ramblings might have tricked them into believing he was pure genius, suggesting that incredible thoughts could be distilled from the great fog of words that issued from his mouth. But he needed no tricks. They were convinced of his high calling because he was convinced of it. His belief in himself ensured their awe.

Ervil realized that he could not continue to placate followers with impossible idyllic visions. At some point, he had to persuade them to accept a cut in their lifestyle for the good of the community. While assuring them they were sacrificing a minor good for a greater good later, he developed an esprit de corps, a sense of community that worked to erode individuality. When he did that, he also reinforced their allegiance to him. Once they had sacrificed, Ervil was needed to justify their actions—like giving up mansions in America for the poverty of Mexico. In supplying that justification, Ervil used the most potent force known to move man: religion. "Religion is the ruling power," said Brigham Young, who could easily have been LeBaron's mentor. "The conscience of the masses in regard to religion, to politics and social life is molded from the pulpit."

Religion carries a risk, though. Ervil's necessary revelations could have backfired on him but they didn't, for a simple reason. As an observer of human nature, he was perceptive enough to predict what a person would do under given circumstances and correctly receive a revelation to forestall it or foretell it. And people who, by dint of circumstances, were impelled to believe in Ervil of their own volition, would hearken to and frequently recount his fulfilled prophecies, while the unfulfilled ones seemed to escape away unnoticed.

Ervil also seemed to have a knack for turning flaws into strengths. In choosing the cold Dan Jordan as his confidant and confederate, he may have alienated some. But Jordan's basic inability to communicate warmth to those around him made him an easy and much-needed foil for the failure of any project on which the two ventured together. The LeBaron family, who have suffered most from Ervil's waywardness, persist in placing blame on Jordan. Certainly Ervil needed a totally trusted second-in-command, but others were available. Even his illness, which served as the excuse for his torpid attitude toward work, enhanced Ervil's believability. Other historical leaders, like Caesar, suffered from epilepsy or other ailments which, seen by the public as their single chink, added credibility to their humanness and, in overcoming the disability, fortified public belief in their godliness.

The flaw that undid Ervil's hold on some followers, which stripped him bare in the eyes of those not deluded by his imaginary grandeur or put off by his more visible faults, was his absence of any empathy toward others. He could feign sympathy at times, but his reaction to wives in travail, to those who crossed or doubted him as well as many callous episodes, revealed him as a man who served himself, not the God he alluded to. Had he been genuinely concerned more about others than himself, Ervil's course would have been different. Without that kind of a proper motive, religious truths can be abused to develop self-aggrandizing power. In the same way atom-splitting can be used for peaceful or warlike purposes, so too the Bible can be used as a guide for good or as an outline for evil. Ervil's own declarations for God may have been sincere enough in the beginning, but at some point he was sidetracked because of personal greed and power lust, and an inability to feel much sympathy for his fellow man.

Ervil could control his Colonia LeBaron flock even if he had little heart for them. In one-on-one situations, his manipulative string-pulling was not always perceptible, but it was always there, like a warm current circling an iceberg, waiting for an enormous sheet to split away. As early as 1958, one Firstborn convert detected this and accurately described the quality in an early pamphlet:

"He has a penetrating and magnetic personality which is at time very charming, but becomes unbearable when it is applied to achieve an end. If you know Ervil, you know what I mean when I say that you can 'feel' him pulling you this way and that. A person has to firmly oppose him, or let himself be found doing exactly what Ervil wants."

In Colonia LeBaron there were very few people who would find themselves capable of opposing Ervil LeBaron.

8.

OF CAIN AND ABEL

The story is told that once while walking through a street in Mexico City, the prophet Joel came upon a decrepit old man, who appeared to be a beggar. Ragged and wrinkled, the man crouched on the ground. He was not noticed by the throngs of passersby for it was a busy time of the day and this was a major highway and there were many poor in the city. In the man's hand, he clutched a piece of paper, waving it and silently entreating someone to read it to him.

Joel stopped, gazed upon the man and drew the paper from his fingers. He read it, and the man's face changed: his fortune was made. The lottery ticket was *the* lucky one, good for one million pesos. As Joel was escorting the man to a nearby bank, he was approached by thieves and robbers. "Cash it yourself," they whispered in his ear. "We will divide it among ourselves and he will be none the wiser." But Joel rebuked the men, saying, "Because the God of heaven granted me the privilege of learning to read and write, do you think I would be found guilty of deceiving this man?"

When friends—and even those who would normally be enemies given his mighty religious claims—are asked about Joel LeBaron, a plethora of Christlike virtues are enumerated: "Kind and meek." "Gentle." "Humble." "Able to get along with all people." "Preferred a modest meal with the lowly than a banquet among the elite." It is evident their descriptions arise not from mere reverence for the dead, but from the facts of Joel's life.

No one is more eloquent in listing Joel's virtue than his sister, Esther:

"Joel was the most perfect and Christlike person I ever knew. I can think of no virtues, great or small, that Joel did not possess and live by.

In all my life I have never found a hair of the spirit of deception in him. He was free from guile, malice, selfishness and false pride. He had charity and love for everyone. From his earliest childhood, Joel was pure inside out—full of truth, sincerity and real integrity toward any job, duty or obligation. He had good control over his emotions and never let his temper guide his actions. He carried the spirit of true peace within his person. Even as a child I marveled at how good and peaceful and safe it felt to be with Joel."

As the embodiment of empathy, Joel was never quick to take the lead in situations. "You had to seek him out. You had to beg him for counseling," says one follower. "His method of counseling was to let you make up your own mind." Some were disappointed, for here was a man who walked and talked with God, who would not give them pre-packaged, TV-dinner answers. He was the same in his public preachments. "When not influenced otherwise," says ore friend, "Joel was very discreet and cautious about ordering people around. He did not bulldoze anyone into things, as does Ervil. Joel, if left alone, would let every other man stand on his own two feet, as God intended. And when it came to abuses rained about his head, Joel is the most long-suffering person I have ever met. Almost too much so."

Joel's attitude was evident even in the early days of the Firstborn Church. When Noel Pratt launched a 1958 diatribe against the church, Joel, as was typical, chose not to respond. Pratt cried out: "What I really want to see is some *Leadership!!* What's that? An unknown substance." It was Ervil, as usual, who took up the church banner and wrote a lengthy essay, which perhaps made a response from Joel moot.

Joel's genuinely gracious personality, with all its commendable virtues, was often misunderstood. Where followers expected a "man like unto Moses"—in all the awesome majesty of that Old Testament prophet—they found only a farmer who seemed as unassuming as soft ice cream. "Joel's name was the dominant force in the colony, but the real dynamic force was Ervil," one of Joel's adherents concedes.

Joel had chosen as his primary counselor Earl Jensen, a constant irritant to brother Ervil, who resented Jensen's wealth. Earl had erected the largest home in the colony when he settled there, flaunting the relative ease in which his six wives lived. His brand of conspicuous consumption was the subject of many over-the-pulpit denunciations by Ervil. Joel, on his part, respected Earl's business prowess and invited his advice more than brother Ervil's. Because Earl was so close to the prophet as to undermine Ervil's influence, he and Ervil never got along. "There was a basic personality clash," says one of Jensen's wives. "Earl wouldn't put up with Ervil, he wasn't afraid of him and he outdid him when it came to making money. In his actions, Earl showed he was a doer, while Ervil was a dreamer."

But despite strenuous efforts, Jensen could not prod Joel into assertive leadership. Joel shied away from revelatory declarations as if they were the devil's instruments, and he was evasive when questioned about his authority-by-vision. "Are you the One Mighty and Strong?" a sister-in-law queried. Instead of answering the question, he deflected the subject, observing that "people should have a testimony of our church first before they believe that." One of Joel's own wives once pointedly asked him if he had ever come face to face with God, something the church expected had happened, since he was as great as Moses. He refused to answer, but told her it had been confirmed to him "beyond a shadow of a doubt" that what he was doing was right. Finally, a Fundamentalist challenged Him: "Now I want you to swear before God's angels and us as witnesses [Ervil was present] that Jesus Christ has appeared to you and ordained you." Joel thought for a few moments, bowed his head, and said, "My lips are sealed."

When a man such as Joel, for whom truth was a conscientious imperative, began evading such basic queries, it could have suggested that he was reluctant to build upon an imagined and false vision which had been the church's cornerstone. That, wanting to create a perfect religion and thereby justifying the initial deception, he had seen what a tangled web he had woven and was anxious to avoid piling one falsehood upon another. However, Joel's followers did not seem to have been persuaded that this was the case. They might recount Joel's renowned response to Earl's prodding suggestions that he be more forceful, and administrate the church of God with miracles, signs from the heavens, including revelations.

"Why don't you use 'Thus saith the Lord' more often when you speak?" Jensen asked, concluding his lengthy discourse on the elements of dynamic leadership.

Joel answered with a question. "Earl, how many times did the Saviour say, 'Thus saith the Lord'?"

Earl thought a moment and replied: "He never did."

Joel weighed his words. "Did that mean he had no revelations?" Checkmate.

From its start, the church that was to end all churches had been in a permanent state of holy hock.

Joel the prophet was shunted here and there by a family friend and pilot, Ossmen Jones, to keep him one step ahead of his creditors. Reported one 1957 neighbor: "Last summer most of the boys had to go into hiding . . . because of the indebtedness they had brought upon themselves. They were deep in debt, and they'd passed a number of bad checks." In the first few years of its inception, the church was a million pesos ($80,000) in arrears. Undoubtedly the most significant contributing factor to their plight was Ervil's truckloads of Mexicans bound for glory to the colony, because Alma had to borrow money to house and feed them. Ervil was chided for his zealousness: he was pushing the gospel faster than the church coffers could afford.

At one point, Ervil thought drastic measures were required to discharge the church's debt. A Firstborn member said he, Ervil and other brethren left on a special mission to Las Vegas. Using an inspired system, they planned to enrich the Firstborn Church and "redeem Zion's bills" at the gaming tables. "The project had the blessing of the prophet and we all had faith that the Lord would help us win," the ex-Firstborner recalls. The group checked into a hotel room where they had a lengthy prayer before solemnly heading for a casino roulette wheel to play the numbers. "We dropped $600 so fast it made our heads swim. And the next night we won only $15. I guess it wasn't the Lord's will that we should win."

Though Joel's generosity was a factor in the sect's impoverishment, church members were often disappointed that their prophet couldn't seem to turn a profit. Instead of money, he offered them consoling predictions. "He'd tell us that God and the angels were just dying to hand us the Kingdom on a silver platter, but we weren't righteous enough yet," according to one member. "Like Moses, he was ready to take us into the presence of God, but we were holding ourselves back." When members still despaired in the colony's dusty poverty, he'd offer additional solace. "Now, don't you worry. Never you mind. We're right on schedule," Joel would affirm. One of his last promises was that the Lord would bless them with prosperity on the day that his people—including the LeBaron brothers—achieved some across-the-board unity. It was asking the impossible.

As funds for the Lord's work were just barely eked out, it became apparent to many that Ervil was the sieve. "Ervil today collects some of the tithing before the bishop ever sees it," Pratt wrote. "He insists on being supported so that he can dedicate himself to the work. But he is going to loaf whether anyone pays his expenses or not." Ervil did not deny what amounted to virtual embezzlement, since all tithing, land and other goods which were given to the church should have gone through Alma or Joel. He claimed he was "working nearly full time for the Church, [and yet] my family is still supported by myself." Knowing the many who'd paid him could call him out if he lied, Ervil added, "However, I do want to be supported in the work I have been called to perform. Furthermore, I am being supported in various ways, and am thankful to my brethren who are giving me this support."

Siphoning tithing became Ervil's standard operating procedure. "What happened was that when someone new came down, everybody would surround [the converts] and kiss their ass," recalls Ervil's daughter Alice. "The people would feel real important. Then, after a while, [the leaders] would just tromp on 'em. It was a snow job. They'd take everything from them—their money, everything. They'd talk people into selling their homes and investing everything in the colony. Then my Dad got ahold of the money and of course he wasn't gonna give them back anything. All these people paid tithing to him—10 percent of whatever they made."

Ervil was not averse to collecting tithing from nonchurch members. Independent Fundamentalist Harold Blackmore says Ervil tried to get him to throw in with the LeBarons, offering as an inducement a promise that Blackmore could have all the tithing of anyone he subsequently converted. Ervil also offered him the pick of the Chynoweth girls one day. When he could see he was getting nowhere, Ervil finally assessed Blackmore $50 for every male member of his family. "I just laughed at him," Blackmore recalls. "I ended up telling him that instead of being out panhandling he should be home taking care of the monstrous [large] family that he had."

Most members felt a healthy financial situation at the colony was a religious imperative. "If we are not economically independent in this land, we will not be able to accomplish the gathering of the Saints," Bill Tucker said during his April 1961 conference speech. "This is one reason God has led his people to a desert land. It will weed the weak from the strong and make the strong stronger and develop everything God has given them."

Tucker and Ervil started a fish business that they hoped would rescue the church from its poverty. Permission was obtained to create a reservoir, and bulldozers worked for weeks digging it out. The pair purchased thousands of fish from the Mexican government, and even obtained some imported Israeli fish. Though the lake provided recreation for the colony, as a business it was a miserable failure. Floren LeBaron blamed it all on Ervil. "He spent thousands of dollars of the people's money in a fish-raising business in Galeana that ended up in the loss of a water supply worth more money than Ervil has made in his entire life." Floren recalled that Ervil and Dan Jordan founded a Chihuahua construction business which "went to pot before even one house was finished. [Ervil also] started a fish buying and selling business in San Diego, spending many thousands again, and only leaving a trail of people holding a bagful of promises."

Ervil's wives said he continually thought up "projects, schemes and deals." For a while, worldwide shipping would fascinate him. Then he'd be obsessed with an interstate trucking venture. Always he promised every one that times would get better, even clearly stating in 1963 that they'd all be millionaires in two years.

One of the oddest LeBaron labor projects—which may have been fruitful because Ervil was not involved—was pine nut gathering.

Verdon Liston, a professonal Utah wholesaler, hired and trained the LeBarons initially for the work. A tasty delicacy similar to cashews, the nuts grow inside pine cones from single needle and double needle Piñon Pines, which generally grow in California, Arizona, and Nevada where the Forest Service charges a fee for picking the cones. With his family, Liston travels to specially selected forests in mid-September. Each member collects an average of twenty-five bushels a day, which they sell on their return in mid-November for about $2 a pound. The Listons came upon Alma LeBaron and his sprawling family at Baker Creek,

Nevada, in 1960. "They were poor as a crow and didn't have no money and we hired them to pick for us," Verdon remembers. Alma's many children were particularly good at picking the cones. He had them working all day, living on this sorghum, which was the size of hen's eggs and made out of molasses. They would chew this while they picked and then come in at night and eat from a big pot of chili beans they made." Each year, Liston lent Alma about $4,000 at the beginning of the season against the cones they would pick. It was such a going business that Verlan, Floren and Joel joined in, and the semiannual October church conference was moved up to August to accommodate those who were "in the pine nuts." The only LeBaron who refused to pick them was Ervil.

He was too busy inventing his own businesses. Apparently, Joel supported him in some of them. In a letter Ervil wrote in 1967, he said that Joel had asked him to be a partner in a "building, mercantile and real estate business. I accepted and am lining up the potential. . . . We want to wheel and deal in everything that will build up the work." Perhaps imagining this business, too, would fail, Ervil wrote about his old standby, tithing. He was not satisfied with the mere 10 percent. "It seems necessary for me to do something to get some of our timid people on the ball. They are beginning to pay tithing good, but the greatest potential in building up the Kingdom is in the 90 percent."

By 1969, Ervil was really hungry for that money. He suggested that those who didn't pay tithing be automatically dropped from the church. He proposed to do this by requiring rebaptism into the church, a privilege which would only be accorded those who were full tithe-payers. When this plan failed, he demanded $2,000 a month from Joel for preaching to the Gentiles even though, at the time, most of the preaching came from his bed. Frustrated in that endeavor, he visited the heads of church families saying he had been instructed to collect their tithing. At the end of one month, Alma, who was responsible for that job, wondered why the tithing wasn't rolling in and found it had been paid to Ervil.

Ervil started to live high off the faithful. "He began running around in $60 shoes and $35 shirts," a friend says. He also acquired a late-model four-door Impala with a shiny tan interior and golden outside. Ervil claimed God had revealed that he should obtain the vehicle because it would be more impressive to potential converts. The contrast between the prophet's modest pickup and his number-two man's elegant chariot was not lost on Firstborn members. They dubbed Ervil's yellow car "The Golden Calf."

No one really knew what Ervil did with the money he received, according to daughter Alice. "Who knows what he did with it. Get new wives. Take everybody out to dinner. Buy a new car. Buy a new house. Spend it. He's a con man. He can con anybody out of anything. I was with him on a couple of conning trips. He was working on land investments. He'd be placed with four or five thousand dollars, supposedly to invest for various people. After we left this one house, he just handed me a $50 bill. 'What do you need, honey?', you know. Very generous with other people's money!"

Ervil LeBaron was, in fact, a religious huckster with a gift for grab. "He could smell money quite a long distance," recalls one of his marks, who had handed over $1,000 for title to a real estate property; he never saw the land, the title or Ervil again. Ervil had so many victims that Floren was moved to issue a signed public warning about Ervil's land maneuvers.

One of his victims was a trusting sixty-three-year-old relative from Canada, Nellie May Gibbs. When her husband died, she sold their home and paid off the outstanding debts, leaving a total of $2,000 in a Canadian bank. She was relatively secure until she visited Colonia LeBaron and met Ervil, who told her that the great and kind prophet Joel had asked for her life savings to purchase some land, and the money would be returned within a week. "He had made me think that they really needed help, and their folks were quite hard up and kind of worked on my sympathies so I gave it to him and he was going to get some property to pay me back." She waited, and waited. Finally she went to see Joel. "I've come to get my money back," Nellie declared.

"Your money?" Joel asked, surprised. "Did I owe you some money?"

"You most certainly do," she replied. "You owe me $2,000."

Joel started to laugh; he thought it was a joke. "What do I owe you for?" He smiled at the elderly woman. "I must have a short memory."

"I just let you take $2,000," Nellie stubbornly responded.

"I'm sorry, but it wasn't me."

At this, Nellie began crying. After Joel comforted her, he asked to whom she had given her money. "To Ervil," she answered. "He told me you were sick and that's why he'd come."

Joel stiffened. "I didn't know a thing about this."

"Well, how can I get my money back?"

"I can talk to Ervil about it, but I didn't ask you to do that," the prophet lamely replied. Some years later, Nellie said she "never heard any more about it."

Ervil did not restrict himself to elderly ladies. Men who should have known better—realtors, doctors, judges, financiers and a minister or two—also felt Ervil's sting.

Take the following ingenious maneuver, related by a New Mexico investor who refused to lend Ervil $5,000. "Then he suggested that I exchange checks for $3,000 with him—just for show. I gave him $3,000 on a bank account I rarely used which had a balance of approximately $8. I knew full well the bank would never honor such a check. But lo and behold LeBaron went to the bank, deposited another check from him to me for $3,000 . . . waited one day so there was ample time for his check to be recorded and immediately followed through with a demand to cash my check. The bank paid the $3,000 to LeBaron and later when the check he deposited bounced, they charged me with an uncollectable check. I couldn't believe how simple it worked and how he outsmarted me."

Another of Ervil's projects was the Judaic Christian Alliance. Working primarily in Las Vegas and parts of Texas, Ervil represented himself as the nondenominational minister for the JCA, an organization he claimed was dedicated to promoting brotherhood and understanding in the world. He pumped corporation executives, ministers, judges and others for $50 to $100 donations, for which he said they would receive monthly literature. Dan Jordan was his partner during the first week when a personal matter called Jordan away. Ervil asked Verlan to accompany him. The honest Verlan agreed, but was disgusted when he learned what Ervil was doing.

He asked his brother what he planned to do with the money, and Ervil said he would use it to support his family. Ervil promised his reluctant brother that the pair could make $2,000 a week and a 50-50 split would make it well worth Verlan's while. "How can you do this?" Verlan asked. "You know you won't send them any literature. It's stealing."

"No, it isn't," Ervil stated.

"How's that?"

"Well," Ervil said, pausing while he thought it out, "the Bible says we shouldn't steal from our brothers or neighbors. These are Gentiles; they're no good anyway. They aren't our brothers, and neighbors are only those who have the same beliefs as us."

Verlan warned him he was rationalizing himself into a devilish practice, and dutifully reported the matter to Joel, who as usual did nothing. His typical response when the brethren berated Ervil in his presence, as reported by one of them, was to say: "People are always criticizing Ervil. I can't see anything wrong with him."

The lengths to which Ervil went, the utter lack of any concern or love toward his own kin, is exemplified in a story told by a LeBaron family member, about their matriarch, Maud, who owned several large Mexican *parcelas*. She grabbed her coat and rushed out of her house one day when she saw a grandson plowing up one of her choicest pieces of land.

When he saw Mrs. LeBaron running after him, waving, he stopped the tractor. Breathless, she panted out: "What are you doing with my land? Why are you plowing it up?"

"*Your* land? Grandma, this isn't your land."

"Since when?"

"I bought this," the grandson said.

"You bought it? Who did you buy it from?"

Looking amazed, the boy said, "Well, I've owned this thing for three months." He thought she might be getting senile.

"Well," Maud said impatiently, "exactly how did you get it?"

"I paid Uncle Ervil $5,000 for it."

Maud could hardly believe her son, Ervil, whom she'd dubbed the most spiritual of her offspring, had sold his own mother's land with neither a word nor a penny to her.

Inevitably, those who were not blinded by Ervil's patriarchal office, his commanding manner and charismatic personality, began noticing similar spots on his character. An engineer who had given Ervil hundreds of dollars and the free use of his Standard Oil credit card cut off the money flow when Ervil made off with his wife.

Another avid supporter, one of his dozen mothers-in-law, turned against him altogether the day he stated, after a lengthy revelation about the future of the gospel, that one of his operating principles was: "You can lie, cheat and steal in the name of God and it is all right." Pilferage by prophecy did not agree with her. Nor was it agreeing with a good many others.

While Ervil came up with new economic schemes, he was developing a new way of looking at Firstborn beliefs which eventually resulted in him and his followers apparently believing that they had the religious authority to take a life.

It was the God that had etched out two tablets for Moses who worked on Ervil to the exclusion of all else, he maintained. Ervil came to idolize the wrathful jealous God of the Old Testament rather than the benevolent Christ of the New. The Ten Commandments, in his mind, were apodictic laws not superseded by Christ's alleged atonement. And the aggregate of laws in Deuteronomy, ordering the minutest details in Jewish life, were applicable to modern times if administered by one who was appointed, such as Ervil LeBaron. He ignored the fact that the original commandments and their corollary statutes were accepted by the Hebrews as a religious covenant and were therefore exclusive laws, not universally inclusive. In LeBaron's warped crystal ball, he soon foresaw the time when he would resurrect the Mosaic codes and such punishments as the death penalty before the believed-in second coming of Christ. The thunder which he lent to this idea—which he called Civil Law—and the authority it would give him as sole judge over people's lives inevitably would inspire horror in the hearts of those who had incurred LeBaron's displeasure—and others who would assiduously avoid doing just that.

The dreaded Civil Law was born on the same mysterious 1960 mission to Mexico City from which LeBaron and Dan Jordan had emerged in so paranoid a state about their safety. As the two developed the new Civil Law line on that mission, they no doubt felt they had come upon a great truth and the devil's forces would necessarily be arraigned against them. Their sermons on the subject, reminiscent of the hellfire and damnation eloquence of Jonathan Edwards, naturally aroused some animosity among those who disagreed with the preaching. In the distorted view of the paranoid pair, the subsequent anger of some of the listeners might have been interpreted as plots against the missionaries' lives, especially since they expected they might be martyred for their cause anyway.

Jordan was supercharged with religious fervor from the trip south. On November 27, 1960, he wrote a lengthy essay to a slight acquaintance in Salt Lake declaring that he and LeBaron had just come from "one of the most successful missions" in the history of religion. Without further details on that mission, he launched into the new doctrine, which divided persons into three groups. The best of them loved God with all their heart and did whatever He asked, even murder. The second-best loved their neighbors and gave all their money to the cause. The third and lowest group did neither. Toward them, all of Jordan's venom flowed. "They must be held in line by the civil government and by brute force. The spirit of the law of this group is 'an eye for an eye and a tooth for a tooth.' In Moses' time, the Ten Commandments were [punishable] by death." He explained that the vast majority of the world fitted into this category, including "most of the members of the sectarian churches, the LDS Church and many of the Fundamentalist people." He added: "Nearly all of this class of people will be destroyed at Christ's coming . . . unless they repent."

Such absolutism was naturally hard for outsiders to swallow—and a number of insiders, church members, had trouble too. Civil Law was a tough line to convert others to at first, prescribing, as it did, the death penalty for traitors, adulterers and murderers. Fearful that he might be declared a false prophet, Joel agreed with the new doctrine but asked Ervil to be its chief apostle, and thus absorb the predictable resistance which would come from Firstborn members. Though some would not let Ervil into their homes for more than a year because of his Civil Law sermons, the greater part of the Firstborn Church eventually embraced the new doctrine and Joel publicly expounded it as revelation.

Ervil was anxious to apply the Civil Law. The first person to face its full—at that time verbal—onslaught was the rival polygamist leader, Rulon Allred.

Not only had Allred ignored the only written revelation of the Firstborn Church, which instructed him to aid them, but he also berated them publicly for their religion. Ervil had to settle for a tract, in the February 1962 *Ensign*, the Firstborn monthly. After charging the Allreds were trying to undermine the great work of the LeBarons, Ervil issued a not-so-hidden threat: "In a spurious and loathsome fabrication . . . 'A Religious Treatise,' reportedly written by Rulon C. Allred . . . and signed by his brother, Owen A. Allred . . . they engaged in the type of character assassination which was punishable by the death sentence under the Civil Law given by God in the days of Moses." Though Ervil's rhetoric was strange and his doctrine convoluted, the Allreds were eventually to grasp the unmistakable intent of such statements.

If Ervil concocted the Civil Law by himself, Joel added to it. He envisioned a time when the "Political Kingdom of God" would be set up—that is, a government that would rule the earth irrespective of any single religion, but directed by the Christian God. The Ten Commandments would be the constitution of that kingdom, a situation which Esther quoted Joel as promising "will actually bring peace on earth and good will toward men . . . stop poverty, prisons, war and corruption . . . stop immorality on all levels."

God had made it Joel's job to unite the whole world and bring them together to set up this kingdom. So he decided to remove the political kingdom concept from the Church of the Firstborn and set up a separate organization, the Alliance of Pastors and Christian Teachers, headquartered in Las Vegas. "He wanted to get it away from the stigma of a religion or a church," said one Firstborn member. "The missionaries turned from theology to more practical, down-to-earth interests. So instead of a tiny little sect, he was opening the truth up to everybody, giving the world broad-principled ideas it needed." Ervil was given sole control of APCT and had only reached a few hundred people when Joel, frustrated with Ervil's inability to recruit, went on an APCT mission and signed up eighty persons in a very short time. Ervil was so jealous of Joel's ability that he asked his brother to stop recruiting, whereupon Joel promptly disbanded the organization and set up a new one, the American Independent Peace Organization. He appointed Earl Jensen to get it under way in California. But when that organization didn't coalesce, Jensen started a third and final one, the Christian-Judaic Evangelical Brotherhood. Founded in El Paso, the Brotherhood preached that its purpose was to resurrect the principles of the Ten Commandments. They received some local publicity in 1971, but did not get far with their professed goal, to prepare the world for the reinstitution of God's law, à la LeBaron.

Back in Colonia LeBaron, Ervil's version of the Civil Law didn't sit well with the ladies. They knew that if Ervil were to dispense it, there would be no equity.

"Ervil believed in the hierarchy of gods among men—that kings or gods are above the law, which was for lower beings," says the member. "Ervil did not believe he was subject to his own laws."

Aside from the expected inequity, Firstborn women objected to the bloodiness with which Ervil portrayed the Civil Law, focusing more on punishment than justice. "He told me about how people should be disemboweled or stoned for this or that," recalls one woman. Said another: "We talked about it at some meetings and none of the ladies wanted Civil Law because they thought they would be killed—wait a minute, there was one who was backing it up, Anna Mae Marston."

Anna Mae was so indoctrinated that she held talks for hours about Civil Law with others. "Every church teaches that it was done away with and love replaced it [the Mosaic law]," Anna Mae later proclaimed in an interview, "That is totally false. . . . If you start spiritualizing those laws, you totally lose the meaning of what God gave them for. That's the foundation of His kingdom. God the Father Himself thundered those laws from Mt. Sinai. Why would He go to all that trouble if they were just some little—it was one of the BIGGEST, MAIN EVENTS that ever happened in the whole world. And people have just written it off, saying Christ came and did away with it. . . . We must put God and His law before any other thing."

In theory, many Christians might agree with the Anna Mae-Ervil line, if a just God directed such law. But Ervil spoke of it in terms of his own right to police it. "He was real bloodthirsty in his conversations—always preaching this blood-and-thunder stuff. You know, if people don't live the Civil Law, cut their damn heads off," recalls leading polygamist Harold Blackmore. Ervil, said Blackmore, informed him that the Civil Law would have to be re-established by force. "He told me he was going to take over the Mexican government first and then up north. And he had laid the groundwork with the Masonic Order and various other organizations down there and he was going to become the president of Mexico before very long and, my oh my, he just had himself built up in the grandest fashion."

LeBaron also had his sights on the United States. Ridiculous as it sounds, he truly believed the Lord was on his side—a force more powerful than a dozen armies. Then too, he considered his task similar to Noah's, preparing the world for its final flood with only a few followers. And so the Church of the Firstborn consistently preached that the United States, as the new Babylon, would soon incur a terrible punishment. "We were God's people," recalls Kim Jensen. "We were down there to escape the destruction of Babylon, which was imminent." Firstborn ministers predicted armies of Mexicans and Indians would march into America and take it over. Joel and Ervil even discussed the day when one among them would be in the White House. Ervil alone thought it might take a revolution similar to the American Revolution before the "last days," and he felt personally connected to such a prophecy because he had been born on February 22, George Washington's birthday.

In the meantime, it seemed advisable for the LeBaron brothers to stay away from the United States. The FBI had begun developing files on Joel, Ervil and Alma. The boys had avoided World War II, and Uncle Sam wanted to know why. Alma claimed a revelation persuaded him not to register for the draft in December 1943, when he became engrossed in brother Benjamin's ill-fated work, which made him subject to draft evasion charges. As for Ervil and Joel, both had been regularly deferred when they served as Mormon missionaries, but their status changed the day they were excommunicated. Neither elected to report to Selective Service boards. The saintly Joel, on the other hand, always ready to face church or legal charges head-on, turned himself in to El Paso federal authorities in November of 1948 and pleaded guilty to failing to complete and return his Selective Service questionnaire and also failing to report for induction. He was sentenced to a year and a day imprisonment, but the sentence was suspended and he was placed on three years' probation.

Ervil avoided facing any charges. The dual citizenship he held because he was born in Mexico to American parents was lost in June 1955. The certificate of loss of U.S. nationality, filed from Colonia Juarez, said he was expatriated for "departing from and remaining outside of the jurisdiction of the United States in time of war for the purpose of evading or avoiding training and service in the Armed Forces of the United States." The expatriation, like many others, was later ruled unconstitutional by the U.S. Supreme Court. However, immigration records still showed Ervil as a noncitizen, and those who traveled with him noted he had a Mexican identification card which only allowed him in America for seventy-two-hour intervals.

The activities—or rather, inactivities—of the LeBaron brothers suddenly came to light when Kennedy was assassinated on November 22, 1963. Five days later, the Salt Lake City FBI office filed a report suggesting the Firstborn Church leaders as possible suspects in the assassination. An informant told the FBI that a Firstborn Church member, Ralph Higbee, had told him since the previous July that "one of the aims of this church is to assassinate the top government officials as well as the top officials of the Mormon Church. [He] believes this group was responsible for President Kennedy's death and he was very concerned about other officials being killed by that organization." A man who attended Firstborn meetings reported that one Firstborn leader, known as the "Avenging Angel," planned in spring 1964 to: "1. Disrupt all civil authority. 2. Destroy all communications, public utilities, and powerplants. 3. Engage in secret undercover operations." Investigation of the church continued until at least February 1964 though its leaders were never seriously considered suspects. It would be fifteen years before the FBI would devote its agents and money to another active investigation of the LeBarons.

Throughout history it has always happened that when a cohesive group is formed—be it religious, political or ethnic—a core of that unit will be comprised of militants wishing to use the group to effect quasi-military goals.

So it was the Church of the Firstborn. Their own version of a militant band began forming under the leadership of Ervil LeBaron. Many were the local teenage boys, like Kim Jensen, who he assumed would be impressionable.

"Ervil had movements like Adolf Hitler when he talked," remembers Kim. "His voice was booming. He would talk about chopping off people's heads. He and Dan [Jordan] were very violent, like a volcano. Ervil's eyes were just active all the time. Dan, his crony, was the same way. There was talk among the young guys about what it would be like to be a [religious assassin]. I always thought that was neat. To have to go around and waste these people who didn't live up to the word of God. . . . It was firmly believed by the younger guys that if a man broke his covenant with God, he would have to die. My father told me this was bullshit, but we believed it anyway."

Jensen taught his youthful companions Arturo, Ervil's son, and Eddie Marston, Ervil's stepson, how to shoot in preparation for the day they would be called on to do so. It was no game to them. Two of Ervil's relatives would later tell police that Ervil's evil roots were in the halcyon days of his teenage militant band. "We were raised in Mexico and I knew him real well," said one of them. "I don't think there was any such thing as kicking anyone out of Ervil's group—they would blow them away. One day he took me out to do some work on the road and he was talking about the apostates from the church and he said he done away with them." Ervil asked the pair several times if they'd kill for him, and they nodded in obeisance. "He has such an incredible ability to influence minds, overwhelm minds," explained one. "The last time I saw his . . . head henchman . . . Dan Jordan . . . was back in 1968. I was arguing with him. He was trying to convince me of Ervil's doctrine. I just wasn't going for them at all. He reached in his pocket and pulled out a .45 and started juggling it from hand to hand and I got the idea."

LeBaron knew he needed some strong adults in his private, loosely organized militia and he acquired several, like Chuck Henderson, by preaching his Civil Law. An indepenent fundamentalist, Henderson recalls: "I was learning a lot from Ervil. He spent his whole life studying the Old Testament especially and I was interested in this—Civil Law and the basic government that would one day be established again. . . . I accepted his talk in very general terms [like] God's army being established someday . . . something I consider very definitely will happen. . . . I didn't understand what Ervil was contemplating—raising an army himself."

LeBaron also cultivated an ex-Los Angeles policeman, who had retired from the force in 1958 after a series of physical, marital and "job-related problems," according to one report. At the time he joined Ervil, in the sixties, the ex-policeman was usually accompanied by a trained police dog and carried a long-barreled .357 magnum. A semi-automatic rifle or shotgun was generally nearby. He felt himself so proficient a marksman that he offered to instruct Colonia LeBaron residents in shooting. His personality is fairly evident in a 1970 letter he wrote the colony announcing he'd be available to give lessons:

"Again, I would like you to seriously consider the impending and serious danger that faces this Colony. . . . If you think the Lord gives a revelation for the fun of it, or just to be making with words, think again.

"If you think that you know how to shoot well enough, then I can't help you. If you think you know WHEN to shoot, legally, ditto.

"If you want to learn more, either in how to shoot, or when, get word to me as soon as possible. The time is NOW. We must not sit and wait till the bullets start flying to act. . . ."

One of Ervil's temporary colleagues, John Lawton (not his real name), told of an exclusive Firstborn priesthood group called "The Sons," from whom Ervil culled an even more exclusive group of his own. "These were clandestine meetings we had," recalls Lawton, who is reluctant to detail them because "Ervil's still alive and capable. He has that group of loyal Mexicans who'd walk right up into a fire for him."

Lawton had some reason to fear LeBaron since he had twice defied him. On one occasion he was arguing religion with LeBaron in the latter's favorite mobile-home hiding place in Santa Ana, California. The discussion heated up until Ervil asked Lawton point-blank if he would kill Joel for him. Enraged, Lawton pushed Ervil onto a nearby bed and straddled him. "Absolutely not! If you ever bring up the fact you want me to kill someone—it's totally repulsive to me! You are repulsive to me!" Ervil was subdued, said Lawton, but as he himself walked out in a huff, he heard LeBaron rise from the bed and ask a third person there if he would murder Joel.

Lawton confronted Ervil the second time at Bill Tucker's funeral. Lawton told him he was "not so sure you didn't do this." He threatened LeBaron that he never wanted to hear from him again, or any of his schemes or else he would "blow Colonia LeBaron off the face of the map. Do you understand me?" he asked Ervil, pushing him in the chest. "Yes," was Ervil's simple reply, almost unruffled. Lawton later joined the Unification Church, and became personally acquainted with the Reverend Sun Myung Moon, to whom he related his experiences with the LeBarons. The discussions gave him inner peace, though he says he keeps an eye out for Ervil's followers.

Ervil LeBaron's most indefatigable pursuer in future years, Siegfried Widmar, was the product of a Mormon home in Germany. His childhood was interrupted by the savagery of World War II, and at fifteen, he was drafted into the German Army. Originally slated for the SS because of his prominent Aryan features, Siegfried resisted and was punished for three weeks at a Hitler Youth concentration camp. His grandfather was gassed in a camp and his father died in 1952, leaving him the man of the family. Though the Mormon Church tactfully discouraged convert immigration to Utah, the Widmar family, what was left of it, headed for Zion in 1955.

Siegfried passed up an opportunity for a graphic design career in New York City and instead worked up to the position of art director at Salt Lake City's most prestigious advertising firm. While gaining stature in the city's German-Mormon society, he spent his spare time investigating "the mysteries," church doctrine not commonly discussed in Mormon meetings. His route of study finally brought him to his first contact with the Church of the Firstborn, a discussion with their heavyweights, Ervil LeBaron and Bill Tucker.

Tucker impressed him, but it was Ervil who really caught his attention. LeBaron laid out the doctrine and boasted of his hallmark mission to Mexico City in 1960. At the conclusion of the meeting, Siegfried decided that Ervil was brilliant. "He would get my certificate for genius without hesitation." Widmar's conversion was an invigorating boost to the Firstborn Church, which hailed his coming as partial fulfillment of father Dayer LeBaron's prophecy that persons from the four corners of the earth would beat a path to Colonia LeBaron. A young girl reported the day of Siegfried's arrival (July 20, 1963) in her journal, noting he was a "very rich German" who was "head of 5,000 Germans in the U.S."

An ardent admirer of Ervil's intelligence and Joel's calling, Siegfried was in a unique position to observe the interplay between the two. "They didn't have much to do with one another," he recalls. "Each did his own thing." To the church, they presented a rosy picture of their closeness, hugging each other, testifying of their mutual love and respect for one another. It was not a total sham, but those on the inside, like Siegfried, recalled the relationship as adequate but distant.

At first, Joel and Ervil must have seemed the perfect pair to begin a church. They were two opposite poles: each attracting the other because of their differing strengths and weaknesses.

According to the admiring Widmar: "Joel was the most generous character you can imagine. He could walk with anybody and feel at ease. We liked each other. We were friends. Ervil was the next classiest thing to Joel. Ervil had class. But most couldn't appreciate him. He was a man. With all the trimmings." Ervil's "manliness" also made it inevitable that the two brothers would separate.

Basically Ervil resented his position as the number-two man, and this resentment began controlling his actions more and more. Widmar had sensed something amiss the first time he met Ervil, even though LeBaron had converted him. "I did not take everything he said for granted. I felt he was dramatizing. I could read him that much at the start." As time passed, he put his finger on the problem: Ervil's ambition. "Ervil saw himself as the king and eventually he fell prey to his own ambition. No question." To enhance his power, Ervil would trick, flatter and cajole people to get them in the church and under his domination. "When I caught on to this, I realized that there was something basically wrong with the man, because I learned in Germany that the ends don't justify the means!"

The hardest wedge Ervil inserted between himself and Joel was the doctrine of Civil Law. Joel would preach that the law was an eventuality, preceded by a period of amnesty before it would be strictly enforced. But Ervil would insist on immediate implementation of the rules and their consequences. Ervil would attempt to influence Joel with such statements as, "If we just put the law of God into action, we'd scare the others into line." Joel, unruffled, would cryptically respond, "If any man wants to go faster than I'm willing to go, he'll find himself alone."

One man who observed firsthand the tug-of-war between the two was Harold Blackmore. He said that he "got the impression that Joel was quite happy to have Ervil create an image for the church if it would strengthen his cause in any way." Blackmore thought Joel's fatal mistake was never contending with Ervil openly when it was still early enough to change his course. "That was Joel's big problem. No matter how out of line things got, he would never come out and oppose anything, see?" So it was inevitable that "the only contention I ever detected between them—over who would be boss, who was supreme"— would come to a head.

Preliminary sparring had occurred over Ervil's marriage brokering, and a disagreement over use of church funds in the school and restaurant. But the first major head-to-head confrontation occurred in August 1967, with Joel the winner by a wide margin.

Expecting to isolate Joel entirely, Ervil taught that he was now the head of a "celestial administration," which meant he had control over the church. Joel got wind of it, he ordered Ervil to abandon "celestial administration." He told several inmates that the one thing he would never stand was for anyone, including Ervil, "to get between myself and the people." Ervil persisted, and the two brothers met privately for a showdown. Siegfried was the lone witness.

Ervil began by saying he'd received a revelation, which infuriated Joel, who was never very accepting of his brother's revelations. Ervil had seen a rock with inscriptions on each side in his vision, indicating that the time was ripe for a sharing of power. Joel said it would be a "two-headed monster" and held his ground. Exasperated by the surprising strength Joel was showing, Ervil finally said, "Don't you remember when we wrote *Priesthood Expounded* together, we understood it my way?" "Absolutely not!" Joel replied and walked out on him.

Joel called a gathering of eighteen "general authorities" of the Firstborn Church and kindly but definitively denounced Ervil's celestial administration, paring it down to nothing. "Ervil was insulted and cut to the core," recalls Widmar. "You have to understand that Ervil doesn't show any emotion. You've got to know him to understand what's going on . . . even at the worst. He probably has more self-control and discipline than any man I've ever met." As Joel continued his tirade, Ervil, still cool, finally stood up very quietly and said, "I don't have to take this any longer," and walked out. Joel had taken Ervil unawares, showing much more determination than Ervil had suspected was possible. The confrontation served notice to Ervil: taking over the church would not be easy, and it might be necessary to eliminate Joel before it was possible.

The community had sensed bad blood between the brothers, but were afraid to acknowledge it. In Ervil's home, his daughter knew violence was coming. "There was a lot of pressure. You should have seen it," says Alice. "My dad would get us so convinced that another person was evil that I would actually lie in my bed and think about how I was going to go out and kill this guy!" Jordan and Ervil stepped up the tempo of the Civil Law classes they were teaching. Bill Tucker was one of the first to see what was coming. He told his Sunday School class in Chihuahua City in 1966, "I can prove by the scriptures that Ervil is the man who will rise up to seek Joel's life."

Perhaps the biggest catalyst for violence between the two brothers was the settlement of a Baja California beach community about 180 miles south of San Diego, which the LeBarons called Los Molinos. Joel had been impelled by divine revelation to found the town as part of a controversial Brigham Young prophecy which stated that the Mormons, after they left Missouri, would travel to Utah and carve a horseshoe pattern through the southwestern states, and possibly Mexico, before returning to Missouri. Some of the Firstborn brethren had fought Joel on his new project, but he was adamant. He envisioned Los Molinos as an agricultural paradise where the poor could come and work the land, raising their station in life. He planned to apply for its acceptance as an *ejido*, a communal or collective farm allowed by Mexican land reform laws. The laws stipulated that native homesteaders who farmed pieces of land would own them.

Several dozen Mexican and American families settled in Los Molinos in 1964 at Joel's behest, constructing adobe huts on the flatland of scrub grass on which they raised wheat and tended goats. Ervil had no interest in Los Molinos for several years until one day he realized the potential of the town as a multimillion-dollar beach resort. Trusted by Joel to acquire property for the church, Ervil used Firstborn funds to buy up beachfront property which he placed in his own name and that of his daughter, Silvia Esther. Together, they owned 8,500 acres, including nine miles of beachfront property.

It wasn't hard to get nonchurch members excited about the development possibilities. About March 1970 he contacted a brother-in-law, who began lining up Arizona investors. When Joel got wind of it, he opposed Ervil's plans. Los Molinos was to be a haven for the poor, not a resort for the rich. Ervil persisted. He stood up in a Los Molinos church meeting and spoke on the subject. Ervil promised the members that "we would all be millionaires if we followed him into his big land projects," recalls one in attendance that day. "He kept saying we would all be wealthy and then said he was going to beg, borrow, steal or kill to get the ends he wanted."

Ervil's constant comrade, Dan Jordan, followed him to the pulpit, asking everyone to get behind their project. "We will become rulers of Baja California," he stated. "We will do in Mexico exactly what Hitler did—only for the good!"

Joel's vision eventually won out for the simple colony, still in existence today. But that realization came at great cost, for with the fallout over Los Molinos, it was obvious that the pace of confrontation was picking up rapidly.

That summer (1970) Ervil and Dan met with Joel and the rest of the church leaders at Colonia LeBaron. Joel warned the pair that they must stop trying to force members to attend their Civil Law classes by threatening excommunication if they stayed away. After a short speech on the necessity for "free agency," or freedom of choice among the members, Joel left.

Ervil stood pat and loudly proclaimed: "I know as sure as the Lord lives that my program is the only one that will put over the kingdom. And I also know that there are men in leading positions in this work who oppose me." He concluded, "And I tell you that blood will have to run to settle our differences." At first, the men present thought Ervil was referring to a recent altercation with the local Mexicans. About fifty armed men had come from Casas Grandes and torn down the fences around Floren LeBaron's *parcela*. Ervil advocated armed retaliation, but Joel vetoed it, declaring that he would abandon the entire colony before joining in a battle against the Mexicans. What Siegfried Widmar, who was present, thought was a statement that Ervil was going to fight the Mexicans anyway, suddenly took on more horrifying clarity when Dan Jordan said, "We're gonna take the dry wood in this church and break it into little pieces and burn it!"

Widmar hastened to Joel's home and related the events of the meeting, observing that Joel had an open rebellion on his hands. Joel asked Siegfried if there was any doctrine that stated members could be forced to attend the church and, when Widmar admitted there was none, he sat back and said, gurulike, "I'm watching things."

Two days later, Joel called for Siegfried, apparently troubled by a new report about Ervil, and asked Widmar his opinion of the situation. Siegfried confessed that he considered Ervil to be a Judas, and that violence could be expected. At the end of the session, Siegfried said, "Joel, let me just ask you one thing. You think you have this Ervil situation under control?"

"Let me answer you this way," Joel replied. "When I first went to Salt Lake in 1955, you know that I invited [brother Ross] Wesley to be part of this. It lasted about a week. I told him at the first meeting that if he ever tried to get between me and the people, it would be all off. . . ."

"That's good enough for me, Joel."

The October 1970 semiannual general conference was postponed until November because Joel and others were still picking pine nuts. In October, Ervil visited Siegfried in Los Angeles, where he was living at the time. He explained the changes in his doctrine and reiterated how his position as Patriarch entitled him to run the entire church. He told Siegfried that he was going to release Joel and others from their positions—at which point Widmar stopped him short:

"You know where I stand, man! Don't waste your time. But I'll make you an offer. I'll take you up to see Joel in the pine nuts and you can convert him. I'll take you in my air-conditioned car; I'll pay your expenses."

Ervil declined to confront Joel. Two days later, however, he returned and went through his same routine with Siegfried. Widmar then went alone to Needles, California, and related the latest details to Joel, urging him to give Ervil another chance. Siegfried hoped to save the inevitable split in the church that would have to come from Ervil's ouster, and he thought the prophet Joel might still bring Ervil around.

But Joel finally commented, "I have very little hope left for Ervil." Siegfried was surprised by Joel's uncharacteristic bluntness and his expression of futility.

Back in Colonia LeBaron, Joel had another pre-conference meeting with Widmar. Siegfried told him he'd learned Ervil had, in fact, "released" the First Presidency, or disfranchised the ruling triumvirate of the Firstborn Church. Joel was quiet for a moment. This had gone beyond sibling rivalry. He called a meeting of the brethren who had gathered for conference and told them he had released Ervil as Patriarch. Ervil had not yet arrived. The men were stunned. Joel then proposed a new First Presidency with Verlan as president and Patriarch; Siegfried and French missionary John Stephens would serve as counselors.

Argument broke out. "There were many men there that Ervil had brainwashed," Widmar recalled. "And they believed that we'd just conducted a hatchet job on Ervil, and that I was the hatchet man. And they told me so," despite Siegfried's protestations he had tried to act as peacemaker. He told those assembled that he was not a political opportunist and he would only serve in the First Presidency if it was the desire of the Lord, Joel and the brethren, in that order.

Joel called a recess. He cornered Siegfried and urged him "to bite my tongue a little longer." When the men returned, Joel said it was either the new First Presidency or none at all, at which point the Ervil loyalists gave in and reluctantly approved the new leadership trio.

When Ervil arrived for the conference, he was told to see Joel as soon as possible. He hurried to their mother's house and into the bedroom where Joel was sprawled out and relaxed on the bed suspecting nothing. Ervil was cheerful in his greetings.

Verlan, the only other man present, pulled a chair over by the bed and closed the door. Joel wasted no time in getting right to the point. He turned to Ervil and said, "Ervil, I've been told to release you from your office."

Ervil was stunned. "Naaaahh," he said, in disbelief.

"I'm serious," Joel said. "From this moment on, you no longer hold the patriarchal office."

As Ervil realized his brothers were in earnest, he threw both his hands over his face and wept like a child, as did Joel and Verlan.

Nothing was said as the three brothers cried silently for almost two full minutes. Then, all of a sudden, Ervil dried his tears and smiled. "Joel, it's such a relief to me. You don't know the burden I've been under." He asked Joel who would be his successor, and Joel nodded in Verlan's direction.

Ervil embraced Verlan, crying again, as they all did. Each knew the full import of this action and the lifetime separation it meant.

The trio headed for the church house where Joel made a simple announcement: "With regret, I must announce that Ervil has been released from his office because we are no longer in agreement." There was no other explanation. Ervil stood up and graciously accepted his ouster. Weeping some more, he expressed his love for his brothers and explained what a great burden had been removed from his shoulders. Now he would be free to pursue other interests. He shook hands with those assembled after the meeting, sometimes crying again. Those were possibly the last tears he shed. From that day forward, he began plotting, moving from light to dark like astronomy slides of the moon, skipping phases in between.

Ervil's removal from office (though not as a member of the church) produced the expected split in the Firstborn Church. Families like the Chynoweths, the Aurelio Rioses and the Benjamin Zarates dropped on Ervil's side of the fence. So did a Vietnam veteran, John Dylan, who had come to the Firstborn Church in 1963 from a Fundamentalist background. "The argument was over who would be head man, and Ervil *was* the church for me," Dylan explains. "Sure Ervil was working people, he really was. He was working me. People that needed to be fed a line, he was feeding a line. People that had to feel they were getting something, were getting something. There were deals for wives, women, money, land . . . a lot of people have told me I was a damn fool. Everyone else was dealing for something; I wasn't dealing for anything. I was just handing over my money."

One of the most astute Firstborn members, Conway LeBaron, also went with Ervil, taking with him some of the financial records of the church. A cousin of Ervil's, Conway had graduated from Utah State University in Logan with a major in applied statistics. A lifetime friend (and subject of the FBI-Kennedy investigation), Ralph Higbee, had converted him into the Firstborn Church in 1964. During the next four years, he became an experienced computer programmer in Salt Lake, rising quickly in company positions. Anxious to be closer to his church, he applied and received a transfer to the National Cash Register branch in Spring Valley, California, near San Diego.

Conway was impressed with Ervil who, in 1969, arranged for Conway to marry his niece, Esther's daughter, Pauline Spencer. "I received a dream and she [Pauline] also received a dream" that she should be Conway's second wife, he would recall.

When his branch president died of cancer, Conway "took it upon myself to get the branch going." He acted as ex-officio leader of the group, as well as bookkeeper and, in addition, handled tithing for the whole church—which brought him in direct conflict with Joel.

"As treasurer," Conway recalls, "Joel constantly was going against the procedures and draining the funds. . . . They laid down a policy and the next thing Joel was going contrary to this policy. Ervil asked me to freeze the funds, which I did. Joel then came for money and I told him to forget it. I then went over and talked with the presiding bishop [Alma] and Ervil was there. The bishop wanted to talk to me alone . . . I told him until this problem was solved, [the funds] would remain frozen. [Alma became] a raging maniac. At that point, I severed all relationships with the Church of the Firstborn because I could see they didn't have anything." Conway said Ervil was always more reasonable in his advice than Alma or Joel.

But Ossmen Jones, Ervil's boyhood friend and a Firstborn stalwart, got a different impression. Ossmen had quit the church when Ervil was released because he couldn't decide which side to choose. In April 1971, in San Diego, he chanced to ride along with Ervil and Jordan to Chihuahua. Along the way, Ossmen was surprised at the dark changes that had occurred in Ervil as he talked about Joel's doctrine, how opposed he was to it and if Joel didn't change his attitude he would soon be "erased from the map." The next morning, in a motel restaurant, the same topic dominated the breakfast conversation. Ervil was anxious to know where Ossmen stood.

"What would you do if we told you you had been the chosen one to kill Earl Jensen?"

"I don't know. Are you ready to kill him?" Ossmen played along to discover Ervil's intentions.

"I don't know for sure. We might even have to kill Joel. What about it?"

"When you get ready to kill him," Ossmen stalled, "let me know and I'll give you my answer then."

Ervil's lust for the leadership role Joel held coupled with his plans for becoming a millionaire. He was pushing his brother-in-law along on the Baja resort project, and the relative found Stan Spence, an experienced promotor who was particularly knowledgeable about Mexican resort properties. Spence got the project rolling, authoring a letter which enticed into the financial venture a lawyer who fronted for four wealthy Arizona doctors. He described the property that Ervil and daughter Silvia Esther, over whom Ervil had power of attorney, owned—about 180 miles south of San Diego, and totaling 8,500 acres of land fronting on the Pacific.

He explained that Ervil had acquired the property, parcel by parcel, over a three-year period "with the plan of developing a luxury resort area with an inland lagoon, marina, resort hotel, waterfront lots, commercial and industrial areas. . . . All of the beach frontage from the border to Ensenada is in a state of very active development at the present time and the cost of this property is astronomical. South of Ensenada the highway goes inland and does not approach the beach until in the vicinity of our property. From Ensenada to this property the land is almost entirely owned by the Mexican government and is under the *ejidal* program, whereby the land may not be sold, leased, subordinated or hypothecated in any manner."

It was precisely this *ejidal* program that Ervil felt stood in the way of his project. He knew he had acquired the property using church funds and perhaps feared he would lose a court battle if Joel pushed for an *ejido* covering Ervil's land as well. And Joel wouldn't budge at all on Ervil's one chance to really make a monetary killing. Ervil was shaken by Joel's adamant position, particularly angry he could not prove his economic prowess over somebody like Earl Jensen.

It was Jensen who obsessed him when he headed for Colonia LeBaron in May 1971 with Dan Jordan. Joel had asked him to come for a last chance at reconciliation, but Ervil was sure he was planning an excommunication trial. The duo stopped in Las Cruces, New Mexico, at the home of a friend, Chuck Henderson, on their way down. They spent the night and the next day talking to Henderson, but their primary message wasn't revealed until after dinner. Ervil explained they would soon face a fixed excommunication trial where Earl Jensen would be the star prosecution witness. LeBaron then added that Jensen had committed such open and rebellious deeds against Ervil that he deserved the death penalty. "He suggested that I follow a plan [they had formed] and go across the border with a passport—which is no problem to do—and do the deed," recalls Henderson. "[I was] not to show up or let anyone know I was there . . . come back out and [make sure] no one ever knew I was in Mexico."

Henderson remonstrated, but not forcefully. "Look, this isn't my job," he told Ervil. "I'm not interested. I don't care for Jensen, but I don't know anything about him deserving to die. You want him out of the way, you do it yourself.

"That's a pretty serious thing to contemplate," Henderson reiterated. "I'll tell you the only way I would ever consider such a thing and that would be if there was a legitimate [religious] priesthood trial, that there was definite, direct revelation that [Earl] had committed such crimes that the death penalty was just punishment. And then, if I was appointed by revelation—and it would have to be something where there was no doubt at all—to do it."

"Well, there is going to be a trial," Ervil said, "but I'm the one accused."

"*You* better look out then," Henderson observed, meaning it as a warning, rather than a threat, that the death penalty might be assigned to Ervil after such a trial. But LeBaron took offense and the pair left for Chihuahua through Texas.

*   *   *

If Tennessee Williams had wandered through the town of Colonia LeBaron, he would have found his Blanche DuBois. She might be more ample than his character, but nevertheless as removed, at times, from the facts of life as Blanche was. One could imagine Esther LeBaron Spencer sighing her lines: "I never was hard or self-sufficient enough. When people are soft—soft people have got to shimmer and flow— they've got to put on soft colors, the colors of butterfly wings, and put a paper lantern over the light." But Esther would add some new refinements, the paper lanterns over her own realities. "I'm a concert pianist," she'd say, when she was an above-average pianist who occasionally played for others. "Hollywood producers are after me," she'd say, when a man who was more promoter than producer would suggest she had talent. "Everybody I met when I was young fell in love with me," she'd say, full of Blanche's imaginary airs. When illusions replace reality, someone is avoiding the colder truth for a joy that can be found only in a creative netherworld.

For years, Esther was relatively peaceful. The two brothers she loved more than any other men in the world, Joel and Ervil, were progressing well in the church they started. Floyd Spencer was a good husband, and the couple had fourteen healthy children. But when Floyd died in a 1965 tractor accident she suffered a nervous breakdown—her first. By 1967, she had recovered somewhat. A second husband married her and left her later. She suffered another nervous breakdown. When she recovered, Esther focused her full devotion on her brothers, particularly Ervil. "I saw him every chance I got. People around here just worshiped the ground he walked on. . . . He was so tender, loving, kind and sweet, people just loved to have him come around." She was more loyal to Ervil than most of his own wives. She ascribed to him all virtues, such as the belief "he felt right at home with the most brilliant of men."

She continued to support Ervil after he broke with Joel, feeling he had taken the demotion with great humility. But the last paper lantern of illusion was to be torn from her on May 7, 1971, when Ervil and Dan met with her for four hours after arriving in town. The pair wanted her to buy up some land which she would hold in her own name for them, since she was moving to the United States anyway. And then came the shocker, as detailed later in her sworn testimony: "Morrel [Ervil] and Daniel . . . talked to me several hours trying to get me to go with them and be one with them in their Baja California business and land projects.

"Morrel said the reason he was getting boats to run a fishing business was so that the boats could be used to haul dead bodies out into the ocean, when they started to execute everyone who opposed his doctrine.

"He said they would also have some kind of a cement business going so they could make cement boxes to seal the bodies in because, he said, if you drop a dead body into the ocean as it is, the body oils will come up to the surface of the water and the body can be found. But he and

Daniel planned to put all the bodies into cement boxes and haul them far out into the ocean and drop them in. Then no one would ever know who did the killing or where the bodies went to.

"Morrell said he planned to execute lots of people—just everyone who opposed him in his thinking and did not uphold what he taught and did. While Morrel was telling me this, about [10 P.M.] Kim Jensen came down the street in his pickup. Seeing him, Morrel growled:

" 'The dirty son-of-a-bitch! The dirty traitor! He is one of the first to be up for execution!'

"When Kim came near us he stopped his car and shook hands with Morrel in a friendly manner. Morrel smiled sweetly at him, shook hands and said:

" 'How do you do, my friend?' and Kim drove on. Morrel then said, 'That's the way we do it! We first make real good friends with them, then quietly kill them and put them out of the way when they least expect it.'

"Then he explained to me how the corpses would be taken care of so that no evidence or traces of them would ever be found. At those words my blood ran cold, because I sensed that Morrel had the spirit of murder to some degree, and that he was taking some satisfaction and delight in the executions he had planned."

Ervil and Dan left Colonia LeBaron May 8 after talking with Esther the previous night and ignoring the Firstborn leadership entirely. Their departure for El Paso was a clear signal to Joel that there would be no reconciliation. But Joel convened the Sunday council meeting anyway. He began by expressing his sorrow that the two subjects of the meeting, Dan and Ervil, were not present. Siegfried was called on to diagram the basic priesthood platform of the Firstborn Church on a blackboard. Only John Stephens argued for Ervil's "celestial administration," but when Siegfried reasoned with him, Stephens abandoned his stand. Joel then stood and stated clearly the authority he held, against which Ervil had been contending.

Joel asked his First Presidency—Verlan, Stephens and Widmar—to stay behind for a separate meeting. Stephens caused a sensation at this private session when he revealed that while heading for Colonia LeBaron, Ervil and Dan Jordan had met with him in his El Paso home for six hours and told him that his two compatriots in the presidency, Verlan and Siegfried, had been sentenced to death "and the executioners had been appointed." Angered by the statement, Joel immediately ordered Jordan's removal from the Council of the Twelve. "What about Ervil?" Siegfried asked. Joel asked Verlan to reach Ervil with a last-chance offer. The meeting was adjourned.

Joel headed straight for his first wife's home where he put his head in his hands and wept the entire afternoon. "He told his wife things about their childhood, how Ervil always had to have his way no matter what and Joel had to take the brunt of things often—do things around the farm that Ervil didn't want to do," Esther related. "He was extremely sad that afternoon. Nothing could stop his crying. I feel sure that he knew this was the beginning of the end for him."

Ervil and Dan parted ways as they headed back to San Diego. LeBaron, accompanied by a daughter, stopped at Henderson's home again, very agitated. After dinner, he and Chuck began discussing Joel.

Ervil detailed his ambitions for the Baja land project and complained that Joel had hired a lawyer, made a down payment on Ervil's land and somehow "tied it up." "Joel was trying to protect his people that he had encouraged to move there and gone in and built homes, put a lot of their life into it," said Henderson. "Ervil somehow finagled or maneuvered or otherwise acquired legal papers on the land and Joel wasn't going to allow Ervil to run roughshod over him and his people." As Ervil ranted, his language became more coarse, a surprise to Henderson who had only known him to be a God-fearing man who never swore. Suddenly, LeBaron pounded on the table and stated, with a stern look in his eye, "I'm going to kill him if that Goddamned son of a bitch doesn't straighten up!"

On May 15, Ervil and Dan took the influential Firstborn Mexican leader, Fernando Castro, for a brief ride in the area of Los Molinos, and told him that Dan Jordan had been released as an Apostle at the Colonia LeBaron meeting and, for this reason alone, Joel and Verlan deserved to die. About the same time, Ervil took Castro to a promontory overlooking Los Molinos and, apparently unaware of the likeness the situation bore to the hilltop temptation of Christ by Satan, offered him all the land and riches beyond measure if Castro "would line up the Mexican members of the church behind [Ervil]."

The die was cast when Joel traveled to southern California and met with Ervil, explaining that from that point on, he was officially washing his hands of his younger brother. "I cannot carry any responsibility for any of your actions any further," he stated.

In mid-May, Ervil received a revelation which told him to start his own church. "I am sure it was an extraordinary manifestation," concedes Siegfried, who pieced the events together from the accounts of others. "He was imposed upon by a messenger from the other side and told to go ahead with the political Kingdom of God in its fullness, in its full power. In other words, under this revelation about Civil Law, Ervil now had divine power over life and death." Only a powerful supernatural occurrence, he feels, could have given Ervil the "rather cool, calculating disposition" he began to show in his actions.

"On May 20, 1971, in San Diego, Ervil severed himself from the Church of the Firstborn and at that time he started calling them to repentance," recalls his cousin, Conway. "We set up a new platform and a new stage for what [we] called 'The Church of the Lamb of God.' " Conway observed several years later that by leaving the First-born Church and going with Ervil, "I jumped from the frying pan into the fire."

Only one official action to confirm the split between Joel and Ervil was left—the excommunication of Dan and Ervil. It was a moot point by that time.

Verlan LeBaron and another Firstborn member were dispatched to Ervil's residence in San Ysidro, California, for the "express purpose and interest of summoning [Ervil and Dan] to a hearing before the local church authorities on charges of apostasy." The pair arrived at the home July 22.

Verlan recalls Dan and Ervil "made it very plain that they would not honor any summons to appear and answer charges that had been laid against them. They said they could care less about their church membership, that it was not worth a dime to them and other such statements."

Verlan told them he considered Dan and Ervil excommunicated from that moment and departed. The action was formally announced at the Firstborn conference August 8, and notices were sent the pair August 16 with a wishful last paragraph included: "We would like to express our hope that you will in the future reconsider your stand and have again the desire to join us for the furthering of God's Kingdom."

Watching her beloved Ervil darken, mother Maud could stand it no longer. Clearly siding with Joel, she tried to imagine what she could do to prevent further enmity from Ervil. She said she was forcefully prompted in the latter part of July to take some action when she had her first and only vision, a visit from her dead husband Dayer. Her course of action lay in a series of letters to Ervil, nephew Conway and grandson-in-law Dan Jordan. "It was her custom, whenever she wrote a letter, to come over to my house and let me read it," said Esther. "She'd ask, 'Is this fit to send? Is it worth anything? Or does it sound stupid? I had such a strong feeling to say this, I got up at daybreak and started writing.' " Esther coaxed her mother into allowing her to copy the remarkable and heart-rending letters before they were sent.

The first, dated August 3, was addressed to "My Precious Ervil [and] Conway:"

"It has been revealed to me plain as can be that you men have lifted your heels against the Lord's anointed and betrayed him [Joel]. . . . The last two Sundays we have prayed for unity and humility. . . . Your father came to my bedside last week and asked me to help remove the sorrowful condition.

"I think you have lost the gift of the Holy Ghost. What have you done? What are you doing? I realize that your life has been too hard. I never realized we had all imposed on you—you have been so grand and noble we thought you big enough to stand it all.

"I asked you if you were humble enough to endure it all and still make things go, and you said yes, so I trusted you.

"And now this.

"Right now is the time to be humble and start over. No one can keep you from being the first and best missionary in the world. The world needs a great leader like you. You can't build tearing Joel to pieces—this I am sure of.

"The man who takes the place of God can't be dictated to by some lesser officer. He is subject to God only. Dear son, don't break your own heart. You must be all I expect of you. I never realized how much I loved you—come. Lovingly, your mother."

In another letter to Conway, written August 22, she detailed the vision. "My husband, Dayer, came to me for the first time since his death twenty years ago, and made it known to me that Ervil's revelations are straight from hell, and he is going to have innocent blood on his hands if he doesn't right about face, and stop following the revelations of Satan like [older brother] Ben has for years. Please don't repeat this, but Ervil is apt to lose his mind if he hasn't partly already . . . when he was here last, we plainly saw that he had come under the same spirit Ben follows—his sentiments in piling honors upon himself, his vocabulary, his mannerisms, his tactics, and the things he threatened. . . ."

She concluded with an interesting note. "Since Ervil got into trouble, it seems like my love for him has doubled. I willed everything I have to Ervil and his family. I gave him my city lots, and I'm willing to do anything I can to help him. But it seems now that you are the only one who can help him."

Her next letter, which struck a harsh tone, was to Dan Jordan on August 25:

". . . first I want to tell you that you went clear over backwards in your planning deeds under the Civil Law of God, and you are in a great way responsible for Ervil's pitiful condition.

"You should be able to detect that everything that is going against Joel is from hell. I can feel the spirit of revenge in all you are doing—I hope you will do all the shooting. Ervil may not be as responsible as you are."

Ervil seemed far more interested in making money than making his mother proud of him.

In June, a trio of investors found by Ervil's brother-in-law flew in a private plane to Baja. "I saw some of the prettiest beachfront land in Mexico—a developer's dream," recalls one investor. Stan Spence, three investors and Ervil met in Phoenix on June 15 and discussed the development possibilities. A recent Mexican presidential decree allowed Americans, for the first time, to own land on the basis of thirty-year leases and those present were optimistic they could show profits within five years. The five signed a "letter of intent" June 17 which sealed them to building "a fully livable luxury resort community in the nature of a marina atmosphere." On July 27, they formed the Baja Yacht

Club, Inc., in Arizona, giving Ervil a 30 percent share because, though he provided no capital, he was bringing them land which only a native-born Mexican could obtain. Spence was named president of the club.

Spence wrote a detailed letter August 20 to an attorney who represented four wealthy doctors interested in resort investment. In it, he projected sales of individual lots for the first three months—twenty lots at $3000 each the first month; fifty lots at $3000 the second month; and 100 lots at $4000 the third month, for a total of 170 lots sold for $610,000. Spence listed other details and concluded: "I will project that within six months from commencing sales, we will be selling a minimum of 300 lots a month at approximately $6000 per lot, averaging a gross sales of approximately $1.6 million a month." The attorney and his investors bit—and hard.

The original incorporators flew to Mexicali to meet with Ervil and Dan Jordan, and to hire a lawyer. The pair acted strangely during a meal in a restaurant. "Ervil bragged how easily he could have someone eliminated in Mexico for just a few pesos," recalls one investor. "He even went into detail of how one day a man could cross him and the next day be found floating facedown in the ocean. He bragged about how easily he could pull strings with high political friends in Mexico City and walk out of any trouble or any jail, all through *mordida* [bribes] and political pressure. Needless to say, we were a little hesitant to puruse any business with him, but the prospects of development were too good to back down."

For the first time, Ervil was actually close to becoming a millionaire and making others rich, as he had long promised. There is considerable irony in the fact that once he was close to doing so, he simply got cold feet. Though Ervil owned the land, he complained to the investors that he must get Joel's approval. "All we needed was Ervil's signature and he'd have been a millionaire within a year," said his brother-in-law. "Because after that time another development, worth $150 million, was put in just south of there. Two appointments were made with the Mexicali lawyer, but Ervil balked at signing both times. Dan Jordan, always at his elbow, said the businessmen were "taking Ervil" and not giving him enough. Finally, Ervil signed papers disbanding the Baja Yacht Club in September 1971.

Though it was a choice piece of property, the investors were generally glad to be out of it. "It was sickening to walk away from it all," concluded Spence, "but I'm still living. I'll be honest. There have been very few times in my life when I was afraid, and this was one of them. Ervil was a religious nut, and I pegged Jordan as a pistolero."

At least $30,000 was lost by all the investors, but they took it philosophically. "[Reading about Ervil years later] I recalled our conversation in a small Mexican café in Mexicali and realized how sincere he was when he said, 'All who oppose me or stand in my way can easily be eliminated for a few pesos.' I can also vividly recall his companion with the unexpressive eyes whom I personally felt uneasy around," adds another investor. "I know now neither of them was joking—life really didn't mean much to either of them. So for that reason I took my loss and walked away from it. Money is not so important as to lay your life on the line. . . ."

Maud continued to refuse to give up on her son Ervil. On November 3, before a long silence, she wrote her most potent missive:

Dear Son Ervil,
The crimes, murder, you and Dan expect to commit are in the name of religion. When I was young I heard that more crimes had been committed in the name of religion than for any other reason. Is that still true?
. . . As things develop they get more terrific. All in the name of YOUR religion. Why can't you let me have peace? Why can't you bury your revenge, pride, ambition? Why can't you answer the prayers of the honest in heart?
You know it's a lie that Joel is a fallen prophet! How are you going to live down the worst lie that ever was told? . . . Am I about to have a Cain in my family? . . .

As the prophet Joel began nearing his appointed end, he did not publicly doubt his success as a minister. Speaking of the morality which would some day change the heart of a world, his words rang with conviction and affection. He was proud of his people, the ones who were with him still and, because of his abundant capacity for love, those who had left him. He advised all to earnestly pray with the Lord: "Thy kingdom come. Thy will be done."

In February 1972, in an expansive gesture, Joel assured a number of selected individuals that they had been so valiant in the cause of truth that they would have an assured place in the kingdom that was to come. If they had been rated on a religious report card, these would have been the A students whose average could never again drop. Those same students gathered around their teacher in private and urged him to name a successor, just in case . . . but he didn't.

Outsiders were not often kind to Joel. They chided him for the pitiful members he'd gathered around him after the seventeen years his church had been in existence. But he was unruffled. In response to one, who asked if he had been successful in his mission, he said: "Yes. I have been able to prepare a few men."

John Dylan was convinced Ervil was simply blowing off steam with his innumerable threats against the lives of others. "I spent one whole night talking to Ervil and he said he wanted to get rid of someone," Dylan remembers. " 'Oh, you and who else?' I said, making a joke of it, because he always talked like that. I thought it was a bunch of bull."

Ervil's mutterings finally moved from intention to action when his group forcefully took over a Church of the Firstborn meeting in Los Molinos. It was the Firstborn tradition on Sunday mornings to rest for about ten minutes between meetings. During a break, Dan Jordan walked up to the pulpit, slammed his Bible upon it and announced that the meeting would begin. Rena Chynoweth strode in and sat at the piano, beginning the opening song which her mother directed as chorister, "Do what is right, let the consequence follow . . ." Other Lambs of God arrived and sat in the congregation: the Rios boys, Gamaliel and Raúl; Andres Zarate; Ervil's second wife, Mary Lou. As the meeting proceeded, uninterested Firstborners began drifting out until Jordan ordered everyone out of the building. Outside, Dan pulled out his gun and began toying with it. "This is all Ervil's land," he claimed, and Charlotte LeBaron remonstrated. She was assured she could keep her own house, but the church and government school would have to fall to Ervil. "You could see his cockiness, his smartness. He just sat there grinning with those black twinkling eyes, little small eyes which he was always blinking. He was like a little child, absolutely delighted," an observer reports.

Even though some Firstborners urged Joel to take the land issue with Ervil to court, Joel told them it was of no consequence. "If Ervil wants to be a thief, I will not try to stop him by [legal or] violent measures," he said.

Around April, an interesting meeting took place in San Diego between Ervil and his brother Alma, who was probably more sympathetic intellectually to Ervil than Joel, but believed in the latter as a prophet. Both Ervil and Dan Jordan asked Alma where he stood, declaring Joel to be a false prophet. Alma refused to believe that. Ervil offered Alma a high position in the Church of the Lamb of God, but Alma declined it. As a last resort, Ervil threatened Alma. Not wanting to provoke outright hostility, Alma told Ervil that he might join him in four or five years if he could see, by that time, that Ervil was a prophet. Ervil was indignant. "I want you to know I'm not going to wait four or five years for you to make up your mind," he said ominously.

Even though Alma had withstood his smarter brother, he had "the strangest feeling" after Ervil left. "It didn't seem like I was the same," Alma recalls. "It seemed like a complete change had come over me mentally and physically. It took hours to get back to normal. . . . My mind couldn't think clearly. . . . It was like an hypnotic spell." Shaken by what appeared to him to be spontaneous possession, Alma told Joel that Ervil had gone off the deep end, was in the hands of the devil and would kill soon. "Just don't worry a thing about it," Joel reassured him. "I don't think Ervil and Dan would be that stupid."

Following a long line of sputtering pamphlets, Ervil launched a major opus, *Priesthood Revealed*, on June 6, 1972. Most of the eighty-two page legal-sized document, co-authored by Dan Jordan, propounded Ervil's position over Joel, hoping to win others to the Lamb of God

Church. He recounted the history of himself and his brother, as if they had been alternately placing their hands, one above the other, on a baseball bat to see who would end up on top.

LeBaron barely disguised his conceit by writing in the third person.

Full of the persecution complex, Ervil noted that he had "suffered the drastic consequences of revealing and establishing [civil] law under the adverse conditions that then existed. [I] was hated and rejected for so doing more than for any other thing." True enough, Joel began expounding the same law once the heat had died down, and had rewarded Ervil with the office of Patriarch on May 20, 1961. "Brother Ervil was eminently well qualified to occupy this position," he wrote of himself. "He, at that time, was probably the greatest student of the scriptures of the twentieth century; and he subsequently was to become the most knowledgeable man in Mormondom since the prophet Joseph Smith."

However, because of the rejection of Ervil as the one true leader of the church, the pamphlet continued, he cut himself off from that church—exactly ten years to the day he'd been dubbed Patriarch and started his own. In this pamphlet, LeBaron took a few shots at his chief enemies. Widmar was "a smooth, sophisticated habitual covenant breaker," who coached Joel into rejecting Ervil. Verlan, who'd replaced him in the patriarchal position, was nothing more than a hard-working incompetent.

Joel LeBaron was held totally culpable for the apostasy of the Firstborn Church in Ervil's eyes. It was he who was teaching worship of himself, unsupportable doctrine and was thus expounding "crime as religion . . . of a nature to lead directly to the shedding of blood."

The intensity of Ervil's threatening proclamations increased toward the end of July and into the fateful month of August 1972. His daughter Alice visited him in San Diego about that time, accompanied by her husband-to-be to seek her father's permission for marriage. And an extra honor was requested—would he perform the marriage himself? Ervil virtually ignored the petition and preached for two hours, citing bloody scriptures and talking about "riding through and swatting off heads with a sword," recalls Alice. "He was paranoid as hell and thought I was a spy." He told Alice she'd have to choose up sides soon because bloodshed was coming. They left unmarried and unblessed.

The subject of Ervil's most fervent threats, Joel was aware of the fate being prepared for him but he could not change his passive nature so late in the game, nor would he have, had the choice been given him. Siegfried offered to live with him and be his twenty-four-hour body-guard, but Joel refused the offer without a second thought. In a Juarez hotel in early August, the two discussed all the events that had occurred. "I've come to the point in my life where I judge no man," Joel told Siegfried. The Firstborn Church was "a church for martyrs," a fate it had been decreed in a previous existence, he added. As the conversation closed, not only did Joel show little animosity toward Ervil, but he offered praise. "Siegfried," Joel sighed, "I could never have done it without Ervil."

It was that very Christ-like attitude that unnerved Ervil and was the substance of a tirade in his second opus written with Dan Jordan, *Message to a Covenant People*, this one a 128-page document dated August 10. Ervil finally tipped his hand publicly as he explained that "God, in the fierceness of His anger, will cause His hand to be felt upon transgressors and rebels." For Joel "to disregard and walk over this [Ervil's patriarchal] authority is an act of treason against heaven that carries the penalty of death in this world." After pages about the destructions of the "last days," Ervil ended by saying that "the period of time, during which the holy people [Ervil's] would be trodden under foot by the . . . false patriarchal [Joel's] reign over them, is nearing its end."

The four key LeBaron brothers were in or around Los Molinos, Baja California, during the third week of August 1972. Joel and his aides, Verlan and Alma, were preparing to attend the semiannual Church of the Firstborn conference in Chihuahua. Ervil was also planning to attend—but as the lone LeBaron to take the pulpit there and undisputed titular head of the Firstborn Church.

During that week, Ervil held forth for a time at Thelma Chynoweth's home in Los Molinos. Verlan's wife, Irene, angry at his *Message to A Covenant People*, went over to talk with him. She felt the message was full of lies and, if Ervil's name were substituted for every reference to Joel, then it would be all true. As the two argued, Ervil sprung a new claim on her:

"I am the One Mighty and Strong, not Joel."

"*You* are? *You* are?" Irene was incredulous.

"Yes, I received the mantle from my father. And I have witnesses who were there."

Irene collected her thoughts. "Ervil, how could you have gotten it when you were, first, a witness that Ben had it, and, second, you came out and said Joel had it and now you come out and tell the world you have it. You're crazy!"

At that point, Thelma ordered Irene out of the house. She was not about to have anyone using "that kind of language" against her Ervil. Irene continued her conversation with Ervil in another home. There he became more particular about his plans.

"Verlan and Joel will be put to death," he said.

"Ervil, those are your brothers! How can you say such a thing?" demanded Irene.

"Huhh," Ervil returned. "God's no respecter of persons!"

Part of Ervil's reason for his temporary residence at Los Molinos was a last-ditch and nearly successful attempt to woo back one of his younger wives. Because she thought his intercession would help avert this, Irene ran to get Joel, who was in the community building a foundation at one of his homes.

He responded immediately and, according to one witness, was as forceful as anyone had ever seen him. "In fact, it was the strongest I ever heard him talk against Ervil," said the mother of the girl Joel was trying to "save" from Ervil. "He was the type of man who didn't talk that strong. I guess he could, if he had to. He just called Ervil a 'fork-tongued liar'—that was his strong talk—and a 'coward.' " Ervil had been drilling his recalcitrant wife on a number of doctrinal points, and Joel patiently discussed each one, convincing her to leave Ervil forever. It was Tuesday, August 15.

A day or two later, Irene visited Joel once again, and this time related Ervil's comments about killing Verlan and Joel himself. At this, Joel threw his hands up to his face and started crying. After a minute, he wiped his tears away. "They've got to be given the rope," he said. "If they want to hang themselves, let them go ahead. They have a right to see how far they'll go. If they go that far, we'll find out."

Irene was shocked and, after he cried a little longer, she asked, "Joel, do you think they'll go that far?"

Her surprise emanated from the deeply imbedded belief of all First-borners that Joel Franklin LeBaron was the man who would bring Christ into the world for the second time. He would usher in the millennium and set his hand upon the whole world. Testimonies had been continually given on the subject; the church was built upon it. So great was this belief that one member always felt safe when Joel was flying with him in one of his planes, because this was the prophet who would never die.

Joel paused after her question, and she asked again. "How far is it going to go?"

"Irene, I want to tell you something," he replied, looking her in the eye. "I *will* be killed."

A long moment passed. "But Joel, I thought you were going to live up until the time Christ would come."

"No, every testator that comes has to seal his testimony with his blood," he said, "and I will be killed." He began weeping quietly again, and Irene left, greatly dismayed.

Joel always enjoyed Sundays. It was the Lord's day, and many of the good things that happened to him in his life had happened on a Sunday. He expected the Sunday of August 20 to be no different, as he departed early in the morning with two wives and several children from Los Molinos. There had been some minor trouble two days before, but it was of little consequence. A sign of Joel's persistence in setting up an *ejido*, the government had placed a notice on a Los Molinos post that day. All parties with claims on the land of the projected *ejido* were notified to show title to their lands to local authorities. One of Ervil's followers had been seen tearing the notice off the post in anger, which seemed harmless enough.

Not long after Joel's departure, three of Ervil's closest followers—Daniel Jordan, Gamaliel and Raúl Rios—arrived in Los Molinos and began knocking on doors, asking where Joel, Verlan and Alma were. They explained they were hoping to arrange a doctrinal discussion. Alma was off attending to some personal business. Verlan, who had planned to drive with Joel, had found another ride and sent word to his wives in Los Molinos that he wouldn't be back until after conference. Both later recounted their absence as a miracle. Ervil's trio left shortly after finding out that Joel was headed for Ensenada, over an hour's drive to the north.

The last errand Joel planned to run in Ensenada involved a stop at the Espinosa and 2nd Street house of Benjamin Zarate. Though the Zarates, particularly son Andres, had joined Ervil, Joel was still friendly with the family. In fact, one of his wives had left Joel's purple 1966 Buick at their home earlier, and the Zarates promised to fix it. By the time Joel stopped by about 1:30 P.M. to pick up the car, the home seemed abandoned, except for Andres Zarate and Gamaliel Rios, who sauntered out to meet him. They explained the car hadn't been repaired and the keys had been left elsewhere, since father Zarate had moved from the small mint-green adobe house two days before.

Andres volunteered to drive Joel's two wives and some of the children in search of the keys, which he thought a younger brother, Cutberto Zarate, had somewhere.

Only Joel and his fourteen-year-old son, Ivan, remained behind. Ivan later recounted the events that followed in court testimony and interviews. He said it was a hot day, and they were both bored. Joel opened the hood of the broken-down car and began tinkering, thinking he might be able to fix it, while Ivan watched.

Gamaliel came out of the house and began arguing religion with Joel. "Why don't you come into the house and preach to me?" he invited.

"I don't have time," Joel replied, tapping on a screw.

"But I'd like to hear what you have to say," Gamaliel insisted.

"I'm sorry," Joel said. "I'm trying to get some work done. I've listened to you folks, and I'm really not interested." Gamaliel walked the few steps back into the house.

Joel determined the car couldn't be repaired on the spot, so he attached a tow-bar to it, planning to pull it to a service station with his other car, when his family returned. An urge to use the bathroom sent him inside the house. "I'll see you in a few minutes," he called to Ivan, knowing he'd have to stay and briefly chat with Gamaliel.

After several minutes passed, Ivan, too, had to go to the bathroom and walked into the house. He saw his father seated on a chair, astraddle, with the back in front of him, conversing with Gamaliel. The talk wasn't interesting, so Ivan went back to the car and partially lay down in the back seat. About twenty minutes after Andres had left with Joel's family to find the keys, Daniel Jordan strode up to the house and saw Joel through the open window. They each waved hello through the window, and Dan walked inside to join the discussion, according to Ivan. Ivan knew him from the days in northern Mexico mountains when Dan and his father had been so close.

Almost immediately after Jordan walked into the room, Ivan heard what he believed to be a fight going on inside. Later, a chair was found broken, Joel's nose was smashed and a nearby window shattered. Ivan, hearing glass break, popped up from the back seat of the car and saw, through the open window, three men fighting.

Despite his injuries, Joel must have continued struggling for a short while. One of the two assailants shouted, in a voice that could be heard in the street, "Kill him!", according to Ivan. A revolver was pushed up to Joel's throat and fired; as he slumped to the ground, a second shot tore through his brain. He was dead before he touched the floor.

Ivan was startled by the shots and began to get out of the car. He saw Gamaliel leap out a side window and run for Conway LeBaron's white station wagon parked nearby.

Dan came rushing out the front door, slowing down when he saw a crowd gathering. He coolly strode across the road toward the same station wagon, and the car quickly sped away from the scene.*

Ivan ran inside the house. His father was lying on the floor on his back with his arms up, and blood was running down the side of his face. "I ran down the road to find Mama and [the rest of the family]," he remembers. "I couldn't find them, so I came back to wait. In a few minutes the police came."

The boy was hysterical and crying when police arrived, which was quickly since they were only a few blocks away when the shots were heard. Meanwhile, Andres had taken Joel's wives on a wild-goose chase throughout the city for two hours. As they returned, Zarate dropped them off several blocks from the home, casually explaining he was planning to buy tacos because he was hungry. Joel's wife Jeannine was surprised at the crowd around the house, and, unaware of what had happened, walked inside to find her husband lying in a pool of blood, his papers and comb strewn on the floor. A broken piece of chair lay near his head. The prophet was dead.

---

*Jordan was eventually extradited to Mexico, but never stood trial for the crime. Conway could not be persuaded to travel to Ensenada to testify, fearing that the Mexican promise of immunity for his testimony would not hold once he crossed the border. Jordan was released, and has repeatedly, both in person and through his lawyer, refused to discuss the Joel LeBaron murder or his association with Ervil LeBaron those many years.

9

HOLY COMMANDOS

With Joel's death Ervil still felt himself in a position to totally take over the Firstborn Church. His man, Bud Chynoweth, was ready to lead the Los Molinos segment. To Colonia LeBaron, itself, Ervil had dispatched Mark Chynoweth and two new followers, Lloyd Sullivan and his son, Don. On August 19 in nearby Galeana, the trio told a friend they were going to take over Colonia LeBaron the next day. They moved down to the colony and stayed with an Ervil convert until Joel's death was reported late Sunday, when they were told to leave. A mob, led by Floren LeBaron, threatened their lives that night. The trio, realizing a takeover was not possible, fled back across the border to Babylon, which embraced them.

Colonia LeBaron had received the news of its prophet's death about 9 P.M. of the day it occurred. At first, Siegfried Widmar didn't believe it and phoned the Ensenada police, who confirmed the report. Verlan drove into Colonia LeBaron late that night and saw dozens of people grouped around Joel's house. He rolled down his window and stopped one of the members, "What's happened?" "Joel has been killed," he was told. "Joel, Jr.?" he asked. "No, Joel." "In a wreck?" "No, he's been shot."

Stunned, the grieving Verlan nevertheless took charge, ordering Joel's body returned to Chihuahua, his home.

The plane bearing Joel's coffin and several passengers took off at 6:30 P.M. and crossed the Gulf of California in the dark. At the Casas Grandes airfield, a throng had gathered, intent on accompanying the body of their prophet on his last drive to Colonia LeBaron. "Into the night they peered," Charlotte wrote at the time. "Each in his heart bore the burden of the fact that shortly would arrive the body of a beloved friend, brother, husband or father who had been murdered in cold blood. . . . Minutes passed that seemed an eternity. Suddenly to the south, someone saw a light moving. It came closer. Huge lights flooded the runway. Overhead the plane circled and then landed."

As the plane's door opened, Joel, Jr., stepped into the arms of his weeping mother. The crowd pressed in. Ossmen's pickup backed up to the plane, and Joel's bronze casket was gingerly lifted onto the truck bed. Verlan, Siegfried Widmar and Ossmen Jones drove the truck to the colony, at the head of a long funeral procession in the dark but starry night.

The viewing of Joel LeBaron occurred in his first wife's home, in the middle of an unfinished adobe addition. Church members and Mexicans from surrounding towns filed in to pay their respects. The black suit he wore in death was better than any he had worn in life. His clasped hands showed fingernails worn down from the fruit orchards planted, the fields tilled and the wells he had dug.

Joel's widows met around the casket at 1 P.M. Wednesday. Verlan opened the glass lid of the coffin, kissed his brother and held his hands for the last time. Each of the seven wives spoke words of endearment to their husband and offered a prayer. Upon finishing their private salutations, the women embraced, weeping upon each other's shoulders.

A second funeral service ensued in the little Colonia LeBaron church house, which was filled and overflowing. Siegfried Widmar offered a eulogy: "We loved him and we hope to stand by him and go with him. . . . He stands with Abraham, Isaac and Jacob. He stands with Abel, who was murdered by his brother Cain. He stands with John the Baptist and Jesus Christ, with Joseph and Hyrum [Smith, both brothers martyred]."

The coffin was solemnly conveyed to neighboring Galeana. Some of Joel's large family—seven widows, forty-four children—gathered around the newly dug grave, and pictures were taken. The youngest was a three-day old boy who would never see his father. Verlan blessed the grave and prayed for the fledgling church. Mother LeBaron staggered, and one of Joel's daughters fainted. Even Charlotte was at a loss for words—"the agony and grief of those present is impossible for me to describe."

That night, Verlan finally got to bed at 3 A.M. His wife didn't hear him undress, but she felt him get into bed. He buried his head in the pillow and sobbed like a child. She held him, running her fingers through his hair. "My brother is gone," he cried. "I have never in my life wanted to die but now I wish that I was in the grave with him."

The Church of the Firstborn needed a Brigham Young if it were to stay a viable religion, but such a man was not forthcoming. By general agreement, Verlan LeBaron was chosen to lead the church since his position had been church president when Joel was alive. But Verlan was more farmer than leader, more father (nine wives, more than fifty children) than church commander. He had many appealing attributes except one: assertiveness. He could never claim Joel's position, nor a single revelation. As one of his wives astutely observed, "He is a prince, not a prophet."

On August 24, Verlan met with Siegfried Widmar and others to plan a course of action. Because of Siegfried's media experience and the ease with which he moved in the Gentile world, Widmar was chosen to deal with the law enforcement agencies searching for Joel's murderers. The group had decided not to seek their own vengeance. Instead, they issued a seven-paragraph statement, "Proclamation Against the Assassins of Joel F. LeBaron," signed by Verlan, Alma, Siegfried and Ossmen Jones, which charged that Dan Jordan had killed Joel on Ervil's instructions because of "a doctrinal conflict which resulted in [Ervil's] excommunication." The "black deed" was an outrage to the memories of Benito Juarez, Mexico's George Washington, and other noble patriots who had fought for the kind of freedom Ervil had trampled upon. "For this reason," they wrote, "we consider these criminals and those who support them as accomplices to murder, traitors to the country, and urge all honorable men to assist in promptly bringing them to justice."

The previously planned Firstborn Conference went ahead as scheduled, August 25 and 26. The most notable incident at the conference, was the prominent testimony of a humbled Aurelio Rios, the septuagenarian father of Gamaliel and Raúl. He stood up and, in emotional Spanish, promised to drag his children from Ervil's clutches where they were hiding in Baja California. "I knew that he was a very poor man," Chuck Henderson recalls. "He was a hardworking man, very loyal to his ties of friendship. At the time I felt so sorry for him I gave him $50 to help finance his way to get his children out of Ervil's influence. The next thing I heard he had joined with Ervil." In fact, Aurelio Rios would continue to provide a hideout for LeBaron in the village of Atlixco, south of Mexico City.

Police investigation of Joel's murder was notably slow until an unidentified Texan friend of Joel's offered a $24,000 reward for information leading to the apprehension of seven men believed connected to the killing—Dan Jordan, Ervil LeBaron, Gamaliel Rios, Raúl Rios, Andres Zarate, Conway LeBaron and Mark Chynoweth. A wanted poster was widely circulated which included their names, pictures, description and a prominent notice of the reward. They were to be considered armed and dangerous. An immediate air and ground manhunt was ordered by Baja state police chief Salvador Hirales Barrera. He told a San Diego newspaper, "We are combing the entire peninsula of Baja California, mile by mile. If they are still in Baja, we will find them." But he was too late. Gamaliel Rios had been discovered behind a truck near a Firstborner's Los Molinos house, but had escaped. The rest of the group had fled across the border. The FBI was alerted, but they were frankly bewildered by the confusing religious aspects of the murder. One of the agents immersed in the case almost from the beginning summed it up: "The minute you step into this, you're in another world. [The] whole case is a mess. M-E-S-S. That's the word for it. The followers change their names and refuse to talk. Everywhere you push, there's jelly."

The first break came when a onetime Firstborn associate accidentally ran into Dan Jordan and Conway LeBaron at a post office in Salt Lake City on August 23, three days after the murder. "I was walking out of the post office and scared them half to death," he recalls. He told them he'd heard Joel had been killed and that they were involved. They denied it, but then detailed how they heard it occurred. "They said that when Joel was in the house, [the killers] got hasty, threw him to the ground, fought him and, while one held his head, the other shoved the gun in his mouth and blew his brains out," he says.

As the three stood on the post office steps, the ex-Firstborner also learned from them that Mormon Church president Harold B. Lee was in danger, which removed the case from an inner-cult squabble to a spare-no-expense police hunt. Unaccountably, the associate didn't attempt to detain the pair, though he did inform the FBI of the meeting, and of the Lee warning. A Salt Lake City police intelligence officer said they already "had indication [from other] intelligence sources at that time that the LDS leadership and others had been targeted, so we kept watch."

One intelligence source was Rulon Allred. Allred had called a friend in the Firstborn Church two weeks before Joel was killed and related to him an amazing story. He said Ervil LeBaron had contacted him by phone and told Allred that Joel would be killed soon, as well as Lee. Putting the pieces together, Widmar, even though he was a leader in an "apostate" LDS group, personally called Lee August 30 and in a half-hour phone call, provided background on the Firstborn strife and its implications to the Mormon Church. The next week, Widmar drove to Salt Lake and met with police to give them the same information. The Salt Lake newspapers picked up a hint of the threats and ran stories about a new, three-man guard assigned to protect Lee.

The danger was real and it was close. A Salt Lake County Sheriff's intelligence report said LeBaron had met with several Fundamentalists in the county in late August. "He offered them high [religious] offices," the report read. "He also wanted money. He also left a few books with various people that pertained to the new doctrine he was preaching. In the books were veiled threats toward anyone who opposed him. It was reported that in his conversations he had been quoted as saying that if he could get rid of Joel and his following, then the . . . Fundamentalist groups, he could then take over the LDS Church, and then the world. . . ."

* * *

When Lloyd Sullivan joined Ervil's retinue in July 1972, one month before Joel's murder, LeBaron's effectiveness for carrying out his plans increased a hundred fold. Sullivan was "river people" stock, born in Vincennes, Indiana, and orphaned as a child. By his first wife, Lloyd had sired two girls and five boys, one of whom, Don, became his shadow. Stripped of any personal ambition, Lloyd became an idealist of the most dangerous kind, ripe for any cause. He first joined the John Birch Society, his son Don following, but they both found its doctrines too lukewarm for them and departed by 1970. At the end of the year, he married for a second time, to a divorcee. Lloyd became obsessed in early 1971 with "finding the truth." He discounted the possibility that the Mormon Church might have it, and began to actively investigate various Fundamentalist groups.

One of his favorite pastimes was tuning into a notorious Salt Lake City radio show—Bob Salter on KSXX. The talk show host was an ultraconservative whose views no doubt ran parallel to Lloyd's. (One day while calling into the show, Lloyd made the mistake of saying Richard Nixon should be "slit from ear to ear," a comment which began a Secret Service investigation of him. In their report, they noted he had been a frogman and demolitions expert in World War II, which caused some concern but they finally dismissed his remark as not serious.) One of the frequent callers to the Salter show was Ross Wesley LeBaron who, for years, had been proclaiming himself as the world's greatest prophet. Lloyd became impressed with Ross's scriptural knowledge and, with Don, joined him briefly.

They were not long in his camp before they journeyed to Colonia LeBaron in 1972, and resided at Galeana for three months. Lloyd was impressed enough with Joel to be baptized into the Firstborn Church, again with Don. A meeting with Ervil finally occurred in Ensenada. Don remembers they were immediately impressed by Ervil's scriptural knowledge, arguments and charismatic personality. Intensive religious discussion between the two continued for four straight days at the home of one of Ervil's younger wives, at the end of which time Lloyd and Don were baptized.

Lloyd saw little of Ervil after his baptism; LeBaron was on the run with Dan Jordan and cousin Conway, traveling "about 10,000 miles to keep one step ahead of them," Conway recalls.

Ervil used Conway's credit cards for the motel bills as "we covered the Southern states, down through Texas and over to Tennessee and then north." During this time, Ervil never wanted to stay in one place longer than three nights. "He'd go to a place until he got a feeling we should move. We'd be driving along and he'd say, 'Hey, stop, I've had a vision saying not to go in this direction.' I [also] received several directions myself warning me of the dangers."

The trio busied themselves writing new pamphlets, the first published September 21, 1972: *An Open Letter to the Faithful Remnants of*

Modern Israel, subtitled *An Appeal for Justice*. The document was interesting in that Ervil claimed Verlan and the Firstborn Church "have recently accused us falsely in the public press of a number of very serious crimes." He never denied involvement in Joel's murder, nor the involvement of five others who signed the ten-page statement—Gamaliel and Raúl Rios, Dan Jordan, Conway LeBaron and Andres Zarate. He did stoutly defend the seventh person on the wanted poster—Mark Chynoweth—against whom there was little evidence anyway.

Ervil claimed that the public had it all wrong—it was Joel who had been threatening him, and whose "incredible control over the minds of his followers" had caused them to form an underground military organization whose mission was to exterminate the Lambs of God. This story became a stock one for Ervil, even among his own followers. By totally reversing the truth, he threw some people off. He would take some small item—for instance, Joel's Council of Fifty, or "Sons," who were, in fact, charged to support and protect their prophet. Then he would blow it all out of proportion, charging persecution and convincing his fellow Lambs that they were in danger and only Ervil could save them. And, sometimes, Ervil would mislead the Mexican police, who would rather that the American polygamists find another country in which to live, anyway.

Ironically, the day after the open letter was issued, September 22, Mark Chynoweth and Donald Sullivan were arrested by Ensenada police for Joel's murder. They had been visiting Mark's father, Bud, in Los Molinos, to obtain clothing and money. Mark said he had asked Don, who was caught with a Titan Tiger F-38 gun, to act as his bodyguard since he claimed to have been threatened, and feared being in Los Molinos unarmed. Having little evidence against the pair, Mexican police shortly released them.

When Ervil learned of the incident, it must have dawned on him that the only real dangers he had to fear were followers in a position to condemn him if they talked. That was probably the root cause behind the issuance of one of his most inflammatory writings on October 26, *The Law of Liberty*. It was written in Elko, Nevada. His words were circuitous: "Every deliberate miscarriage of justice by the judicial powers and every deliberate failure of the people to apply the law is regarded as an act of treason and is punish[able] by death." Since Ervil's people were the "judicial powers" who felt empowered to carry out self-styled sentences—including executions—under the Civil Law of God, such a statement meant anyone who failed an Ervil-ordered mission or turned traitor would be killed by fellow Lambs of God.

The consensus of the Firstborn Church council that convened after Joel's murder was that Verlan LeBaron was the next person Ervil would try to kill. They urged him to lay low, good advice since, according to Lambs of God, Verlan was the number-one target then and now.

Siegfried Widmar left with Verlan for an extended missionary tour shortly after the conference, exchanging cars so Ervil wouldn't recognize their vehicle, and resolving to stretch the $40 they had between them as far as possible. They drove to Denver where they stayed with a friend for several months and obtained two guns, which they discarded after a while. Neither felt comfortable with a weapon. They were gone a total of four months before returning to Colonia LeBaron.

In December, Ervil pulled an amazing rabbit out of the hat—himself.

He walked into the Ensenada police station on the 13th, accompanied by two lawyers, and asked that the charges against him be dropped. The dumbfounded police, chagrined they couldn't collect the sizable reward, nevertheless jailed Ervil immediately. From there, the ball was in the Firstborner's court.

If the relatives of a murdered person in Mexico want justice, they must often push for it—and pay for it. The Firstborn Church hired a lawyer who, in effect, acted as prosecuting attorney. Spearheaded by Widmar, the Firstborners amassed enough evidence within the required seventy-two-hour period for the judge to bind Ervil over for trial December 16.

Under Mexican law, officials may hold a prisoner up to a year on a charge. During that time, they obtain depositions from witnesses for both sides. The defendant is not always present during these proceedings. Sometime during this period, the judge decides the guilt or innocence of the accused. Such trials are wide open to bribery, particularly on the city and state levels.

Thus it was that several prosecution witnesses arrived in town July 2, 1973, to give their testimony, but could not find their lawyer, who was out celebrating his previous night's election victory as the new president of the Ensenada Bar Association. As a result, they were late for their court appearance, and officials therefore refused to take their testimonies at all. Their statements were only duly recorded when they agreed to pay $50 in fines. "In Mexico," recalls one of the witnesses, "the officer you're dealing with *is* the law." Eventually, a few dozen witnesses from the Firstborn Church were presented by the prosecuting attorney. Esther Spencer, John Dylan, Floren LeBaron, Fernando Castro, Alma LeBaron, and Ossmen Jones repeated the gist of their conversations with Ervil in which he had threatened to kill Joel.

Though the trial seemed to be going well for the prosecution, there were some disturbing signs. Reports had reached Firstborners in early August that part of an $80,000 bribe had been raised by the sale of Utah land owned by one of Ervil's followers and was being offered to ensure an acquittal. Widmar, Alma LeBaron and two other Firstborners met with the president of the Tribunal of Justice, the State Appeals Court of Baja California, and relayed the information. He promised to look into the allegation, but never reported back.

It was also apparent to the Firstborners that their case would be strengthened immensely by the appearance of either or both of the men charged with the actual murder—Dan Jordan or Gamaliel Rios. They were seeking the conviction of Ervil as the "intellectual author" of the crime when they had to first prove who actually committed the murder, and the murderers' link to Ervil.

The Mexican police completed their official investigation into Joel LeBaron's murder on August 7, after which defense witnesses were presented. Without exception, those paraded before the judge said they had only learned about the murder through the newspapers, and had not heard Ervil make any violent threats toward Joel, or even have differences with him. Duane Chynoweth, who testified August 14, went a step further, saying he had heard Ervil preach "more than a hundred times" over a five-year period and "in none of those instances [had he] heard Ervil say anything about murdering his brother." Only Bud Chynoweth was out of sync with the others. On August 14, he said he knew of disagreements between the two brothers but they were "always settled as brothers." He'd also heard them argue religious doctrine, but not violently. The same day, one of Ervil's wives attempted to establish an alibi for Dan and Ervil. She said the two of them, along with Conway LeBaron, had arrived at her Ensenada home about five days before the murder to work on the translation and publication of some pamphlets. Dan had become ill, and would eat nothing. About noon, August 20, an hour before the murder, she said he left for San Diego, still under the weather.

Finally, Ervil testified in his own behalf. He began by stating he had never had any personal disagreements with Joel or the Firstborners, but this defense slipped away. According to court records, he finally admitted to the judge that he and Joel "didn't agree in their religious beliefs. Ervil went his own way. Ervil then thought his brother Joel had too many fanatics among their family and friends, and decided to end such fanaticism by distributing pamphlets to show the difference in the doctrine and convince people his (Ervil's) was the right one. Joel didn't like that at all, and following the incident, Ervil felt somebody wanted to kill him—one way or another. Ervil knew there was another reason why they would try to get rid of him—an apparently worthless piece of land in San Quintin (close to Los Molinos) had caused several fights . . ." The case was closed on September 11.

It took Judge Antonio Salas Carrillo two months to deliver the verdict and sentence. He did not take any of Ervil's writings, some of which had been introduced as evidence establishing motive, into consideration. "His writings were very extensive and very confusing," says Carrillo. "I looked at them but decided that they should not have been taken into evidence." His legal secretary during the trial, Gustavo Reynoso Moreno, who would later take the bench to judge Ervil in another trial, says LeBaron was an astute courtroom performer, perpetually "serene." Moreno said "Ervil knew the law. He never attacked.

He let every accusation pass, obliging his enemies to prove the relation between him and the murder."

In handing down his guilty verdict November 8, Carrillo said the defense witnesses' testimony was not "enough proof to save Ervil from responsibility in this case." He ruled that the homicide charge against Ervil LeBaron had been legally proven, adding that he "found that Ervil Morrel LeBaron induced his followers, among them, Daniel Jordan, Gamaliel Rios, Raúl Rios, Andres Zarate and Conway LeBaron to kill Joel," in effect, condemning the co-defendants even though they hadn't been present for the trial. He said they were still all "considered material authors of the crime." A deciding factor in his verdict, the judge noted for the record, was Ervil's own "confession in admitting to have had strong disagreements with his brother Joel, not only concerning religion but also in material matters."

The district attorney urged leniency in the sentence. Carrillo said he had to take into consideration that Ervil was a religious minister, a farmer, a married man and a father, a nondrinker and non-drug user, as well as the fact he had no previous record, had confessed to a motive "and several incidents which demonstrate the defendant's fear of inferiority." He sentenced Ervil to a twelve-year prison term beginning December 13.

LeBaron served only one day, officially, of that sentence.

A Mexican supreme court in Mexicali overturned the lower court verdict December 14, without hearing from the prosecutor. The two justices who signed the decision said the verdict could have been overruled on a number of technicalities. For instance, there was the problem of determining if LeBaron could induce others to be criminals when the latter were not available for examination. They quoted a jurist who said "an exhaustive set of psychological and behavioral tests should be done on the individual or individuals thought to be the criminals, to establish a weakness in character, which would allow another person to influence the individual's mind so much as to induce him to commit a serious crime." Another jurist outlined the difficulty in establishing "when a person has successfully taken over the willpower of another person, and blame the first for a crime committed by the second."

They ruled the charges against LeBaron were invalid because the alleged murderers, Rios and Jordan, were not present. Without their testimony, Carrillo "had to base his resolution on mere suppositions," the justices wrote.

Responding to the higher court decision, Carrillo later noted "it was a very particular case. There were dozens of witnesses but no one said he saw Ervil order Joel to be killed. No one said he saw Ervil give anyone a pistol. A very difficult case."

The Firstborn Church, having celebrated their victory, were stunned by this reversal, and the release of a dangerous man. They presumed a bribe had been finally accepted, given the speed of the court's decision.

Those familiar with the Mexicali court say many of the cases are bribed out.

Whatever the true reason, Ervil LeBaron was free.

And though a court had ruled he had not been found guilty, his mother had made her own decision. Her final letter to Ervil, dated January 1, 1973:

> Dear Ervil, Son,
> You have paid no attention to my letters as far as I can tell—you never answered them.
> Somewhere along the line you turned yourself over to the buffetings of Satan and caught the disease Ben had. Only Ben never had the evil spirit of murder.
> Don't you know it was crazy to kill Joel? . . .
> Don't you know it was crazy to write articles and tell Floren and Verlan that if they didn't accept your baptism they would be killed? . . .
> There are many people who have told that you have tried to hire them to kill Earl Jensen.
> Why can't you see this is all crazy? You should not be in jail, but in a mental hospital.
> Now, Darling Son, today I have been told that you are a Judas, a son of perdition.
> I shall never stop praying until you repent and stop lifting up your heel against the Lord's anointed. Repentance is a gift of God. Pray for it.
> Surely now you can come to, and help poor Dan understand you were a misled leader.
> I love you truly,
> Mother

Ervil LeBaron was in no loving mood when he was finally released on Valentine's Day 1974. He had languished in jail for fourteen months, enough ignominy for any prophet. However, it had given him time to form plans in his new position as leader of a God-ordained death squad.

The first thing he did was travel to Yuma, Arizona, where he met with the most loyal of his followers—Dan Jordan; Anna Mae Marston; Ervil's son Arturo [sometimes called Morrelito—"Little Morrel"]; and Lloyd Sullivan. When the judgments of God were carried out in the future, he pointed out, the Lambs of God must pay meticulous attention to avoid leaving any telltale clues.

"He told me and the others present to make sure there [were] no fingerprints on any of the bullets, on any of the guns or any of the weapons for anything else that had ever been used," Sullivan later testified. LeBaron advocated use of surgical rubber gloves in future murders because, according to Sullivan, "you could have more feeling in your fingers, you could do things much better [than] you could with [the regular] cumbersome gloves." Ervil himself began carrying his favorite weapon—a .38 caliber revolver—which he left behind only when he went on some harmless errand; the bulge was noticeable in his clothing.

His followers began calling Ervil by a number of saintly names. He was the One Mighty and Strong, the presiding Patriarch and the Prophet of God. His wives sometimes called him the Lord Anointed. His followers, trying to win converts or speaking in awe among themselves, referred to him as Tío (Spanish for uncle), King David, Israel, the Modern Moses or the Deliverer of Israel.

LeBaron cautioned his followers to be constantly on watch for the members of the Church of the Firstborn. "What I understood was that [we were] hiding from Verlan's group, the CFB, and you had to lay low," recalls one follower. "You never knew when somebody was going to shoot you." The Lambs of God were now on the alert. All church records, even marriages and births, were to be kept in their heads, and never written down. All members were to operate only on a need-to-know basis—one Lamb of God should not know about the mission carried out by another. Each was asked to pick a suitable alias and obtain driver's licenses and other records under the new name. And all long distance calls were to be made only from neighbors' phones or pay phones so that no one could monitor or trace the conversation. The Lambs of God had begun to resemble the Mafia more than a religious sect.

Ervil attempted to formulate a doctrinal basis for all these actions. The kingdom he commanded, according to earlier scriptural interpretation, had been divided into three branches, religious, economic and civil (government). New light Ervil received indicated that another division was required, a military branch. Lloyd Sullivan, who had served as LeBaron's lieutenant on matters of doctrine, was asked to assume the temporary role of military expert. His purview was now the Bible—and bullets. Lloyd took to the job. "I used to be a connoisseur, you might say, of weapons. I love them. I love guns. I love to shoot targets and different things. I've been in demolition; I've handled weapons quite a bit in the Navy. They've always fascinated me. So I know just about every gun that was ever made."

Now, whenever he came across a fine gun, and purchased it, he tithed it over to Ervil, and sometimes never saw it again. But he never complained. LeBaron was commander-in-chief; Lloyd was only a general. Ervil commanded him to teach wives and children how to shoot, but the women were not interested in learning and only acquired the rudiments. The three who became the most proficient under Sullivan's tutelage were Don, Eddie Marston and Ervil's son Arturo. The trio surpassed their master, and were soon able to alter their weapons, for instance, converting an M-1 carbine into a machine gun of sorts. The group was taking on new dimensions entirely.

Imprisonment had changed Ervil in subtle ways, and, after several weeks of freedom, his devotees began detecting a hurried earnestness that he had lacked before. For example, he had become virtually humorless. "We might tell him the funniest joke—a real howl—and get absolutely no response out of him," Don says. Eddie Marston, rarely one to complain, recalls that Ervil had also acquired an irritating habit of repeating things a hundred different ways.

But the group readily forgave the new Ervil any character defects, chalking it up to enigma rather than an indication that something more was amiss. "In a lot of ways he is not a logical man," concludes Don. "But he is a super genius in most ways." So while LeBaron was not considered perfect, he was still looked upon as the authority on everything.

The group came to understand that any failures in their religious and military missions would occur because of the members' failures, not Ervil's. LeBaron apologist Anna Mae noted that it was not even necessary for Ervil to be charitable toward his people. The fact that he was willing to give his life for God's truth was more important than all the luxuries he enjoyed while the group starved. "That is the greatest love that a man can show [sacrifice his life]. It's not me taking my shirt off my back and giving it to somebody," she says.

The assassination of Joel had effectively weeded out those adherents who were not totally dedicated to Ervil's work. Eddie Marston was an unveering disciple, particularly because of the iron hand his mother held over him. No independent thinker, Eddie was molded by Anna Mae and Ervil. "Eddie would treat you like a brother unless you did something wrong [or against Ervil]," says an associate.

Mark Chynoweth was a close runner-up to Eddie in loyalty, but for different reasons. Certainly his mother's heavy influence counted for a lot, but Ervil fed Mark's own fires of self-importance. When he was fifteen, Ervil took him along on a mission to Mexico City. "Ervil bragged him up and it just kind of went to his head," recalls one associate. "He came back like he was the biggest priest next to Ervil." Mark was attracted to Ervil's power as a way of increasing his own.

LeBaron held his men in thrall for a number of reasons, including doctrinal justifications. Lloyd Sullivan had come with a burning desire to know that Ervil was the One. He was convinced of Ervil's divine mission, which made him a natural candidate for leadership in the Lambs of God. Raúl Rios was a total believer in Ervil's godly origins, having once gone on a forty-day fast to understand religious points which would prove Ervil was right. Raúl's joining had influenced his younger brothers, Gamaliel, Guillermo and Carlos, as well as his father, Aurelio, to join Ervil's church. Raúl had enough zeal for all of them.

But controlling Dan Jordan was to be a more complicated matter for Ervil. Dan had been present at the inception of the Divine LeBaron, and he knew Ervil's secrets. He was perhaps the only group member to whom Ervil was so transparent. Being Ervil's intellectual equal, Dan was a potential rival in religious affairs. But while Ervil couldn't dominate him mentally, there were other areas where Dan was more vulnerable. Ervil graciously provided Dan with his first two wives. As long as he could keep Jordan—and the other men in the group—supplied with wives, they would stay loyal to him, particularly if the marriages were between his offspring or relatives. This familial tie could prove stronger than any claim by Dan to religious office.

So, on returning from jail, Ervil made it quite clear no marriages in the group would be permitted unless he authorized them. Jordan asked for, and received, one of Ervil's stepdaughters. Only temporarily satiated, Dan soon had his eye on two of her sisters, but Ervil held them out like a carrot. He instructed Sullivan that Jordan was in a state of apostasy at one point and was a man most miserable and was not worthy of more wives. "You don't see me giving him more wives, do you?" However, when Dan's obedience was vital, Ervil turned over both teenage stepdaughters on the same day. "I don't have any word [from God] on it," LeBaron said, "but if you think it's right, go ahead." As usual, Ervil left himself an out; should anyone be dissatisfied later about the double marriage, he could explain it had not been a revelation, just a favor. And he could call for an instant divorce or rearrangement of marriage relationships.

The women were easiest for Ervil to control, according to his shadow, Eddie Marston. "Women don't give him a lot of static, but men do," Eddie would conclude later. Don Sullivan says Ervil's female followers were fanatical because their hearts ruled over their heads: "They were deeply *emotionally* involved and they believed in what they were doing."

Among his wives, LeBaron used his own form of domination, meting out punishment, or apathy. "If they didn't do what he said for them to do, why he wouldn't go to bed with them for a year, maybe two years." recalled Don. "He'd treat them just like a man. I've seen this happen, like they were a man, not even show them any affection. Not even say, 'Hi, honey,' or kiss them on the cheek or anything, just absolutely alienate himself from them. He's a hardened man, I'll tell you, very, very, hard. He tried to get me to be the same way."

Ervil's two Mexican wives had always been troublesome to him. During the 1973–1974 period, Mary Lou, who often complained about their marriage, was assigned to live in Los Molinos. When Ervil came to town, he stayed with the Chynoweths, and didn't even visit her. She was forced to beg food and clothing from Firstborn neighbors. His first wife, Delfina, left him a number of times. But her continued involvement with Ervil, according to daughter Alice Rose, was "not all my dad's fault. It has to be her fault too, because if she'd have been stubborn and said, 'Hey, I'm gonna leave you,' he would have thought twice [before mistreating her]. She let him take advantage of her. And if people take advantage of you, it's your own fault." Two other wives, Linda Johnson and Rosemary Barlow, who had both begged to marry him, remained devoted to Ervil but showed signs they might defect if he continued to ignore them.

Vonda White was one of his most unflinching followers. As for Anna Mae, she had earned a category of her own. She lapped up the new Ervil and his teachings with relish. A true fanatic, she pronounced years later in an interview: "There is no gray. There is no gray. It's black or it's white. You either worship God or you don't." Worshiping God, according to her, had nothing to do with love or kindness, but everything with following every Old Testament law. "That's what [God's] interested in—He doesn't want you to love Him; He wants you to love His law. He wants you to put the law He taught—[take] Christmas, Christ's birthday, celebrate Christ's birthday and we'll have peace on earth. It's a bunch of MALARKY!! What Christ is interested in is that you live the law that His father gave, and not celebrate-His-birthday-and-Happy-Birthday-Jesus!"

The fact that Ervil alone had been teaching the truth, made him the world's unchallenged ruler. "He is personally responsible for educating people [to the law]," Anna Mae continued. "And he takes it seriously. . . . I know he has the authority for the simple reason he is the only one that is teaching the true principles that are going to do any good to anybody. 'By their fruits ye shall know them.' He's the only one. . . ."

Such things were clearly stated and believed by Lambs of God as they prepared, after Ervil's release, for their next mission. And no one flinched when Ervil claimed the Biblical angels who would "reap the earth" and destroy it, were supposed to be mortal men—men now living who were charged with the destruction and killing of God's enemies.

It also came as no surprise when Ervil revealed that these very "angels" were they themselves, the Lambs of God. Once over that hurdle, LeBaron regularly discussed the missions these angels would have to perform, for which he used a variety of terms. Sometimes he was Biblical—so and so deserved Old Testament "justice."

In an obvious reference to his particular weapon fetish, Ervil sometimes dubbed someone as targeted for the "Law of the .38." And he used even more colorful expressions, such as this religious criminal needed a "one way ticket to hell" or that Lamb of God traitor was up for "hot lead and cold steel." The meaning was all the same—death. The list of those pegged for such punishment at one point reached as high as twenty-one names, according to Sullivan.

The varying degrees of obedience to the Lord's commandments (via Ervil) carried both rewards and punishments. Commandments "of major magnitude," like planned executions, carried special remuneration. Those who successfully carried out such assignments were promised high places in heaven. If a Lamb of God failed, however, he or she was liable to be killed.

Fear of punishment began to impel many of Ervil's followers to continue on with him. Love for LeBaron and respect for his mission held others in line. Ervil now had a core group that was suitable for the most dangerous of exploits, perhaps reluctant to kill, but nevertheless willing to see it done if it was necessary—if they were commanded to do so by the Lord, or his appointed representative, Ervil Morrel LeBaron.

Knowing he was first on Ervil's "Ten Most Wanted" list, Verlan LeBaron embraced a certain truth: it is harder to hit a moving target than a stationary one. Verlan thought if he kept on the move—entrusting only a few family members and Firstborn leaders with knowledge of his whereabouts—then he could safely foil any pre-planned hit Ervil might conceive.

One of the best places Verlan found to "hide out" was Nicaragua. A nephew had been the first to go there "to get away from the law when out on probation [for polygamy] with his wife," according to a relative. "He came back to the States and returned to Nicaragua a second time, finding it a real haven, a refuge which didn't cost very much." The nephew began purchasing tracts of land, and set up his own bakery business. Back from the lengthy trip following Joel's murder, Verlan accepted an offer to visit the nephew in Nicaragua. Verlan and others left in early December 1972 to see what the place was like. He had an interest beyond mere refuge, for Joel had told Verlan around 1965, that within seven to ten years, Verlan must pioneer colonization in Central America. Thus Verlan felt he was fulfilling his dead brother's prophecy in going to Nicaragua. By luck, they missed the massive Managua earthquake that December, walking into the city the day after the disaster.

Verlan enjoyed a relatively peaceful 1973 while Ervil was in jail. He bought lots in Nicaragua, while his brother, Floren, became a semipermanent resident. Ervil's release broke the quiet, and it was not long before the Church of the Firstborn saw a new firebrand pamphlet, *Hour of Crisis—Day of Vengeance,* authored by Ervil in May 1974. The pamphlet carried a Colton, California, post office box number, in case any would-be Lambs of God wanted to follow up on the message.

The eighty-seven-page notebook-sized essay had a blue-and-white cover with the doomsday title and a gleaming hand-held sword emblazoned in red ink. (Lambs of God referred to it among themselves as the "sword book.") "The sword of vengeance [will] hang over the heads of all those who should fail to hear the word of the Lord," LeBaron wrote. "Willful failure to comply with its minimum requirements [as interpreted by Ervil] constitutes the crime of rebellion against God, which is punishable by death in this world." The tone was far more threatening than any previous documents. "[The Lord] has also said that at the time His messenger would come forth [being Ervil], whosoever would not hear His word that He would send forth among His covenant people in this manner would be destroyed from off the face of the earth through the pouring out of judgments and destructions."

Ervil was particularly angry he wasn't getting all the money he should.

"It is a criminal offense, punishable by death, for an enlightened people to pay tithes and offerings to thieves and robbers," or certain Mormon or Fundamentalist leaders, he wrote. "From this very hour, every man and woman . . . including responsible children . . . found living among or associated with any of these groups in Mormondom is required to . . . remove themselves from the midst of this corrupt society. Those who do not heed this warning will be subject to the overwhelming judgments and destructions of God that are shortly to be poured out."

This was the wrathful God of the Old Testament coming back for a return engagement, Ervil explained. "God, even from times of old, has destroyed entire nations and peoples for the crime of rejecting [his servants, Moses and Ervil]." Instead of an army, God was choosing His only "true church," the Church of the Lamb of God, to help Him out.

Finally, LeBaron said a show of fire would be called for as the only way to ensure that those who wanted to join Ervil and his "liberty," could. "God has said that He would give his people protection . . . even though it should require the exercise of the military might of His kingdom to the point of bringing down fire from Heaven to destroy the wicked."

Two months later, a weary Ervil had a long conversation with Conway which Conway never forgot. They were traveling in a car, and Ervil "mentioned at the time we finished [*Hour of Crisis*] that we had written all the major documents of the church. He said this was sufficient warning to them [the Firstborn Church]—by reading that they no longer had reason to stand blameless before the Lord. . . . The purpose [of all the pamphlets] was to call the Church of the Firstborn to repentance . . . to uphold the Lord's kingdom." Conway began an extensive period of missionary work with Ervil, concentrating in Colorado, Utah and California.

August 23, 1974, was a day for cheering in Los Molinos. After two long years the Mexican government officially recognized the *ejido* at Los Molinos, and it was given a Book of Mormon name, "Zarahemla." Now all who homesteaded on the property, and were Mexican citizens over fifteen years of age (including Mexican-born Anglos), could join the collective farm, vote in its monthly meetings and share in its profits. The action was destined to infuriate Ervil, who had actually ensured the recognition of the *ejido* when he failed to dispute the move for it by showing the land titles he had obtained, acting as an agent for the Firstborn Church. That August day, through the *ejido* formation, Ervil lost 1,200 of his precious acres to his enemies.

His rage was two months in coming, but come it did, in the most damning of all his documents, *Contest at Law,* subtitled, *The Great Whore—The Persecutor of the Church—Summoned to Mount Carmel.* In October, the spiral-ring 151-page green-and-yellow notebook, co-authored by Dan Jordan, was dispatched to the residents of Los Molinos and Colonia LeBaron postmarked Ogden, Utah. The most unusual essay Ervil had ever written, it is understandable only after considerable study. The writing is labyrinthine; one sentence may go on to over a hundred words broken into ten separate clauses, losing its original meaning along the way. The confusion this caused was deliberate, says Conway LeBaron, who helped write this and three other tracts with LeBaron, editing and even typesetting some of them. "I asked [Ervil] a hundred times why he just didn't write our church stuff simple. He told me several times that it was double-talk so he could avoid any legal problems—so they couldn't pin anything on him," said Conway.

This was wise, since *Contest at Law* was to Ervil LeBaron what *Mein Kampf* was to Hitler. It outlined what he planned to do in the future, and offered the general thrust of his plans, presenting a three-and-a-half-year timetable in which to accomplish those designs. The timetable was derived from a prophecy in Daniel 7, which said the "saints," which Ervil interpreted as Mormonism and its splinter sects, would persecute him "until a time and times and the dividing of time." He took this to mean that, as the persecuted, he would purge the Mormon groups during a "time and time and time and a half," or three and one-half years, and rule at the end of that time, when "three kings" or leaders had died.

No doubt feeling safe since he had already been acquitted for Joel's murder, Ervil railed against his dead brother. He listed seventeen "spurious" and "capital crimes" Joel had committed, noting that Joel "had become an imposter and a false prophet" and "had come under severe condemnation [which made him] subject to civil judgment by the law of God, which, in some cases, requires the penalty of death." Ervil concluded, ominously: "The death of this wicked man [Joel] was to be the first of the judgments of God that were to begin to be poured out upon His house."

Ervil, the defamed servant, then got to the crux of the matter. The Firstborners hadn't fallen into his hands, as expected, and had thereby incurred God's wrath. This publication was the Firstborn Church's last chance to repent, Ervil noted, "because we have solemnly testified to the world that God has sent us to overthrow their apostate church and kingdom."

Ervil concluded by summoning Verlan and his followers to "this contest at law, even as the priests of Baal were ordered to come up to a contest with Elijah the Prophet at Mount Carmel." In the Biblical account, Elijah beheaded the 400 priests after his sacrificial pyre was consumed by heavenly flames. Firstborners, if they did not repent, could expect a show of fire followed by summary executions. . . .

Toward the end of November, Verlan drove across the border from Tijuana to San Diego, accompanied by his first and second wives, Charlotte and Irene.

After they passed the first American gas station, Charlotte, momentarily startled, grabbed her husband. "Verlan, that was Ervil I saw back there in the phone booth."

Verlan whipped the car around, headed back to the service station and pulled in next to a car in which Anna Mae Marston was placidly seated. Ervil, in a large coat and with his back toward them, was conversing on the telephone. Verlan stepped out and strode over to talk with Anna Mae. When she saw him she clutched the steering wheel briefly and then flashed a broad smile. Ervil turned around about the same time and "freaked out because he thought we'd probably come there to kill him," Irene recalls. He began talking furiously to the unknown caller, gesticulating wildly in the booth.

"Ervil looks pretty worn and haggard since Joel was killed," Verlan observed to Anna Mae, who began laughing, and said she was "100 percent behind whatever Ervil does."

Shortly thereafter, Ervil pushed out of the phone booth and hopped into the passenger side of his car, slamming the door. "You don't have to listen to what he says," Ervil told Anna Mae, and she began rolling up her window. Verlan placed his fingers on it, trying to hold the window back and, searching for an appropriate invective, finally stared at Ervil and said, "I think you're chicken shit!" It was the worst thing one LeBaron brother had ever called another. Ervil and Anna Mae drove off.

Every *ejido* needs workers like a hive needs bees, and the new Zarahemla was no exception. A Firstborn leader left in December for Mexico City to find Mexicans willing to work the land, homestead it and vote the way the Firstborn Church indicated. He arrived back at Los Molinos Friday the 13th with seventy-three Mexicans packed into two trucks. "They got out of these things like sardines," says Irene. "I just was ready to cry because it was so stupid. They'd talked them all into coming to Zion when there was no place for them to live or food to eat." The group was divided and apportioned to various homes, which caused some complaints from the crowded inhabitants.

The disillusioned new arrivals ate meager meals in the church house, but seemed to enjoy Sunday services. Two boys were particularly excited about being there—Morone Mendez, sixteen, and Edmundo Aguilar, whose family had arrived two months before. They both cheerfully chipped in when Irene needed help packing her things to leave Los Molinos December 16. She was most impressed with Morone, who was "thrilled to death to think that I'd give him a Bible in Spanish." His gratefulness encouraged her to offer another gift, a dresser, which he gladly accepted. It was the last she saw of Morone or Edmundo.

Siegfried Widmar made little headway interesting U.S. authorities in the troubles of the Firstborn Church.

On Verlan's instructions, Widmar had collected excerpts from *Contest at Law* and explained their significance to the San Diego FBI office, whose agents replied that there was little they could do. When Siegfried noted that the threats were being made against a legal U.S. organization (the Firstborn Church was incorporated in Utah), and against people, most of whom were Americans, the FBI suggested Siegfried approach the U.S. Attorney's Office on the matter. In El Paso, the U.S. Attorney's Office advised him to speak with the U.S. Postal Inspector.

On December 20, he met with the El Paso inspector, displaying a mailing wrapper for the book he'd obtained, showing it had been sent from Ogden, Utah. The inspector leafed through postal laws and told Siegfried that was "no violation" in sending the publication through the mail system since no person had been threatened by name. "An organization threatened does not constitute a violation," Widmar was told.

The next day, a Sunday, Siegfried felt "moved upon" to speak to those attending Sunday School about the impending dangers that faced Colonia LeBaron and church members. He reiterated the conversation with Joel in which the latter had noted that the Firstborn Church was one for "martyrs only."

On December 22, Siegfried was told that Ervil LeBaron was announcing to Fundamentalist leaders "that before New Year's every adult man in Colonia LeBaron would be killed." A message was sent to Los Molinos, to ensure they would be on guard as well.

Peace on earth and goodwill toward men was still ringing in the ears of Los Molinos residents the day after Christmas 1974. Charlotte LeBaron took all her children still living with her—five out of nine— and a nephew down to the beach for some winter frolicking. They scrambled along the beach, while some waded into the perpetually warm Pacific Ocean, despite a nip in the air. "We were a pretty happy bunch that day," she recalls.

Not long after the sun went down, an ominous caravan of cars slowly approached Los Molinos, switching off headlights as it turned into the town. A brown GMC pickup truck carried several of the front-line Lamb of God soldiers.* They were armed with shotguns, carbines and a variety of revolvers. The truck bed was loaded with Molotov cocktails. According to eleven-year-old Isaac LeBaron, close behind was a late-model dark green Fiat driven by sixteen-year-old Rena Chynoweth, with Isaac and a friend of his riding along. The small car was also laden with firebombs. Just before turning into Los Molinos, Rena stopped the car and told the two boys to run into the hills, from which point they would be able to see the fireworks. Ervil had explained to his small son

---

*Primary material was provided by participant Isaac LeBaron, according to several police reports on extensive interviews of Isaac.

Ervil LeBaron:
Mormon missionary

LeBaron being booked in-
to jail (March 1976; Ensenada, Mexico)

Colonia LeBaron, Mexico, in 1979 view (*Photo by Ben Bradlee, Jr.*)

THE LeBARON CLAN

Matriarch Maud LeBaron

(Photo by Dale Van Atta)

Five of the LeBaron brothers at a Church of the Firstborn conference in Colonia LeBaron, 1965. *From left:* Ervil, Joel, Verlan, Alma and Floren. Not present were brothers Ben and Ross (*Deseret News*)

(Deseret News)

Ben LeBaron

Ross LeBaron

(Deseret News photo by O. Wallace Kasteler)

From the desk of Ervil LeBaron, circa 1974

Two who were wounded in the 1974 Los Molinos raid stand amidst the rubble of their homestead. *Left:* Fernando Castro. *Right:* Joel Castillo Lima (*Los Angeles Times photo by John Malmin*)

Robert Simons

Desert area near Price, Utah, where Simons' body was discovered (*Photo by Dick Forbes*)

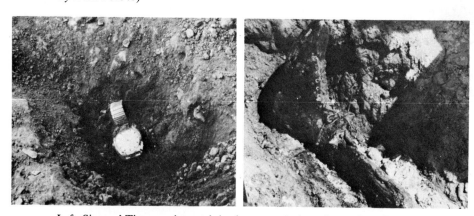

Left, Simons' Timex wristwatch in the ground where it was found. *Right,* Simons' boot and a portion of his leg as found in the excavation of his grave (*Photo by Dick Forbes*)

Mourning disciples crowd around the open casket of Rulon Allred at his funeral in 1977 (*Deseret News*)

THE FOLLOWERS

THE CHYNOWETHS

Victor Chynoweth

Mark Chynoweth

Rena Chynoweth

THE SULLIVANS

Lloyd Sullivan

Don Sullivan

John Sullivan

THE MARSTONS

Eddie Marston

Ramona Marston

(Deseret News)

that they were planning to burn the town down because he [Ervil] owned the buildings and didn't want anyone using the structures anymore. Ervil had told Lloyd Sullivan that he'd had a revelation that it was time to wipe out Los Molinos—particularly since God told him their archenemy, Verlan, would be present and could then receive his "hot lead and cold steel." A war council involving Ervil, the nearly seven-foot Dean Vest, who'd had some military experience, and other group members had meticulously plotted the commando raid, even including the use of a diversionary measure.*

The moon was bright that Thursday night, one of the coldest evenings of the year. The thirty families (about 200 persons) living on the quiet communal farm at the time were all huddled around stoves in their homes or tucked into bed by 9 P.M. A few were planning to attend a church meeting at Virginia Lopez's home, a three-story house, the town's largest, which sat at the northernmost and highest point of the generally flat colony.

About 9:20 A.M., a firebomb came crashing through her window, and another struck the door. The house and a large sixty-foot water tower next door were instantly on fire. Mrs. Lopez and her two children were temporarily trapped until Fernando Castro, Jr., came at a run and freed them. His primary concern after ensuring the family's safety was to pull down the highly flammable butane tank which sat atop the house. A few other people came hurrying over on bicycles or on foot. One tossed a lasso up to the tank and yanked it down. It smashed to the ground and exploded, burning several persons.

Raymond Dambacher arrived and took immediate command. He formed a bucket brigade to pass water from a well and toss it on the flaming structure. About three dozen neighbors had come to help by this time. As the fire appeared to diminish, Dambacher, along with brothers Fernando and Joel Castro, clambered up the house to a first-level outcropping. From above they tossed sand and dirt onto the fire. Always helpful, sixteen-year-old Morone Mendez leaped to to the second level. It was about 10 P.M., and they'd been fighting the fire for nearly a half hour.

Suddenly, startled onlookers below saw Morone's legs buckle, and watched him topple over the roof and bounce off some outside stairs. Several seconds after he landed, he began crying for his aunt: "Tía! Tía!" He'd been shot in the legs.

The group heard a barrage of bullets whizzing by, some finding their marks. They were easy targets, silhouetted against the blaze. At first, Dambacher hit the ground, thinking ammunition stored in the house

---

*Don Sullivan later told police some details about the Los Molinos raid, and wrote an account of it for Verlan LeBaron."Ervil actually participated in some of the . . . testing of Molotov cocktails," one police confidant of Sullivan's said. "They were to start a fire, hoping that everyone would run to the fire, and that Verlan would be one of those at the fire and they could get him there."

was exploding. He felt a nudge at his legs as he fell. The sharp pain told him he'd been shot in both legs.

Fernando, on the roof, heard the noise, but couldn't comprehend until a bullet struck *his* leg. He hobbled to the edge of the roof and peered into the darkness, where he saw a number of men with rifles emerge from behind parked cars. "Jump, Joel!" he shouted to his brother, as he followed his own advice. Joel had already realized the danger and was in the midst of leaping. He landed with a jolt and sprinted for cover behind a low pile of adobes. Before he reached the heap, Joel was crippled by a bullet that struck his right leg. Another spattered into his right hand as he reached down to his leg. Breathless, he fell behind the adobe bricks.

While the Castro brothers were jumping from the roof, Benjamin Zarate, gazing at the fire, was knocked down by a shotgun blast which struck his neck. He stood up again, thinking the fire had exploded something in the house, and a second later, more shotgun pellets pounded into his head and he fell. "It's the Ervilistas!" his wife, downed by a rifle bullet a few feet away from him, whispered. "Play dead!"

From the ground, Benjamin could now see his attackers, shooting from twenty yards away. They were clad in heavy clothing, with Arabian-style cloths hanging down at the sides of their heads, partially obscuring their faces.

A half dozen men stood and calmly continued firing into the crowd. Few words were uttered.

More volleys of gunfire struck the downed bodies, and the cries of women and children magnified in the otherwise still night air. Morone was crying the loudest. One man walked over, raised a shotgun, and blasted the sixteen-year-old in the chest. Morone was silenced. After less than two minutes, one of the religious commandos shouted in a muffled voice, "Let's go!" The marauders clambered into the waiting Fiat and the GMC truck. The two vehicles headed in different directions through the community.

At least ten of the wounded were unable to rise from the ground. Almost all were in shock. Benjamin dragged himself up to a standing position. He saw Mrs. Fernando Castro, who'd been shot in the legs, and lifted her gently and placed her next to her injured husband, who was also on the ground. From the group of strewn bodies, Morone, barely alive, was still crying for his aunt. "Hold on," Benjamin begged. "Someone's gone for Ray's truck."

When the pickup arrived, Zarate and Dambacher painfully lifted the wounded into the truck bed. It was laborious. Precious minutes passed, and finally they were ready. "I can't drive," Ray told Benjamin, "my legs are shot." Benjamin sat in the driver's seat, even though he didn't know how to operate the gearshift. Dambacher edged in beside him. He manipulated the shift while Benjamin worked the gas and clutch. The truck lurched toward the center of town, and they looked for more wounded.

While neighbors were picking themselves up, their assailants were stopping in front of each residence as they drove out of Los Molinos. They lit firebombs and tossed them through windows and onto roofs. The Aguilar home was badly damaged. A seventy-eight-year-old woman was struck by the bullets which ripped through the curtains of her window. Twenty-four-year-old Edmundo was completely taken by surprise. He'd slept through the fire and gun blasts. One of the firebombs landed on his bed and he woke up on fire, frantically flailing his arms at the flames. He turned to the window for a moment, saw a shotgun aimed at him. The blast shattered his head, knocking him unconscious but not killing him.

The truck, with several men in the bed clearly outlined by their torches, then barreled toward their main object—the home of Verlan LeBaron at the far end of town. He had left for San Diego earlier that day, but Charlotte and six of their children were still there.

Charlotte had been feeling cheerful after a good day. She had put several of her children to bed, and she followed them to bed about 9:15 P.M. Steven, her oldest boy, her teenaged daughter Laura, nineteen, and their cousin, Doug, were staying up late to finish a prolonged game of Monopoly by the light of their new kerosene lamp, a Christmas present.

By chance, Steven stood up and looked through the window at one point and saw the brightly lit Perez home, totally ablaze. "I thought it was the Ervilites right off," he recalls. Laura ran and woke her mother, "Mother, Mother, the tall house is burning," she said, shaking Charlotte. While she dressed, the family began hearing popping sounds, which resembled fireworks. Charlotte and her son knew immediately that guns were being fired.

A million things raced through Charlotte's mind. Verlan had told his first wife on many occasions, "If the time ever comes that this place is attacked, yours will be the first place they'll come to." Looking out the window, Charlotte saw a truck moving away from the blaze, with men bearing torches in the bed and "I knew they were coming after us."

She gathered her children quickly and pulled two pistols out from a dresser drawer. They all ran outside and got into Doug's Toyota.

They drove only a short distance, because the truck with its heavily armed passengers was already bearing down on the house. Doug stopped by a backyard well and they all tumbled out. "It would have been easier to hide behind tumbleweeds than my three-foot olive trees," says Charlotte. She hurriedly handed each of the guns to Doug and Laura, telling them how to use them. "Don't use it until they've shot first," she urged. The truck had come much closer now and Charlotte could clearly see five men in the back with rifles, shotguns and pistols. "I knew we didn't stand a chance," she says.

The vehicle pulled up in front of their house, the brief silence an eternity. They shot through Charlotte's windows eighteen times and threw thirteen firebombs on the roof. But she and her shivering brood somehow escaped detection, only fifty yards from the house, and in full view. The family stood rooted to the spot after the attackers left, thinking they might come back.

But Steve dashed to the house, leaped onto a fence and to their roof and began tossing the firebombs off, thereby saving the building. He and others then made hasty rounds of all Los Molinos homes, stamping out fires with wet overcoats and tossing explosive bottles off roofs. An angered Pat Mackie, who hadn't been struck in the initial hail of bullets, started to chase the GMC truck out of town but his car nearly turned over when his four tires were suddenly flattened by nail boards the Lambs of God were tossing from their fleeing vehicle.

Gathering as many of the wounded as possible into the pickup, Dambacher and Zarate picked their way out of town between the boards. They passed Charlotte's home, "making a noise, like teenagers having a good time," she thought. When she realized the groans and screams came from wounded friends and neighbors, she began to cry. "Thank God we're alive," she said to her children, and uttered a long prayer.

When the Dambacher vehicle arrived in San Quintin, about fifteen miles south, and began unloading at Hospital Buen Pastor, the police were notified and a large detachment of Mexican Army soldiers were dispatched to the colony. They arrived about 3 A.M., and stayed for nearly two months; another detachment was posted around Colonia LeBaron in Chihuahua, hundreds of miles away.

The attack had lasted no more than twenty minutes. Morone Mendez and Edmundo Aguilar died within a day, and the faithful of Los Molinos said there was an earthquake tremor within minutes of each death. Thirteen others—nine men and four women, one of them pregnant—had been wounded in the shootings. Seven buildings were destroyed. When Dambacher was transferred to the Veterans Hospital in San Diego, the local press was shocked as the story of the polygamous cults began to unfold. *Newsweek* picked it up. The raid was variously identified as a "commando mission," "a scene straight out of a Peckinpah Western" and a "despicable bushwacking."

The aftereffects, years later, of the raid at Los Molinos, are still evident in those who lived through it.

Some of the children, including Charlotte's, continued to have nightmares. A few drop to the ground at the sound of a loud blast, but the Firstborn homes are safer now because the windows are higher. Veterans of the raid learned that bullets wouldn't penetrate adobe walls, just the windows.

Fernando Castro, the eloquent pastor of the community, rises when asked about it and uses expressive hand movements and words to convey the impact of such a calamity. Ervil LeBaron, to him, is less than a man, lower than any he has known. "As far as I'm concerned," he says in peculiar Spanish idiom, "Ervil, as he went among us, the Lamanite people, I consider he's a man who constructed his house, but after the edifice was quite high began to tear it down." And here his hands move down in a quick chopping motion. "As a father who raises sons, he [Ervil] raises them and turns around and eats them," Castro concludes, turning his back symbolically on Ervil.

To everything there is a season, and
a time to every purpose under the heaven:
  A time to be born, and a time to die;
a time to plant, and a time to pluck up
that which is planted;
  A time to kill . . . (Ecclesiasticus 3:1-3)

10.

FRENZY

In the six-month period from December 1974 to June 1975, five persons connected with Ervil LeBaron were left dead: the two boys slaughtered in Los Molinos and three later. Several others narrowly escaped. The evolution from fanaticism to barbarism had been easy and fast.

All the warning signals had been there, including crazy talk. Once or twice Lloyd Sullivan was put off by LeBaron's comments that a number of people "deserved cement overcoats" and dumping into the sea, so their bodies would never rise. "With the Lord's help he was gonna sink a lot of automobile bodies . . . and some cement coffins . . . down in there and change the current in the Gulf [of Mexico]," Lloyd would recall. Ervil talked about buying a farm in Wisconsin where, with the help of other farmers, he would haul enough manure to manufacture tons of explosives (deriving sodium nitrate from manure) to be used against his enemies.

Zion beckoned LeBaron and his retinue in 1974, or so he said, and they heeded the call to come to Utah, where the new Lamb of God headquarters was established.

The belated support of Victor Chynoweth was a factor in the move to Utah. Hired as a body repairman at an establishment called Lincoln Auto in Ogden in 1972, Victor had swiftly moved up the business ladder to salesman and buyer. When he joined the Lambs of God in 1974, he was head and shoulders above the rest of Ervil's group; he was a man with proven money-earning ability. Ervil's attraction to Victor was plain as the way to the parish church. "Victor's a good thinker, moneymaker and salesman. He likes to flaunt it if he's got it, and he usually does," says his brother, Glen. "He's blunt and sometimes vulgar. He doesn't fit the prototype of any of the others in the group." Whatever the reason,

Victor did become indispensable to LeBaron—the left-hand man, as it were, while Dan Jordan still sat on Ervil's right.

This Utah period was a nervous one for LeBaron and his crew. Ervil assured his followers, though, that his revelations would always save them from the law. "He's told when there's danger and when there's not," claims Ervil's stepson, Eddie Marston. Ervil told his followers when it was very hot, in so many words. "When something gets hot," Lloyd Sullivan recalled, "the Lord showed Ervil a picture of it real, real red." Sullivan was angered once, when, after checking into a motel and getting settled, Ervil informed him the Lord had just tipped him off that the place was hot. They had to vacate the premises immediately; it wasn't safe. Sullivan thought the Lord should have had the simple courtesy to reveal that to LeBaron before they had paid in advance for the room.

Elden Kingston had been happy enough with a good job during the Depression at an Idaho Falls railroad yard. But one day when he was out walking, he later recounted, he had a revelation urging him to quit his job and head for Salt Lake City. The family pulled up stakes and arrived in Salt Lake where, soon enough, Elden got further word, again from a nonearthly being. He was to start a United Order, a communal-living situation, not particularly aligned to any church. Obediently, Elden incorporated the nonprofit Davis County Cooperative Society in 1941. From the 1950s on, it prospered into what Salt Lake County sheriff's lieutenant John Llewellyn describes as "a very close-knit, impregnable polygamist group."

By the 1970s, the co-op had successfully purchased and was operating at least thirty businesses in Utah. The Kingstons also owned several farms, including a 300-acre dairy farm in Woods Cross, a 1,000-acre general crop farm at Tetonia, Idaho, and a cattle ranch in Utah's Emery County. Add to that list of only the known businesses, their largest operation, a bituminous coal mine in Huntington Canyon, Utah, and a coal trucking business, and the group easily achieved the kind of self-sufficiency that Elden had only dreamed about back in 1941. In 1974 the group had about 500 members—some fifty families—who were worth, altogether, about $50 million, according to the best estimates. Oddly, these wealthiest of all polygamists live as the poorest, in a lifestyle described by Llewellyn as "inconspicuous prosperity." Leaders and followers alike live in middle- to lower-class housing and ride around in run-down cars. "It's an ascetic deprivation thing," explains a Fundamentalist friend. "Whoever gives up the most is viewed as the highest."

Few not born into the highly secretive society are allowed any contact with it anyway.

Ervil LeBaron had periodically visited the Kingstons since the late 1950s, occasionally using Harold Blackmore as an entrée. Besides the Kingston wealth, LeBaron was interested in the family's interaction with another polygamist leader, Rulon Allred. The naturopath was a family doctor to many of the Kingstons. In turn, Allred was allowed large loans and other privileges at the United Bank.

At first, LeBaron worked at the edges of the group, approaching middle-level leaders, moving higher all the time. One of the co-op members, Arnold T. Pratt, distinctly recalls his meeting with Ervil in early November of 1974 in a Salt Lake café. While Ervil's prodigious appetite surprised Pratt, LeBaron's statements were even more astonishing to him: "He told me he was the One Mighty and Strong, commissioned by God to set things in order," recalls Pratt. "He said he needed money. He wanted to know if I had any influence and I told him I didn't have any." Then LeBaron moved on to weightier matters. He told Pratt that the Lord protected him and "that if I shot at him with a pistol it wouldn't do anything—the pistol wouldn't even work."

LeBaron boasted to Pratt that within a year he would be head of a separate nation which would have power over the whole earth. To do that, he had to "cleanse these other [Mormon spin-off] organizations by killing the leaders."

"Even the Mormons will fall," LeBaron said. "The president and his twelve apostles must come under the Civil Law. They are knowingly teaching false doctrines, and false prophets receive the death penalty under Civil Law."

"But how are you going to do it?" asked Pratt. "Isn't that a big order?"

"When the Lord gives me a job to do," LeBaron arrogantly replied, "I don't ask how I'm going to do it. I just do it."

Pratt called a friend in Mormon Church security and alerted them. LeBaron had given the Mormons a two-month deadline to repent, a deadline which would end January 1, 1975.

Finally, LeBaron began meeting with the Kingston leaders. Elden had died and his brother, John Ortel Kingston, known by his middle name, was appointed prophet and co-op president. But Ortel was weak with cancer in late 1974, and brother Merlin virtually took over the co-op. Ervil arranged a meeting with Merlin at a Salt Lake restaurant, the Chuck-A-Rama. He brought Conway LeBaron along. Ervil explained that the Lord had given the Kingstonites twelve years to line up behind LeBaron and they had not done so. He was giving them a last chance. The "dire consequences" of not paying tithing to Ervil would include the burning of Kingston businesses by the Lord. Conway said, at the time, he didn't consider it extortion because "Ervil had a right to do what he was saying the Lord was going to do."

Merlin met another time with Ervil. LeBaron again demanded 10 percent of the Kingston income as tithing. During this late November meeting, he threatened sabotage against five specific Kingston businesses and stated the order in which they would occur, with the Huntington mine at the top of the list. Merlin was not impressed. As a police report noted, the Kingstons were not sheep. They had "extensive security capability and will expend whatever measures are necessary to ensure adequate protection of their facilities." If it came to confrontation, police put the odds on the well-armed Kingstons, who would not be defenseless, like the members of the Firstborn Church had been.

Interested in learning more about LeBaron's plans, Merlin allowed him to meet with brother Ortel in the latter's home on December 17, 1974. Dan Jordan came as Ervil's second. As an ice-breaker, Ervil offered to heal Ortel, who was so sick with cancer that he couldn't lift his head from the bed. "He asked me if I wanted him to intervene, to call down powers from heaven and have my brother healed," says Merlin. "I didn't believe he could do it." When the offer was rejected, Ervil got to the business at hand. Merlin recounted the conversation later in police reports and on the witness stand:

"Ervil mentioned he had spent twelve long years calling on us and teaching and his patience was coming to an end. He said he was the head of the political Kingdom of God and that the world would be under their jurisdiction and their rule. We were to start obeying the laws of the political kingdom [or we] would have to suffer the death penalty."

LeBaron was most angered that he wasn't getting any money out of the Kingstons, Allreds and Short Creek groups. "He said we had been breaking the law of tithing," Merlin remembered, "and if they didn't pay tithing they'd be killed or done away with."

Ervil got even more explicit at the meeting. He issued a January 1, 1975 deadline for the payment of this money. "If we didn't start [giving it to him] before the first of the year," Merlin recalled the threat, "there would be bloodshed and our businesses would be burned. He expanded the threat at this time to include even the Mormon Church, closing with the definition of tithing as "anything you are able to pay."

Ervil's speech took the Kingstons aback. Before they had time to plan, Ortel's phone was ringing. Lieutenant Llewellyn warned Merlin that "LeBaron and two armed men are about to stop in and pay you a visit. Be careful. They are armed and dangerous." Merlin politely thanked his police friend and explained that the Lambs of God had just left. He asked Llewellyn to relay the threat to the Mormon Church. Merlin himself warned his friend Allred, sent word to Short Creek and also called Rhea Kunz, asking her to spread the alarm to the Church of the Firstborn, whose community of Los Molinos was to be attacked only nine days later on December 26.

Because of the heightened LeBaron activity, Sergeant Dell Mortensen of Salt Lake City police intelligence arranged a personal conference with Merlin Kingston on December 21. Kingston noted that he had several meetings with Ervil—which were sometimes attended by Conway LeBaron, Dan Jordan and Raúl Rios. Planning to turn down Ervil's offer to join the Lambs of God, and pay tithing, the Kingstons were busy upgrading the security at their facilities. Merlin told police the group would "retaliate defensively if attacked," and asked law enforcement for a permit to carry a weapon, which was rejected. Kingston agreed to tape-record any future meetings with Ervil, but refused to help in any LeBaron-extortion investigation. A police report filed on the conference said Merlin was reluctant to help since he was "sure that LeBaron's arrest would only temporarily delay his carrying out of threats, and that danger to co-op leaders would be greatly increased if LeBaron were to be arrested at this time."

Finally, the report noted that Ervil consistently harped on the theme of world conquest, using a step-by-step plan. "He envisions accomplishing this goal by first assuming control of the financial resources of the Davis County Co-op. He would use this group as a base for attacking and assuming control of the Mormon Church. When asked how he planned to deal with the Mormon Church's [simple] arrangement for replacement of fallen leaders, he has replied that he has a plan which would involve killing at one time all members of the Mormon Church hierarchy. This plan supposedly includes the use of Mexican aliens and guerrilla-type tactics. Assuming he is successful in taking control of the Mormon Church, LeBaron has indicated he would then move on to greater heights." Since, up to the point of that report, only Joel LeBaron had been murdered, the police higher-ups could only scratch their heads or laugh at reading such incredible intelligence reports.

Still, they thought it serious enough to alert Mormon Church Security, headed by the former Salt Lake City Police Chief. At first, some Mormon leaders thought the Kingstons might be inventing threats to the church in order to ensure active law enforcement and protection for themselves. "This was the first dialogue that ever opened up between the [splinter] groups and us," says one Mormon leader. "We shared information for our mutual protection." He compared the Mormon Church to a "mother hen. When all the little chicks were in trouble they came to us."

About the same time as the warnings came, Fundamentalists were reporting a mysterious new LeBaron scheme, called the "Plan of Seven." Ervil told confidants that seven dedicated Lambs of God would be sent to slay President Kimball and the Quorum of the Twelve, either by hiding near their cars or homes. If the seven failed, seven more would be sent. "Seven upon seven upon seven upon seven," Ervil said, in mesmerizing cadence.

On December 30, cars were seen prowling around several residences of Allred's family. One of Rulon's sons reported that rocks had been thrown at the windows of his Bluffdale home, which also served as the Allred school. Once the power switch had been pulled, cutting off the electricity in the house, after which one wife received a call in which a chilling voice said, "You think you are very secure, don't you?" That night, at another Allred home, an unknown person scratched in the snow on their driveway the words, "We will be back."

Llewellyn reported these incidents to his superiors—four days after Los Molinos—writing that "at this point I don't think there is much danger. Ervil told my informant that they wouldn't bother Rulon Allred or the others until they get things taken care of in Mexico. The harassment received by Rulon Allred's family is real enough, but it doesn't make sense. I fear someone is capitalizing on the LeBaron scare. It doesn't fit with the general pattern of things."

Verlan LeBaron, the main target of the Los Molinos raid, had been missed, and the Firstborners knew it.

In Chihuahua, Siegfried Widmar received news of the raid at 5:30 A.M. the next day, December 27. A town meeting was called for 10 A.M., during which Widmar prayed for the Lord's help, adding he hoped the Mexican government would become a "protecting wing" over the church members. Everyone was ordered to take extra precautions to lock their doors, close their curtains and have their weapons ready and dogs on alert. The secret group, "Sons," met and planned a defense for the town.

After ensuring the protection of Colonia LeBaron by government soldiers, who stationed themselves at the entrances to the town on December 29, Siegfried went to San Diego, where he discussed the tragedy with several news agencies. Then he checked out a ranch Ervil had obtained from a Mexican general, which he suspected was Lamb of God headquarters during the raid. Widmar found a cement-block home littered with cow dung, burnt cans, new flashlight batteries shot up with rifle bullets and the packing box of an American-made bicycle. Neighbors recognized pictures of Dan Jordan and Ervil LeBaron.

For the local police, Siegfried provided background on the conflict and descriptions from his people of the attackers and the cars they had used. He also reported that many unused firebombs had been discovered after the raid in bushes, storage bins and next to homes still standing. Evidence of firebomb manufacture had been found in the house of one of Ervil's supporters the day after the raid, but a mysterious fire that night destroyed the residence, and that of Ervil's wife Mary Lou. Ervil blamed the Firstborners for setting fire to his property, but the Firstborners retorted that the blaze had been set by the Lambs of God to destroy evidence of their culpability. Neither was right. Eyewitnesses watched as some of the Mexian Army officers, for some unknown reason, set them ablaze.

Two days after the raid, December 28, Rena Chynoweth was stopped as she tried to cross the Baja border into San Diego in the dark green Fiat. Since Rena was sixteen, she was detained as a juvenile. A San Diego policeman, Detective Ron Collins, who interviewed Rena at the time, reported she "admitted being at the village during the attack but she denied any involvement." She provided the Ogden telephone number of Victor Chynoweth as a way of contacting her parents. Later that day, after police conducted surveillance on Chynoweth's home and learned from a neighbor there had been many strange "comings and goings" in recent weeks, a sergeant called Victor and told him his sister was in custody at San Diego. Victor thanked the officer and said his parents were not home, but he would reach them.

While Rena Chynoweth was in custody, overnight, Detective Collins received a call from a LeBaron follower who demanded the girl's immediate release because he planned to marry her. Thelma, the Chynoweth matriarch, showed up at the station December 29, and Rena was turned over to her. Within a short time, a border station guard called Collins and said Thelma, Rena, Linda Johnson and another woman had tried crossing into Mexico, and he had detained them. While Thelma was allowed through, Collins drove to the border and interviewed the remaining women.

"They all admitted being friends of Ervil LeBaron," said one police report. "They all became quite excited and protective when Ervil's name was discussed. They further stated that the attack in Mexico had its origin in disagreements between Ervil LeBaron and Verlan LeBaron regarding ownership of property near Los Molinos . . . that Joel LeBaron was killed because he had strayed from the true doctrine." Collins finally allowed them to cross because he had no warrants for their arrest.

The people of Los Molinos remained on guard for several months. They slept on the floors of the houses left standing in the colony, with their guns nearby. Suspicious things continued to happen. In early February, one of Alma LeBaron's homes was set ablaze by a firebomb. An *ejido* tractor was stalled after someone put sugar in its gas tank. Linda Johnson and Thelma were seen twice taking license numbers of Los Molinos cars in the churchyard.

For a while, the Lambs of God concentrated on Firstborners in San Diego, which actually was then Verlan's place of residence. They scouted homes suitable for burning, acting under a Biblical injunction to trample the enemy into "ashes under the soles of feet." Ervil's women, particularly Vonda, disguised themselves as men with beards while checking on license numbers and homes in southern California and Baja California. Ervil's Plan A was to throw five-gallon cans of gas on the homes and set them afire, shooting the residents as they came running out. Plan B was to dig a large hole under the Firstborn Church building in San Diego and blow it up with explosives made from manure. But neither plan was deemed realistic, so the schemes were abandoned.

Ervil concocted other ways to get Verlan. Once he asked a follower to rig up a fake police car, rent a home on the Baja highway and come screaming out of the garage with a siren when they saw Verlan go by. He'd think they were police and stop, giving them the perfect opportunity to shoot him. Several of the male Lambs of God, including even old Aurelio Rios, began having divine dreams which told them where and how they would kill Verlan, no doubt expecting Ervil's highest approval. It was an open contract, and the reward was a calling and election made sure. Ervil had ordered his military to kill Verlan on sight, even if a million people were around, Sullivan later said. Ervil expected the Church of the Firstborn would naturally fall to him if Verlan could be done away with.

Early one morning in late January, sixteen witnesses to the Los Molinos raid gathered at the Ensenada courthouse to offer their testimony, demanding justice for the death of loved ones and the wounding of others. Some of the witnesses, sporting wounds from the raid, were anxious to make sure the judge would hear what they had to say. They were shuffled outside to await their turn giving depositions. One of the witnesses, Alma LeBaron's son Nephi, said they were outside about half an hour, passing the time with small talk. A Baja state senator drove up in his truck shortly before 10 A.M. and parked it near them, getting out to converse with his friends in the Firstborn Church.

Only one or two of them saw Raúl Rios walk down the sidewalk, a shotgun raised and pointed at them as if in a scene out of *High Noon*. As he prepared to fire the first round, he tripped on a crack in the sidewalk and the shot hit the ground, sending pellets into the legs of Nephi, the senator and another man, and flattening one of the senator's tires. "The BBs had hit the ground before they hit me, so it felt like a firecracker," said Nephi. He looked up to see Rios trying to pull the trigger for a second shot into the crowd, but Rios hadn't pulled the bolt all the way back so it wouldn't fire. In disgust, he threw it to the ground and started running. Nephi and a hefty Firstborner chased after him.

After a fifty-yard dash, Rios turned to see his enemies closing on him, and pulled a pistol out of his shirt. Incredibly, as he was ready to fire, not looking where he was going, his hand smacked into a telephone pole and his gun was thrown to the ground. The chase continued down the street, with Nephi gaining on Rios. Meanwhile, the local police began racing the runners in their police car, finally halting next to Rios and knocking him to the ground. He was jailed for about five months in Ensenada, and released.

Thus yet another of Ervil's plans had failed. This one had been first discussed at Yuma, Arizona, about February 1974, according to Lloyd Sullivan. Incredibly, the chosen victim was the state senator, whom Ervil considered as a sworn enemy. Sullivan later said he took the shotgun to Raúl and his father, Aurelio, before the January 1975 attempt. Raúl was ordered to empty the shotgun at the senator, and hoped to kill some of the witnesses at the same time. That no one was hurt was deemed a miracle by the Firstborners.

Sometimes, women irritated Ervil LeBaron. He told Delfina often that if she got any further out of line, he'd have her killed, weigh her down with stones and toss her into the ocean. Ervil liked the sound of that so much, that he used the same threat against Naomi Zarate Chynoweth, plural wife of Bud Chynoweth. Ervil had once courted all of his seven sisters, but their father objected to any marriages between LeBaron and his daughters. Apparently it was different when Bud Chynoweth came a-wooing.

Though her brother, Benjamin, Jr., says that Naomi loved Bud, Irene LeBaron insists this was not true. She'd given Naomi an ironing job when Naomi had first come to Los Molinos, and learned her true feelings. "She had already been married to a Mexican, loved him and wanted to stay with him but her father wanted her to marry Bud," said Irene. In an effort to stop it, Irene protested to Joel about the marriage, noting Ervil planned to perform it. "No way," said Joel. He was leaving for Chihuahua at the time and instructed Irene, "If I don't get to see Ervil, you personally give him this message. You tell Ervil that he is not to marry that girl to Bud. If she divorces her present husband she still has to go her six months." He was referring to the required post-divorce waiting period among members. She repeated Joel's words to Ervil, who said it was none of his brother's business. The marriage went ahead as planned.

Brother Benjamin recalls that Naomi was an obedient, jolly and pleasant wife to Bud for a time. They had three boys. But after Joel's murder, she became frank and outspoken, opposing the Lambs of God and her husband Bud's involvement. She threatened to turn them over to the police if they didn't abandon future plans.

Apparently Naomi was safe until the raid at Los Molinos. Shortly after, one of Dan Jordan's wives was kidnapped by two of Ervil's wives and disappeared. Given that precedent, Naomi would have been wise to hide, but she didn't. Firstborners saw her talking to Anna Mae Marston and Thelma Chynoweth. She was last seen being driven away from Ensenada by Vonda White, about the time the raid witnesses were shot at, in late January.

Vonda later recounted briefly to Lloyd Sullivan what happened. Sullivan would later tell police that Vonda, together with one of Ervil's followers, shuttled Naomi around in the blue 1970 Dodge the Lambs of God lovingly labeled "Puff the Magic Dragon." Finally, they drove to a remote spot near Ensenada where Vonda shot Naomi several times with a .38, as Naomi stood next to the right rear taillight of Puff. One bullet drove through her with such force that it broke off a section of the light. Vonda and her companion heaved Naomi into the trunk and drove to a nearby hillside where they dug a hole and buried her. "Rather gruesome, isn't it?" Sullivan commented to authorities after relating the story. Ervil, on the other hand was delighted that Vonda had carried out her mission, beaming about her calling and election to heaven being almost sure. Ecstatically, he assured her, "You don't know how pleased the Lord is that that traitor is dead!"

Like a shark smelling blood, Ervil was in a perpetual frenzy during this Utah period. He ranted on endlessly about impending deaths and about the Lord's imperative three-and-a-half-year timetable. He was a man possessed.

No one saw this more clearly than Carol Jensen, his longtime devotee who had left him before Joel's murder. Thelma Chynoweth contacted her in February 1975, since both were living in Ogden. Carol said she'd be glad to see Ervil; she proceeded to meet him in local restaurants three times.

It was *déjà vu* for Carol and Ervil. "The last time I met with Ervil I sat there and he thought—I had been away for so long," she says. "But I sat there and looked at him and listened for hours and hours. And he became more and more vociferous, and more and more intense and told me more secrets and I didn't say anything. He must have thought he really had me hooked 'cause he told me many things that he must have felt sorry for later."

Ervil explained that the final battle was at hand, a battle for the control of the Kingdom of God. He needed Carol on his side to help him. There were people who opposed the coming of the Lord, the millennium, who weren't letting the angels do their bit. The Lambs of God had to eliminate these enemies "so the Lord can roll forth his prophecies and this world can receive its ultimate paradisiacal blessings," Carol continues. The group members were murdering "for the sake of the world, not for themselves. [And Ervil] just wanted to carry out prophecy . . ."

At that point, he told her, the Mormons were first on his list. The LDS First Presidency and Apostles would be attacked and killed— "they would disappear somewhere between their cars and either their homes or the office." Then the Church of the Firstborn would be wiped out, and the Short Creek group. Ervil told Carol about the meetings he'd had with the Kingstons "giving them all their last chance, because things were going to happen." Finally, Ervil said Rulon Allred must die. Years before, Allred had ignored Joel's revelation instructing Rulon to join them. "Ervil always said he'd be the one to do it [cause Allred's fall]." All this had to be accomplished in three and a half years, according to Daniel 7, Ervil told Carol. He did not say when the period began, she adds, because "he always had to have a way to edge out of it if it didn't come about."

About this time, Ervil lost one of his most faithful followers, Conway LeBaron. As an example of Ervil's influence, Conway's first wife, Betty Ann Jones, remembers that the Patriarch ordered the couple not to pray to God anymore in their home: "He said it was a ritual, and shouldn't be done every day. Just like a little child coming up and asking their mommy and daddy for the same thing over and over again. It becomes very irritating."

The new order of things miffed Betty Ann, but no more than when Conway took his second wife in 1969. Ervil had arranged a marriage with his niece, Pauline Spencer; and the new twosome was very pleased.

But Betty Ann was discomfited by the polygamous relationship, particularly since they lived in the same California house, and Betty Ann had to earn a living for them all.

Betty Ann left Conway in 1971, gathering her children and heading for Los Molinos. Ervil visited her trailer there often, acting as the go-between and sometimes bringing child support money from Conway. "He tried very hard to convert me, almost threatening. He wanted me to join [the Lambs of God] and leave the other group [Firstborn Church]," says Betty Ann. When Dan Jordan was there for conversion attempts, Jordan would talk about "an awful lot of bloodshed that would happen when people didn't come along with them." Finally, Betty Ann left Los Molinos and the Firstborn Church for good in October of 1971 and remarried in Utah.

Left alone with Pauline, Conway was content for a time. Occasionally, he was annoyed by Ervil's incessant use of his credit cards and the fact that he was always expected to foot Lamb of God bills. Then too, after Joel was murdered, Conway found himself unwelcome in Mexico. "I went on the run and haven't been into Mexico since then," he says. "I couldn't cross the border."

While Ervil was in jail, Conway was in Utah putting publications together, aided by other Lambs of God. But "all of the missionaries went against me and left me with a printing bill we agreed to pay. My name was on the papers. I couldn't get a job. I took an assumed name and got a fake Social Security number. I had the bill paid by the time Ervil got out of jail."

Things were rosy on the surface for a time, but it became apparent that association with non-Lamb of God friends in Salt Lake had a telling effect on Conway and, particularly, his wife Pauline. In late 1974 and early 1975, "she said she could no longer go with Ervil. She said she had found something in her mind that proved Ervil wrong," recalls Conway. "I couldn't see it. I went on a three-day fast . . . [Then] I talked with her. She said we were never [really] married. We agreed to work it out." LeBaron had previously instructed Lambs of God that, according to a mysterious "13th Code," members must turn in friends, relatives, even spouses, when treachery surfaced. "According to [the code], if a wife or someone goes against you, you are to turn them in," Conway confirmed. So he "told Ervil what was wrong. He told me how to handle the situation."

Conway is silent on Ervil's final solution, but his wife Pauline has not been. A close friend, in whom Pauline confided, says Ervil ordered Conway to kill Pauline.

"Pauline was a smart girl," the friend explains. "She could see through Ervil and she couldn't stand him. So Pauline was leading one of Ervil's men astray. It was a fight for power with Conway. It was either Ervil or Pauline. That's what it came to. [Ervil gave] Conway explicit instructions. . . . He was supposed to take Pauline out in the desert and kill her and leave her body there. Then he was supposed to take the kids away. . . . Ervil was real suspicious [at the time] and he was keeping close guard on them to make sure they didn't get away. So they had about a fifteen-minute period in which they could escape . . . before anybody found out . . . and they just jumped in the car with the kids and went with nothing. They escaped with their lives."

Of all LeBaron's relatives, former friends and defectors, Conway LeBaron remains the most frightened of Ervil. Conway's reluctance to talk to anyone, including police, is formidable.

One of the greatest mysteries among the Lambs of God, even among the elite, was whether Ervil LeBaron had ever married Thelma Chynoweth.

Civil Law—the Old Testament—prohibited it. Anna Mae Marston said the Lord's plan is "definitely against" the marriage of both a mother and a daughter, Lorna Chynoweth in this case.

But, Ervil, like Anna Mae, never seemed to deny the allegation point-blank. Ervil, when queried repeatedly by wife Delfina who "always asked because of the things I saw," responded that it was "against the law to marry a mother and a daughter." Others in the group, like Isaac LeBaron and Pauline, Conway's wife, said it was common knowledge that the two were married, or sleeping together, and the situation revolted Lorna enough to leave Ervil once or twice.

Thelma herself told a Firstborn member before Joel was killed that she had "made a blood covenant with Ervil." And when, in late December, she met with detective Ron Collins, she proudly boasted she was, in fact, married to Ervil.

Whether the marital tie bound them or not, Thelma was instrumental in arranging for her second daughter, Rena's, marriage to Ervil during this Utah period, on February 3, 1975. A bubbly, outgoing and attractive sixteen-year-old, Rena agreed to the match reluctantly. She had several boyfriends and had grown quite attached to the latest, Dean Vest. "They were in love with each other," says Don Sullivan. "I seen them holding hands and hugging each other at one time prior to that and she had plans to marry him. [But] Ervil wanted to marry Rena and said that it was a commandment from the Lord that she marry him because he was the only one who could save her."

She became one of his most influential wives because she talked back to him and bossed him around. "She's cool," says one associate. "As long as you treat her right, she'll treat you right. She's a friend if you need a shoulder. I think she was forced into doing what she did . . . she hated Ervil." Her resentment was evident to all, particularly when she sparred in front of Ervil in April of 1975, two months after marrying him, about killing Verlan. He told her Verlan was a false prophet and when the time came, she was to walk up to him and shoot him. By this time, she was accustomed, as Ervil's latest wife, to getting away with giving him more lip than most anyone else in the group.

"I'll play hell doing it," Rena told her husband, refusing to carry out the assignment.

"You will, or you'll get a one way ticket to hell," said Ervil, slightly taken aback. It was a favorite phrase when dealing with balking Lambs of God.

"I will *not* do it."

"Well, then, you can go down like the rest of them."

In March, Ervil took a last crack at the Kingstons and failed. He called a Kingston leader and was told the man wouldn't return for a week, so he hung up, leaving no number. But the next day, he met with Merlin Kingston personally in Salt Lake. Kingston reported that LeBaron was "very congenial and indicated no hostilities" except toward their printer who refused to publish LeBaron-authored literature. They parted on a friendly note, but Ervil had some of his followers drive straight to the Huntington mine. "They were planning a hit but chickened out," said one Utah law enforcement leader. "Kingston's people were on the mountainside with rifles and scopes. The LeBarons wouldn't have stood a chance."

The Lambs of God were slowly changing in character. As eldest son, Arturo was considered the future prophet if Ervil fell. Victor had taken Conway's place in the hierarchy, had started carrying a small blue gun he'd purchased from a convict and even brazenly introduced the elusive LeBaron to his Lincoln Auto boss, ostensibly to discuss the sale of Mexican resort land. But Ervil harangued the man with three hours of religion instead. Victor's wife, Nancy, seemed even more enamored of Ervil than Victor. So when LeBaron was unable in early 1975 to persuade a Pioche, Nevada, ranch owner to allow the Lambs of God the ideally isolated location for military maneuvers and training, it was only natural he would head for Ogden, Victor's stronghold.

Victor's new eminence pushed Lloyd Sullivan into the role of a lackey, temporarily. Lloyd was asked to deliver Ervil's latest pamphlet in April.

Prior to the pamphlet's publication, Siegfried Widmar had been in Salt Lake for several months launching a massive campaign in lectures, billboards, newspapers, radio and television to explain Joel's idea of the political kingdom of God. He had sent a message to Ervil through Victor to arrange a meeting, but LeBaron wouldn't chance it.

So Siegfried urged Verlan to issue a declaration of their still-peaceful intentions toward Ervil, which Verlan did in less than 200 words:

"Having been twice attacked on our lives and properties, the first attack resulting in the murder of our beloved Joel F. LeBaron, the second attack resulting in the murders of Edmundo Aguilar and [Morone] Mendez, and the wounding of thirteen other men and women and the burning and damaging of homes in Los Molinos in the Ejido Zarahemla, Baja California; we the members and officers of the Church of the Firstborn of the Fulness of Times make this offering of peace to the people under the leadership of Ervil M. LeBaron and to himself. We ask them to restrain themselves from any further acts of violence against our people, to respect our God-given rights to life, property and the free exercise of conscience and no more proceed criminally against us in treading down our inalienable civil rights.

"This we do according to the word of the Lord of God of Israel (Doctrine & Covenants 98) and with the world as a witness, following the order and law of God in these matters and to justify our restraint in the eyes of all honorable men in not retaliating against our offenders." It was signed, Verlan M. LeBaron, "Patriarch over the Church."

If Ervil was not exposed before as unjustifiably paranoid, his fervid reaction to this simple statement did so. He called the paper a "spurious publication," "a fraudulent document," "a pernicious plan of attack" which demonstrated "such an overt and premeditated act of war," that Ervil had to answer. He said that, by their statement, "these ruthless and unprincipled men" had made "militant threats." True to form, Ervil entitled his eighteen-page rampage *Response to an Act of War— From the Church of the Lamb of God to It's [sic] Attackers*. The red-and-white cover supposedly symbolized the blood-serious response to such an "act."

Ervil reiterated his Civil Law in the pamphlet, as well as the dire penalties for disobedience. A separate section was devoted to the necessity of paying tithing to Ervil and, true to his obsession, LeBaron spent pages throwing more dirt on his brother Joel, even though Joel had been buried for three years.

LeBaron ordered Lloyd Sullivan to personally deliver the pamphlets to Fundamentalist leaders and instruct them that soon those who disobeyed Ervil's orders would be "destroyed" or "wiped from the face of the earth."

Lloyd hand-wrote threats on the white back page of the pamphlet which were delivered to Salt Lake leaders April 6. The most lengthy and detailed was to "Rulen [sic] C. Allred." Allred was instructed to "Repent & live the Constitution of the Political Kingdom of God lest the sword of the Lord fall upon you. Then how hardly shall you escape the wrath & indignation of an almighty God? The day is at hand. Repent ye therefore or suffer destruction at the hand of God! There shall be left neither root nor branch. Repent immediately!"

One of the Lamb of God threats was dropped off at the private Allred polygamist school: "You are all commanded to repent & commence living the constitution [etc.] or suffer the wrath to shortly follow."

LeBaron had assigned a pamphlet given to Allred's sister Rhea Kunz, sixty-eight, ordering her to follow this constitution or "God shall not suffer you to continue to live—" He handed similar notes to Rhea's sons.

On April 9, Lloyd distributed the same publication, uttering the same kinds of threats verbally, to the people of Colorado City (Short Creek), the closed polygamous community, where he was "detained" by the sheriff. "He told the people who confronted him that they better repent or the judgment of God would fall upon them," said a police report.

* * *

Verlan's mother-in-law Rhea Kunz received a call at 8:30 P.M. on April 19 from a woman who said she wanted to learn about Fundamentalism, and, in Las Vegas, had been given Rhea's name as a contact. Rhea, always anxious to unfold the "fullness of the gospel," including polygamy, to anyone who was interested, explained she'd only talk to the woman if her husband were along. That was her policy.

The caller suggested they meet secretly (polygamy was still underground) near a riding stables at the extreme southern end of Salt Lake County, and her husband would arrive a little late. Rhea asked how she'd recognize the lady, and was given a description. Rhea drove near the stables in the dark when she was overcome by a feeling of foreboding, which she ascribes to a guardian angel's whispers. She never left the car, and drove away immediately.

It would be three years before Rhea learned she had, in fact, been set up to be killed. While staying with Lloyd Sullivan in 1974, Ervil awoke one morning and said he'd had a vision which had come in the night. "He stated he saw Rhea Kunz dead at her funeral and that Verlan LeBaron had shown up and they were able to kill Verlan," Lloyd later related. The long-term plan to knock off the sometimes troublesome Rhea and lure Verlan to the funeral at the same time since he was her son-in-law, finally reached fruition in April 1975. Arturo drove Lloyd to a ditch near the stables, where he was deposited with a nine-shot .22 caliber revolver. While he lay in wait, both Arturo and Lloyd's son Don drove around in circles to provide the getaway after the murder. Lloyd had been told a woman would call Rhea and entice her from her residence to the stables.

After waiting for a time, Lloyd called Arturo in and pointed out numerous cars passing by, some of which he thought could be a trap for the Lambs of God. Lloyd decided to abandon the plan. Arturo called him a coward for backing out of the hit, and would have left but Lloyd threatened to throw Arturo out of the car if he didn't drive Sullivan away right then. The pair departed.

Meanwhile, Ervil was waiting at a Salt Lake residence, where he melodramatically proclaimed to Dan Jordan, "I heard a shot. She is dead."

Jordan was enraged when Lloyd walked in and explained the failure. He called Sullivan a "yellow coward," while Arturo added that Lloyd was a traitor to the Kingdom of God. But in four days, Sullivan would redeem himself in a perfectly executed murder. And six weeks after that, a new Lamb of God enemy would be dead.

11

HOT LEAD AND COLD STEEL

Robert Hunt Simons loved the land. The son of a farmer, Simons had grown up under the clear, crisp skies of central Utah, and the passions of his life were hunting and fishing. Any woman he married would have to get used to this, and Mary Jane Anderson of Salt Lake City did, although she was an attractive and gregarious Mormon girl who felt more comfortable in an urban milieu where she could socialize easily with her friends, dance, or have ready access to the arts.

But as would any good LDS wife, Mary learned to control her own desires and accommodate to Bob's more introverted tastes. Mainly she invested her energy in rearing their five children and taking an active role in church affairs. Though Bob adhered strictly to the Word of Wisdom, he was an inactive Mormon, in part because he dreaded being drawn into social functions at his local ward.

"We led a quiet life," remembers Mary, "and though Bob didn't like to socialize that much, he was the kind of man everyone liked. I don't believe he had an enemy in the world. He was down-to-earth and honest."

In the fifties, they lived in Salt Lake City, which then was still rural enough to suit Bob. In 1958, opportunity dictated that Bob move his family to California, where he took a job for more money as a machinist in a manufacturing plant. But Mary remembers her husband had difficulty from the outset adjusting to the congestion and the quicker pace of life on the West Coast. To bridge the difference, she urged Bob to broaden his spiritual base and show more of an interest in Mormonism. She wanted him to become an Elder.

Bob agreed, somewhat reluctantly, and one day the local bishop tapped him to address his fellow Mormons in the ward—a kind of baptism by fire, as it were. Never having spoken to any group but his own family, Bob was petrified. This was just the kind of experience he'd taken pleasure in avoiding back in Salt Lake when he didn't go to church. But when he stood up to tell the assembled brethren about his testimony of Mormon gospel he acquitted himself honorably. It was not vintage fire-and-brimstone stuff, but Mary recalls that Bob nonetheless made a fine impression.

Two days later, completely without warning, he had a nervous break-down. Growing increasingly violent and muttering repeatedly to him-self, "I'm an old, old man," Bob was admitted to a mental hospital where he spent the next five days chained to a bed. Then he was transferred to a state facility where, over the course of a month, he was given twenty-two shock treatments which left him drained and docile.

He was never the same again. No one seems certain precisely what caused the breakdown, but Mary speculates her pushing him toward religion had a good deal to do with pushing him over the brink as well. Bob became imbued with religion. He started having visions and would often speak to his wife in verse.

The Simonses left California and moved back to Salt Lake City, where for the next ten years Bob drifted in and out of lunacy. A daily 350-miligram dose of the depressant Thorazine somewhat facilitated the business of coping with life, but Bob found it difficult to hold down a job. His orientation was no longer in the here-and-now, but in the spirit world of religion. He continued to have intense visions. Once, Mary recalls, Bob imagined himself an Indian and proceeded to virtually become one. She says his countenance turned beet-red and he began alternately speaking in tongues and a gibberish she thought sounded like an Indian dialect.

It soon became apparent that Bob wasn't merely playing at being an Indian. He confided to Mary that he believed Indians to be the chosen people, and that he was the man who would rise up and lead them in "the latter days," according to Mormon prophecy. He was nothing less than a prophet, Bob later concluded.

Bob sought out and met Indians from various Utah tribes, befriend-ing many and becoming schooled in their religion, culture and ritual. He grew acquainted with venerable old tribal leaders, as well as young turks from the American Indian Movement, including AIM leader Russell Means and several others who would participate in the occupa-tion of Wounded Knee in 1973.

He also immersed himself in Indian history. He staked out mining claims on an island in the Great Salt Lake, where he was convinced there were precious metals, artifacts, and a lost civilization to be found.

His insanity liberated his inhibitions. As he became more and more convinced he was a prophet, Bob tried to give Mary and his children away to other men, for he said they kept him from doing God's work. And he became attracted to polygamy, reasoning that a prophet was entitled to several wives. He told Mary if she didn't agree to let him take another wife, she would be damned.

At this point, Mary—who had loyally stood by her husband for ten years after his nervous breakdown—finally decided she had had enough. A doctor had told her that Bob would never recover from his mental illness and suggested it would be best to divorce him and let him

"Headless Hex Ranch." He went to work for a lime company in nearby Tooele, and continued his involvement with the Indians. In the fall of 1972, at an Indian gathering in the Salt Lake Valley, he met the woman who was to become his second wife. Samantha McKinnan was tall, blond, attractive, and, at fifty-six, ten years Bob's senior. She was immediately attracted by Bob's rugged good looks, and she perceived his evident abnormality not as insanity but as a deep spiritual asset. She quickly came to believe that he was, indeed, a prophet. The couple began living together and were soon excommunicated from the Mormon Church for "unlawful cohabitation."

Bob and "Sam"—as Samantha liked to be called—were married October 10, 1974, in Ely, Nevada. Samantha had two children by a previous marriage—Reid, thirty-three, and Linda, twenty-nine—who were soon captivated by Bob's "spiritual presence." Both left their own marriages and children to come live with Bob and Samantha in Grantsville. Now guru to at least three persons, Bob decided it was high time he became a polygamist. He took Linda as his first plural wife.

One day that same fall, a friend of the Simons family found a flier on the windshield of his car. It was from Ervil LeBaron's Church of the Lamb of God. The flier was of no particular interest to this man, but he thought Bob Simons—obsessed with religion and intrigued by various cults—might be interested.

"I've never heard of that one before," Bob remarked upon glancing over the flier. But he suggested to Samantha that she prepare three pertinent questions that any group claiming to have the truth on its side should be able to answer clearly. Samantha drew up the questions and sent them to the return address noted on the flier—a post office box in Colton, California.

They received no specific answer to their three questions—just a pamphlet spelling out basic Lamb of God doctrine. Bob thumbed through the booklet, concluded with some irritation that "they don't have anything," and put the cult out of his mind.

But two weeks later, Ervil himself suddenly appeared on Robert Simons' doorstep. With him was Dan Jordan—wearing a wig, looking stern, nervous and bodyguardish. Ervil introduced himself as Ellery Steelson and Dan as Al Perry—missionaries for Ervil LeBaron's Church of the Lamb of God. People who had expressed an interest in the church often rated a personal visit from Ervil—especially if he was in the area. Ervil looked at Robert Simons and his land and saw an asset for his group. If he could convert Simons, Ervil hoped to have him either sell his property and give the proceeds to the church, or simply turn over the land itself. An isolated and substantial piece of property, it would make an ideal "military staging area" for Ervil's soldiers as well as a good place to hide out if necessary.

Ervil politely asked for a moment of the Simons' time to discuss the Church of the Lamb of God. Bob—himself now selling his own image as a prophet—was always curious to see another's approach, and so he invited the two men inside. Ervil launched into an animated discussion about "this man LeBaron" being the only true prophet on God's earth. This fact had naturally prompted such pretenders as Mormons, First-borners and other enemies to want to kill LeBaron, but he did not let these constant threats deter him from pursuing the justness of the Lord's cause. Ellery Steelson, as Ervil's number-one missionary, proceeded to explain the prophet's doctrine and basis of authority in some detail. All the while, Bob sat in rapt attention. Samantha wandered in and out of the living room, bringing refreshments, and pausing occasionally to listen. Dan Jordan sat silently, eyes cold and intent, regularly looking over his shoulder toward the window and door, ever alert for unusual noises—real or imagined—that might signal the approach of an enemy.

Finally, after hours of listening to Ervil hold forth, Bob asked the two men to stay for dinner. Ervil quickly accepted. After dinner and more talk, Ervil again cited the great danger he and Dan faced as emissaries for LeBaron. When they were on the road, they didn't deem it safe to stay in motels. Could they stay there overnight? Bob—whose patience by this time was wearing thin—reluctantly agreed, if they would be on their way first thing in the morning. Ervil coiled his long body atop a short sofa, and Dan contented himself with the floor. In the morning they left, having been politely, but decidedly, rebuffed in their efforts to bring Simons into the fold.

But Ervil didn't give up easily. Over the succeeding months until April of 1975, he, posing all the while as Ellery Steelson, returned to Grantsville several times with various members of his troop—including Lloyd Sullivan, Mark, Victor and Thelma Chynoweth. Ervil kept returning despite the fact his sessions with Simons were growing more and more acrimonious, and Bob let him know he was less than welcome. The encounters were bizarre—especially one witnessed by Bob's son, visiting at the ranch, in which his father and Ervil were rolling on the floor talking in tongues, as women cried and wailed watching two would-be prophets trying to outdo each other.

That was the nub of the issue. For if the Lord would not accept two prophets on earth, then two in the immediate area or under the same roof was certainly too much to bear. Ervil, in his magnanimity, might entertain another's delusions that he was a prophet until the errors of his ways were pointed out to him and it was explained that the true

laughing uproariously at the man she still knew as Ellery Steelson.

Steelson said he had come to deliver a revelation from Ervil LeBaron: if Bob would renounce all claims to being a prophet, Ervil was prepared to make him second in command in the Church of the Lamb of God. Bob continued to howl. Ervil quietly steamed.

"Look," said Bob, "if this Ervil LeBaron is so great, and he's claiming he has revelations for me and wants me to be his second in command, why doesn't he come here and deliver the message himself?"

"Well," replied Ervil, "he can't."

"Why can't he?"

"Because he's hiding."

Bob laughed again, contemptuously. "You mean he's doing the work of the Lord and he's afraid to come out in public to deliver me a revelation? That's the most ridiculous thing I've ever heard of, but tell him to keep hiding. I'm not interested."

In December of 1974, after the Los Molinos raid in Baja California, Ervil thought he would take one more shot at impressing the Simons family with his prophetic credentials by playing the role of a clairvoyant. Bob wasn't home when Ervil arrived, but, undaunted, he sat on a piano bench and told Samantha, Reid and Linda that around Christmastime something "astounding" would happen on the Baja peninsula. Ervil was circumspect about what that would be, but he sounded somber and authoritative so they would be able to clearly link the calamity with his prediction.

"We just thought, well, he's probably bragging about an earthquake or something," Samantha would remember.

It soon became apparent that Ervil, still posing as Ellery Steelson, was glad Bob wasn't around. Always on the lookout for new wives, Ervil found the two Simons women attractive. He had one of his underlings subtly inform Linda that Ervil LeBaron would be pleased to make her acquaintance.

When this news was relayed to Bob Simons, he was livid, and quickly concluded what he had suspected for some time: that Ellery Steelson was, in fact, Ervil himself. On December 26, 1974, the date of the Los Molinos raid he still knew nothing about, Bob sat down and wrote the following letter to

> Mr. LeBaron/Mr. Steelson:
> You are now dealing with the man you claim to be. You solicited this relationship . . . I did not. I sent a letter to you asking for some of your literature, but you saw fit to send some of your people as well . . . .
> You and your people, through revelations from the darker regions, have professed, by the mouth of one of your servants, in my home, a desire to remove from me something very precious that God has given unto me—namely Linda, one of my women.
> Consider this letter to be an open challenge to your power and your authority.
> Do with it what you may.
>
> Sincerely,
Robert H. Simons

Affidavits would later speculate that this letter—utterly defiant with no hint of contrition—was what prompted Ervil to decide Bob Simons would have to be killed.

Based on the statements and testimony of witnesses, particularly the Sullivans, police later provided the following account of what happened next:

In the spring of 1975, Ervil called several of his followers together to make plans for Simons' murder. Most of the strategy was conceived at the home of Don Sullivan in Salt Lake City. Other discussions were held at Victor Chynoweth's house some forty miles to the north in Ogden. Present during these meetings, at various times, were: Ervil, Dan Jordan, Lloyd Sullivan and his son Don, Victor, Mark and Duane Chynoweth, Ervil's son Arturo and Eddie Marston.

Ervil announced to the assembled that the Lord had revealed to him that Robert Simons should be removed from this earth, and that they were going to "blow him up like a balloon." He noted that in several visits to Grantsville, Lloyd Sullivan had appeared to get along with Simons. Ervil told Lloyd it would be his job to return to the ranch, establish trust, then lure their unsuspecting victim away to the desert where Eddie Marston and Mark Chynoweth, lying in ambush, would kill him.

After some discussion, it was decided that Simons should be driven to the desert area near Price, Utah—some 150 miles southeast of Grantsville. Lloyd, Eddie and Mark drove to Price and agreed on a spot for the murder. Lloyd would take the main road south of Price for twelve miles until he came to a dirt road marked by an old tire draped around a post. He would drive down the road—used by the local utility to service gas lines—for a little over a mile. There, not far from a piñon pine tree,

Mark and Eddie would erect a rockpile where Lloyd should stop the car.

Ervil instructed Eddie and Mark to leave for Price before dawn on ~~the appointed day so that they would have plenty of time to dig a grave~~

spending much of his free time lately meeting with various Indian groups, Lloyd would explain, and he was now involved in the search for the white prophet who would come forth to lead the Indians to the latter days, as spoken of in Fundamentalist circles.

On April 21, 1975, Samantha Simons was behind her trailer feeding the rabbits when she heard a man's voice around front talking to her German shepherd puppy. She walked to see who it was and recognized Sterling Thomas, the alias Lloyd had used in his previous visits to the ranch with Ervil. Her husband wasn't home, so Samantha told Lloyd to tag along with her as she fed the horses and did her other chores. Samantha motioned for her son Reid to join them. Though Lloyd had impressed her as perhaps the most reasonable of Ervil's group, she still wanted a man nearby when she dealt with any of the Ervilites. The Baja prophecy had come horribly true in the form of Los Molinos, and Samantha knew she wasn't exactly dealing with a pillar of society.

After some small talk, Lloyd moved to the nub of the issue: he told Samantha and Reid he had lost the testimony he once had that Ervil LeBaron was a prophet of God. He had given considerable thought, in the meantime, to Bob's claims and concluded that they had some merit. He wanted to talk again with Bob, but, more importantly, he knew five Indian leaders who were very anxious to find the white prophet mentioned in scriptures and prophecies. He had told the Indians about Bob and promised he would try and set up a meeting. It was important that the meeting be arranged soon because one of the leaders was in his nineties and about to die. If Bob was in fact a prophet, then this chieftain wanted to pass on his authority to him, as well as a sacred book of some sort. Lloyd added that the Indians' impressions of Bob would help clarify his own search for the truth. He had taken a leave from his job in Las Vegas to try to get some answers once and for all, he said. Lloyd was flattering and therefore convincing. Samantha urged him to come back that evening when Bob would be home.

"He returned about 5:15 to see Bob," wrote Samantha in her journal of the period, "and right away, Mr. Thomas seemed to sense the spirit of the Lord in Bob. Even when Bob went under the spirit and spoke in tongues, it didn't throw him, as it nearly always does people, if he lets the spirit show forth."

Bob was delighted to put on a show for anyone who was interested in him, especially one of Ervil's followers. Afterward, as a gesture from a leader to a disciple, Bob presented Lloyd with a rock from one of the mines he had worked in on Stansbury Island in the Great Salt Lake. In appreciation, Lloyd deftly said that the old Indian leader had told him that when he met the true prophet, he would be offered something like this. Lloyd added, indulgently, that the Indians have visions and dreams of a valley surrounded by mountains and a large lake with islands rich in gold and other minerals.

"So he left," Samantha recorded in her journal. "It seemed he felt good, and so did all of us—Bob, Reid and myself."

Lloyd returned the following evening to cement Simons' trust. He had a tape recorder with him, and told Bob he had been making a tape for the Indian leaders in which he described Bob and the land which surrounded him. Bob spoke into the tape, too, at Lloyd's request, and told of the hidden springs beneath his property, and that this was "the land of many waters" spoken of in the scriptures. He then launched into another dance and trance.

Afterward Lloyd told Bob he had been in contact with the Indian religious leader the night before. An Indian woman named Mona had relayed messages to him. Lloyd said he had let it be known that he would "have something for them" in Bob. The Indian leader had wondered how soon Bob could come.

"Right now, if you want!" Bob blurted, gushing with enthusiasm.

"That's what he said you'd say," Lloyd smiled. "But the old Indian told me the day after tomorrow."

They would leave tomorrow night, Lloyd announced, not mentioning in which direction they'd be traveling or to what state. No one asked. The old Indian had assured him all their needs would be taken care of once they arrived, so Bob needn't worry about bringing anything. But Lloyd said he would need $60 for gas.

The arrangements thus made, officials were later told by Sullivan that Eddie Marston and Mark Chynoweth left early the following morning for Price. South of town, they spotted the rubber tire, turned onto the dirt road and drove to the spot where they planned to murder Robert Simons later that night. They stopped the car and set about gathering some medium-sized rocks which they arranged in a pile as the landmark for Lloyd. But for the sound of an occasional car passing in the distance along the main road, everything around them was still, and though it was springtime, there was still an early-morning chill in the air.

They walked fifty to 100 feet from the rockpile and started digging. They were on a high desert plateau, less than ten feet from a cliff which dropped off sharply to a ravine six or seven hundred feet below. It was clear and they could see for miles.

After peeling off six to eight inches of topsoil, Mark and Eddie struck

feet wide, and two and a half feet deep.

Mark and Eddie broke up the drudgery around noon by driving into town to have a few beers and shoot some pool.

The Simons family was anxiously awaiting the arrival of Lloyd Sullivan the evening of April 23, 1975. When Lloyd finally appeared shortly after 6 o'clock, Bob asked him if Samantha could come on the trip with them. Lloyd quickly said no, tactfully explaining that he had received strict instructions from the Indian leaders to come alone with Bob. The would-be prophet gently put his arm around his wife and asked if she was disappointed. She smiled and said she wasn't. She hadn't really thought she'd be asked to come.

The two men climbed into a 1972 copper-colored Lincoln Mercury owned by Victor Chynoweth and drove away. Samantha Simons waved goodbye to her husband—never dreaming this would be the last time she would see him alive. She went inside her house, threw a log on the fire and sat down to write in her journal. Concerning Bob's mission with Lloyd, she wrote: "I feel so good about the whole experience."

It took Lloyd more than three hours to drive the 150 miles to Price. He was in no hurry to get there, and he would later assert that an attack of conscience prompted him to intentionally overshoot the turnoff to the ambush site by several miles, hoping that when he returned, he would be so late that Mark and Eddie would have given up and left. Many thought this story hard to believe, however. One hundred and fifty miles afforded plenty of time for the wheelman in the plot to turn back if he wanted. But Lloyd hadn't turned back. He was well aware of the penalties Ervil imposed on those who failed to carry out an order or a mission for the Church of the Lamb of God.

As the van finally pulled off the lonely highway around 10 P.M. and started down the desolate dirt road, Robert Simons might have been pardoned for wondering how many Indian chiefs he was likely to meet in such an area, at such a time. And for a moment, Lloyd later told police, Bob *was* unsettled enough to remark: "If I didn't know you better, I'd say you might be bringing me out here to kill me." Lloyd had enough presence of mind to laugh off the comment, hoping to put Simons at ease, but he felt a quick sinking feeling in his stomach, and his heart was racing.

Bob's anxiety seemed to pass quickly. Perhaps he allowed himself to conclude that the remoteness of this area conformed with the nature of his mission. After all, the kind of Indians he was going to meet were not likely to be found on Main Street.

Then, Lloyd would remember, Simons began to hallucinate. He started crying out excitedly that he was seeing Indians hiding behind rocks and bushes. And when they finally arrived at the rockpile landmark, Bob was ecstatic: "There's an Indian marker!" he shouted. "They've gotta be around here somewhere."

Lloyd quickly stopped the car, leaving the engine running and the headlights on, as if to illuminate the area and facilitiate the appearance of the Indians. Then he opened the car door and walked over beside a nearby tree to urinate. His hands were shaking with tension. Lloyd looked around and saw neither Mark nor Eddie, nor their car. He wasn't sure if they were still there or not. But if they were, his present location would put him well out of the line of fire.

Bob Simons stepped out of his side of the van and slowly walked around to the front of the vehicle, in the full glare of its headlights. He bent down and scooped up a handful of the desert soil and felt its texture as he looked about him and surveyed the scene.

According to Lloyd, Eddie Marston and Mark Chynoweth crept out from behind the thicket where they had been lying in wait. Weapons drawn, they tiptoed up to within five feet of their target, who, obligingly, was standing with his back to them.

Then, Sullivan would assert, Eddie raised his 12 gauge shotgun and Mark his .357 magnum. Eddie squeezed the trigger. Nothing happened. He realized he still had the safety on, so he quickly lowered the gun and clicked the device off. Mark, who was to stand as backup in case Eddie for some reason failed to deliver the fatal shot with his higher caliber weapon, still kept his gun trained on target, but quickly glanced over at his partner, wondering if he'd chickened out. Then came a deafening crack from Eddie's shotgun, along with a muzzle flash so bright it made the headlights on the van seem like a faint candle. From point-blank range, Marston's shot burst into the back of Simons' head, smashing him to the ground. Mark didn't need to fire. This pretender was dead.

"I thought you never were gonna shoot him!" Mark gasped with relief.

"I had the fuckin' safety on," explained Eddie in a soft, slightly quivering voice.

Lloyd walked over and quietly reached for Simons' left arm. Mark grabbed the right arm and Eddie the feet. Then they carted the body over to the grave which had been so laboriously dug. Eddie stripped

Simons of three things which might identify him—his wallet, a suede-type jacket with fur collar and a watch with a silver waistband—before

heel of his boot, then dropped the watch inside and filled the hole back up with dirt.

The three men then drove back to Price where they stopped at a restaurant, drank coffee and talked of the murder. All things considered, they decided that the hit had gone off swimmingly.

They were scheduled to report directly to Ervil that the mission had been accomplished. So the three proceeded to drive—Eddie and Mark in one car and Lloyd in the Mercury—some 230 miles north to Ogden, arriving at the Chynoweth home about 3 A.M. April 24. Ervil praised them all for a job well done. Also up were Dan Jordan, his wife Elsa, and Mark's wife Lillian.

As Lloyd, Eddie and Mark told of their work, the contents of Simons' wallet were examined by all. This included $4, some letters and a few photos of naked women with heads partially cropped to conceal their identities. Ervil speculated that the women were Samantha and Linda. Lillian and Elsa seemed fascinated by the photos and did a lot of giggling. Then Ervil ordered the burning of both the wallet and the jacket.

12.

LAW OF THE .38

As a prophet of God, Ervil's command alone was considered reason enough for devoted followers to commit murder. A "judgment" might "come down" from Ervil against someone who was a false prophet, or who worshiped a false prophet and failed to heed a call to repent, or who was generally rebellious and disobeyed the word of God (i.e., Ervil) or who was a traitor and decided to defect from the Church of the Lamb of God. Ervil found these lines of reasoning enumerated in the Bible's book of Deuteronomy and he was fond of quoting from it to underscore his own authority.

The beginning of the thirteenth chapter, he would often remind his flock, warns of a false prophet and "dreamer of dreams" who would lead the people to "other gods." The Bible says such a pretender "shall be put to death . . . ." But Ervil's favorite section was the sixth verse of that thirteenth chapter, which read: "If your brother the son of your mother or your son, or your daughter, or the wife of your bosom, or your friend who is like your own should lure you secretly saying let us go serve other gods which you have not known . . . you shall not consent to him or listen to him, neither shall your eyes pity him, neither shall you spare, neither shall you hide him.

"But you shall surely kill him. Your hand shall be first upon him to put him to death. . . ."

A major problem was still the Church of the Firstborn. After Joel's murder in 1972, Ervil had been greatly distressed that the Church of the Firstborn did not simply fall into his hands, a body without a head. Instead the church had continued and, worse yet, another of his brothers, Verlan, had assumed the church presidency. Another brother claiming to be a prophet who would have to be rudely brought to his

senses. Ervil complained about Verlan constantly and often told his
followers that one day Verlan would have to be killed. The Lord would

Dean had grown up in Oregon, near Eugene, the second of four
children and an epileptic. After completing two tours of duty in the
Navy, he and his wife, Emily, moved to San Diego in 1970. His second
Navy stint had taken him to Vietnam where he sustained a shrapnel
wound in the head. He had recovered from the injury, but not from the
effects of the war. It had left him alienated and confused. "He was
trying to find out why he was still alive," remembers Emily. "He didn't
understand why he'd survived and others hadn't."

The couple moved in with Vest's sister, Karen. Dean worked at odd
jobs in construction and drew a disability pension from the Navy. Later
that year he became friendly with Ervil LeBaron, who had just been
excommunicated from the Church of the Firstborn.

Dean was no stranger to the Church of the Firstborn, and had
actually met Ervil years before. Dean's father, Leonard, had become a
convert to the church while the family was living in Arizona. They
moved to Colonia LeBaron, but Leonard was an independent sort and
did not thrive under the colony's rigid social and intellectual regimen. In
addition, the murders of Mauro Guttierez and John Butcherelt unsettled him; and then there were the rumors of church members going into
the mountains and never coming back. Ervil scared him.

So Leonard got out and moved to Alaska. But in 1970, his son Dean
had a Firstborn hangover, of sorts, and came to find Ervil LeBaron's
message appealing—especially in the wake of the Vietnam experience
when he badly needed a sense of purpose. Ervil took Dean under his
wing. He taught him the gospel, ordained him into a top church
quorum, and in time made him the church's "military leader."

Dean was enamored of Ervil and basked in his powerful spiritual
presence. Troubled by a world of gray populated by fence-sitters fond of
hedging their bets on life's most vital issues, Dean admired Ervil for
articulating concepts in black-and-white, absolutist terms. For he
believed there *were* certain universal truths that simply couldn't be
ignored. Perhaps the most fundamental of these truths was the reality of
God and the laws He promulgated through Moses for His children to

live by: the Ten Commandments. It was a sacrilege for artificial entities, like countries, to enact laws separating church and state or otherwise minimize the influence of God on people's daily lives. For God *was*
life.

But if Dean found this message appealing, the self-reliant Emily Vest
found Ervil and his group decidedly unpalatable. She didn't need
anyone or any movement to fill a void in her life. Ervil and his followers
repelled her. She took pains to avoid them whenever possible, but since
Dean was very much involved in the group, she often couldn't. She
rarely talked with Ervil, but sometimes she would get trapped into a
discussion with some of his wives, and these conversations left her
unsettled.

Emily distinctly remembers an encounter with Vonda White in February of 1975. Vonda had an eleven-year-old son named Craig whom
the group deemed "troublesome" because the boy often paid little
attention to his mother's requests and did what he pleased. This kind of
rebellious conduct from a child, or anyone else for that matter, was
considered intolerable in the Church of the Lamb of God.

"If kids in the church don't behave and do what's right," recalls one
teenaged defector from the church, "parents were supposed to whip 'em
or something first. Then if they didn't straighten out, they were to be
killed. These were the last days, and there wasn't time to mess around
anymore."

Emily had heard talk that such drastic action for Craig was imminent. She asked Vonda if she would ever allow her son to be killed.

"If Craig hasn't become a human being by the time he reaches the
age of responsibility, then his fate would be a priesthood matter and I
would abide by whatever was decided," replied Vonda, adding: "If a
person's calling and election was to commit murder, and a direct
message from God came to that person, it would be his or her bounden
duty to do so."

Emily was appalled. She was, and would always remain, an unindoc-
trinated outsider unable to fall in with the cult mentality. This made it
difficult, if not impossible, for her and Dean to remain married, and
indeed after the murder of Joel the two of them had separated for a time
over that, as well as Dean's continued involvement with Ervil. The
killings at Los Molinos were the last straw for Emily. Shortly after the
raid, she left San Diego and moved to Seattle, telling Dean he could
choose between her or the group.

This was not an easy choice for Dean to make since so much of his
identity was now wrapped up in the group. He was the military leader
and Ervil had shown his appreciation of Dean's dedication by quietly
providing him with a second wife. But despite their philosophical differences, Dean was still devoted to Emily and wrote letters to her in Seattle
during this period. He loved her, he said, but needed time to think things
through.

While wrestling with his demons, Dean began spending less and less time with the group and more and more time aboard an old fifty-

had made his decision, and was making preparations to leave San Diego.

He would fix up his barge once and for all and sail it up the Pacific Coast to Seattle, where they would settle. Dean did not broadcast his intentions, since he was well aware that Ervil did not suffer defections lightly. He could not possibly have realized the danger he was in.

One winter night in early 1975 at the home of Victor Chynoweth in Ogden, Ervil motioned Don Sullivan over to a couch in the corner of the room and said he had something to confide to him. Ervil liked Don. The twenty-three-year-old's tall, angular frame, sandy blond hair and choir-boy face all belied his inner toughness. And Don could be trusted with sensitive information, Ervil thought.

They both sat down; the prophet leaned over and quietly said: "I've had a revelation." Don perked up and listened intently. It had been a winter full of murder and talk of murder. From the severity of Ervil's tone of voice, Don guessed another killing was going to be ordered up.

"In this revelation," Ervil continued, "the Lord told me that Dean Vest is going to defect from the church; that he is going to go to the police, if he hasn't already, and reveal the secrets of the Kingdom of God. Those who betray the kingdom must be condemned to death, but the Lord has let it be known to me that to save his soul, Dean should be blood-atoned."

Don knew that blood atonement, in the strict sense of the term, meant that the sinner would have to knowingly cleanse his soul by shedding his own blood. But somehow he didn't see Dean Vest as a likely suicide candidate.

Then Ervil confirmed as much: "The Lord," he said, "has named Vonda White to carry out the blood atonement."

Vonda had just moved up to San Diego from Ensenada and was living with Linda Johnson, another of Ervil's wives. Dean stayed at the house occasionally when he didn't sleep on his boat. Ervil said the Lord had told him to move Vonda back to Mexico, and get Dean to help her in the move. When they finished, Vonda would serve up a hot meal for Dean. As he ate she would approach from behind and shoot him in the back of the head.

Since Ervil had now chosen Vonda to commit the murder and no one else figured in the plans, Don would later tell police he wondered why he had been asked to listen. Ervil was not known for telling people in the group anything they did not need to know. Ervil looked at Don briefly as if waiting for some sort of reaction to his plan. But Don said nothing. One simply did not comment on a revelation. If the Lord was speaking it was a *fait accompli* and remarks from mere mortals were presumptuous.

Though he had already decided, Ervil seemed to want Don's advice on what kind of gun Vonda should use to kill Vest, since Don was a weapons expert. Ervil spread four revolvers out on a table. There was a .45, a .357 magnum, a .25 caliber and a .38 special. Ervil rejected the first two as too big and powerful for a woman to handle. Vest was a big man and the .25 might not pack enough wallop, so Ervil said he thought the .38 was the logical compromise—strong enough, yet small enough for Vonda.

Don knew the .38 Colt revolver with the four-inch barrel well. It was his. He had been carrying the weapon for two years and he had built a new firing pin for it. He assured Ervil that the gun would do the job.

A few months later in Denver, Ervil had a similar conversation with Don's father, Lloyd Sullivan, in which Dean Vest was again condemned to death. Although Dean had once been a valuable member of the church, now there were indications that he was "getting too big for his britches" and contemplating defection. Ervil also noted he had relied on Vest in the past to procure weapons for the group, but now he suspected Dean had absconded with several guns.

Ervil offered no evidence to support any of his charges, and Lloyd thought it was difficult to tell if the prophet's fears were real or imagined. Lloyd did know one thing. Dean Vest was romantically involved with Rena Chynoweth.

Lloyd suspected that Ervil's displeasure with Vest stemmed more from banal jealousy than from any loftier spiritual transgressions.

In any case, Ervil proceeded to tell Lloyd Sullivan, as Sullivan would later testify, that the Lord had decided Dean Vest was a traitor to the Kingdom of God, and as such, he would have to be done away with. Vonda White had been appointed to carry out the blood atonement.*

On May 25, Ervil and Dean's plural wife set out to leave Denver and drive to San Diego via Ogden, where they would spend a few days with

---

*Despite Lloyd's testimony that Vonda murdered Naomi, Zarate's body has never been found and White has not been charged with any crime in connection with Zarate's disappearance.

the Chynoweths. Lloyd Sullivan would remember May 25 well, for it

pen while he was gone, Dan would be in charge. Dan flashed a rare
smile in appreciation.

After completing the circuitous drive to San Diego, Ervil delivered
Don Sullivan's Colt .38 special to Vonda along with specific instructions
on how to carry out the murder of Dean Vest.

Vest awoke on his boat early the morning of June 16, got dressed and
left to do some laundry. On his way back, he stopped at Del Ocheltree's
boatyard, as was his habit, to check on his mail and any telephone
messages. Ocheltree told Vest his wife had called from Seattle and
wanted him to call back right away. Dean did, and learned that Emily
and his daughter had been in an automobile accident. Neither was
seriously injured, but Dean decided he should be with his family anyway. He called the San Diego airport and booked a flight to Seattle for
four o'clock that afternoon.

Around noon, Vest locked and secured his boat, then drove to National City, the suburb south of San Diego where the Lambs of God rented
a four-bedroom house shared by Vonda, Linda Johnson, several of their
children and occasionally, Dean himself. He still kept a lot of his
belongings there. Though this would not be his final trip to Seattle, he
thought he would use the occasion to take back a few trunkloads of
clothes.

Dean arrived to find Vonda at home with six of the children—three
of hers and three of Linda's. They were having lunch. Linda was at
work. Dean told Vonda what had happened to his wife and said he was
flying to Seattle that afternoon. He brought a few trunks into the living
room and began tossing in his belongings. He chatted briefly with some
of the children. Vonda told the children they were getting in the way of
the packing and shooed them all upstairs. Vonda knew that Dean was
planning to move to Seattle in the near future, but she assumed he'd
have to return to the house several times to gather up his things, thus
giving her more than one opportunity to do what she had to do. Now

however, as she watched him pack more and more clothes and other odds and ends, she wondered if he would ever be back at all. She concluded she would have to kill him now.

Vonda asked Dean if he would mind taking a look at the washing machine. It wasn't working properly. Dean had almost finished his packing when he went out in the backyard to try to fix it. He disassembled a few parts, turned the machine over and tinkered with it, but couldn't figure out what was wrong, and he told Vonda so.

Vonda didn't look disappointed. She thanked him for trying and suggested that he might want to clean up a bit before he left for the airport. Dean stepped to the kitchen sink and began washing his hands.

It has become a cliché in murder scenes that the victim never knew what hit him, but chances are that Dean Vest knew what was happening when Vonda sent first one shot and then another slashing into his back. Dean quickly whirled his massive frame around and may very well have caught the eye of his murderer for a moment before he fell to the floor. Hands trembling, Vonda walked over to the fallen man to administer the coup de grace: a third shot behind the left ear.

She wiped the .38 handle clean of fingerprints, then tossed it on the floor near the body. Finally, leaving the water running in the kitchen sink, she walked upstairs and called the National City police.

Vonda told the dispatcher that she and her children were upstairs and they had heard shots fired downstairs. The dispatcher who had eight years' experience, recalls that she had never heard a person reporting a shooting sound so calm and collected. She noted the time: 2:47 P.M.

Officer Gary Pierwola responded to 439 East Eighth Street and found the front door locked. The back door was open. He walked into the kitchen through a laundry service room and saw Vest's body sprawled out on the floor, lying in what were now pools of blood. A gun was near Dean's head. Shaken, Pierwola went out the back door and used his car radio to call for more officers.

Lieutenant Wayne Fowler arrived shortly and took charge of the investigation. Fowler is a short, stocky and amiable man with a reputation as a methodical, thorough investigator. Except for the carnage in the kitchen, the house impressed Fowler as meticulously clean, almost sterile.

Fowler walked gingerly past the body, careful not to smear any of the blood. Vest bled so much, Fowler would later discover that one of the pools had soaked through the kitchen floor and was dripping into the basement below.

The detective ordered a thorough search of the house. He went upstairs and met Vonda White, who had remained on the second floor after calling the police. Fowler immediately noticed that Vonda was very pregnant. She was wearing white sneakers, blue jeans, and a loose-fitting blouse covered by a large smock. Upon close inspection, Fowler noticed what appeared to be bloodstains on her sneakers and the bottoms of her jeans. The smock was wet and turned inside out, as if

as well as a letter to Ervil from Verlan LeBaron written after the Los Molinos raid. The letter called on Ervil to stop the bloodshed and let the Church of the Firstborn live in peace. Vonda cited the letter as evidence of a threat.

But as Fowler later began immersing himself in the mysterious world of cults, religious fanatics and polygamists, he had occasion to talk with Verlan LeBaron and quickly determined the letter was not a threat at all. Verlan explained he had written it because Mormon scriptures said that when you are attacked, you should not retaliate, but simply warn your assailant and appeal for peace. Using such restraint, salvation shall then be yours.

Vonda White was taken to the police station and booked on suspicion of murder. Her clothes were impounded and sent to a lab to be analyzed. If the blood on her sneakers and jeans was the same type as Vest's, Fowler had a case. But the report came back inconclusive. It was human blood, all right, but there wasn't enough of it to type. Asked to account for the blood on her clothing, Vonda rather lamely explained that Dean had had a nosebleed. Some of his blood must have dropped on her when she went to assist him.

Fowler also ordered a test of Vonda's hands to determine if they had fired a gun recently. This test, called neutron activation analysis, isolates barium and antimony—two elements used in the manufacturing of gunpowder. If they are found on the skin or clothing of a person, it can be concluded the person recently used a gun. But no barium or antimony was discovered on the skin or clothing of Vonda White.

Fowler gave Vonda the thousand-watt-bulb treatment during hours of interrogation, but came away with nothing. "I've never interviewed anybody who seemed to have such a complete lack of emotion as Vonda White did," he would recall. "I applied just about every trick known in interrogating to try and evoke some emotion and get closer to the truth . . . but I can honestly say she had no fear whatsoever. She didn't fear going to jail. She didn't fear anything at all. I attribute that to her religious beliefs. She wouldn't tell me anything about the organization. I asked her who her husband was and she flatly refused to say."

This, despite the fact that Fowler pointed to the birth certificates of her children which had Ervil's name on them. She said it was none of his business who the father was. She was always calm. Never angry.

"I came away with the opinion that the followers of Ervil LeBaron would readily die for him," adds Fowler. "They don't fear any other type of authority, because he's the ultimate authority, as far as they're concerned. He's the ladder to heaven. The more honors they do, the closer they'll sit to his side."

Linda Johnson, after getting a call at work from Vonda, had arrived at their National City house shortly after the police did. She was as tight-lipped as Vonda, and Fowler's efforts to elicit information from her were no more successful. Linda was quickly eliminated as a suspect in the killing since detectives placed her at her job when Dean was shot.

Interviews with the children established that they had all been in a bedroom upstairs when the shots rang out downstairs. Some thought the noises were Dean banging on a door in anger. Then they heard Vonda come upstairs about four minutes later. She opened the door and said: "Come on, kids, let's go in Audrey's bedroom. I heard shooting in our house." They all went into another bedroom and Vonda called the police. Police found the children reluctant to talk about the shooting, and especially wary of saying who their father was.

As for the .38 special, Fowler found that he could not link it to Vonda, Ervil or anyone else in the Church of the Lamb of God. A trace of the serial number showed that the weapon had been stolen from a Colt manufacturing plant in the east. There were no suspects in the theft.

Despite a lack of tangible evidence linking Vonda to the murder, Fowler thought there was abundant circumstantial evidence—certainly enough to charge her formally with the crime. But the San Diego District Attorney's Office disagreed, so after a seventy-two-hour holding period, Fowler reluctantly had to let Vonda go. Trying desperately to develop enough evidence to satisfy the DA, he asked her to stay in touch with him for the next few days.

But almost immediately, Vonda packed up and left town altogether. Under the circumstances, Ervil deemed San Diego unsafe for his wife, so he had another of his trusted wives, Anna Mae Marston, pick up Vonda and her children and drive them to Denver.

There, Vonda assumed the alias of Jean Wolfe, and she and her brood moved into one of the group's houses presided over by Lloyd Sullivan. A dozen or so church members lived in the house at various times so the quarters were cramped. But Vonda didn't mind. She had proven herself one of the most important cogs in Ervil's wheel, and she was more than willing to endure inconveniences while doing the work of the Lord.

Vonda's life had taken a curious evolution from a sheltered, innocent

Sullivan. As the number-four man in the organization after Dan Jordan and Victor Chynoweth, Lloyd was considered trustworthy. As Sullivan would later relate, the two were in the kitchen cleaning fish when Vonda casually confided to Lloyd that it had been she who had blood-atoned both Naomi Zarate and Dean Vest. Though Lloyd already knew as much, he gave this confession the attention and respect it deserved. He seemed less interested in the gory details than in how a woman could have summoned up the strength to do such a thing. Vonda gave short shrift to the Naomi affair, saying she'd been nervous, but not nearly so much as right before the time she leveled her gun at Dean Vest.

Vest had been fidgety, she said. He knew others in the group were aware he was planning to defect, and he certainly knew the penalty for defection. But he probably never suspected she would be the one to do him in.

"Were you scared?" asked Lloyd.

"I was scared clear out of my wits," Vonda whispered, telling Lloyd to keep his voice low as children wandered in and out of the kitchen.

"What did you think of the idea of killing Dean? Did it bother you?"

"Well, yes, it did. I never really had anything against Dean."

"Then why did you do it?"

Vonda turned and looked at Lloyd as if he were crazy. "Why did I do it? It was a command of God. I had to do it or suffer the consequences."

Of course, thought Lloyd, what a stupid question. "How did you go about it?"

"Well, I was getting more and more scared all the time," Vonda gushed. "He was packing up all his things, and it looked like he might not have to come back to the house before he moved to Seattle for good. So I thought, it's now or never. But I could just hardly bring myself to do it! My heart was pounding. I must have chickened out a dozen times. Then, finally, I simply made up my mind I had to go ahead with it. So I maneuvered him over to the washbasin in the kitchen. Told him to freshen up before he went on his trip, or something like that. I don't remember exactly. And while he was washing his hands, I came up from behind and shot him three times with a .38." Vonda looked up at Lloyd, flashed her right thumb to the ceiling and wiggled her index finger to describe how she had squeezed the trigger.

Lloyd, ever the technician, said: "That's no way to use a .38. When you pull on the trigger, the gun will kick up and you can miss the target. The thing to do is cock it first, then drop the hammer. You get better control that way. But at close range, I suppose it didn't matter much."

"No, it didn't matter. I hit the target all right," Vonda said, slightly irritated at Lloyd for impugning her abilities and disrupting the flow of her story. She continued to hack away at a catfish. "So, after I killed him, I wiped the gun off, dropped it on the floor, and went upstairs to call the police."

"What did you tell the police?" Lloyd asked. "Did they give you a hard time?"

"Sort of, but I didn't tell them anything. They kept me in jail for three days. They questioned Linda and all the kids too. The only thing that worried me was that I picked up some of Dean's blood on my sneakers. I told them he had had a nosebleed. I don't think they believed me, but apparently they ran some tests on the blood, and there wasn't enough to type it to Dean. I told them I had nothing to do with the killing and was upstairs with the kids when I heard shots downstairs. I said it was probably someone from the CFB [the Church of the First-born]."

Lloyd shook his head in a mixture of admiration and amazement. Vonda had really earned her colors as a foot soldier for the church. Ervil was very pleased with her, too, Lloyd added. The prophet had told him he thought Vonda had displayed great courage in carrying out the two assignments, and she had gone a long way toward securing her calling and election in the Kingdom of God.

A contented half-smile spread across Vonda's face as she finished the final preparations on the fish before placing it in the oven.

"Ervil told me I *was* an elected lady," she said softly.

Besides Vonda's arrest following the blood atonement of Dean Vest, Ervil's soldiers had survived two other brushes with the law after the murder of Robert Simons.

On April 27, just four days after that killing, Eddie Marston and Ervil's son, Arturo, were confronted by Rulon Allred outside Salt Lake City as they passed out literature in front of the Allred group's church. The tract that caught Allred's eye was Ervil's less-than-subtle *A Declaration of War*. Both of them coolly denied to Rulon that they were part of Ervil's group. They were being paid to pass out the literature and didn't know what it said. They added that they were from out of town and were staying at a local motel, but they refused to say which one. Allred's threat to have them arrested and turned over to the Sheriff's Office was met with ridicule. The police were called, but since Eddie and Arturo had broken no law, they weren't arrested.

On June 19, two detectives investigating what was then still being called the disappearance of Robert Simons traveled to the Ogden home of Victor Chynoweth. Several days after her husband drove away with Lloyd Sullivan, Samantha Simons reported to police that a man had fired shots at her while she was on her ranch, then escaped in the same car she had last seen her husband in. This time she had been able to take down the license number, and a check showed the vehicle was registered to Victor Chynoweth. In examining photos of people known to belong to Ervil's group, Samantha had also picked out Lloyd as the "Sterling Thomas" her husband was last seen with.

So the detectives went to Ogden that June day hoping to interview both Lloyd and Victor. They arrived to find neither man present, but they did talk to both Eddie Marston and Mark Chynoweth. Neither man admitted to having seen Lloyd in the last year. They acknowledged being affiliated with LeBaron and passing out literature for him, but Eddie said he hadn't seen Ervil for three months. Mark was a little more helpful on that score, telling the officers he had seen LeBaron two weeks ago at Victor's house in Ogden, and that Ervil had been driving a blue Datsun or Toyota at the time. Asked if they had been down to Los Molinos recently, Eddie and Mark coolly replied they hadn't been there for a year.

Then Victor drove up. The police recalled, ". . . it was very apparent that he had been called by someone inside the house." Victor, not known for his fondness for police officers, demanded angrily to know if the lawmen had a search warrant or a warrant for his arrest. When they admitted that they didn't, he ordered them off his property and refused to answer any questions. Though Victor's behavior aroused their suspicions, the two detectives had little choice but to leave.

As Ogden in particular, and Utah in general, started to get hot, Ervil ordered his troops to pack up and move to Denver, where they would concentrate on making money to finance the Kingdom of God. Ervil thought Denver—the commercial hub of the Intermountain West—would be a good place for the group to melt into anonymity and work on "economics"—as he referred to any financial venture. In addition to religion and politics, economics was the important third link in the kingdom, and its dollars enabled the other two branches to function. The trouble was, there were never enough dollars, so now that they were in a new city, the prophet exhorted his followers to make a concerted effort at generating a steady flow of money.

Lloyd Sullivan had by now convinced Ervil that a good way to do this, given the group's talents and its mobile lifestyle, was to go into the appliance business—repairing, overhauling and selling washers, dryers and refrigerators. Lloyd had been in that business back in Indiana, and he assured Ervil there was money to be made. So Ervil ordered Arturo, Don Sullivan, Eddie Marston, Guillermo Rios and others to learn the trade from Lloyd and generally be at his disposal. Ervil also told Lloyd he would have the use of dozens of children in the group—at little or no expense—to perform repair, delivery, sales and clerical chores. Work for the group would be the children's highest priority, and all other activities—including school—would be placed on a back burner. (Actually, few of the children attended school anyway.)

Lloyd soon established an enterprise called Michael's Appliances. Warehouse space was leased, newspaper ads placed and a fledgling business was born. They bought old washers for as little as $5, overhauled them, shined them up and put them on the "showroom floor" at $50 to $75. Occasionally, people even gave away perfectly good washers. In the beginning, someone had to buy new parts for old washers, but as their inventory grew they could take parts off one washer and fit them to another. Receipt blanks were issued and work guaranteed for

Ervil. . . . One day, I got fed up and told Lloyd I was walking out. He said, 'No, no. Don't do that.' He arranged for me to talk to Ervil. Ervil told me to calm down. Things weren't the way I saw them—communistic. He said I was doing this for the Lord. It seems amazing now, but everyone really believed that then. He ate steak while we ate mush."

The Lambs of God supplemented their meager daily rations by engaging in a practice they called "gardening." This involved going to the rear of their favorite supermarket and burrowing in the trash bin for fresh vegetables. What was waste for others became a staple of the dining room table for them, and they came to count on "gardening" as a necessity.

But across town, Victor Chynoweth did not live so hand-to-mouth. Victor—whose unabashed devotion for the dollar and indifference toward Ervil's gospel was causing some dissension in the group—had been able to persuade his Ogden auto salvage employer to let him open up a branch office in Denver. Owner Peter Lindeman saw executive talent in Victor and deemed the move to Denver a promising venture.

The new business was launched with an investment of $20,000—$10,200 of it Lindeman's and $9,800 Victor's, giving Lindeman a 52 percent controlling share. Victor involved his brothers Mark and Duane in the business by splitting his investment and lending them each $4,900. Technically, this made Mark and Duane 24 percent shareholders, but it was Victor's money, and as the chief executive officer of the Denver office, he ran the show. In the agreement worked out between Victor and Lindeman, profits from the Denver office were to be split between them, plus Victor would be paid $1,500 per month and have the use of a new Lincoln Continental.

Such a display of affluence did not sit well with the far more austere Lambs on the other side of town; but Victor didn't care what they thought. If he was going to belong to this strange church, he would do so in his own way, and he would live the style of life to which he had become accustomed. This attitude might have offended Ervil were it not for the fact that Victor soon began turning over a substantial share of his earnings from Lincoln Auto to the church. Ervil didn't like anyone else in the group rivaling, or surpassing, his own standard of living. But with Victor providing him a large part of his income, Ervil could hardly complain.

On the contrary, the prophet showed his appreciation by naming Victor the number-three man in the church, and bestowing upon him a rather grandiose title: minister of finance.

So the Church of the Lamb of God now had two salvage businesses. Victor did to cars what Lloyd Sullivan et al did to washing machines and other appliances. Though Victor and Lloyd were hardly charter members of the Denver Rotary or Chamber of Commerce, they were doing their best to quietly assimilate the group into a large metropolitan area during a period when maintaining a low profile was the watchword for all concerned. This was all the more important since both operations could easily come under official scrutiny.

Police habitually keep a close watch on auto salvage businesses as likely outlets for stolen cars, while Michael's Appliances had to worry about harboring a number of Mexicans who were illegal aliens, violating child labor laws and illegally keeping children from attending school.

But in the meantime, the work of the Lord was being adequately financed and Ervil was pleased. Victor's boss back in Ogden, Peter Lindeman, was pleased too at his own foresight in spotting Victor as a budding executive talent. Lindeman knew his partner was involved in some weird church, since he had met Ervil once. And Lindeman was also aware that Victor had recently taken a second wife. Though he didn't approve of what Vic was doing with his private life, Lindeman concluded that theirs was a strictly professional relationship, and what Victor did after hours was his own business.

Victor's second wife, Rebecca LeBaron Chynoweth, was not happy. One of nine children born to Ervil and his first wife Delfina, Rebecca had been reared in abject poverty by her Mexican mother. Living in America, being married at age sixteen, and being surrounded for the first time by relative affluence, were all taking their toll on Rebecca and she was finding the transition difficult. Her situation was not helped by the fact that Nancy Chynoweth, Victor's first wife, who was ten years older than Rebecca, treated her more like a visiting babysitter than a sister wife. Though Nancy was committed in principle to polygamy, she did not like Rebecca and jealously guarded her primary relationship with Victor. Rebecca felt like an outsider, rather than a new addition to the family, and she soon came to the conclusion that Vic's only interest in her was sexual.

Materially, Rebecca had to admit she was more than well taken care of. She had never known anything like this before. Vic gave her all the money she needed to go shopping; anything she wanted, within reason,

"Some of us other kids got shipped around to other families in the colony, but my mother raised Becky, and she never had anything. But she was beautiful. She was thin, with long, brown hair, and always seemed happy. When I saw her in Ogden (I hadn't been asked to the wedding) I couldn't believe it. She had put on about fifty pounds, and she seemed miserable.

"I blamed Victor for what happened to her. That man is obsessed with sex, as are so many of the polygamists, I think. Vic's been trying to make me since I was a kid, and his dad, 'Uncle Bud,' proposed to me when I was twelve. A little girl has no defense against an older man trying to take advantage of her. Basically, these are the kind of pressures that Becky faced. She was fourteen when my dad decided that she would marry Vic. I told her, 'Please don't. Why don't you come and live with me for a while?' But the family wouldn't let her.

"When I went to Ogden to visit that spring of 1975, Vic promptly took me and Nancy off water skiing and made Becky stay home and babysit. I was there to see Becky! Vic said she wasn't mature enough to be with the adults."

When they returned from water skiing, Alice quietly took Rebecca aside and urged her to leave Victor. She broached the issue very carefully for Alice was afraid to cross the Chynoweths or anyone else in her father's retinue. "I was very cautious about it. . . . When I got up there, I saw Becky, at age sixteen, was carrying a gun in her purse, and there were guns everywhere throughout the house. I didn't dare ask any questions about why they had an arsenal because I might have aroused their suspicions."

Becky told Alice she didn't want to leave. She wanted to stay and "make it work." The two sisters then went shopping together, and Becky, with Victor's ample supply of cash at her disposal, offered to buy Alice anything she wanted.

Delfina and her three youngest children—Isaac, Pablo and Delia—were still living in Colonia LeBaron. In February of 1976, the group in

Denver heard reports that some residents of the colony were beating up Isaac in an attempt to elicit information from him about the Los Molinos raid. Ervil thereupon deemed it too risky for his wife and children to remain at the colony, so he dispatched Nancy Chynoweth to drive to Mexico and bring them back to Denver. Since Delfina and the children would be more likely to trust their own flesh and blood, Alice was asked to go along.

The drive with Nancy was unpleasant, Alice recalls. Nancy spoke contemptuously of Rebecca, as if she were oblivious of the fact that Alice was the teenager's sister. And incredibly, Alice thought, Nancy laid claim to Rebecca's forthcoming child as her own.

"She said, 'That's my baby. There's no way Becky's gonna get that baby. It's mine.' I don't know why she thought I'd be more sympathetic towards her than I would be towards my own sister. All it made me do was hate Nancy. She also tried to convince me that I should marry Vic, and together we could share him."

When they arrived in Colonia LeBaron, Delfina at first declared that neither she nor her children would go to the United States. Delfina rarely saw Ervil anymore, especially now that he was persona non grata at the colony. It had been a long, difficult and wearisome marriage, and she didn't particularly care if she ever saw him again. But she did want what was best for her children, and Alice was able to convince her mother that there was no future for Isaac, Pablo and Delia in Colonia LeBaron. Delfina finally decided that maybe the U.S. wouldn't be so bad after all. So she and the children packed their things, managed to get across the border without proper papers and drove on to Denver with Alice and Nancy to start a new life.

Alice thought that life in Denver with the Church of the Lamb of God was no life at all. As her mother and siblings moved in with Mark and Lillian, she told them wistfully she would like them all to come back to Utah and live with her. But Mark was quick to nip that idea in the bud. He took Alice aside and said: "You're not gonna cause us any trouble, are you?" Getting the message clearly, she said she was not.

Before she left Denver, the rebellious Alice tried to instill a bit of spunk in her pregnant sister Rebecca. She urged her to leave Victor once and for all. She also urged her to become more self-reliant, get an education and get a job. She even took the liberty of enrolling Rebecca in a beauty school, but Alice recalls that the Chynoweths ". . . didn't like that one bit, and told me to mind my own business."

Alice returned home to Utah, never to see her sister again.

After his soldiers' spate of violence spanning from Christmas of 1974 to June of 1975, Ervil had spent the last six months of the year in relative peace. There had been time to write and time to carry out the will of the Lord. But LeBaron would never let an apparent sense of calm lull him into carelessness or complacency. He was all too well aware that police officers in several states and Mexico were looking for him.

He took care never to stay long in any one place, choosing instead to

was suddenly spotted by a member of the Church of the Firstborn named Jay L. Ray.

Beside himself with excitement, Ray tore into a nearby hotel to alert Siegfried Widmar and Alma Dayer LeBaron III (brother Alma's son, known as Alma D) to what he had just seen. Though Widmar had an advertising business in Chihuahua, he and Alma D. were in town to talk to police about reports that Ervil had been seen in the area. The three men raced out of the hotel, grabbed the first policeman they saw and piled into Widmar's Volkswagen. Weaving in and out of traffic and running red lights, they caught up with Ervil as he turned down a dirt road where his daughter lived. By this time, another Firstborner driving a Datsun had joined the chase and was following behind the Volkswagen.

As Ervil pulled his car to a stop, he suddenly found himself boxed in by both the Datsun and the VW. When he looked out to see that he was surrounded by his adversaries and a policeman, his face turned white. Neither he nor his companion had a gun and there was no hope of escape.

The Chihuahua State Police officer, Ramón Chacon, jumped out of Siegfried's VW, leveled his gun at Ervil and ordered him out of the car. Ervil didn't move. No longer concerned about escape, he was now worried about staying alive. His captors would probably just as soon kill him right here—a victim of Mexican frontier justice—as arrest him, Ervil thought. He could imagine the adrenalin surging through their veins. Their eyes were intent and wild, especially Alma D's. The situation was explosive.

Finally, after a long pause, Chacon stepped forward and yanked open Ervil's car door. Ervil promptly pulled it shut again, telling Chacon in Spanish to summon more police officers. He didn't want to die at the hands of a band of vigilantes. Finally, assured by Chacon he would not be killed, Ervil stepped slowly out of his car. Alma D immediately frisked his uncle and removed the car keys from a pocket. Then, acting authoritatively as if he had just been deputized into the Chihuahua State Police, Alma D proceeded to launch a methodical search of Ervil's car. But Chacon called him off, noting it was illegal.

The officer ordered Ervil into Siegfried's car for the trip to police headquarters. But Ervil hesitated, still wanting more police on the scene before he entrusted himself to the automobile of an archfoe.

"Shoot him in the leg if he doesn't move!" screamed Alma D.

Ervil promptly got into the car, followed by Zarate, who seemed oddly unperturbed by the arrest. Alma D did his best to unsettle him a little.

"What are you gonna tell 'em *this* time?" he hissed.

"Just the truth," replied Zarate, still unruffled.

"Just the truth like last time?"

At the police station, Siegfried told Pasquale Villaverde, a high official in the Chihuahua State Police who was acting chief while the Chief of Police was out of town, that Ervil LeBaron was wanted in Ensenada for murder, assault and the destruction of property in connection with the Los Molinos raid. Villaverde said that to hold Ervil for any length of time, he would need official confirmation from Ensenada that there were charges pending there.

As Siegfried would soon learn, Chihuahua authorities were reluctant to pay for anything that did not involve crimes committed in their state. So Siegfried placed a call to Ensenada to get the confirmation, but he couldn't get through because of problems with the phone system. Villaverde promised he would hold Ervil overnight, but he ordered Siegfried and Alma D to return at six the following morning.

Widmar was worried that Ervil might again summon up the resources to bribe his way out of jail. But if the arrest was widely known, it would make a bribe more difficult to arrange. So Siegfried and Alma D beat a path to Chihuahua's main newspaper and reported the arrest in detail, along with considerable background on Ervil himself.

The paper's account the next day infuriated Villaverde, and he angrily accused Widmar of undermining his authority. But the commandante's temper blew hot and cold. It wasn't long before he jokingly recounted an interview he'd had with Ervil the previous night until 2 A.M. in which Ervil had disgustedly referred to Siegfried as a "Gestapo agent." But Villaverde said that as far as he was concerned Siegfried had proved himself a crack police officer in giving chase to, and arresting, Ervil. Maybe Siegfried would be interested in coming to work for the Chihuahua State Police?

Villaverde said that he needed confirmation Ervil was wanted in Ensenada. He warned Siegfried that unless he received that confirmation by nightfall, he would release Ervil and throw his two captors in jail.

Siegfried wasn't sure if that threat was real or just bluster. But he wasn't going to take any chances, so he spent the next several hours on the telephone. He called Ensenada authorities and urged them to

Chihuahua, the prisoner could not be legally detained for more than seventy-two hours—there were twenty-four hours remaining. In addition, two Baja police officers would have to come to Chihuahua to escort Ervil and Zarate back to Ensenada, but Ensenada authorities let it be known they would not cover this expense. If the Firstborners wanted justice, they would have to pay for it.

Widmar, accepting outstretched palms as a fact of Mexican life, got on the phone and made arrangements for Ossmen Jones, now the head man at Los Molinos, to provide air fare for two Ensenada police officers to fly to Chihuahua. Though Widmar stressed time was of the essence, Jones either misunderstood that part of the message or ignored it. In any case, he put the two Ensenada policemen in his pickup truck and leisurely drove all the way to Chihuahua, arriving three days later on March 6—forty-eight hours after Villaverde's deadline.

Widmar, furious with Jones, had nonetheless been able to persuade Villaverde to extend his deadline and not release Ervil. Siegfried feels Villaverde took this step, while his boss was out of town, at considerable risk to his own job and out of a sense of fairness and decency.

The transfer of prisoners at Chihuahua airport was made on March 6, shortly after Jones arrived with the Ensenada policemen.

Siegfried purchased four one-way tickets for Ervil, Zarate and their two official escorts. He stood out on the tarmac near the plane and photographed the scene as Villaverde officially released custody of his two prisoners to the Ensenada policemen. The four men walked on board, and the plane took off, landing safely in Ensenada a short time later.

As the transfer was going on, Widmar noted two other things, but attached no particular significance to them at the time: Villaverde was being repeatedly paged over the airport public address system, and a small, yellow-and-white, twin-engine Cessna with a Nevada registration was parked nearby . . . its engine running.

The following day, March 7, Villaverde told Siegfried that in their search of Ervil's car, police had found a list of people Ervil had marked for death. Villaverde refused to identify the names on the list, but hinted that he might provide the names to U.S. authorities if he received an official request. As for the airport happenings, Villaverde said when he was paged, one of his aides responded since he was busy with the prisoner transfer. The aide later reported the message was from the pilot of the Cessna, who was willing to pay Villaverde a sizable amount of money if he would simply walk Ervil to the private plane instead of the commercial flight and allow him to escape.

THE SOCIETY OF AMERICAN PATRIOTS

In May, two of Ervil's wives—Anna Mae Marston and Rosemary Barlow—walked into a post office in South Pasadena, California, and rented Box Number 1412. The rental was routine. Two citizens wanted to use the mailbox as headquarters for a newly created organization called The Society of American Patriots. The name was innocuous enough, and at the time, postal officials would have had no reason to suspect anything but the start of another Southern California right-wing group.

But within six months, box 1412 and its renters had aroused the attention of the FBI and become the focus of a nationwide U.S. Secret Service investigation. During that time, the society—or SAP, as it came to be called—harangued against rival polygamists, the press, taxes, welfare and gun control. It maligned Pope Paul, Billy Graham and a high official in Nebraska state government. It threatened to launch an invasion of Mexico and threatened the life of the Democratic nominee for the presidency of the United States—Jimmy Carter.

All this, of course, was vintage Ervil—packaged in eight pamphlets totaling forty-nine typewritten legal-size, single-spaced pages.

Ervil knew that under the ponderous Mexican criminal justice system he could be held in jail up to one year while his trial was being conducted, and that if he were convicted, it might be some additional time before he could arrange to have his conviction "overturned." In the meantime, though he had been forced out of sight, he was determined not to be forced out of people's minds. So he created SAP as his mouthpiece from exile, a vehicle through which the American people might learn of the wisdom contained in the political realm of God's Kingdom.

213

As with other Ervil writings, the SAP tracts were pedantic, outrageously presumptuous, tedious and riddled with redundant rhetoric. Sentences packed with dozens of words and punctuated by several separate clauses were common. But the confusion this caused was deliberate, begun after the murder of Joel in 1972. Onetime follower and typesetter Conway LeBaron said that before writing a pamphlet then, Ervil told him to be obtuse so they could avoid culpability. The deliberate ambiguity of the threats in the SAP publications succeeded in stumping the Secret Service, who couldn't prosecute Ervil for writing the Carter letter. "We know it's a threat," explains one agent, "but because of the way it was written, it'd be hard to prove in court."

SAP sought a world government run by God through his "chosen servant" LeBaron. The basis of this government would be a fusion of church and state grounded in the Ten Commandments—what Ervil referred to as Civil Law or the Law of Liberty—violations of which would be punishable by death. SAP announced that it was the legal arbiter of right and wrong, of proper religion as opposed to "criminal religion," and it called Ervil LeBaron a martyr to the cause of freedom who it alleged was being persecuted as part of a U.S.-Mexican conspiracy to stifle the truth.

SAP's most closely read tract was its nine-page tirade entitled *The Candidacy of Jimmy Carter vs. American Liberty.* In the document Ervil took issue with "the representing of Jimmy Carter by scores of thousands of posters, as well as in the press, as coming in the similitude of Jesus Christ with power to save America. . . . This would exalt him, as president, higher than God and attribute to him, as well as to our government, the status of false gods."

Ervil said that death was a "just punishment" for such an act.

Whether Ervil really had the inclination or the means to carry out a threat on Carter was open to question, but the Secret Service—mindful of the FBI's investigation of LeBaron and the Church of the Firstborn in connection with the Kennedy assassination thirteen years before—took notice.

Said one official who had been investigating Ervil for years: "He's certainly capable of an attack on Jimmy Carter if the opportunity presented itself."

When Carter was elected president in November of 1976, Ervil was still languishing in an Ensenada jail cell, and he decided to write the vice-president, Walter Mondale, in hopes that Mondale would "control" Carter. The letter, which was never sent, said:

"I clearly recognize that you will have problems with Mr. Carter if he is a 'hard-shelled' Baptist as one is led to believe. If Mr. Carter is inclined very strongly to be a Baptist, in preference to being a Christian, or in preference to being an honorable citizen of the United States, the country is in real trouble. This is probably where you can be of the greatest service to your countrymen, as well as to Mr. Carter. . . ."

cover letter which berated him for "willfully engaging in carrying on psychological warfare against one of the foremost champions of liberty of all time [Ervil]. You are charged with criminally disregarding and disobeying [LeBaron's] minimum law."

The letter said Allred would get "one opportunity to willingly submit" to Ervil's law, and it ordered him to distribute the SAP's pamphlets and "hold an open testimony meeting once each month" on basic LeBaron dogma. If Rulon failed to follow these instructions, SAP would "bring further attention to your case, as a matter of due process, through our legal council."

The letter, copies of which were sent to four other Utah polygamist leaders, closed by saying: "We have very *impressive* methods of causing the rights of honorable men to be recognized, respected and upheld."

Despite his protestations, Ervil did not really mind Mexican jail life that much. He was treated well, and had enough means to assure that he would continue to be treated well. He had time to write, and with the help of SAP, he was actually maintaining a higher profile in captivity than when he was free and living underground. He received a steady flow of conjugal visits from his various wives—a practice which provoked chortling and envy from Ervil's guards and fellow prisoners.

Ervil also preached, since prison literally afforded him a captive audience. Many quickly dismissed him as a fanatic and would have nothing to do with him, but some were attracted by his charisma and his simplistic blood-and-thunder approach. One of the latter was Leo Evoniuk, a Californian sentenced to eight years for drug smuggling. Shortly after they met, Ervil sent word back to some of his followers that Leo was infected with the spirit of Satan, and that he [Ervil] was tiring himself out trying to instill the spirit of the Lord into his fellow inmate. But Leo soon came around to Ervil's thinking and the two became frequent companions—reading scriptures and talking for hours—and Leo even began helping Ervil with some of his writings. The prophet also converted Evoniuk to polygamy, and it was not long before he arranged for a thirty-eight-year-old Rios family member to be Leo's second wife. Ervil officiated at the prison wedding.

Ervil confided in another prisoner, Brian Peters, to his detriment. The forty-year-old was in on a weapons possession charge and had a history as an informer. Many of the statements LeBaron made to him eventually found their way into official FBI reports. According to Peters, LeBaron claimed SAP was affiliated with both the Minutemen of America and the terrorist 23rd of September League in Mexico. After a large unidentified arms cache was located in late 1976 outside Los Angeles, Peters was interviewed by the FBI. According to an agent's report: "[Peters] stated that LeBaron advised him that Los Angeles is the main area from which arms are shipped to Mexico, and LeBaron advised [Peters] that the arms cache [later found] in the desert was destined for shipment to Mexico . . . where they would be turned over to Tino and Alfredo Navarez, known 23rd of September terrorists and currently being sought by the Mexican government as such. The 23rd of September League is trading narcotics for weapons in an effort to increase their arsenal and ultimately effect the overthrow of the Mexican government. . . . He finally advised that LeBaron [continued] to work towards the ultimate overthrow of the Mexican government."

Occasionally, while in the Ensenada jail, Ervil would grant an interview to someone outside his Lamb of God family. Two National City, California, detectives investigating the 1975 murder of Dean Vest dropped in to chat with Ervil about his relationship with Vest and Vonda White, but LeBaron coolly refused to provide any substantive answers—this at the same time as he was boasting about killing Vest to Watson, according to the inmate. LeBaron skillfully maneuvered the questions into a safe topic like religion, quoted scripture by chapter and verse, and even began proselytizing a little. The two detectives went away thinking Ervil a formidable, intelligent and fanatical adversary.

A session with San Diego *Tribune* reporter Laurie Becklund made Ervil considerably more nervous, however. By now, he'd become used to dealing with police and officialdom, but he had little or no experience with the press. Becklund, who then did not know nearly as much about LeBaron as she later would, says Ervil was again able to keep virtually their entire discussion on safe religious ground, which did not exactly yield page-one material. He had a commanding physical presence, she thought, but it was something far more mundane that she would remember most: his breath. It reeked of onions and seemed to color everything he said. Though the talk seemed highlighted by halitosis and dogma, Becklund, who now writes for the Los Angeles *Times*, remains the only reporter ever to have gotten an audience with Ervil.

Through visits with his wives and other followers, Ervil kept abreast of the doings of his flock. And of all the pieces of news that he received money—to achieve that end.

Siegfried thought it plausible that Dan would be in Mexico City, lying low and working for some industrial firm. When the two men had been close friends several years before, Siegfried had helped Dan land a job as an engineering consultant to a Mexican-American firm in Chihuahua that manufactured cooling compressors. But after the murder of Joel, Dan had abruptly fled, leaving, Villaverde told Widmar, 300,000 pesos in unpaid debts around Chihuahua. That was reason enough for Villaverde to be interested in Dan's arrest, not to mention the murder charges still pending against him in Ensenada.

Widmar urged Villaverde to take action on Jordan immediately. But Villaverde would not be pushed. He promised he would take care of Dan in due time, but meanwhile the Chihuahua Legal Department needed all the official records on file against Ervil because of his arrest in Chihuahua, and in case any future prosecutions were brought against LeBaron in that state. Villaverde hinted that Ervil could be charged in connection with the hit list found in his car. Would Siegfried mind going to Baja and getting Ervil's records from the courts? Siegfried balked, wondering why Villaverde couldn't handle that chore through official channels, but when the officer assured him he would begin moving on Dan's case in the meantime, Widmar agreed to make the trip.

After spending several days navigating the mysteries of Mexican bureaucracy, Siegfried came away with what purported to be the official file on Ervil LeBaron in the state of Baja California. The file contained records of Ervil's ongoing trial in connection with the Los Molinos raid, but no mention of his arrest in Chihuahua or his subsequent transfer to Ensenada. There was an official request from authorities in Ensenada to authorities in Mexicali—the Baja state capital—for any prior records on Ervil. And Mexicali's reply was also included in the file: no prior records on LeBaron existed.

For Siegfried, this confirmed the Church of the Firstborn assumption that Ervil had bribed his way out of jail and had gotten his records expunged as part of the deal. There was no mention whatsoever of the fact that Ervil had been arrested and tried for the murder of his brother Joel.

Villaverde, upon looking over the skimpy file, agreed it was fraught with "irregularities." He then said that he would arrange for the arrest of Dan Jordan in Mexico City and his transfer back to Chihuahua. He also showed Siegfried a telegram he had written to Ensenada authorities telling them charges were pending against Ervil in Chihuahua. He said this would serve as insurance in case Ervil again managed to walk away from any substantial jail time.

Just as Widmar allowed himself to think his problems were over, Villaverde delivered the kicker: both these investigations would cost Siegfried or his church "lots of money." Villaverde explained that Chihuahua could not pay for expenses incurred outside its own state.

Widmar decided to go to Salt Lake City and the Short Creek polygamist colony in Arizona on a fund-raising mission. He tried to explain to skeptical police, Mormon and Fundamentalist leaders—all of whom he felt had a vested interest in the successful prosecution of Ervil and Dan—that there were now excellent opportunities to put away both men for a long time, but there was a fact of Mexican life that had to be overcome first: *mordida*. Justice south of the border often had to be bought, it was as simple as that. Siegfried told his would-be benefactors he thought it would take about $10,000. But Widmar faced a tough sell. He couldn't guarantee that justice would be had and no one was willing to trust him with that kind of money. He returned emptyhanded.

A few days later, on June 4, 1976, Siegfried and one of his wives met with Villaverde in Deming, New Mexico, where Villaverde revealed how much he would need to arrest Dan and ensure a Chihuahua prosecution for Ervil should he manage to evade the Ensenada charges. On June 8, Siegfried delivered the money to Villaverde in Juarez.

On July 15, Villaverde and Widmar met again in Juarez, and this time the police officer had startling news to report: he had heard that Dan Jordan had been arrested in Mexico City by Chihuahua authorities, but a funny thing happened on the way back to Chihuahua. The transport car had stopped in Durango. Dan was complaining about his handcuffs being too tight when he suddenly pulled out a gun he'd concealed in his boot and shot one of the officers in the leg. Then, when he tried to escape, Jordan was shot six times and killed by another officer.

Two months later, Villaverde came to Colonia LeBaron with a newspaper clipping which documented that Dan was dead. The clipping was a large classified ad from *El Heraldo de Mexico*—a Mexico City daily—which offered a 20,000 peso reward for information on the whereabouts of Dan Jordan. The ad had been placed by Victor Chynoweth, which seemed to prove that the Church of the Lamb of God *was* looking for Dan.

With the misspelled name, the lack of a Chynoweth registered at either of the two hotels, the lack of a gringo-killing at Durango in mid-July and, most importantly, the lack of a body, Widmar was quickly coming to the conclusion that Dan Jordan was still alive. Wouldn't Jordan have paid handsomely, first for his freedom after he was arrested, and second for a false death certificate so that officials of a country where he was wanted for murder would no longer pursue him? Siegfried thought Dan probably wouldn't mind if American officials also thought he was dead.

Siegfried decided to try one last thing. He had Vern Ray, a fellow Church of the Firstborner but also Victor's uncle, inquire if Victor had been in Mexico City any time that summer. Word came back that he had not.

Siegfried now believed Jordan was alive, but as far as Mexican and U.S. officialdom were concerned, he was dead. It would not be long before the FBI pronounced him as such.

And when Ervil heard of all this, he must have smiled a rare smile. For he knew better. Dan was alive, well, and managing the church's appliance business in Denver.

Ervil's Los Molinos trial droned on, as depositions and witnesses trickled in. The prosecution relied heavily on the circumstantial weight of Ervil's 151-page tract, *Contest at Law*—published two months before the Los Molinos raid—which had warned that unless Church of the Firstborn members justified their dogma they would be slain, as were the 450 priests of Baal.

In addition, the state called dozens of witnesses—most of whom had also testified at Ervil's first trial—who reiterated the circumstances leading up to the Joel-Ervil split and spelled out the brothers' differences over how the church's land at Los Molinos was to be used.

There were, however, some new witnesses, including Robert Simons's second wife, Samantha, and her son Reid—wife and son-in-law of one of Ervil's victims. Both testified they had heard LeBaron predict, in the first part of December 1974, that something "astounding" would happen around Christmas in the Baja peninsula, and they should watch the news to see if his prophecy didn't come true.

Appearing in Mexico to testify against Ervil was traumatic for Samantha and Reid. Both were now convinced Ervil had ordered Bob Simons murdered. When Reid took the witness stand he couldn't contain his rage, and according to witnesses suddenly leaped across the courtroom toward Ervil, screaming, demanding to know what he had done with his father-in-law. Police quickly stepped between the two men.

But perhaps the most emotional moment in the trial occurred when eighty-four-year-old Maud LeBaron, the defendant's mother, appeared to testify against the wayward son she had not seen in five years. As Maud was helped into the courtroom her eyes, still keen, fell on Ervil and they looked at each other for a moment.

Maud looked beautiful, many thought. She was wearing a brand new blue, polyester dress which she had bought for the occasion and would never wear again. Her gray, wispy hair was pinned back. Her pale blue eyes were intent, her jaw jutted proudly and her right hand shook constantly but unobtrusively.

The spectacle of Maud softened even the hardened Ervil, and he reached out to hug his wrinkled mother as she went slowly past him. "When I'm rich, I'll make you rich too, Mother," he said incongruously but not without feeling.

Maud's testimony—consisting primarily of a rehash of her many letters to Ervil, together with a maternal view of how her two sons had re-enacted the Cain and Abel story—was largely irrelevant. Her appearance was the thing. And it was that to which Ervil primarily addressed himself in a deposition he prepared for his own defense.

He accused the Church of the Firstborn of mounting a "violent campaign of unfounded defamation" against him, and singled out his three Firstborn brothers—excluding the mentally ill Ben—as "depraved."

"Nevertheless," said Ervil, "the strategy that has most incited the spirit of hate and violence among the followers of the leaders of the apostate sect, has been in large part produced by the deceiving and continuous inciting of my innocent mother of more than eighty years and at the brink of her death due to her heart condition. They have taken advantage of her emotional and intellectual state, leaving her completely defenseless to the agitation and deception of my bitterest enemies, those principal leaders of the opposition sect, my own brothers. . . . As a way of defaming me and taking away my prestige, they have accomplished the shameless task of having my mother give this absurd testimony . . . they converted my aged mother—trusting and innocent—into one of those who most frequently accuse me. . . ."

Ervil also noted that none of the prosecution witnesses had linked him directly to the Los Molinos murders, and though he was charged with

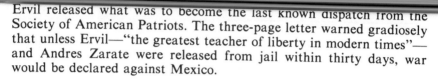

Ervil released what was to become the last known dispatch from the Society of American Patriots. The three-page letter warned grandiosely that unless Ervil—"the greatest teacher of liberty in modern times"—and Andres Zarate were released from jail within thirty days, war would be declared against Mexico.

By early November, Ervil and his follower were free—their charges dismissed by a judge for "lack of evidence." The jurist stressed that there had been no eyewitness testimony to corroborate the state's allegations. Lloyd Sullivan said that during this period the workers at Michael's Appliances back in Denver had "orders to sell anything necessary to get [Ervil] out of jail." Peters, the former cellmate, adds to a presumption of bribery by stating unequivocally that Ervil told him "he laid $50,000 on a judge from Mexico City" to get out of jail. In one FBI report, Peters "advised a woman named Thelma [Chynoweth, who was affiliated with] a new car Ford agency at Littleton, Colorado . . . is the main supplier of money to LeBaron as she brought a lot of money while LeBaron was in jail in Ensenada. This money was used to buy LeBaron's release."

Siegfried Widmar, brother Verlan LeBaron and the rest of the Church of the Firstborn—not to mention interested U.S. observers—were shocked at the news of Ervil's release. Their immediate assumption was that Ervil had managed to buy his freedom.

Ervil, for his part, would not have his victory cheapened by sordid, bitter talk of bribery and influence peddling. And while coincidence was generally this prophet's best friend, he would duly remind his flock that he was released well within the thirty-day deadline set by the Society of American Patriots, and this would reap him considerable mileage and add further to his divine mystique. As Anna Mae Marston waited with open arms, Ervil walked out of jail bathed in glory, a free man once again. And before Siegfried Widmar could get Pasquale Villaverde to honor his promise to arrest LeBaron and try him in Chihuahua, Ervil was gone.

15.

DALLAS

Ervil and Anna Mae repaired to Yuma, Arizona.

There the prophet held court and received some of his wives (Rena, in particular) and other followers.

Two followers summoned to pay their respects were Don and John Sullivan. John, twenty-four, was a distant cousin of Don's from Indiana who had recently joined the Church of the Lamb of God. As part of an economic expansion program ordered by Ervil, both young men had been sent to nearby Phoenix to open an appliance business. Ervil's new goal was to set up a nationwide chain of Lamb of God appliance stores.

Don and John had been called to Yuma because John—a slender, blue-eyed redhead the group called "Red Jack"—had never met Ervil. LeBaron took certain liberties with new converts—going so far as to tell John that the Mexicans had released him from jail because he had warned them that unless they did, their country would be destroyed by a comet.

Despite his claim of being in communion with the heavens, Ervil made a poor initial impression on John Sullivan. John had heard so much about Ervil, he'd expected his first encounter with the prophet to be an uplifting spiritual experience. But Ervil seemed tired, preoccupied with his own thoughts and indifferent to John's presence. He offered a little small talk, but then, after a ten-minute audience, Ervil abruptly waved Don and John out of the room and ordered them back to Phoenix.

"I thought that was pretty low of him to do that to us," John would recall. "But I didn't question it."

John was coming to the realization that there were a lot of things he

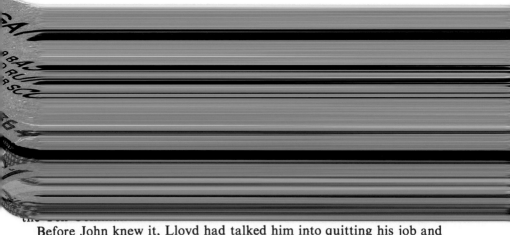

Before John knew it, Lloyd had talked him into quitting his job and turning over the $700 he had in his savings account. Lloyd took the money and promptly left town, not to be seen or heard from until a week later when he returned to Vincennes and told John he had used the $700 to start a church appliance business in New Albany, a southern Indiana community across the Kentucky border from Louisville. John went to New Albany and tried his hand at fixing appliances; he found himself taking home about $300 a week—not exactly twice his previous wage, but a promising beginning nonetheless, he thought.

A short time later, John was told that his services were required in Denver—that summer of 1976. John dutifully joined Dan Jordan, Eddie Marston, Arturo LeBaron, Lloyd and Don Sullivan and the rest of the group at Michael's Appliances. The business in Denver was fairly prosperous, John soon discovered, but little of the profit ever filtered down into his pocket. Arturo regularly collected everything beyond minimal living expenses, explaining that the proceeds were being used to pay Ervil's lawyers in Mexico and to print Society of American Patriots literature.

Lloyd hadn't told John the part about Ervil gobbling up all the profits while the rank and file ate crumbs. Lloyd found that as a recruiter—his official title was chief missionary for the eastern states—it was best to be initially discreet about the inner workings of Ervil's cult. In taking this tack, Lloyd was in step with recruiters for other cults who generally conceal the nature of their group at first, as well as the role the recruit is expected to play in it. More information is dispensed later when the convert's capacity to analyze it has become low, his suggestibility-quotient high and his previous life a fading memory.

The word "cult" was directly applicable to LeBaron's Church of the Lamb of God. Traditional churches may differ in doctrine but are united in their support of prevalent social mores; sects only partly secede from society in an effort to change existing dogma. A cult completely secedes from society in order to practice an esoteric doctrine under the leadership of a charismatic and authoritarian figure. That was the Church of the Lamb of God.

Ervil was a charismatic energumen in the tradition of Charles Manson and, more recently, the Reverend Jim Jones of Guyana fame. All shared a Messianic view of themselves. All had a paranoiac obsession that outside enemies were constantly plotting their destruction, and did their best to maintain this tension in the cult by fostering a "we-versus-they" mentality. They possessed hypnotic personalities, and were adept at seducing and manipulating people. Once their authority was established, they used harsh practices and coercive measures to maintain control in a totalitarian model. In a world filled with gray, complexity and uncertainty, these men offered up black-and-white, simple and absolute solutions.

Rooted as it was in three families—the LeBarons, the Chynoweths and the Sullivans—the Church of the Lamb of God could hardly be called a broad-based movement. But it sustained, if not multiplied itself, through polygamy, generating at least enough dedicated followers to keep Ervil in money and to do his bidding.

Of the estimated two million Americans somehow affiliated with cults, most are white, between the ages of eighteen and twenty-five, and from upper-middle-class backgrounds. While Ervil's hard core were decidedly white and young, most came from impoverished, blue-collar backgrounds and had little or no formal education. Many, in fact, could be characterized as poor white trash—chronic losers drawn to a megalomaniac like LeBaron who could lend some structure and stability to their lives.

Since freedom—the laying out of choices, opportunities and responsibilities—had proved to be too dizzying a prospect to cope with for most of the would-be Lambs of God, they were happy to surrender it to a man who could make their decisions for them and bring order out of chaos. In joining up with Ervil, they sought a return to the comfort and carefree years of childhood. In such an atmosphere, Ervil's totalitarianism—like a father disciplining a child—seemed more palatable.

Historically, periods of social turbulence are often accompanied by the emergence of cults, and some scholars believe that the upheavals of the sixties gave rise to the proliferation of cults in America today. There was rebellion against the war in Vietnam, the U.S. role in the world, economic monopolies, racial injustice and materialism in general. But the people that waged those battles for the most part possessed a reasonably well-developed social consciousness and a leftist political outlook—neither of which would be characteristic of an Ervil LeBaron follower. By inclination, education and temperament the Lambs cared little about what was going on in the world around them; their politics, if they had any, inclined to the extreme right.

Politics, more precisely, was a matter which fell under the Kingdom of God. For Ervil a separation of church and state was not possible. Politics was merely a function of establishing an adequate framework for the administering of the Ten Commandments.

LeBaron shielded his flock from some of the moral dilemmas of the seventies, the erosion of traditional family ties, permissiveness and increased decadence. Besides such protection, as well as relief from the burden of having to fend or think for themselves, most of the Lambs of God took comfort in their communistic, all-for-one, one-for-all life-style—sheltered from the competitive harshness of the outside world and warmed by an extended family system of caring involvement. Ervil was referred to as "Tío"(Spanish for "uncle") with the same adulation that led Jones' flock to call him "Dad." In this atmosphere, people—who, left to their own devices in the outside world, would likely have failed—succeeded. The cult offered an insurance policy against failure, since, even if the group did fail at something, an individual could always blame it on someone else.

Ervil's offspring and other children born into the cult evolved and grew with it. But the Chynoweths, Sullivans and others who converted to the movement had had to totally divorce themselves from their previous lives. Isolation from friends and most other contact with the outside world is the first step in cultic assimilation. Eventually, dependent on LeBaron for decisions, and lacking free association with nongroup members, the Lambs of God became a herd that would unthinkingly follow their leader over the cliff.

One might wonder why John Sullivan—disillusioned with having to turn over all his earnings to an invisible leader and then less than star-struck with the leader himself after finally getting to meet him—did not simply pick up and leave. But rarely is the proposition as simple as that. He had suffered his own personal failures, so broken promises and unfulfilled dreams were nothing new. Then too, he may have been physically prevented from leaving, in a joking way at first to finesse what he later would learn was the penalty for defecting: death.

In addition, joining a cult is usually such a major commitment that the recruit will find it hard to admit that he has made a mistake, and will often go to great lengths to rationalize his decision. The cult exploits this and tries to make the convert feel guilty about his previous life and recognize the need to be born again in his new family.

Step by step—brainwashing, as such, is seldom necessary—the recruit surrenders his conscience and will to the cult leader.

To bind the cult even closer together, the leader creates a siege mentality—an image of an outside enemy or enemies constantly plotting the group's destruction. For Manson it was the Blacks. For Jim Jones, it was the FBI, the CIA and the Ku Klux Klan. For Ervil, it was the Mormons, the Catholic Knights of Columbus and a religiously duped array of law enforcers, from the FBI, Secret Service, immigration and welfare investigators reporting to the Baptist Jimmy Carter, to the Utah Police Department presumably working for the Mormon Church. But, most of all, it was the Church of the Firstborn under Ervil's brother Verlan that was the primary enemy. "These people were constantly warned that the CFB was out to get them, and kidnap them, or kill them, that they had to watch out," an attorney for one of the Lambs of God stated later in court. "The men had to know how to use guns . . . this atmosphere of fear was complicated by confusion." Thus the threat of death, both from without and within, was omnipresent.

The threat from within—death or serious injury to defectors—is usually withheld until the cultist has been in the group for a time, and then fear is often the instrument that keeps him in. Manson and Jones made their policy on defectors perfectly clear. Ex-Scientologists speak of a "2-45 solution" for deserters of that group: getting shot with two .45 caliber slugs. Likewise, LeBaron spoke of his "Law of the .38," "Hot Lead and Cold Steel" and "A One Way Ticket to Hell."

Besides threats, cult leaders share more conventional ways of controlling their followers' lives: spiritual influence and sex. Like Manson and Jones, Ervil was both a prophet and a matchmaker. Followers commonly share the belief that they are valuable only when they're serving the collective good of the cult as defined by the leader.

People on the outside commonly view such cultists as hostages of deranged leaders. But the insiders themselves think it's the outsiders who are imprisoned. That is when the "us-them" mentality comes into clear focus, and the cult grows increasingly paranoid about "them" trying to destroy "us." Prophecies of violence then often become self-fulfilling.

It is not that the cultists are necessarily psychotic—experts say they probably are not. They merely are convinced that what they are doing is right and essential to their own salvation and perhaps even to that of the rest of the world. To increase the importance and urgency of their mission, cultists play at the drama of Apocalypse and "the last days," urging people to come aboard with them as Manson and Jones did, for they will be the ones to usher in the millennium. Ervil had been playing his last days fiddle for so long, some wondered when one of the strings would break.

LeBaron arrived in Denver and basked in the adulation of his flock. They greeted him like a returned conquering hero—a martyr who had served time in jail for the greater good. He told them that he had done considerable writing for the cause while he was locked up, that his trial had been a farce, but that when it came down to the crunch, Mexican officialdom had heeded his warning about an imminent invasion and let him go.

Ervil's presence rekindled the passions of many of the Lambs of God. While they had not been listless during his absence, they had hungered for new directions, new adventures. Ervil gave them what they wanted.

He said that their Denver appliance business (with considerable help from Victor Chynoweth's Lincoln Auto tithing) had generated enough capital to warrant expansion, and he had decided to open a major new operation in Dallas. Dallas was a large and growing metropolitan area, Texas offered a hospitable business climate and, not incidentally, it was closer to Mexico, where Ervil still liked to spend much of his time. He announced that Dan Jordan, still considered the number-two man, would stay in Denver to anchor Michael's Appliances and Victor would continue his business. But most everyone else would go to Dallas and make a concerted effort to get the new enterprise off the ground. This included Mark and Duane Chynoweth, both of whom had been fired by their brother Victor and the auto company's majority stockholder Peter Lindeman. Business was business, Victor felt.

The first envoys were Ervil's son Arturo and wife Rena. Rena later recalled that Arturo "came to me and asked me if I would go to Dallas with him to start [the] business, and he talked with me for about a week before he convinced me that we weren't going to screw up like we did in Denver, because I left the business because of mismanagement—I couldn't stand the way it was run." Sister wife Anna Mae was there before them, and the small group began "Budget Appliance." Rena acted, for a time, as "the salesperson. I kept the books, cleaned the washers, supervised the whole thing." About a week before Christmas 1976, the men came to rent houses for group members to live in and to lease a large warehouse for the business.

Though some thought they were stretching their Denver-generated dollars far too thin, Ervil was in an expansive mood, and he soon decided to launch three more Lamb of God appliance businesses in Indianapolis, Oklahoma City and Jackson, Mississippi. In terms of a commitment of capital and employees, Ervil's idea of launching a new washing machine business was not exactly comparable to, say, Maytag's. He would send one or two people to a city, have them rent a house, put an ad in the local newspaper, and then claim to have opened a new branch. These branches were usually fly-by-night operations that opened fast and closed faster, before the dissatisfied customers could come in waving their worthless guarantees.

The Phoenix venture, for example, had gone under. John Sullivan came to Dallas, while Don was sent to Indianapolis to crank up the church's on again, off again Indiana presence. But by late February of 1977, Indianapolis was written off too and Don was called back to Dallas. Lloyd Sullivan and Arturo were dispatched to work in Jackson, and later that spring, Thelma Chynoweth, her son Duane and his Mexican wife Laura would try Oklahoma City.

Another who was sent off to Mississippi was Delfina. On February 20, in Dallas, Ervil told the woman, who had become his least favorite and most bothersome wife, that she would take their two youngest children and move to Jackson, leaving their older son, Isaac, in Dallas. This was a "military order," Ervil added—gravely, grandiosely and irrelevantly.

He and Delfina operated on totally different wavelengths. She was basically a stout and amiable Mexican peasant who wanted a tradition-al husband who would love her (only her) and their children. Instead, she had wound up with someone she considered a promiscuous megalomaniac with a penchant for murder. She regretted that she had decided to come to the U.S. and live with the Lambs of God. The group knew she wasn't loyal to its cause, and for the past year in Denver and Dallas, she had been watched closely.

But in Jackson, Delfina soon realized that she was being kept a virtual prisoner. Arturo, her own son, watched her constantly. He warned her that she couldn't leave the house, or the group, under any circumstances. The example of Dean Vest was enough to drive the point home.

She called a Mormon bishop in Jackson named Daniel Boone and asked him if he would send some missionaries out to her house. Boone promptly dispatched two young "Elders" who listened, transfixed, as Delfina poured out her tale of woe. The missionaries verified Delfina's identity and other parts of her tale by calling her mother, Luz Salido, in San Diego. Satisfied that her fears were real, they assured Delfina they would help provide her with bus fares for her and her children. But when the two young Saints took the matter up with Bishop Boone, he felt it was too dangerous for them to be seen at Delfina's house by Ervil's followers, and counseled them to renege on their commitment, which the young men did.

Delfina waited for the Mormon response that never arrived.

One of those who had come to Dallas from Denver was Rebecca Chynoweth—Ervil and Delfina's teenage daughter, who had been awarded to Victor as a second wife. She did not want to be in Dallas but Victor wanted nothing to do with her anymore. Becky's relationship with her husband and Nancy Chynoweth had gone from bad to worse since she gave birth to her first child, a son she named Victor, Jr.

It seems Nancy had wanted to name her son Victor, Jr., too, but Vic himself refused to allow it. When Rebecca was in the hospital, however, she somehow managed to have Victor, Jr., put on the birth certificate. Vic and Nancy were enraged, and Nancy apparently proceeded to make good on the statement she had once made to Alice Rose—that Becky's child would be "her baby." For now that Rebecca was in Dallas, her baby was still in Denver with Nancy.

Rebecca's frame of mind had not changed much since she'd last seen her sister Alice in the spring of 1976. Vic and Nancy always seemed to want her out of sight and out of mind, and she was largely ignored in her own house. Usually isolated from the rest of the group, Rebecca grew suspicious and openly questioned some of the group's activities. She was told to mind her own business, and once was locked inside her room for a week. Recalls one former Lamb: "They thought Rebecca was rebellious. She often wouldn't do what she was told. But she seemed normal to me."

Alice called her sister regularly from Utah, but was always told by Victor or Nancy that Rebecca was out running an errand. Alice asked them to have Becky call her back "one of these days," but the calls were never returned.

Rebecca worked briefly at Michael's Appliances, under Lloyd Sullivan's wife Bonnie, but Bonnie complained that Becky was flighty, didn't want to work and whined constantly about the problems she was having with Victor and her baby. One day, in exasperation, Bonnie sent her home, then told Dan Jordan never to assign Rebecca to her again. Dan told Becky not to come back at all.

Rebecca, who by the spring of 1977 was three months pregnant with her second child, did not flourish at the Dallas warehouse either. John Sullivan remembers that she "hollered a lot" and often caused customers to leave. She was becoming an increasing embarrassment to the group, and there were whispers that Ervil's daughter was mentally ill again, that her previous stint in a Denver mental institution had not been long enough. Orders came down that Rebecca should be watched carefully at home, and that under no circumstances should she be allowed to borrow anyone's car. There were fears that she would leave. She was threatening to go to the police and inform on the group unless she could be reunited with her child in Denver.

Finally, according to statements later given police, Ervil LeBaron decided to cut his losses and order yet another murder—that of his own daughter. He was in Lloyd Sullivan's office at the Dallas warehouse when he picked up the phone and told someone on the other end of the line that the deed should be done. Lloyd was present in the office at the time, and heard the order, but didn't question whom Ervil was talking to. The Lambs of God knew their bounds.

At about 8 A.M. the next April morning, Lloyd was in the Perth Street warehouse when he noticed Ervil's pride and joy, a green-over-white LTD, was sagging measurably. "I wonder if Rebecca's in the trunk," Ervil commented idly to Lloyd, who opened the trunk about four inches and was stunned to see Rebecca Chynoweth lying there, blood running from her nose. She was obviously dead.

Later, Ervil called and instructed Lloyd to tell nephew John Sullivan to get a shovel and bring it over to Thelma Chynoweth's house immediately. When John arrived, he also noticed Ervil's sagging Ford, this time parked in the driveway.

Inside the house, John remembers seeing Ervil, Eddie Marston and Duane Chynoweth. He simply told them the shovel was outside in his car, and one of them went outside and put it into the LTD. Then John drove Ervil back to the warehouse.

On the way, Ervil said to John: "If anybody asks, Rebecca ran off to Mexico. . . . Delfina's gonna come back and wonder where Rebecca's at, so if she wants to know, she ran off to Mexico with a lover."

John tried to make idle conversation with the prophet, but they couldn't communicate. "He was just sitting in the car," Sullivan recalls. "He's a scary man. You've got to know him to know what I'm talking about. He was just sitting there thinking. He thinks all the time. Just sits there and concentrates. He was just talkin' to himself, kind of."

Two Lambs of God left town for a few days, and when they returned, they were vague about where they had been. But Don Sullivan would later recall Ervil's fury over the condition of his LTD when it got back from its body burial mission. Sullivan and LeBaron had been talking together when one of the Lambs entered the room "and Ervil chewed him out for using [his] car in that case [when he was supposed to use another one] and said something about . . . having tire tracks or something on the ground and [having to] change the tires because of the tracks that they could probably trace to the car." In a lengthy statement to police later, Don said Ervil also railed about bloodstains in the back seat that had to be cleaned, and the fact that "Oklahoma mud" was "different than Texas mud"—another reason to chuck the tires. The police could analyze soil contents and discover the site of the "military mission." Sullivan received the distinct impression that something had occurred about 200 miles away in Oklahoma, but he didn't know what yet.

LeBaron also ordered that the bloodstained mat in the trunk, where his pregnant daughter had been lying, be burned. He told Lloyd that reminded him of Dean Vest's blood spots found on the sneakers of Vonda White which so easily could have convicted her had there been enough blood to type. "That's inexcusable!" Ervil railed. "It's just stupidity. We can't have any more of it." He traded in the car for another green-over-white LTD shortly thereafter.

The prophet could not have been proud of this particular murder, and therefore information about it, even within the cult itself, was hard to come by.

Whatever the motive, however, particulars of the crime itself soon began to leak out. John Sullivan overheard Eddie Marston saying he'd learned a new rope trick that enabled him to strangle a person "real quick."

And Don Sullivan heard more from two principals within the same week—Ervil and Eddie Marston. Sullivan would recall that the talkative LeBaron was a passenger in a car Don was driving, when Ervil began a conversation with the blunt statement that he had "gotten rid of Rebecca."

"What do you mean you got rid of Rebecca?" Don asked hesitantly.

"Well, we sent her a one-way ticket," LeBaron replied. "She couldn't get along and the Lord ordered to send her a one-way ticket."

"Where did you send her to?"

"Well, we know what a one-way ticket is," Ervil chided his driver. But Sullivan was still incredulous at the implication. He later confessed "astonishment at the idea that he could kill his own daughter." At the time, he pressed as if he were a prosecutor: "Well, what do you mean exactly by a one-way ticket?"

"The Lord ordered her to be blood-atoned, so He had her blood-atoned," LeBaron replied still cryptically. Finally, as if taking pleasure in his oblique comments, Ervil said, matter-of-factly, "Rebecca is no longer with us."

There could be no doubting now that she was dead and, feeling garrulous, LeBaron spun out some of the details. Sullivan would later relate to officials that Ervil's daughter had packed a suitcase because he was sending her down to Mexico for a rehabilitative visit with some relatives. Then he had Eddie Marston and Duane Chynoweth drive her in the direction of the airport. At some point, LeBaron said, Eddie strangled her in the back seat, per command of the Lord.

A few days later, Don heard it straight from the horse's mouth—Eddie himself. The two were friends, and Marston felt an apparent need to unburden himself of his secret.

"He wanted to talk it over with someone," Don later recalled, "so he told me that him and Duane had gone up to the mountains and had carried out a blood atonement on Rebecca. They was ordered by the Lord and he was ordered to carry it out." Eddie told Don that Victor Chynoweth had bought a tent for the burial mission, which they practiced setting up in the warehouse. Later they drove to a site in the mountains where they dug a hole underneath the tent. Some hikers wandered by and saw them, but there were no other incidents and the burial went off without a hitch. Eddie had only one complaint. He said "his arms were [still] sore because he had performed the strangulation on Rebecca."

Three and a half years before, Ervil had made much ado about his "time and time and time and a half " prophecy—that by May 3, 1977, either Mormondom or the Church of the Firstborn would be "totally obliterated." In the interim, his Lambs of God occasionally asked about the prophecy, and Ervil would tell them to be patient. The Lord had not yet consulted him on how the prophecy was to be fulfilled.

Now it was mid-April and the May 3 deadline was only a few weeks away. Sometimes, Ervil must have wondered why he boxed himself in with specific dates, but he had, and now he had to do something about it or risk losing face with some of his more hawkish Lambs. As he surveyed his options, Ervil realized that the four-million-member Mormon Church, with its billions of dollars in assets, was in no imminent danger of total obliteration. The Firstborners were a more realistic target, but how would he go about destroying them?

A Los Molinos-type raid on Colonia LeBaron would likely be ineffective since there was no guarantee that any of the gypsyish Firstborn leaders would be there at any given time. Since Ervil was on record as having threatened their lives, they kept a low profile and rarely perched anywhere for very long. Ervil wanted to kill a key Firstborn leader, and the man he most wanted dead was the new head man: his brother Verlan.

Killing Verlan as a means of destroying the Firstborn Church was questionable strategy since Joel's murder had not resulted in the dissolution of the group. But Ervil could argue that things would be different this time—the beleaguered cult could not reasonably be expected to survive the assassinations of two of its leaders. Verlan's murder would satisfy the rank-and-file Lambs that the May 3 prophecy was being fulfilled, and also give Ervil great personal satisfaction.

How to do the deed when merely finding Verlan was so difficult? The best way, Ervil concluded, would be to create an event that Verlan would be likely to attend, then ambush him. And Ervil had just the event in mind: a funeral for Rulon C. Allred.

LeBaron had been threatening and stalking Allred for years now, but the seventy-one-year-old Fundamentalist leader had steadfastly ignored Ervil and his demands that the Allred group start beating to the Lamb of God drum or suffer the consequences. As the leader of the second-largest polygamist group in the United States, and as heir to the Fundamentalist legacy, Allred had thousands of followers and was something of a polygamist legend in his own time. Ervil reasoned that killing Allred would be a coup that would serve to reassert the LeBaron stature and credibility and create such disarray within the Allred group that many of its followers would decide to turn their loyalties—and their tithing—to the Church of the Lamb of God.

Ervil knew thousands would come to Allred's funeral. Polygamists may not all be united, but, like the Mafia, they generally all turn out for a leader's funeral. Ervil wasn't a betting man, but if he was, he'd bet that Verlan LeBaron would be among those in attendance. He would tell his Lambs of God that the Lord wanted Rulon Allred killed, and that Verlan should die at Allred's funeral—along wth anyone else who got in the way.

After a period of dormancy, Ervil was about to let the world know that he was still around.

On April 20, LeBaron, using his favorite alias—Ray Johnson—flew from Denver to Dallas along with his minister of finance, Victor Chynoweth. They were met at the airport and driven to the home of Thelma Chynoweth where, that night, Ervil convened a meeting of some twenty-five persons, including children—a meeting police would later refer to as "The Dallas Conspiracy."

According to witnesses, those in attendance included: Ervil; Victor, Thelma, Rena, Mark, Lillian, Duane and Laura Chynoweth; Isaac LeBaron; Lloyd, Don and John Sullivan; Eddie Marston; Gamaliel Rios; and Jack Strothman—another of Lloyd's recent Indiana recruits.

The meeting was opened with a prayer, followed by further religious indoctrination. Some of the smaller children in the room were then ordered out as Victor stood and delivered a fifteen-minute lecture to the group on how to deal with police. They should remain calm and collected, he said, and remember that they were under no obligation to answer any officer's questions. In fact, it was better to say nothing at all, and if they were under arrest, they should deal with officials only through a lawyer. Always ask to see a search warrant if a policeman came to one of their houses, and if he didn't have one, he should be ordered off the property immediately.

Some wondered what the purpose of Victor's discourse was. Others with prior "military" experience, however, sensed that a new and dangerous assignment was in the offing.

Though he was in new territory in Dallas, Vic was asserting his authority within the group. Before the session began, he took Don Sullivan aside and warned him to watch his step with Ervil. It seems Don had been badgering the prophet a bit too much about his plans for May 3. "You're out of line," Vic had warned.

After Victor's police lecture, Ervil stood to address his flock. The recollections of four who were in attendance would differ slightly as to precisely what transpired next, but there is agreement on the substance. Ervil announced that the Lord wanted them to undertake an important mission in Utah. He said that on May 3 there would be a funeral at which God had decreed Verlan LeBaron should be killed.

Ervil looked toward Don Sullivan, the man he'd appointed his "military leader" after the murder of Dean Vest. It was taken for granted Sullivan would lead the Utah mission. Ervil asked whom he wanted to take with him. Don thought for a moment, then answered that Eddie Marston and John Sullivan were reliable.

There was someone else the Lord wanted removed from the face of the earth, Ervil continued: Rulon Allred. Allred was a false prophet who had defied repeated warnings to stop holding himself up to idol worship, and to fall in with God's chosen: the Lambs of God. Now, he had to be killed, and Ervil said it had been revealed to him that the murder should be done by the group's two prettiest women.

The prophet opened the floor to nominations. One of the Rios brothers suggested that the prettiest was Lillian Chynoweth, Ervil's own daughter, who stood five-feet-eight and had radiant dark hair that reached far down her back. Lillian smiled self-consciously. Ervil looked over at his daughter proudly, but quickly dismissed her as a possible murderess. She was pregnant, he noted.

Ervil was sensitive to suggestions that he might be saving his own family from combat duty (there were rumblings from some group members that Arturo had not pulled his weight in this regard) so he abruptly stopped soliciting names and announced the two murderesses himself. First would be Rena Chynoweth, a choice Ervil knew would quiet talk that he covered for his loved ones, since everyone knew she was his favorite wife. And accompanying Rena would be Ramona Marston: Eddie's sister, Ervil's stepdaughter and one of Dan Jordan's wives. Ramona, twenty, was an attractive five-foot, five-inch brunette. She had just had a baby and was in Denver.

Ervil felt using women for murder had its advantages, especially in a state like Utah, where the mere suspicion that a woman might kill someone cut against the grain. If Rena and Ramona *were* seen, and clearly identified as women, Ervil guessed that the police investigation might center on Allred's own wives (two who might have been jealous and disgruntled) or, more likely, polygamist Alex Joseph's women all of whom were young and attractive, like the two Lambs of God.

Ervil wound up the public phase of the meeting. Each hit team could meet to discuss details of their assignments later. Before he dismissed his followers, the prophet issued a warning, just for the record: anyone who chose to leave the church after being privy to the conspiracy would "get it right between the eyes." As he spoke those words, Ervil gazed directly at the man in the room he knew least: the newcomer from Indiana, Jack Strothman. He wanted to make certain Strothman realized he hadn't just joined the Junior League.

Strothman, twenty-two, dazzled no one with his intelligence. He was a slender, bespectacled strawberry blond who was easily manipulated. He was an improverished tenth-grade dropout, a dead-ender with no prospects who had been easy pickings for a salesman like Lloyd Sullivan who promised a better way.*

Strothman had been reared an indifferent Catholic, was not religious, and did not seem ripe or receptive to Ervil's fire and brimstone. Actually, he didn't understand it. He had done a stint at Michael's Appliances in Denver toward the end of 1976, but he tired of turning all his money over to Ervil—the elusive prophet he still hadn't met—and went back to Indiana. In February of 1977, he was arrested for drunken driving, and decided to jump bail and rejoin the Lambs of God in Dallas. By the time of the April 20 conspiracy meeting, he recalls that most of the group—with the exception, perhaps, of Ervil, who barely knew him—"started trusting me good, you know. They took my word."

After the meeting broke up, one participant would remember that Don and John Sullivan, Eddie Marston and Mark Chynoweth all went over to the group's warehouse and testfired guns into an old dryer-drum filled with sand. They also began sawing off shotguns, modifying them for quicker, easy handling.

The atmosphere in the warehouse was professional and businesslike, but there was an unmistakable feeling of esprit de corps, as well. Things finally seemed to be moving again. They had direction.

But Ervil promptly broke the momentum he had created. Unaccountably, he left Dallas after the meeting and did not return for several days. The hit team, which had no specific plan or idea when it was leaving for Utah, grew disillusioned and finally exasperated. Then they began to doubt if they could get to Salt Lake City and kill Allred in time for the much prophesied May 3 funeral when Verlan was supposed to be murdered.

*Strothman had been a friend of one of Lloyd's wives.

So on April 29 Don Sullivan and a few others confronted Ervil in Dallas and pleaded with him to make a plan if the May 3 deadline was going to be met. They said they would not go in unprepared.

Ervil—boxed in—thought for a long moment, then looked at them and said: "Want to know a secret? The Lord always gives us a date in advance, to prepare us for the *real* date."

He thus conceded the failure of the prophecy he had made more than three years ago. When May 3 came and went uneventfully, Lloyd Sullivan asked Ervil why nothing had happened.

"I can't question the Lord on these things," LeBaron replied impatiently.

Don was even more skeptical that his father, openly suggesting to several in the group that Ervil was a false prophet. But he found no one who would go that far. Many even defended their leader and blamed themselves for not being righteous enough. Under such circumstances, they said, it was unrealistic to expect the Lord to meet rigid deadlines.

Finally, under duress, Ervil re-established some direction to the plot. He would personally counsel with Rena and Ramona, draw them maps of Allred's office, home and church and discuss disguises, types of guns to use, as well as a modus operandi. The two girls and the three boys would go to Salt Lake City together. Don Sullivan and his two hand-picked accomplices would be responsible for the hit on Verlan at Allred's funeral. Don would check the newspapers to see where the funeral was to be held and devise a plan of attack accordingly. They would all be armed with machine guns and cut down Verlan in a hail of bullets—anyone who stood in the way should be killed too, Ervil instructed.

As insurance, in case Verlan did not show up at the funeral as expected, LeBaron decided to send another hit team to El Paso, the border crossing point for those entering the U.S. on their way from Colonia LeBaron. They would stake out the home of Siegfried Widmar, the Firstborn official Verlan would be most likely to stay with while passing through El Paso. Don Sullivan would notify Dallas if Verlan did not appear in Salt Lake, then the border card would be played. Named to go to El Paso were Mark and Duane Chynoweth and—a change in plans—John Sullivan.

Ervil decided to take John off the funeral mission and replace him with Jack Strothman. John felt he'd been replaced because Ervil didn't think he had the guts to kill. Whatever the reason, Strothman's choice came as a surprise to Don, Eddie Marston and others in the Lamb of God military. Like John Sullivan, Strothman had not yet received his baptism under fire, but, more to the point, he had only been in the group several months, and his loyalties did not yet seem above reproach.

Strothman had gone back to Jackson, Mississippi, where he was helping to run the group's appliance outpost along with Lloyd Sullivan and others. Mark Chynoweth called and told Jack that Ervil wanted

him back in Dallas immediately, and that he should bring his snubnose
.38 revolver with him when he came. Jack told Lloyd about the phone
call, and both speculated he had been tapped to go to Utah. Strothman
felt a surge of importance.

Arriving in Dallas, he was taken directly to an audience with the
prophet.

"Are you ready to join the military service?" Ervil inquired.

"Yeah, I guess I could," said Strothman, less than authoritatively.
"What do I have to do?"

"We'll get in a discussion later about it." LeBaron dismissed his new
recruit to the custody of Don and Eddie.

Jack handed his .38 to Eddie, who had asked for it. Don asked Jack if
he knew why they would choose him for such a mission.

"No," Strothman admitted, "why did you choose me?"

"I'm assigning John to another mission and you're taking his place,"
said Don. "Do you know how to use a gun?"

"Yeah."

"Do you have the guts to use it to kill somebody?"

"Sure I do," promised Jack, sounding like the proverbial underaged
hood begging for acceptance into the neighborhood gang. The three
then began loading guns into the trunk of a Ford El Camino for the trip
to Utah.

Another recent arrival in Dallas from Mississippi was Delfina LeBaron. But this was no liberation, merely a transfer. She was taken to stay
with two of Ervil's other wives, Vonda White and Lorna Chynoweth.
Soon, Ervil came to visit her. Long out of love, the prophet and his first
wife no longer even liked each other, so their conversation was strained
and brief.

"What am I going to do here?" Delfina would later tell authorities
she demanded of her husband.

"Take care of children," replied Ervil, simply. With two of the
group's women going to Utah for a time, more help on the domestic
front was needed. And Nancy Chynoweth, who would figure indirectly
in the Salt Lake plot, was coming to Dallas soon with her children, so
more babysitters were needed.

"You've taken most of my children already," Delfina snapped. "Why
don't you just take the last one and let me go live with my mother?"

"No, you can't. You have to stay here and take care of these
children."

Delfina, at least, was comforted by the presence of her daughter
Lillian in Dallas. Lillian, though Mark's wife and firmly in her father's
camp, nevertheless went out of her way to look after her mother, and she
sympathized with her plight.

It was perfectly obvious to Delfina that the Lambs of God were
preparing for something big. They made no attempt to be discreet in
front of her. She saw Don and Eddie wrap rifles in a blanket and store

them temporarily in the house where she was staying. They talked of "getting ready to go to war," and the women of the group worried that their men might not return safely.

Suddenly, Delfina thought of the Los Molinos raid, and wondered if this time the group was going to attack Colonia LeBaron—where she still had loved ones. She summoned Lillian and asked her about it.

"Don't worry, Mom, they're not going to Colonia LeBaron. They're going to go get some men in Utah. Important men," Lillian said.

Ervil decided that he and Arturo would accompany the two hit teams as far as Evanston, Wyoming—a small community at the southwest tip of the state, ninety miles from Salt Lake. There they would spend the night at a motel and map their final plans. Then, in the morning, Ervil and his driver would head safely south again. The prophet always said he was indispensable to the cause, and as such, could not risk becoming personally involved with any of his own capers. His presence in Evanston—that far along in the plot—would be merely a gesture of support for the troops.

On or about May 5, the principals fanned out from Dallas in different directions. Marston, Strothman and John Sullivan went to the Oklahoma City residence of Duane Chynoweth. Duane gave Sullivan a military-issued arms manual that he kept hidden in a compartment behind a wall mirror. John then drove back to Dallas and gave the manual to Arturo, a gun mechanic, who consulted the book while finishing the conversion of two .30 caliber carbines into fully automatic rifles. Jack and Eddie drove on from Oklahoma, heading directly for the rendezvous point in Wyoming.

Ervil, Rena and Don Sullivan spent the night of May 6 in an Albuquerque, New Mexico, motel on their way north. Don registered under his true name. From there, Don began driving to Evanston by himself, while Ervil and Rena drove to Denver to pick up Ramona Marston.

Apparently worried about his arsenal, Ervil acquired another gun legally while he was in Denver. On May 7, Nancy Chynoweth went shopping for the weapon and stopped at the Shooting Shop, not far from the group's flagship appliance business. Nancy struck up a conversation with the shop's owner, Buzz Ward, and asked about buying a .25 automatic.

"What do you want the gun for?" inquired Ward.

"Self-protection," Nancy said.

In that case, Ward said he would recommend a larger caliber gun. Nancy demurred, saying she wanted something light and easy to handle. Ward said he didn't have anything like that, but he referred her to a few other stores in the area which did.

Nancy left, but about three hours later, she returned to the Shooting Shop and told Ward she had decided on a larger caliber gun after all. She settled on a used Smith & Wesson .38 special, then paid $140 cash for the gun, $10 for some ammunition and filled out a standard federal firearms form—to which she signed her name.

Arturo arrived in Denver to chauffeur his father the final leg of the trip. They set out for Evanston in Ervil's new 1977 Ford LTD, while Rena and Ramona drove separately in Bud Chynoweth's 1970 Mercury station wagon.

Evanston is a Wild West railroad town, its main street lined with bars and motels. Don Sullivan had arrived early, checked into one of the motels—the Dunmar—and then called Dallas to have them tell the others where he was staying. Everyone else drifted in on Sunday, May 8.

Ervil and Don promptly got into a tiff about the accommodations—they weren't to the prophet's liking. He said he thought he'd told Don to rent a house so they could have more privacy. Don said he had checked but couldn't find anything. Besides, he added, it wasn't practical to rent a house for one or two nights. Ervil grumbled but agreed to stay where they were. He, Rena and Don shared one room, while Jack, Eddie, Arturo and Ramona took another room.

Police would later allege that they then all convened to review their assignments one final time. Ervil took the two girls to one side and gave them a physical description of Allred, and drew maps showing the locations of Rulan's office, house and church. The first choice for the hit would be the office—chances were he would be there and the number of witnesses would be minimal. Both Rena and Ramona would wear wigs and heavy makeup to help conceal their identities. The boys would steal a pickup truck for them which they would use to drive to and from the office. Afterward they would dump it nearby, get into their own Mercury station wagon and drive immediately to Denver.

Ervil was confident that his favorite young wife and his stepdaughter would carry out their mission successfully. But Don Sullivan, the military leader, was not. He thought the women would simply chicken out. Don had asked Ervil several times why he insisted on using Rena and Ramona. "Because the Lord said to," LeBaron responded each time.

Ervil turned and chatted with Strothman for a while, wanting him to feel included. He asked how Jack was doing, and how economics in Mississippi were progressing. Finally, Ervil got around to the issue at hand: did the young man know why he was here?

"I got a little idea what I have to do," Strothman replied earnestly—talking like a team player. "I come up here to kill somebody, but I'm looking forward to getting more information from Don."

Don ignored this, indicating Strothman would know all he needed to know when the time came. Strothman was anxious to please, and he hung on Sullivan's every word. Don ordered him to start wiping the guns and ammunition clean of fingerprints. Arturo, meantime, was sitting on a bed drilling serial numbers off the guns.

Ervil had one final comment for Don, Eddie and Jack about the murder of Verlan LeBaron: "The Lord wants this guy more than anything. Find out where Allred's funeral is going to be held, then simply do whatever has to be done. Anybody gets in the way—men, women or children—it doesn't make any difference."

Then the prophet peeled off four $100 bills and handed them to Don for expenses during the mission. More money would be forthcoming if needed, he assured Sullivan.

Before dawn the following morning, Ervil and Arturo got up and began driving south again. The others spent the day in Evanston, then headed for Salt Lake City the morning of May 10 in a three-car caravan. Don, Rena and Ramona rode together in the station wagon while Eddie and Jack each drove an El Camino.

They reached their destination after an uneventful hour and a half and proceeded to drive out to the salt flats west of the city, not far from the Great Salt Lake. There, totally secluded, the two hit teams got out and test fired their weapons to make sure everything was in good working order. Don and Arturo had conducted test firing in Wyoming, but the military leader felt one couldn't be too sure. Eddie Marston was careful to pick up the expended shells afterward.

Then they drove to Murray, the suburb south of Salt Lake where Rulon Allred lived and worked. Don—having lived in the Salt Lake Valley in 1975—was familiar with the area, so he drove Rena and Ramona past Allred's office, so they could size it up.

Nearby was Deseret Industries, a Mormon-owned secondhand store where the five Lambs of God proceeded to go shopping for disguises that the girls would use. They bought white shirts, dark pants, a light-blue parka, wigs and wire frames for glasses. Rena and Ramona would put the shirts and pants on over their regular clothing, then get rid of them after the murder.

Next, the group decided to get something to eat at a Skaggs drugstore. On the way, Rena told Don that the inspection sticker on the station wagon had expired. Did he think they should have the car inspected? Don thought for a moment, then told her to go ahead and have it done. It was stupid to risk being stopped by police on a technicality like an expired sticker. Rena drove to a Phillips station in Murray to have the job done, while her comrades ate. The attendant performing the inspection did not notice a blanket which Rena had carelessly left in the back of the car. It was covering the group's arsenal.

Early that afternoon, the men checked into one motel and the women into another. They had separate missions so they would have separate accommodations. The men chose the Holiday Motel, where Strothman registered under the name of Fred Tompkins. The two women decided on the Lone Pine, with Rena signing in as Patti Sanders.

The men then went out to a Murray shopping mall and stole a Ford pickup truck that Rena and Ramona would use in the murder. They had a Ford ignition switch (with a key to match) so it was simply a matter of finding a Ford pickup, changing the ignitions and driving away.

Leaving the truck at their motel, Don and Eddie decided to go out to a discount store and buy some gloves. On the way, they spotted Rena and Ramona in the station wagon. They each honked their horns, smiled and waved to one another.

After getting the gloves, Don and Eddie decided to check on the women before going back to their motel. Both men poked their heads inside Rena and Ramona's room and asked if everything was okay. They were assured that everything was fine.

A few hours later, around 4:30 P.M., the two hit teams rendezvoused at the men's motel room and discussed last-minute details. Don told Rena and Ramona while they were in Allred's office, he himself would be parked across the street in one of the El Caminos. If anything went wrong, they should run outside and jump in the back of his car since there wouldn't be time to go back and get the truck they were unfamiliar with. If everything went off as planned, they would drive the truck to a Skaggs parking lot a few blocks from Allred's office where Eddie would be waiting with the station wagon that the women would immediately drive to Denver.

Rena and Ramona—wearing wigs, makeup and their newly purchased shirts and pants—climbed into the stolen pickup. The men wished them luck, especially Strothman, who had been ordered to stay behind in the motel room. Don had decided there was no sense involving Jack in murder any more than was necessary.

The girls drove off, easing the pickup smoothly into traffic for the trip to Rulon Allred's office, just a few miles away. Arriving at their destination, they found a place to park in a rear lot which was not particularly crowded. No one seemed to notice them as they stepped out of the truck and walked calmly into the doctor's office to perform God's work.

16.

FLIGHT

"How'd everything go?" Don would later tell police he asked Rena, as the group reconvened in the Skaggs parking lot.

"It went okay," Rena replied, her chalk-white face belying the coolness with which she spoke the words. Ramona appeared even more shaken.

"You got him?"

"Yeah, we got him."

Ramona volunteered that a man in the waiting room had attacked her, and that Rena had had to put her gun to the man's head to get him to stop.

Quickly the two girls slipped out of the pants and shirts they had bought to wear over their regular clothing, and handed them to Don. Then they climbed into their station wagon, waved goodbye and drove off toward Denver.

Leaving the stolen pickup in the parking lot, Don and Eddie drove one of the El Caminos back to the Holiday Motel, stopping along the way to dump a paper bag full of odds and ends into a large trash bin. As they arrived at the door of their motel room, they were laughing.

"Beautiful!" they both said in unison as Strothman inquired how things had gone. "Rena emptied her gun into him, and he said, 'Oh my God,' as he fell," Don reported, as if to give the Lamb who stayed home a play-by-play.

"Did the girls get away okay?" Jack wondered.

"They're long gone by now," Eddie assured him.

All three felt heady with the accomplishments of the moment. They went out to buy hamburgers, french fries and soft drinks, then took them back to their motel room and ate with gusto. A few hours later, they admired their sister Lambs' doings on the nightly television news.

The following day, May 11, Don and Eddie clipped an account of the Allred murder from the Salt Lake *Tribune* to save for Ervil. They dumped a second bag of trash, this time full of incriminating evidence, into a dumpster at a mall and then retreated to Evanston and checked into another motel to await news of where the funeral would be held.

May 12 was a big day for the police.

At 7:10 that morning, two employees of a Murray printing shop, were routinely rummaging through the trash bin located near the shop, looking for aluminum cans that could be turned in for cash at a recycling center.

On top of the trash, both men immediately noticed a tightly stuffed brown Safeway paper bag. Inside were a light-blue parka with a Deseret Industries tag on the sleeve, a gun box for a Smith & Wesson .38 revolver with the cleaning kit still intact and a serial number stamped inside, three live .38 bullets and two expended rounds, four hand-drawn maps, a can of Mace, a can of anesthetic spray, a Jack-in-the-Box advertisement clipped from a Texas newspaper, a crumpled-up package of Marlboro cigarettes and, finally, four aluminum soft drink cans.

Since this was not exactly their everyday find, they decided to call the Salt Lake County Sheriff's Office, which, in turn, summoned the Murray Police Department. Responding was thirty-nine-year-old Sergeant Paul Forbes, head of the thirty-man police force's detective division, and the man who had assumed investigative jurisdiction over the case.

Forbes was a genial, bald, meticulously dressed man who enjoyed a reputation as a good policeman and something of a bon vivant. A "Jack Mormon" (a nonpracticing Mormon), he had been asked to withdraw from Brigham Young University for violating the honor code: he smoked, drank and chased women.

Forbes worked for the Kennecott Copper Company for seven years as a security guard, but in 1966 he took a $300 a month pay cut to join the Murray police.

Forbes was well aware that the Allred case involved murder, polygamy and cultist intrigue and that public and press interest would be high. There were already rumors that in investigating the Allred murder, police might well uncover clues to other unsolved murders linked to polygamy, in general, and Ervil LeBaron, in particular. The case was a detective's dream.

Thus Forbes was elated at the dumpster find. He immediately suspected that the light-blue parka might be the same one described by witnesses in Allred's office. The hand-drawn maps were of areas where the doctor worked and held prayer meetings. And the .38 gun box with a serial number inside looked like an investigative jackpot. They had found two .38 shells at the scene of the crime. He called his brother,

Dick, and asked him to have the serial number traced through BATF (the Bureau of Alcohol, Tobacco and Firearms).

Dick Forbes was an investigator for the Salt Lake County Attorney's office, who had recently returned from a three-month training stint with BATF in Washington. He had established contacts at the agency which enabled him to get a gun traced within a matter of hours, where otherwise it might take more than a week.

Both Forbes brothers were natives of Salt Lake. Dick had for a time been a deputy sheriff for Los Angeles County, but had decided that he wanted his five children to grow up in Utah. He was a Mormon and he considered the pro-family sheltered atmosphere of the Salt Lake Valley a "better environment" to rear children than a den of iniquity like Los Angeles.

So he moved back to Zion in 1971, became active in his suburb's community affairs and soon went to work for the Salt Lake County Attorney's Office (the equivalent of a district attorney's office) as an investigator. Forbes was tireless, relentless and thorough, with a fanatic's eye for detail. Nothing was too insignificant to be noted and filed away for possible use later.

The execution of Gary Gilmore notwithstanding, Dick Forbes felt that Rulon Allred's murder would probably be the biggest case Utah had ever seen. Though it was the city of Murray's case, Dick Forbes' peg for involvement, technically, was that he was the investigative assistant to the man who would prosecute the case, David Yocom. But jurisdictional disputes could be finessed by fraternal ties, and within four months, Dick would have left his unmistakable personal stamp on the Allred investigation, and on a larger scale, the investigation into Ervil LeBaron's murderous history. For it would take the Allred case to drive a wedge into the other murders and put an official focus on LeBaron for the first time. And it would be Dick Forbes who would emerge as the pivotal figure in a multistate investigation and an international effort to track down Ervil and his accomplices.

By the afternoon of May 12, Forbes had gotten an answer from BATF. The original owner of the .38 revolver in question was a Denver man, who had bought the gun January 14, 1976.

Police would later learn of something else that happened on May 12: Ervil and Arturo crossed into Mexico from Arizona, driving LeBaron's 1977 Ford LTD.

It soon became apparent that Ervil was not merely taking refuge in Mexico, but that he had a mission as well. Wanting to strike while the iron was still hot, Ervil and a bodyguard appeared at an Allred polygamous colony in the village of Ozumba—at the base of a volcano some thirty miles southeast of Mexico City—and announced to its 250 inhabitants that they must now either follow LeBaron or be destroyed.

The people of Ozumba were still in shock from having heard that

Allred had been murdered by Ervil LeBaron's followers. Over the years, Allred had visited the colony frequently to preside over conferences and help administer his church's programs. He was loved and respected, and the colonists were still mourning his passing when LeBaron appeared. It was a bit like Lee Harvey Oswald stalking Hyannis Port.

Ervil knew Ozumba well. It was the home of Margarito Bautista, the late Fundamentalist leader who had been affiliated with Allred and who had once been revered as a prophet by the LeBaron brothers. In fact, Ervil was well acquainted with the entire area south of Mexico City. He had served his Mormon mission there and had widespread contacts through the region. He felt he could make an appearance at Ozumba with impunity.

Under the circumstances, LeBaron's mere presence at Allred's colony was an outrage to the local residents. But they were also afraid of him. Ervil spoke with a pistol displayed in his waistband and his bodyguard was probably armed as well. So the people of Ozumba suffered his sermon in silence.

Several of those present later told Utah freelance writer Frank Matheson what Ervil and his bodyguard, Aurelio Rios, said. They recalled that LeBaron made such statements to the assembled as "you must accept this doctrine or die" and "the kingdom of God must exist by force." Rios thundered that they must follow Ervil "*si no por lo bueno, por lo malo*" (if not for the good, then for the bad). He added: "*Ustedes tienen que aceptarlo por su voluntad o por blazos*" (you must accept this voluntarily or by bullets). Rios also said that the Mosaic law—an eye for an eye—had been restored through LeBaron.

On May 13, Paul Forbes dispatched two Murray detectives to Denver with orders to find the original owner of the .38, an electrician, from Denver. The man admitted he had purchased it, but he said he had sold it a few months before to the Shooting Shop, which in turn told the detective they had sold the gun to a Nancy Chynoweth six days previously.

Back in Salt Lake City, the name Chynoweth was well known in police intelligence circles. Here was the definitive lead in the Allred case which pointed officials toward Ervil.

As far as the Church of the Firstborn was concerned, there was no doubt who had killed Rulon Allred. The leaders of the church hoped that the sheer luridness of the murder would bring enough national attention to prompt the first comprehensive official investigation into Ervil's doings over the past five years.

As LeBaron had predicted, brother Verlan did come to Salt Lake for the Allred funeral, scheduled for Saturday, May 14, in the auditorium of a suburban high school. On the 13th, Verlan and Siegfried Widmar met with police and began filling them in on the complex evolution of Ervil Morrell LeBaron.

* * *

Don Sullivan, Eddie Marston and Jack Strothman left Evanston, Wyoming, early the morning of May 14 and arrived in Salt Lake in plenty of time for the early-afternoon funeral.

They stole two pickup trucks and took them to the parking lot of a Mormon chapel just west of the high school auditorium where the funeral was to be held. When the time came, they would take one of the pickups on their mission, then drive back to the chapel lot and make their escape in the two El Caminos they had parked there. The second truck was to be used if the attempted murder was botched and they decided to try again.

The men were nervous. Ervil had told them that Verlan's death had been ordered directly by God, and they knew the penalty if they failed to carry out God's will: Ervil might order each of *them* killed. Yet the chances of success in this mission seemed almost nil. The funeral was likely to be crawling with police. They would have to go inside with guns drawn, find Verlan, shoot him, run out again and escape. It was doubtful they could get a clean shot at Verlan without having to kill several other people first. This would obviously alert police, who would then begin shooting it out with them. They probably would not be able to escape. They would have to spray their automatic rifles at random and scores would be killed.

People began filing into the funeral early. When the service began there were some 2,600 people present. Nine police patrol cars were in evidence and undercover men were sprinkled throughout the crowd, alert to the possibility of more polygamous assassinations. Dick Forbes manned a post outside recording the license numbers of every car in the high school parking lot and any other car he saw that looked suspicious. TV camera crews milled about filming the arriving mourners and other funeral doings.

The three men piled into the cab of their pickup truck and slowly began driving to the high school from the chapel where they had parked their cars. They carried with them two .30 caliber fully automatic rifles and one .45 semiautomatic pistol. They also had some 600 rounds of ammunition. Two 30-round "banana" clips were taped together and loaded into each rifle, and each man carried several more clips in his pocket. As they approached the site, they pulled stocking masks over their faces.

They cruised by and surveyed the scene: lots of people, police, and TV crews who might actually film a murder. Don Sullivan didn't like their odds of success. It was a suicide mission, he thought.

"Well, what do you guys think?" Don asked quickly.

"Whatever you say," replied Eddie, bowing to the will of his military leader and speaking for Strothman as well. "You go in there and we'll go with you."

"I wouldn't expect you to follow me in there. No way. This is stupid. We're not gonna do nothin'."

No one argued. No one wanted to die. They drove the pickup back to the church parking lot and left it near the other stolen truck. Don and Eddie got into one of the El Caminos, Strothman into the other and they drove off toward Texas—their mission a failure.

Back inside the Bingham High School Auditorium, mourners listened sadly but attentively to the Allred funeral service, oblivious of the carnage that had just been avoided. The naturopath's brother Owen presided over the ninety-minute service, which saw thirty-six of Rulon's children sing tributes to their father—first the sons and then the daughters.

"Do not seek vengeance on those who did this horrible deed," Owen urged the assembled. "Those who killed him gained no more than those who killed Joseph Smith. . . . Rulon was called to represent Jesus Christ among the children of men."

Perhaps in deference to the policemen and reporters in the audience, there was no reference to polygamy throughout the service, except in the opening prayer, when Clarence Allred—another brother—asked God to bless Rulon's "wives and children."

Still another brother—Marvin—eulogized Rulon as a "man of peace . . . who spent a lifetime of devotion and love. His life was taken by disciples of the devil."

And Louis Allred, a son, said his father was "wealthy in love—not in money." Some in the audience who were familiar with the net worth of the Allred empire might have doubted that latter assessment, but this wasn't an appropriate time to question such things.

Not knowing whether or not Verlan had actually appeared at the funeral, Don and Eddie drove directly to El Paso where they joined Mark and Duane Chynoweth and John Sullivan in a stakeout of Siegfried Widmar's home.

Duane and John arrived in El Paso by way of Amarillo, Texas, where they had met Rena and Nancy Chynoweth in a Holiday Inn parking lot. Rena began talking to Duane near a truck, and John listened in. He later testified: "Rena was telling how it went in Salt Lake, and she showed Duane a calculator that she'd got . . . she said that her and Ramona went in, and she shot Allred . . . and on the way out, some man grabbed Ramona, so she came back in and pointed a gun at him. And he let her go, and at the time during the struggle, Ramona dropped her purse. And she scooped everything up and grabbed the calculator at that time."

The foursome split up, Rena headed for Dallas where she ran into Jack Strothman, back from his unsuccessful funeral mission. Rena asked Jack how things had gone and, in a hangdog shameful manner, he explained it had been too crowded and risky and Don called off the operation. Rena chose not to rub salt in his wounds, and asked about publicity surrounding the Allred murder. Jack told her it was all over the papers and on television. Rena laughed with satisfaction.

He didn't have to ask her for particulars, Strothman would testify. She told him about it willingly and proudly. She herself had killed the doctor, she said. Allred had looked up, saw she had a gun and said, "Oh, my God!" Then she just fired her gun at him until it was empty, and he fell to the ground. Rena also told him about the struggle with Bunker and the gun that was put to his head.

In El Paso, Mark and Duane were not as tolerant with Don Sullivan—the man responsible for the mission—as Rena had been with Strothman. "You blew it!" they told him contemptuously. Don was not known for accepting criticism graciously. He began railing at Ervil, saying the funeral plan had been stupid, ill-conceived and therefore not the Lord's plan. Ervil was a hoax and a false prophet. In addition, Don fumed, LeBaron had promised to provide him with additional money after the Allred murder, but he never came through with anything. Now they were virtually broke. Don demanded to know where Ervil was and said he wanted to confront him with these charges personally.

Mark and Duane ignored Don's ravings and told him simply that they were in El Paso with orders to kill Verlan if he showed up at Siegfried Widmar's house. But after another day of fruitless stakeouts, the Chynoweths gave up and went back to Dallas.

Don, Eddie and John stayed where they were—Don not wanting to be accused of giving up too soon. At this point, John Sullivan also began to complain about Ervil. John had provided Jack Strothman with his El Camino for the trip to Utah, and he was angry to learn that Jack had driven the car back to Mississippi. He got angrier still when Eddie told him that Ervil would soon expect John to sell the car and give the proceeds to the church, or to Ervil himself.

Finally, after two more days of waiting around with no sign of Verlan, Don led his unsuccessful hit team back to Dallas. At the warehouse Don immediately noticed that he was not exactly receiving a hero's welcome. There were prolonged stares and disapproving frowns—unspoken indictments of his performance as military leader in Utah. Don encountered Rena, and was probably pleased to discover a flaw in her murder mission so that her success did not contrast so glaringly with his own failure.

When she told him about the small calculator she had picked up, Don proceeded to thoroughly chew Rena out, reminding her that if any policeman found the calculator on her she could immediately be linked to the murder. He asked her to give it to him, whereupon he took it and crushed it beneath the heel of his boot.

But this small show of authority did not put Don back in the good graces of the Lamb of God hierarchy. Through the polygamous grapevine, Dan Jordan soon learned that Verlan LeBaron had, in fact, attended the Allred funeral. In a Denver-to-Dallas phone call, Dan angrily told Eddie Marston that Don had failed in his mission. He had violated orders by not going through with the plan.

After that conversation, Eddie—always the blind follower—cooled noticeably in his attitude toward Don, even though he had agreed with the decision to abort the mission. Marston told Sullivan of his conversation with Jordan, then gave Don a warning: though they were friends, he would not hesitate to kill him if ordered to.

The military leader knew that Ervil would soon hear—if he hadn't already—that the funeral mission had failed. He would also hear of Don's comments in El Paso accusing him of being a false prophet. And the Marston threat—stemming no doubt from Jordan—was a likely barometer of Ervil's sentiments, that as far as the key Lambs of God were concerned, Don had strayed from the flock. Sullivan settled down to a routine of looking over his shoulder and he began plotting his escape from the group.

Based on the Nancy Chynoweth connection established by tracing the .38 revolver, Dick Forbes, Paul Forbes and two of his Murray detectives—Byron Vranes and Gary Pedersen—flew from Salt Lake City to Denver on May 17. Vranes and Pedersen were to emerge as Paul Forbes' key foot soldiers, and between them, they would log well over 100,000 air miles flying around the country tracking down various leads.

The four arrived in Denver, made contacts with local police and promptly took up surveillance of Victor Chynoweth's residence. All but Paul Forbes, that is. Paul connected with an agent from Colorado's Organized Crime Office, which was investigating Victor's business—Lincoln Auto—for alleged involvement in a stolen car ring. When the agent went over to Lincoln Auto to interview Vic, Paul tagged along. The agent never introduced Forbes, and Victor, uncharacteristically, never asked who Paul was.

The next morning at 8 o'clock, Vranes and Pedersen, Dick Forbes and two Denver detectives went to Victor's house and interviewed him for two hours. Victor quickly made it clear he didn't like the police, and initially refused to talk at all, explaining that he had been "screwed around" too much by the FBI and the Secret Service in connection with Ervil's letter to Jimmy Carter. When he finally consented to be interviewed, he volunteered nothing, and his answers to questions were short and evasive.

When the detectives asked the whereabouts of his wife Nancy, Victor said that Nancy and his sister Rena had left town May 11 (the day after the Allred murder), but he refused to tell them where they had gone. He said that he first heard about the Allred murder the night of the 11th when his boss in Ogden, Utah, called him about it. But he denied that call had prompted Nancy and Rena to leave town. He said he and Nancy had been having marital problems.

As far as the rest of his family was concerned, Victor discussed their involvement with LeBaron briefly, but gave no indication where any of them were.

As for his connection with Ervil, Victor was equivocal. He denied being a member of the Church of the Lamb of God, but he admitted he knew Ervil, got along with him well, and had seen him in Denver three or four months previously.

Asked about Nancy's whereabouts on May 10, Victor said she was home in Denver and witnesses could attest to it. He denied any knowledge of his wife's recent purchase of a gun.

Once during the interview, Pedersen got up to go to the bathroom. Actually, he wanted to look around the house a bit. It was virtually empty, with the exception of a few couches, some end tables and a bed. Victor explained that he was getting ready to move to another house in the Denver area. Pedersen remembers believing little of what Chynoweth said that day: "We could tell that he was lying. There was no doubt. We kept crossing him up."

That afternoon, the detectives canvassed the neighborhood trying to see if anyone knew where Nancy Chynoweth was. They didn't have to go far. Next door, a chatty and cooperative housewife named Esther Ballew volunteered to Gary Pedersen that Nancy herself had told her she was moving to Carrollton, Texas, a suburb of Dallas. Mrs. Ballew said that she was familiar with Carrollton because she and her husband used to live there. A police check with the school that the Chynoweth children had been attending confirmed that their records had been forwarded to Carrollton.

Seeing that Nancy had been packing two cars and readying to leave, Mrs. Ballew recalled that she and her husband, Robert, walked next door the evening of May 11 to say goodbye. Nancy mentioned to Esther that she was tired of the "bullshit" in this neighborhood—people complaining about how she treated her kids. Victor had spoken with Robert and referred to his "little sister" who was going to Dallas. Robert said the sister was attractive, well built and had short brown hair, a description that matched Rena's.

The Ballews said the two women drove off at 10 P.M. the night of the 11th in a Ford pickup and a Ford station wagon. Another witness said they left the following night, May 12. Both cars were loaded with furniture. Nancy had all her children and Rena had one child with her.

Almost parenthetically, the Ballews then proceeded to provide Nancy with an alibi for the Allred murder. Esther said she remembered that on May 10, at about 5 or 5:30 P.M., Nancy came over and asked if her daughter could babysit that night. Diane Ballew went next door and tended the Chynoweth kids from 6 to 9. It was all Pedersen could do to conceal his disappointment. For up to that time, police thought Nancy Chynoweth was an excellent candidate to be one of their two murderesses.

Esther Ballew recalled one other thing that puzzled police. A day or two before Nancy left for Texas, a truck had dumped a load of sand in the Chynoweth driveway. It just sat there for a while, then Nancy methodically took wheelbarrow loads of it out to her backyard. The detectives wondered why she would order a load of sand right before she was moving to Texas, and Victor was moving out altogether.

On May 20, Dick Forbes placed three long distance calls to Victor Chynoweth from Salt Lake City, trying to persuade Vic to put him in touch with Nancy. Though Forbes knew she was in the Dallas area—he didn't tell Chynoweth that—he hoped Vic could make things easier and agree to set up a meeting.

But Victor wasn't about to make things easy for Forbes. He had already called his wife in Dallas and told her that Salt Lake police were asking questions about her and Rena. He instructed her to sit tight and volunteer nothing should they find her, though he was going to do everything he could to see that they didn't. Victor then took Forbes on a verbal waltz.

He said he might arrange for the detective to talk with his wife by phone, but how could he be sure Forbes wouldn't have the call traced? If that was the concern, Forbes suggested that he simply fly to wherever she was and meeet her. In fact, he would rather do that.

"Yeah, but then you'd know where she is anyway," complained Victor.

"Well, what's the problem there?" wondered Forbes, forcing Chynoweth's hand a bit. If he and his wife had nothing to hide, shouldn't he make her available?

"I'm just gun-shy of the sonovabitch," retreated Victor.

"Like you say," Dick coaxed, "she doesn't have anything to hide. There's no problem."

"I just, I've just done it before, and I got screwed before, and I'm not—I don't like doing it again," stammered Victor, again citing his mysterious "prior experiences" with police.

"Yeah."

"When you get screwed one time, it's your fault, you know. If it happens three or four times, it's definitely my fault."

"Vic, the only thing I can tell you is if you have nothing to hide, I'm not going to screw anybody, you know."

And while he was trying to get a foot in the door with Nancy, Forbes also tried to find out where Mark, Duane and Thelma were—without success. Then, shooting for the moon, he wondered if Victor couldn't put him in touch with Ervil himself.

"I'll ask him," Vic offered, disinterestedly. "I kinda got my doubts, but I'll ask."

"Well," Forbes persisted, "you might explain to him there's a hell of a lot being said about him, and we'd like to hear his side of the story. There's two sides to every story, and I'm sure as hell not close-minded enough that I wouldn't be willing to listen to anything he had to say, as well as these other people."

When Forbes called back later that day, Victor quickly said that a meeting with Ervil was not possible, but that he had talked with Nancy and persuaded her to talk. She was reluctant, and didn't see what good it would do, but she would speak with Forbes anyway.

"Good," said Dick.

Victor suggested that he have her call him somewhere, so that he couldn't trace the call.

But Forbes demurred. He wanted to see her in person. Over the phone, how could he be sure whom he was talking to?

"Yeah, that's true," Vic admitted. "Well, God, I don't know how you'd do that. I'm sure you could figure out some way." But as Forbes continued to push for a personal meeting with Nancy, Victor seemed to soften his stand, and agreed that maybe it wouldn't be such a bad idea after all. Perhaps they could meet on neutral ground—just so Forbes couldn't pinpoint her present location. Vic said he would call Nancy back and arrange a meeting place, then Forbes could call him back later.

Forbes agreed, but quickly decided he'd had enough of this dance. He already knew Nancy was in the Dallas area, and through a trace of Victor's phone tolls and a check with local utilities in Dallas, Forbes had come up with an address for Thelma Chynoweth where he guessed Nancy was staying. He and Gary Pedersen flew to Dallas the following day, May 21.

They staked out Thelma's house, saw Nancy and other Lambs of God coming and going, recorded license numbers and learned where the other group members were living. They met with local police officials, FBI and Secret Service agents and mapped plans to arrest Nancy the next day.

Forbes wasn't sure he would detain her and take her back to Utah. It would depend on how she answered his questions about the .38 revolver. But in Salt Lake City, prosecutor David Yocom agreed to teletype Forbes an arrest warrant to facilitate extradition procedures if he did decide to detain her. The charge: conspiracy to commit murder. Despite the Denver alibi established for Nancy, Salt Lake officials were not yet totally convinced she was not one of their two killers. But for now, the conspiracy charge would suffice.

At 2:30 the following afternoon, May 22, Nancy Chynoweth and one of her children got into a brown pickup truck and drove away from the Lamb of God warehouse on Perth Street in Dallas. Officers who had been watching the warehouse radioed this information to Dick Forbes riding nearby in an unmarked police car. Forbes confirmed the identification of Nancy as she passed, and a marked squad unit was ordered to pull her over. An officer did so, roughly jerking her out of the truck, frisking her and demanding to see identification.

"Are you Mr. Forbes?" asked Nancy icily, furious at the way she was being treated.

Forbes walked up and interrupted the frisking procedure. "I'm Mr. Forbes," he said. The two sized each other up briefly, then Forbes asked if they could talk privately. She agreed, whereupon Dick got into her truck and began driving it back to the Carrollton police station, followed by another officer.

As they started to drive, Nancy immediately asked what he wanted to talk to her about. Forbes gave her a Miranda warning, which she waived, then asked her to account for her whereabouts over the last two weeks. She said she'd been in Denver until the night of May 12, when she and Rena left to drive to Carrollton, arriving the night of the 13th. Asked if she had gone out at night during the week before she left Denver, Nancy said she and Vic had gone out for dinner on Wednesday the 11th and had used a babysitter.

This conflicted with the statement of the next-door neighbors, the Ballews, who said their daughter had baby-sat the night of the 10th. Nancy insisted she was home all day May 10—the day of the murder. She said she had read of Allred's killing in the Denver newspapers before she left the city. Forbes noted that Victor had told police his wife did not know of the murder before she left.

At the police station, Forbes told her he had information that she bought a gun in Denver on May 7.

"Yes, that's correct," Nancy replied coolly. She had been expecting that question.

"Do you still have the gun?" asked Forbes.

"Yes."

"Where is it?"

"It's at the house." Here, Forbes later recorded in his police report, Nancy's "facial expression changed noticeably," but he didn't say how it changed. He asked her if the gun was at the house where she was living now, and she said that it was.

". . . What kind of a gun is it?"

"A .38 special."

". . . Does Rena have any guns?"

"I'm not going to tell you about anything that Rena has done," Nancy snapped, changing her quiet tone of voice. "If you want any information about Rena, you can talk to her."

Forbes then decided to play hardball. He told her he now had enough information to formally charge her in connection with the Allred murder, and handed her the warrant for her arrest that he had received from Salt Lake City.

"What does this mean?" Nancy asked, scanning the document.

"It's a warrant for your arrest and it charges you with conspiracy to commit the murder of Dr. Rulon C. Allred," explained Forbes somberly.

"Oh—only conspiracy?" she asked, sarcastically.

Forbes ignored this. She was in a good deal of trouble, he warned, hinting that he still might not choose to serve the warrant on her if she would lead him to the key players in the plot. Nancy was not interested.

"I only want to talk about myself," she said. "Why should I hang somebody else? If you can hang them, go ahead, but I'm not going to."

Forbes went back to the gun. If she still had it, he'd like to see it.

"No, I don't have it anymore," Nancy said vaguely. "It's been ripped off."

"Where did it get ripped off from?"

"I put it in the jockey box of the truck."

"Why did you tell me it was in your house?"

"You already know it isn't there," Nancy admitted. Actually, Forbes knew nothing of the gun's whereabouts.

"Well, has it been ripped off or is it in the house?"

"It's been ripped off."

"Did you report the theft of the gun?"

"No, why should I?"

"Well, it's a valuable gun, and if it was stolen, an owner would obviously want to report it stolen so that he might recover it."

No, Nancy said she hadn't reported the theft. She said she had put the gun in the jockey box of the truck and hadn't seen it since. When Forbes pressed her further on the subject, she cut him off and said she wouldn't answer any more questions without first consulting an attorney.

That was enough for Forbes anyway. He formally placed her under arrest and charged her with conspiracy to commit murder. That done, he proceeded to take her purse into custody as well, and took an inventory of its contents. There was $130 in cash and a receipt for the gun she'd bought in Denver, but by far the most interesting item in the purse was a small electronic calculator—similar to the one Richard Bunker said he had dropped while struggling with the two murderesses inside Allred's office.

Forbes could hardly contain his excitement. Maybe Nancy was one of the killers after all. He immediately called his brother Paul in Utah and had him ask Bunker to describe his calculator in more detail. Paul checked back later with the make and model of Bunker's machine. It matched Nancy's on both counts. Dick's joy at hearing this was tempered only slightly by news that a search of the house where Nancy had been living in Dallas failed to turn up the gun.

Events moved swiftly on May 23. Nancy appeared at a morning hearing, waived extradition proceedings and had bail set at $50,000. Around noon, Forbes got a call from the Dallas County jail and was told that Victor Chynoweth was in town preparing to make bail for his wife. Forbes and Gary Pedersen promptly sped to the jail, checked Nancy out and took her to another jail at the Dallas-Fort Worth airport. If Victor couldn't find her, they reasoned, he couldn't bail her out.

They made arrangements to fly her back to Salt Lake City that night, via Denver. But when they arrived at the airport about 9:30 for their flight, who should they see in the passenger terminal, preparing to board the same plane, but Victor Chynoweth.

At first, the two detectives tried to get Frontier Airlines to bump Victor from the flight, citing a security risk. But the airline officials refused, fearing a civil suit. Airport police then took Chynoweth through the metal detector device again, and into the bathroom where they conducted a strip search. Though this turned up no weapon of any sort, Forbes and Pedersen confronted Victor and let him know they did not like the idea of him riding on the same plane with his wife, a prisoner in transit. They told him they would board first with Nancy and sit at the rear of the plane, while he would board last and sit at the front. He could not talk with Nancy, make eye contact with her or try to transmit signals in an any way, they warned. Victor agreed to these conditions.

The detectives took their prisoner to the rear of the plane and sat her between them. Nancy was friendly and willing to engage in small talk with her captors. The conversation was innocuous, though at one point she did tell Forbes that her only goal in life was to serve her husband and raise her children "for the cause."

They began flying through a storm and it was a bumpy ride. Pedersen, who hated to fly even in good weather, recalls: "It was thunderin' and lightnin'. I was back there like a dog shittin' peach stones, wonderin' what was gonna happen."

Suddenly he noticed a commotion toward the front of the aircraft where flight attendants were huddling around a passenger. At first, Pedersen thought someone was just airsick because of the rough flight. But then he noticed an oxygen mask being administered to a woman, and an attendant asked over the intercom if there was a doctor on board. Finally, the woman was taken out of her seat and put on to the floor of the plane in the middle of the aisle.

"What in the hell is going on up there?" Pedersen whispered to Forbes, leaning across Nancy. "You don't think this could be some kind of a setup, do you?" Crazy as it seemed, they began to entertain the notion that the "sick" woman was an accomplice with Victor, who was sitting nearby. They would force the plane to land at some deserted airport late at night, and more accomplices on the ground would stage a bold, commando-style raid—à la Los Molinos—and free Nancy. Since Victor had learned what flight they were on, he could easily have relayed the information to the other Lambs of God before the plane took off.

"We were kinda hinky anyway, with Victor on board," remembers Pedersen. "It was a big deal because at the time, we figured Nancy could well be one of the killers."

He stood up to get a better view of what was happening down the aisle, but it was hard to see because several people were huddled around the apparently ill woman. Pedersen stopped a stewardess and told her to inform the captain that two Utah police officers transporting an accused murderer interstate were suspicious about what was going on. But just then the captain announced over the loudspeaker that they had a sick woman on board and would have to make an emergency landing at the nearest airport . . . Amarillo, Texas.

This news did nothing to allay Pedersen's suspicions, and he instructed the attendant to have the captain radio the airport tower to have them provide some additional police to assure the security of their prisoner.

By the time the plane landed, it was evident that if this was a plot, the Lambs of God had gone to great lengths for authenticity, because the woman passenger was dead of an apparent drug and alcohol overdose. She was taken off the plane first, and then no fewer than fifteen of Amarillo's finest came on board—the security Pedersen had requested. Surrounded by police, Nancy was taken off the plane, past her no doubt astonished husband.

It was after midnight and the airport was deserted. No terrorist raid appeared imminent, but Forbes and Pedersen were uneasy nonetheless, and urged the pilot to take off again as soon as possible. They arrived in Denver too late to make their connecting flight to Salt Lake City, so Nancy was booked into the city jail for the night. The three finally arrived in Salt Lake the following morning, May 24.

If Dick Forbes' trophy from Dallas was the calculator he assumed to be Richard Bunker's, Bunker himself quickly tarnished it. Shown the calculator, Bunker denied that it was his. Forbes at first was stunned. Then he concluded that Bunker was lying—possibly involved in the plot himself and now covering up for one of the girls.

Could he have had a motive to kill Allred? What precisely did this business deal involve that he wanted to discuss with Rulon? Why had they both been subpoenaed to testify in a civil suit? And could Bunker have known either of the two killers? Why hadn't they killed him—the prime eyewitness—when they had a perfect chance during the struggle? Could the struggle have been staged?

Dick Forbes wanted to investigate Bunker, as did Byron Vranes. Gary Pedersen was undecided, and Paul Forbes was strongly against it. They debated the issue heatedly. Paul, although he considered it a waste of time, finally authorized an investigation. But nothing ever developed to implicate Bunker in any way.

Neither Bunker nor any of the other witnesses in Allred's office the day of the murder, were able to pick Nancy Chynoweth out of a police lineup staged shortly after her arrival in Salt Lake City. But after being shown a photograph of Nancy, Bunker thought she resembled the woman who had killed Allred.

But on May 26, further news from Denver definitely ruled out Nancy as being one of the two who killed Allred. A Denver detective reported that he had interviewed a teacher of one of the Chynoweth children who was positive that she had personally met with Nancy to discuss her child from 3:30 to 5 P.M. the afternoon of the murder.

The conspiracy charge stuck, however, and a preliminary hearing to determine if the state possessed enough evidence to warrant a trial was set for June 15. Bail was set at $20,000. Victor posted it and took his wife home to Denver.

On May 28, Dick Forbes accepted a collect call from Siegfried Widmar in Colonia LeBaron. Siegfried said he had learned from a reliable source that about six weeks previously, two Mormon missionaries had made contact with Ervil's wife Delfina in Jackson, Mississippi. But he said the local LDS bishop, Daniel Boone, had for some reason advised his missionaries to stay away. Widmar told Forbes that Delfina had always been a thorn in Ervil's side, probably wanted to leave the group but couldn't and would likely be very helpful to the investigation if police could get in touch with her.

On June 3, Forbes called Boone in Mississippi and confirmed Widmar's account. Boone said he had advised his missionaries to stay away from Delfina because it appeared that Ervil's followers, who she claimed were keeping her captive, could harm any strangers seen with her. He provided Forbes with the name and telephone number of Delfina's mother in San Diego, which the missionaries had taken as a reference.

Forbes then called Ron Collins, a San Diego detective who had worked on the Dean Vest case, and asked him to contact Luz Salido on the chance that she might have heard from her daughter, Delfina.

Delfina was still confined to Dallas, tending Lamb of God children. Her depression and general fear for her own well-being was mounting daily. She knew she asked too many questions for the Lambs' liking, but she couldn't help herself. She had observed the "preparations for war"; then the arrival of Nancy and Rena in Dallas, along with most of the rest of the boys, signaled that the deed had been done. Victor had called Nancy with instructions on how to deal with the police, and then Nancy had been arrested. Delfina finally cornered her daughter Lillian, the only person who would even begin to confide in her about group doings, and asked about the incriminating succession of events.

Lillian told her mother the police had nothing on Nancy, "but who knows with Rena." Delfina later told officials she wondered if Nancy was responsible for Allred's murder. Lillian refused to answer, but she indicated it had been two of the group's women.

"Did they have an appointment to see the doctor?" Delfina asked innocently.

"No they just walked in there and did it, and left."

"Why couldn't the police get them right then?"

"Well, the police weren't there soon enough. Other people saw it, but they couldn't get them that fast . . . one of the girls shot seven times and the other girl once."

"How did the man die?"

"Well, Mom," Lillian smiled, "if someone shot you with seven and the other one with one, wouldn't *you* die?"

Delfina supposed she would. Actually, Nancy Chynoweth could rot in prison for all Delfina cared, but there was someone else near and dear to her heart whom she cared desperately about: her daughter Rebecca. While she was in Jackson, Delfina knew that Rebecca had been in Dallas, but when Delfina returned to Dallas in late April, Rebecca was nowhere in sight.

That wasn't alarming in and of itself. She might have gone back to Denver to be with her son. But when Delfina asked various Lambs of God where Rebecca was, no one could tell her. In fact, she got different answers from everybody she asked. When Ervil commented to her earlier that spring: "She [Rebecca] is acting up, like you acted up," Delfina had not interpreted that as a good omen. And now, when she asked Thelma Chynoweth, for example, "How's Rebecca?", Thelma just told her, vaguely: "She's just fine. She's doing lots better." Others she asked were just as vague.

Delfina knew her daughter had threatened to inform on the group, so when Nancy was arrested, she began worrying that some of the Lambs would think Rebecca had called the police.

Lillian assured her mother that wasn't so: "No, don't worry about Rebecca, everything's just fine."

Then, on June 7, Delfina was in the warehouse when she asked young Alex Chynoweth if he knew what had happened to Rebecca. Alex was the thirteen-year-old son of Naomi Zarate, who had been murdered as a "traitor" in 1975. Alex told Delfina he had heard that Rebecca was in the same place his mother was now. They were watching stars and airplanes explode in the sky, he said.

Shaken, Delfina left the kitchen where she was cooking and went into the warehouse office where Vonda White was working. Vonda counseled Delfina not to worry. Rebecca was with her brother, Arturo.

Delfina went and found Mark Chynoweth. "Okay, Mark," she demanded. "Where's Rebecca?"

"You know what we've been through with her," he snapped angrily, "and what we've suffered. It's been a big problem and we tried everything."

"You murderer!" Delfina sobbed. "You're all the same thing!"

The next day, June 8, Lillian came to see her mother.

"Hey, Mom, Mark's really upset because you're calling us all murderers," Lillian said. "I need to talk to you and let's talk it out nice."

When they sat down, Delfina immediately got to the nub of the issue. "Okay," she said, "what happened to Rebecca?"

Lillian tried to soften the blow. "You know, Mom, how hard we all worked with her. I took care of her, Thelma took care of her, everyone tried everything with her." Rebecca was mentally unstable, but despite all the problems, she was still a sister, and Lillian said she loved her. Then one day Rebecca disappeared, and Lillian went to Ervil and asked him what happened.

"I went to Dad and asked him, really mad, where Rebecca was," Lillian recalled. "He turned white as a sheet and began crying. He said that the judgments of God fall on the Lord's house first, and that she's lots happier on the other side. He said that it wasn't for Rebecca to live in this life. This life wasn't for her. He said I shouldn't feel bad, that everything was better that way."

Delfina, incredulous, stared down at the floor. Lillian tried to comfort her. "Mom, you have to try and feel good about this. It's not a problem anymore. She's in a better place. At first, Mark and I didn't understand it either. We cried a lot and felt bad too. But then we saw that it was the right thing to do, because it was ordered from the Lord. It just didn't work here for Rebecca. She was such an angelic girl, such a nice girl, that she wasn't able to stand the kind of life that we have here on this earth. She'll be lots better off on the other side."

Then Lillian turned abruptly from condolence to something far more pressing. The Lambs of God were losing patience with all the questions Delfina was asking about Rebecca, and the way she was conducting herself in general. The group's policy toward rebels and recalcitrants should now have been abundantly clear, but Lillian wanted to make sure Delfina knew.

"Mom," she said, "please don't talk any more about Rebecca or say anything. Just be good and do what they tell you. Mark is really upset at how you're acting. . . . You have to be really careful or else the same thing will happen to you."

Here was the final indignity, Delfina thought. Her husband treated her like a piece of chattel for their entire marriage, took other women as wives, took some of her children away from her, ordered one of her daughters killed and finally, another daughter—dominated by her father's persona—threatened her with the same fate. She was too numb to protest, too hurt to cry.

What she did feel more than anything else, was fear. She was now convinced that they would soon kill her no matter what she did, so she made up her mind to escape that night. To make escape possible, she would have to suffer one final humiliation. She would assure them she'd cause no more problems, and she'd even ask to be baptized into the church.

Mark joined them, as Lillian hammered away: "Look," she said, "you've suffered and sacrificed so much up to now, and been through everything. You can stick it out to the end. Please."

"Okay, Mark," Delfina replied, putting on as cheery a face as possible and ignoring Lillian, "what do I have to do? I'm willing to conform, and do what you tell me. Who can baptize me? What do I have to do?"

"Just help us and don't lose your good spirits," said Lillian quickly, pleased that she had apparently turned her mother around.

Mark added: "Be sure if Ervil comes to not get mad at him and not say anything to him. Just be really good, and do what he tells you."

"Okay, I'll be good," promised Delfina, reverting to the role of a child. "Could I go to a show tonight?"

Mark thought under the circumstances that was a modest request. "Hey," he said, pleasantly, "you want to go to a show, Mom?"

"Yeah."

"Okay."

"Who's going to pay?"

"I'll pay, but hold on just a minute, okay? We've got to go to the warehouse for something, and we'll be back soon."

They left the house, and Delfina decided it was now or never. She told her ten-year-old daughter, Delia: "Get ready! Let's go. They're going to kill me now." Within minutes, both had gathered up whatever they could carry and were walking down the street to a small convenience market.

The owners of the market saw right away that this Mexican woman and her daughter were in some distress. Since only Delia could speak English, she blurted out that they needed the police. It was an emergency. They had to go to Mexico. But the owners said the police wouldn't take them to Mexico. They'd have to take a taxi to the bus depot. Delia said they didn't have enough money for both cab and bus fares. Convinced this was a desperate situation, the owners drove Delfina and Delia to the bus station in their own car.

From there, Delfina called her mother in San Diego. The timing of that call was remarkably fortuitous. Visiting with Luz Salido at that very moment was Ron Collins, the detective sent by Dick Forbes. After mother and daughter had talked, Collins, a Chicano, got on the phone and spoke with Delfina in Spanish. She told him that Rebecca was dead, that her own life had been threatened, and that she and her daughter had just escaped from the group. They were preparing to board a bus to El Paso, and from there, on to Mexico.

Collins immediately called Dick Forbes in Salt Lake City and relayed this information. Forbes, in turn, called Siegfried Widmar in El Paso, who proceeded to meet Delfina at the El Paso bus station, along with a local Secret Service agent. She was glad to be met by law enforcement, and law enforcement was more than glad to meet her. Here was a major turning point in the investigation: a chance to get the first inside look at the Lambs of God. The Salt Lake command caucused and determined that she should be interviewed at length immediately. Forbes flew to El Paso and promptly spirited Delfina and Delia back to Utah for "security purposes."

"Delfina gave us more than we'd ever heard to that point about the Allred murder and about the group itself," recalls Forbes. Speaking Spanish, translated into English by Lawreve Widmar (Siegfried's wife),

Delfina, provided police with the names and numbers of most of the players, though she didn't know enough to specifically link anyone to any crime. She told of Rebecca, of Ervil's operations in Mississippi and Oklahoma, of seeing guns and watching the group's comings and goings before and after Allred.*

During the "preparations for war," Delfina told Forbes of her daughter Lillian's statement that the Lambs were going to "get some men in Utah. Important men." (Forbes wondered who else had been targeted.) Afterward, Lillian didn't worry much about Nancy's arrest, but seemed to think Rena could be vulnerable. She hadn't specified who had killed Allred, but indicated it was two of the group's women. Victor had called frequently from Denver with advice on how to handle the police.

Delia offered that Nancy's daughter, Pacey, had shown her some wigs she said Nancy and Rena had used in restaurants en route from Denver to Dallas because they said police were looking for them, Delia quoted Pacey as telling her. She said the wigs were black and orange—neither of which fit those seen by witnesses in the Allred office, but Forbes was heartened to know that they had wigs of any color.

Delia also told Forbes that "all the men"—she named Don and John Sullivan, Eddie Marston and Duane Chynoweth—had their hair cut short after they returned to Dallas from their various expeditions. As for Ervil, Delfina said as far as she knew, he was in Mexico City, and that he had taken $8,000 with him when he left the U.S.—$6,000 of it from Victor Chynoweth and the rest of it from funds at the Dallas warehouse.

Delfina also told of the trials and tribulations she'd had in trying to keep her three youngest children with her at all times. Ervil had taken some or all of them away from her whenever it suited his whim, she said. Now, she at least had Delia with her, but Isaac and Pablo were still in Dallas with the group. She wanted to have legal custody of her sons and have them brought to live with her. Could anything be done? She was certain she could get the boys—especially Isaac, who had been privy to the inner workings of the cult—to cooperate with the police investigation. Forbes promised to petition a juvenile court for a hearing, and see if they could get an order to award custody of the two boys to her.

*Though Laurieve Widmar was helping police in their efforts to capture LeBaron, they accepted her translation of Delfina's Spanish unquestioningly.

17.

INVESTIGATION

In the meantime, the investigation continued on other fronts. Although Richard Bunker—primary eyewitness—appeared quite insistent that the woman who shot Rulon Allred was Nancy Chynoweth, the police were satisfied they had proven otherwise. So they asked Bunker to undergo hypnosis to see if, in his subconscious, there were buried further details which might offer new leads.

The session took place June 24 in Los Angeles, where Dr. Martin Reiser, director of Behavioral Science Services for the Los Angeles Police Department, had established the nation's foremost reputation for hypnosis as it applied to criminal investigations. Though Reiser was present, the session—which was videotaped as well as tape-recorded— was actually conducted by an LAPD captain.

Bunker was hypnotized for two hours and twenty minutes. He recalled that he was reading a *Reader's Digest* in the waiting room at Allred's office when he noticed the door open and two girls walk in. He said this caused a reflection in the glass around the receptionist area. He proceeded to describe the two girls in astonishing detail.

He said that the girl who came through the door second sat down next to him on a couch. He remembered that her head was tipped to the west as if she recognized him. She was attractive, in her early twenties, with medium-length brown curly hair, full breasts, dark eyebrows and dark eyes, fair complexion, smooth skin and red lipstick. She was wearing Levi's, a red T-shirt with a vertical ribbed pattern and woven leather brown sandals with a thick sole. Her long, thin and pale arms were bare. She had a white plastic or leather belt with a brass buckle. Her purse was slung across her body from the right shoulder to the left hip. She was wearing a pleasant but determined expression on her face.

The girl who walked through the door first did so with authority and was definitely the leader, Bunker thought. She was not as attractive as the other girl, and seemed to be shorter. She was wearing loose-fitting Levi's and a robin's-egg blue ski parka with white lining over a white shirt. Her breastline was wrinkled, as if she were wearing a bra that didn't fit, or perhaps she didn't have much there in the first place, he suggested. Her skin was darker than her accomplice's. Her hair was dirty blond, possibly tipped on the ends, unkempt and curling around her ears, partially obscuring them. Her top lip protruded farther than her bottom lip.

Bunker began to talk about the murder as if it were occurring right then.

"I think she knows the doctor," he said, referring to the girl in the blue parka, "because she walked in and didn't talk to Melba, the receptionist. She must know the doctor or be a relative."

Then he heard what sounded like dynamite going off. He used dynamite at his ranch occasionally, and was familiar with its sound. He heard four loud bangs, followed by the words, "Oh, no!" and then three more bangs. He realized the girl had shot Dr. Allred. He watched as she backed out of the reception area, a gun in her right hand at waist height, ready to fire again if need be. The gun was small, blue or black steel with what appeared to be a brown handle. It looked like his own Colt automatic.

As she reached the door leading out of the office, the girl who had been sitting next to him rose and also displayed a gun. Not a big gun. Maybe four inches long at most. He could see engraving on it—a fern or something. Melba shouted, "They shot Rulon!" Bunker put the magazine he'd been reading on a rack and watched the girls walk out the door.

"I don't feel afraid," Bunker remembered at this point. "I'm not panicky. I'm not sick about it. I want to get the license number. I put my hand on the exit door. It opens against me. The girl in the red is leading. The one that did the shooting is not at the door. The girl in red points her gun at me. I grab her hand. Hold it against the door. The other girl comes through. I'm kicking at her with my right foot. The girl who did the shooting is trying to point a gun at me. She is on the wrong side. I twist the head of the girl in the red T-shirt with my left hand. The other girl, or the shooter, reached through and pointed the gun in my face.

"Then I get scared and I'm afraid. The face on the shoulder looks different, looks mean, looks lighter complected. The sun is shining through her hair. She has no makeup. She's mean, scowling at me. Please don't kill me. I'm a father with a lot of children.

"Somehow, I'm able to push them both out the door. The killer still has the same gun in her hand. Looks like a .22. I push the door shut and put my foot against it. I'm trying to find the latch, but I can't. I'm thinking they're going to shoot me through the door. Why doesn't somebody come and help me?

"I back away from the door approximately two feet and it starts to open. I start to run. I'm afraid I won't live through this day. I look back and the door is opening farther. I run into the bathroom and a shot is fired. I lock the bathroom door. The door is very thin. I can't get my breath and it feels like I'm going to pass out. I hear two more shots, and I think they're shooting through the wall or the door at me. I see a window inside the bathroom and think maybe I can crawl out of it.

"Then I think I'm a coward. I couldn't even stand up to them. My friend Rulon has been shot. He's obviously dead. Melba is out there and she needs help. I hear Melba calling for help and walk out of the bathroom. At this point, or shortly thereafter, the police arrive."

As Bunker gave his detailed descriptions of the two women, a police artist sat and prepared composite drawings. The artist began with rough sketches based on pre-hypnosis conversation, then when the session began, he filled in the details. When Bunker was taken out of hypnosis, he pronounced himself delighted with the composite of the shooter. It was perfect, he said. But he was not so satisfied with the accomplice who had sat next to him. The mouth didn't look right. It wasn't tight enough; the lip line was too wide. The face looked too masculine.

For Byron Vranes and Gary Pedersen, who were in attendance at Los Angeles, that last reference was no throwaway line. Taken together with the statement of the witness outside Allred's office, who had seen at least one of the killers remove a wig, police now began to seriously consider the possibility that one or both of their murderers were men disguised as women.

On July 1, back in Salt Lake, Vranes, Pedersen and Dick Forbes met again with Bunker to tell him of their suspicions and to ask him to look through a group of photographs of men. Though his associates might not have gone quite that far, Pedersen did say flatly to Bunker that day: "We think the shooter was a male. We know we have been going after females, but we have turned up some more evidence, and we think it could have been a male, very possibly." This statement was based on Delfina's account of the belicose comings and goings from Dallas of several men in the group.

Bunker amitted that one or both of the women might have been wearing wigs. He also said: ". . . the conduct of the person that did the shooting could have very well been the conduct of a man versus the woman." But he couldn't identify any of the male photographs shown him. And, much to the detectives' chagrin, he still inclined toward Nancy Chynoweth as the actual murderer of Allred.

On July 12, Vranes and Pedersen flew to Dallas to try to take Isaac and Pablo LeBaron—Delfina's two sons—into official custody. They began staking out the addresses which had been linked to the Lambs of God when Nancy Chynoweth was arrested in May. The warehouse looked deserted. So did the next house they checked out, but just as they were leaving, they spotted Vonda White driving an old red Dodge truck. She turned into the house they had just left.

"You couldn't miss Vonda," recalls Vranes, laughing. Privately, the boys of Murray loved to sit around and discuss the sex appeal of some of Ervil's women, then assign them nicknames, Vonda, admittedly no beauty queen, had become simply "Dirty ol' Vonda."

Vranes and Pedersen observed the house for about forty-five minutes from about a block away but saw nothing. Then Pedersen decided to take a closer look. He borrowed a passerby's ten-speed bike and cruised down past the house where he saw Vonda, Isaac and an unidentified Mexican loading washing machines into the back of the truck from the garage. Ten minutes later, Vonda pulled the truck away, got on the LBJ freeway and headed east.

"Off we went," continues Vranes. "We didn't know where the hell she was taking us. I figured maybe Mississippi or someplace." Vonda exited about sixty miles later in Mesquite, Texas, dived into a subdivision and promptly lost her pursuers.

Miffed and slightly ashamed at having been given the slip, the two detectives drove back to Dallas where they took up a position at Mark Chynoweth's house. It was there, the following day, that the big raid took place.

Vranes and Pedersen had briefed various local law enforcement agencies on their mission and had been promised all the support they needed. When Pederson let it be known that the time had come, about fifteen police officers, including the Dallas SWAT team, showed up within minutes.

Having been warned by Vranes and Pedersen that the Lambs of God were armed and dangerous, the local officers were skittish. They moved in on the house, guns drawn, from the front and the rear simultaneously. Isaac was in the backyard working on a washing machine, and Pedersen pointed the boy out to a policeman as being one of the two they were after. Isaac looked bewildered by this sudden show of force.

Inside the house, Mark and Lillian were told that police were taking Isaac and Pablo into custody because the boys had no parental guidance in the area, and their mother wanted them in Utah. Mark and Lillian were quiet and passive, offering no resistance.

But Isaac and Pablo, taught to distrust police, were scared, hostile and confused as they were taken into custody. They thought they were being kidnapped, and didn't believe Vranes and Pedersen when they told the boys that their mother was coming to see them. They would answer few, if any, questions at first.

Recalls Pedersen: "Pablo was only eleven, but my God, it was like trying to interview John Dillinger. He just sat there and stared at you. And hey, if looks could ever kill, you'd a been a dead sucker. I never seen anybody so hard in my life."

The next day, July 14, a Dallas judge awarded Vranes and Pedersen temporary custody of the two boys until they could be reunited with their mother. Paul Forbes escorted Delfina down to Dallas that afternoon, and there was a tearful reunion between mother and sons at the airport.

* * *

After two weeks of adjusting to their new surroundings and, no doubt, being prompted by their mother, Isaac and Pablo volunteered to talk to the police.

Pablo said he had been at the group's Mississippi outpost from March to June, when the business shut down. It seemed that rather than honor the many guarantees made for work done on washing machines, the Lambs decided to cut their losses and leave town. Isaac offered another insight into the group's business ethic: rather than come up with always scarce capital to finance the purchase of necessary equipment, they would often rent whatever they needed, then simply not return it.

Isaac had been in Dallas since the group branched out to Texas, and it was he who provided police with their first details of the April 20 conspiracy meeting. If the dumpster discovery and the linkup with Delfina had been the investigation's first two watershed moments, information supplied by Isaac was surely the third.

Isaac recalled that the meeting began shortly after Ervil and Victor Chynoweth arrived in Dallas from Denver. Ervil had opened the meeting with a sermon, of sorts, after which the "little people" had been asked to leave. At fourteen, Isaac may have been little, but he was trusted enough that he was allowed to remain for what ensued.

Victor rose and spent several minutes lecturing the group on how to avoid answering questions from the police. Then, Isaac said, his father discussed a planned murder wherein someone, an important leader, was going to be killed. He turned to Don Sullivan and asked him who he would like to have accompany him on the murder. Eddie Marston and John Sullivan, Don had replied.*

Ervil also said that there was another murder to be committed, and that two of the group's "young ladies" would perform that chore. During this August 2 interview with the Forbes brothers and Gary Pedersen, Isaac mentioned only one of the women Ervil had picked: Rena. Nor did he say who the two targets of the murders were.

But he did discuss, in considerable detail, the test-firing session in the warehouse which followed the meeting. Isaac said that he and Bill Rios had filled a large dryer-drum with sand so that Don Sullivan and Eddie Marston could test fire a .25 automatic and a .38 automatic. Afterward, he and Rios took the drum to a field about a half mile from the warehouse. Prior to dumping the sand, they picked out some of the expended slugs, including four .25s and two .38s, but he said he thought there probably were some more shells still in the sand that they hadn't been able, or bothered, to find.

The detectives perked up at this. They would love to recover some of those slugs and test them ballistically to see if they matched any of those found inside Allred's office.

Isaac said that the persons who left Dallas "on a trip to kill some-

*During their last trip to Dallas, Vranes and Pedersen had spotted Don at Mark Chynoweth's and excitedly called Utah for instructions on whether to arrest him or not. He wasn't a firm enough suspect at the time, so they were told not to.

body" included Don, Eddie, John Sullivan, Duane Chynoweth and Rena Chynoweth. While they were gone he read an article in a Dallas newspaper about the Allred murder in Utah. Bill Rios mentioned at the time that that was the first hit which they had planned. When the boys returned to Dallas, Isaac noted that Don had cut his hair and shaved off his mustache. He looked like a girl, the teenager thought. Then Rena, looking "tired and ugly," returned with Nancy Chynoweth, but Rena soon left for Jackson with Lloyd Sullivan. During this period of time, Isaac added that his father had contacted the group in Dallas several times by phone from Mexico.

Finally, Isaac alluded to Jack Strothman. Except he said he wasn't sure of the last name. It was either Jack Stroffman or Jack Troffman. In any case, Isaac said that not long after the Allred murder, Strothman had become disillusioned with the group and escaped—probably to Indiana, where he was from. That was all Isaac knew, but it was considerably more than anyone had known before. Vranes and Pedersen immediately began following up all of Isaac's leads.

Delfina's two sons, however, were not to be spared yet another ordeal. That summer of 1977, the strain of all that Delfina had been through in recent years came crashing down on her. She had a nervous breakdown and was committed to a mental institution. The Murray Police Department placed Isaac, Pablo and Delia with a family which volunteered to take them in.

The children adjusted well to their new surroundings. They were given new identifications and began attending school regularly. But Isaac, especially, knew that he had taken a dangerous step by becoming a state's witness. He knew there would come a day when he would have to take the witness stand against his father or the other Lambs of God—whoever was captured first. He knew what his father did to anyone who crossed him.

Isaac's host-family reported to police that he was so terrified the group was going to kill him, that he had taken to locking himself in the bathroom or hiding beneath his bed.

Vranes and Pedersen flew back to Dallas to follow up on what Isaac had said about the .25 and .38 shells being dumped amidst some sand. They found the dumping ground near the warehouse that he had referred to, but the area was a landfill, and Isaac's sand was now probably ten feet under. The detectives called Paul Forbes back in Utah with this discouraging report, but Paul was unconvinced his men had found the right spot. He told them he would fly down that night with Isaac to make sure. When he arrived with Isaac, the boy led them to the same landfill. Slightly red-faced, Paul Forbes took Isaac and flew immediately back to Salt Lake City.

But this Dallas trip was not a total loss. Vranes and Pedersen discovered that the Lambs of God had vacated their warehouse, and they persuaded the owner of the building to let them go inside and look around. There, they came upon a piece of paper which was to set up the next major thrust of the investigation. The paper made reference to a Jack Strothman. This was the man police had never heard of until Isaac phonetically spelled his last name and mentioned that he had been present at the Dallas conspiracy meeting. Now they had the correct spelling, and one other piece of information as well: the paper indicated Strothman was living in Indianapolis.

All things considered, the investigation in Utah was progressing well, officials felt. But there were problems too. The case—with its scores of players, elaborate polygamous interconnections and extensive LeBaron family history—was complex. Reams of reports were being generated and inadequately digested, work was being duplicated and organization was shoddy. The prosecutor-designate, David Yocom, perceived the need for someone who could see the forest for the trees, someone not directly involved in the day-to-day legwork of the case who could organize and correlate information as it came in, then analyze it, interpret it and assemble it to establish patterns, strong points, weak points and project what was needed and what was likely to occur in the future.

In the increasingly specialized world of law enforcement, such a person was called a "case analyst" or an "intelligence analyst." Yocom had just who he wanted in mind: Norma Glover, a bright twenty-three-year-old Idaho native who had been doing such casework for the Salt Lake County Sheriff's Office for over four years. Yocom told her the Allred investigation was burying them all. Would she help?

"It was a mess," Glover remembers. "There was a real problem of correlation, and a lot of things were being missed because each thought the other was going to do it." First she organized the reports and interviews chronologically, then built files on each suspect in the investigation—listing every statement he or she ever made and all they knew about the person. When she listed what they knew, it became more apparent what they didn't know. She would then talk to Yocom and others. They would have meetings with the investigation's principals, make assignments, and the duplication started to decrease.

Glover emerged as the clearing house through which all information in the investigation passed. She coordinated contacts between federal, state and local agencies, and as the Lambs of God began hopping from state to state that summer, she began contacting an increasing number of lawmen throughout the nation. Helped by a series of Jack Anderson columns on Ervil and his cult, Norma would usually refer to the Allred case as "the polygamous homicide" when she spoke with officials in various states, and she found they all remembered the polygamy angle. The cooperation from other jurisdictions was generally excellent, but after she finished explaining the complex polygamous interrelationships in the case, whoever she was talking to would invariably laugh and ask: "Do that again?" Said one cop in Wichita, Kansas: "Lady, I don't care who your mother is. Let's just go find 'em."

* * *

While canvassing in the area of Allred's office in Murray, Dick Forbes came upon a registration card for the Lone Pine motel—where Rena and Ramona had stayed—which intrigued him. He was trying to place any of the known Lambs of God near the scene of the crime around the time it had occurred. He didn't think they would register under their real names, so he was looking for names that sounded suspicious.

Of 100 cards at the Lone Pine, Forbes pulled only one: a "Patti Sanders." It was just a gut feeling, but Patti Sanders sounded like an alias. And the address listed on the card was in Ogden, Utah, where Forbes knew the Chynoweth clan had lived for many years. But when Murray officers went up to Ogden to investigate, they learned there was no such address. The registration card had said Patti Sanders was driving a Mercury, with Utah license plate MHA-044. But when Forbes ran that license number down, it came back registered as a Volkswagen.

So he had the state Bureau of Criminal Identification run "near makes" on the number—other license numbers with approximately the same digits. The fifth license number run was MHA-054, and that came back as a Mercury registered to Bud Chynoweth, the patriarch of the Chynoweth family. Buoyed by this piece of news, Forbes had a handwriting expert compare the signature of Patti Sanders against the known signatures of some of the Chynoweth women which existed in state files. The expert said Patti Sanders was Rena Chynoweth. And the motel card was for May 10—the day Rulon Allred was killed.

Forbes also uncovered another piece of physical evidence that linked one of the key Lambs of God to the Allred murder. He was in the daily habit of going over all the evidence that had been accumulated in the investigation to date, and rereading intelligence files. This was a routine he liked to do to refresh his memory, and to see what directions the investigation might take next. While doing this one day, Forbes came across a fingerprint card for Don Sullivan, who had been arrested in Salt Lake City in 1974 on a misdemeanor charge.

Forbes noticed that one of Don's fingerprints had an "arch" in it that was distinctive and unusual. Then he remembered that local criminologists, in dusting for fingerprints the various items found in the dumpster two days after the Allred killing, had also isolated a print with an unusual arch on one of the hand-drawn maps. He asked them to compare that print with Don Sullivan's. They matched.

Responding to a request from Utah, Indiana State Police tried for two weeks to locate Jack Strothman, without success. Then, in late August, Dick Forbes, along with Vranes and Pedersen, flew in to try their luck. Since Strothman had been arrested before, they had a mug shot of him, along with addresses of relatives in Connersville—the community some fifty miles east of Indianapolis where Jack had grown up.

Strothman's father, who lived in Cincinnati, happened to be visiting his sisters in Connersville at the time and it was he who supplied the police with their most valuable piece of information, which was that Jack had been married earlier that month. He said his son and new bride were living in Indianapolis. Jack was pumping gas there somewhere. He wasn't sure of their address, but he gave them an address and phone number of the wife's cousin, who would be able to locate the couple. He also supplied a description of Jack's car.

Back in Indianapolis, Forbes et al found Strothman working at a gas station. When arrested he offered no resistance. On the contrary, he appeared relieved. He said he'd been expecting Utah police to come looking for him. He had left LeBaron's group and would be glad to tell the officers anything they wanted to know.

Based on what Isaac had told them, Forbes and his men thought that Strothman was a low-level conspirator who happened to have sat in on the April 20 meeting in Dallas. They hoped to get another account of that critical meeting.

But within minutes, Strothman made it clear that he was a considerably bigger catch. He had been part of the hit team which had gone to "Utah City."

"You mean Salt Lake?" asked Forbes, incredulous. Strothman nodded.

The three detectives looked at each other in amazement. Strothman waived his rights to an attorney and started to talk or, as Vranes puts it: "He laid down for the whole nine yards. He admitted everything. Everything except having shot or killed anybody. I mean, I've had harder thirteen-year old kids."

The detectives sat and listened to Strothman intently as the serial unfolded. After investigating the case for months, they were about to get a chance to test their theories and suppositions as one of the insiders readied to tell them how the murder had actually occurred. Strothman, aware of his rapt audience, nevertheless proceeded at his own methodical pace, often needing considerable prodding to sharpen his dull memory.

He related something of his background and how he had come to join the Lambs of God. He described the Dallas conspiracy meeting and how Ervil had announced that Allred was to be killed. LeBaron had also ordered another murder, but Strothman now couldn't remember the victim's name. The detectives suggested the names of several polygamist leaders. When they got to Utah's Merlin Kingston, Strothman said, "Merlin! That's it." He didn't know the name Kingston; Ervil had only referred to the man by his first name.

This bit of phonetic misunderstanding was to cause police considerable embarrassment. Ervil had talked of killing Verlan. Verlan LeBaron. But to the vague Strothman, "Merlin" sounded close enough. He told them this murder was to have taken place at the Allred funeral. Though Strothman had the wrong name, it all sounded plausible enough to the police, who knew that Kingston had, in fact, attended the Allred funeral, and that he had been threatened by Ervil in the past.

Strothman told how the conspirators rendezvoused in Evanston, Wyoming, and then, sans Ervil and his sons Arturo, continued on to Salt Lake to carry out their assignments. Rena and Ramona had successfully carried off the Allred killing, but he, Don and Eddie had decided to abort the attempt on Verlan LeBaron at Allred's funeral. There were too many people present.

They went back to a nearby parking lot where they stripped off some of their clothing and disguises and put them in a garbage bag, which Strothman said he disposed of in the same dumpster that had been used before.* Then they split up—Don and Eddie in one car, Jack in the other—and drove south. Strothman said he followed his two accomplices as far as Albuquerque, at which point Don ordered him to continue to Dallas, pick up some money and return to Mississippi. He didn't know where Sullivan and Marston went.

In Dallas he saw Rena, Strothman continued, and she told him she had killed Allred, adding: "I'm glad he's dead."

Jack returned to Mississippi and worked for a few weeks before getting permission to leave the group temporarily to fly back to Indiana and get married. After the wedding, he and his wife returned to Dallas, but life with the Lambs of God was not exactly the new Mrs. Strothman's idea of a honeymoon. Although he now had a wife to support, Jack made no money. Nor was he free to come and go as he pleased. Don ran roughshod over him—often cuffing him about, and threatening him if he should ever dare leave the group. Strothman said Don was afraid he'd go to the police.

This imprisoned, dead-end life grew harder to justify, especially to his new wife. So, around the beginning of July, the two of them sneaked out of the house where they were staying in Dallas with some other group members. It was midnight. They took whatever they could carry, pushed their car down the street so as not to alert anyone inside, then drove off to Indiana. Strothman said he was certain that if any loyal Lamb of God found him, he or she would shoot him.

Strothman was casting his lot with the State of Utah, now. He could be charged with murder, and he knew they shot people in Utah too. But he also knew officials didn't have anyone else in a position to testify to the things he could. He told the detectives he would testify in court to what he had just told them, and that seemed enough for Dick Forbes and his two colleagues. They took him into custody and flew him back to Salt Lake City with them, but didn't arrest him. He wouldn't be charged with any crime.

Strothman was not exactly the well-spoken solid citizen that prosecu-

---

*In addition to Don Sullivan's, police later found Strothman's and Marston's fingerprints on the bag recovered from the dumpster or on various items found inside the bag.

tors love to build their cases around. The police thought he didn't have a brain in his head. He was slow, dimwitted and had such a poor memory for detail that officials found themselves constantly having to jog him with tidbits they had picked up during the course of the investigation—thereby leaving themselves open to charges that they were coaching and programming their key witness.

Recalls Norma Glover: "The Indiana connection in this case was a real eye-opener. The guys who went back there discovered a lot of incest. The people lived in cardboard houses along the riverbottom. They stank. They were terribly backward. This was the kind of area Strothman came out of, and that helped me understand a lot better why he was the way he was. Because I couldn't believe the guy was for real when I first saw him. He was just so slow. And he wasn't retarded."

After interviewing Strothman and listening to his descriptions of other Lambs of God, the detectives were beginning to draw some conclusions about the group's membership. With a few exceptions, they were the have-nots of the cult world. "Most of these people have never had a pot to piss in, or a window to throw it out of," thinks Gary Pedersen. "And so Ervil's their answer. He's taken care of them. . . . The people in that group couldn't make it on the outside. They have to be in a cult. They haven't got the education. They haven't got the guts, willpower, or nothin'. They're followers."

On the plane ride back to Salt Lake in late August 1977, Strothman was absently flipping through the current issue of *Time* magazine when he chanced to come upon a full-page story about none other than Ervil LeBaron. His jaw dropped and his eyes bugged. Here was the leader of the group he, Jack Strothman, had run with—making *Time* magazine. And now he was about to play a critical role in putting Ervil away. The shacks along the Wabash River, and his twin, pink-dressed aunts back in Connersville started looking farther and farther away. Now, he was about to *be* somebody.

Landing in Utah, Strothman found himself still very much the center of attention. He was a traffic cop of sorts. He directed the detectives to Evanston, Wyoming, where he showed them the two motels that he, Don and Eddie had stayed in. Motel registration cards for the names Don Sullivan and Fred Tompkins—Strothman's alias—were picked up for the days before and after the Allred murder.

Back in Murray, he showed them the motel where the men had stayed—Dick Forbes had already found the women's—and another Fred Tompkins registration card was taken into evidence for the day of the murder itself. He also pointed out the test-shooting site, the Deseret Industries store where they had bought clothing, and the gas station where Rena had gotten her car inspected.

Dick Forbes got the gas station to examine its car inspection records for May 10, and he found a document attesting that Bud Chynoweth's green Mercury station wagon, license plate MHA-054, had indeed been inspected that day.

*   *   *

The state was gathering more and more physical evidence against the Lambs of God, enough so that prosecutor David Yocom concluded that it was time to draw up arrest warrants and mobilize state and federal law enforcement resources for a multistate bust.

Strothman and his wife, meanwhile, quietly began a new life in Utah—courtesy of the Murray Police Department. The police placed their witness in a job with the city's maintenance department and even bought him some furniture to help tide him over until his first paycheck came in.

The summer of 1977 had been an anxious time for the Lamb of God's Sullivan faction. After the Allred murder in May, Lloyd and his wife Bonnie agreed to reconcile after an eight-month separation. But no sooner were they back together than the fifty-year-old Lloyd began an affair with none other than the prophet's favorite wife, Rena Chynoweth, age nineteen. At the same time, Lloyd was becoming increasingly disenchanted with Ervil, and he spoke candidly of his doubts to his son, Don, and his nephew, John. Lloyd had been instrumental in getting Don and John to follow Ervil in the first place, and now, as he came more and more to the conclusion that LeBaron was a false prophet, Lloyd felt it his duty to pass his thoughts on to his family.

Don didn't need much convincing. He had been afraid for his life since his failure on the funeral mission. And before that, he had openly challenged Ervil to explain his failed prophecies. John Sullivan needed more convincing that LeBaron was not who he claimed he was, but finally, he too agreed to quit Ervil.

Don, however, was of the opinion that their most pressing concern was not making a break from the group, but rather the romance between his father and Rena. It was dangerous, he thought. Ervil had killed for much less, and it was folly to provoke him by seducing one of his wives—and Rena, no less. Don urged Lloyd to have nothing to do with her, but Lloyd would not listen. He was in love, he said.

As this relationship developed in Mississippi, Bonnie Sullivan—reconciled with Lloyd to give their marriage another chance—was furious. She even played detective and somehow got her hands on a tape recording Rena had made during this period. Bonnie would recall that in the tape, Rena talked about what she and Lloyd could do together and she said she would like to "get rid of " Bonnie so their romance could flourish. Rena added that she didn't want Ervil to know what she was up to either. She knew that under her husband's system of Civil Law, adulterers were condemned to death. Another tape was one Lloyd made for Rena. Bonnie listened to that one too, and later gave both of the tapes to one of Ervil's wives, for forwarding to the prophet in Mexico. No one knows whether Ervil got the tapes or not, but when Lloyd learned of Bonnie's action—which might have exposed him to serious repercussions from Ervil—he beat her.

The awkward trio—Bonnie, Rena and Lloyd—moved back to Indiana, where Rena received a message from Ervil summoning her to Mexico. She balked; she wanted to marry Lloyd, she told him. Then came a long distance call from Don. He had located Verlan LeBaron, he said, and needed her help for a hit. When he wired her money, Rena flew to Dallas, only to learn that Don had lied to get her away from his father Lloyd. Don quoted to her from the scriptures on the subject of adultery. If she wanted a divorce from Ervil, he said, she should do it legally. He finally persuaded her to join Ervil in Mexico, and got Anna Mae Marston to drive along to ensure that Rena actually reached their husband.

With Rena gone, Lloyd flew back to Dallas and persuaded John and Don that it was time to leave the Church of the Lamb of God. The two cousins tried to persuade two other followers, Eddie Marston and Duane Chynoweth, then living in Oklahoma City, to leave with them, but Eddie and Duane were too solidly entrenched in Ervil's camp. Knowing they had been compromised, the Sullivans all fled to Houston, but were discovered there. They then decided to split up. Don and John headed for Little Rock, Arkansas, while Lloyd and Bonnie went to Wichita, Kansas.

In Wichita, Lloyd began writing voluminously. He wrote letters to people still in the group whom he thought could be persuaded to leave. He wrote long doctrinal dissertations which he felt exposed LeBaron as a charlatan. Lloyd knew this was a dangerous course for him to embark on, since some of his letters were certain to find their way into Ervil's hands. But he viewed it as a necessary cleansing process—a period in which he would seek to liberate his imprisoned religious conscience.

These letters were a prelude to a thirty-six-page open letter Lloyd directed at Ervil, apparently late in August though the document is undated. The letter—notable for its candor—amounted to Lloyd's public repentance, his rejection of Ervil as "fallen," and his call to others in the group to recognize the obvious failures of their leader.

"I have studied, prayed, walked the floor, and studied, prayed again and again," Lloyd wrote. "I find to my hurt, disgust, amazement and great sorrow, that Ervil Morrel LeBaron is a fallen prophet." He then painstakingly detailed prophecy after prophecy that had not been fulfilled, and sought to strip Ervil of any claim to religious authority.

He bemoaned the death of Joel LeBaron, who had never done anything to "deserve the axe," and then revealed the depth of his own LeBaron-inspired activity. He admitted that he had petitioned Ervil to have his wife Bonnie killed in December 1976 as a way to end their marital discord. LeBaron had responded shortly thereafter that he had had a vision in which two of his wives and another follower were to take Bonnie for her last ride. But a few days later, Ervil announced that the Lord had changed his mind. He wanted Lloyd himself to take Bonnie down to the "deep south and deep-six her there." Lloyd decided he could live with Bonnie after all.

He ended his letter by appealing to LeBaron's wives, and pointing out that all the Lambs of God were "divided, backbiting, backstabbing, walking over each other's rights, stealing from each other . . ."

To live, Lloyd tried launching a small washer repair business in Wichita but it never succeeded. So in September, he tried one last move—a curious one to the Lamb of God stronghold in Denver.

On August 2, the State of Utah had been forced to drop conspiracy to commit murder charges against Nancy Chynoweth. The state delayed her preliminary hearing more than two months after her arrest, in the hopes of developing more evidence which would warrant the arrest of additional Lambs of God police knew to be involved in the plot to kill Rulon Allred. The revelations of Delfina and Isaac LeBaron hadn't given them enough to go to trial against any of the others.

Prosecutor David Yocom didn't want to display the evidence police had accumulated for the trial of a minor player like Nancy. When he went to trial, he wanted more and bigger fish than just Nancy Chynoweth. So the charges against her were dropped, with the proviso that the state reserved the right to refile those charges at any time.

But with the addition of Jack Strothman into the picture, Yocom felt the situation changed. Officials now had an insider who could trace the conspiracy from Dallas to Evanston, Wyoming, and finally to Salt Lake City for the murder itself—naming names all along the way. This was the added dimension they needed to complement both the testimony of Isaac and the physical evidence which had been gathered.

On September 15, Yocom and the Forbes brothers met with a Salt Lake City judge and presented their evidence in a sworn deposition. The judge signed complaints against eleven persons for varying charges, including murder, conspiracy to commit murder and the attempted murder of Merlin Kingston—the man Strothman still mistakenly thought was the target of the funeral mission. At the request of Utah Governor Scott Matheson, the Justice Department also issued federal unlawful flight warrants against the Lambs of God. Since the arrests were expected to be made in several states outside of Utah, this was a logistical move which would enable the prosecution to avoid cumbersome state extradition laws.

The eleven warrants were for: Ervil; his son Arturo; Victor, Nancy, Mark and Rena Chynoweth; Lloyd, Don and John Sullivan; and Eddie and Ramona Marston.

With the help of the FBI, Secret Service and state law enforcement agencies, Utah officials had been monitoring the movements of most of the wanted Lambs for more than a month, and they thought they had a good idea where the cultists were. On the afternoon of September 15, in Salt Lake City, a meeting was held between several different local law enforcement agencies and federal agencies. Plans for a multistate, coordinated arrest were made.

On the 16th, Utah officers fanned out to four different cities. Dick

Forbes went to Denver, Paul Forbes to Dallas, Byron Vranes to Oklahoma City and Gary Pedersen to Houston. Local and federal police were to help them carry out the arrests in each city. The event was scheduled for September 17, but Vranes found that Eddie Marston had left Oklahoma City, and Pedersen learned that Don and John Sullivan were no longer in Houston. The arrests had to be coordinated or not go off at all, lest news from one city prompt group members in another city to flee.

The officers in each city communicated with one another via a command post set up back at the Murray police station in Utah. Vranes was ordered to fly to Indiana to follow up a lead indicating that Eddie, Don and John were there, but that trip proved fruitless. He flew to Denver to help Dick Forbes, while Pedersen was ordered to Dallas to help Paul Forbes.

Police finally made their move at 6:30 A.M. September 23. Eighty officers raided seven different locations in Denver, while twenty lawmen entered three houses in Dallas. The arrests went off without incident, but only four of the eleven named were initially arrested: Lloyd Sullivan, Victor Chynoweth and Ramona Marston in Denver and Mark Chynoweth in Dallas. However, later that day, an attorney for Nancy Chynoweth assured police he would surrender her in a few days, bringing the total to five.

The Denver raid netted a bonus: Dan Jordan, whom the FBI had written off as dead, following reports from Mexican police that he had been shot in 1976. Though Jordan hadn't been named in any of the charges out of Utah, Forbes knew he was still wanted in Mexico for the murder of Joel LeBaron. The FBI agreed to hold Jordan on a technicality until Mexico decided whether it wanted to extradite him. It seemed Dan, a native of Oregon, had never registered for the draft, and there was still a federal charge for "violation of the Selective Service Act" out of Portland outstanding against him.

After their federal removal hearings in Colorado and Texas, the accused Lambs were transported back to Utah and were booked into Salt Lake City-County jail. After their arraignments all five were eventually bailed out. Bail for Victor, Nancy and Lloyd was set at $15,000 and only $25,000 for Mark Chynoweth and Ramona Marston, who the state was alleging was one of the two women inside Allred's office. Authorities worried that the bails were too low to guarantee the defendants' appearance for the preliminary hearing.

Dan Jordan, meanwhile, was flown back to Portland where he sat in a jail and sweated out a decision from Mexico as to extradition. After a few days, Mexico announced, inexplicably, that it would not seek extradition. Jordan was released and his draft evasion charge dropped.

Some of the Utah investigators and other prosecution officials were disappointed that their carefully orchestrated series of arrests had collared only five of the eleven people they were after, and they were even more disappointed when those who were arrested had managed to get bail set so low. Nonetheless, the raid was a culmination of a thorough and exhaustive four-month investigation which had spanned about a dozen states, involved some eighty different local, state and federal law enforcement agencies, and made imaginative use of new techniques like hypnosis. The investigation had brought recognition to the Murray Police Department and to Dick Forbes, and was generally considered by the law enforcement community and other observers to have been first rate.

"No one else before these officers had been able to unravel the complex workings of LeBaron and his cult," said one Secret Service agent, admiringly.

And Ervil's doings were to be unraveled still further.

18

THE SULLIVAN DEFECTION

Ironically, the man who was to become the state's star witness, Lloyd Sullivan, was the only one of the five Lambs of God taken into custody who refused to talk. When they had arrested him, officers had also come upon his writings, which showed he had clearly grown disenchanted with Ervil. In fact, Lloyd had even told Dick Forbes before being taken to jail that he had come to the conclusion Ervil was a false prophet and that he felt it his responsibility to prove LeBaron wrong.

But Lloyd was to take his time in revealing what he knew. Despite his stated intention of cooperating, he remained "evasive" through several interviews, according to Forbes. After a while it became apparent that to assuage his conscience for being a lieutenant to an outlaw messiah for the last five years, Lloyd was going to make peace with the Lord before he got around to helping lay lawmen.

His first move was to extend an olive branch to the Church of the Firstborn. In a Thanksgiving Day letter addressed to Ervil's brother Floren, mother Maud and other residents of Colonia LeBaron, Lloyd begged for forgiveness and asked to be rebaptized a member of the Firstborn Church.

On December 5, 1977, Lloyd and his four co-defendants were in a Salt Lake City courtroom for the preliminary hearing in the Allred murder case. That proceeding—barred to the press and held under tight security over a period of five days—was notable for the deficiencies it revealed in the prosecution's case.

Police who investigate a murder, interview witnesses and live with a case personally for months, generally feel they know who committed the crime. But their view of what the evidence conclusively shows often differs from the prosecutor's, who must present that evidence in a courtroom under tight legal constraints.

David Yocom had taken stronger cases to trial in his day. At thirty-nine, he was generally considered the top prosecutor in the State of Utah. His courtroom manner was usually phlegmatic, though he was given to occasional displays of emotion, and was not reluctant to do battle with his opposite number. In seven years with the Salt Lake County Attorney, Yocom had prosecuted most of the murders that the office handled. Of sixteen homicide cases, he had lost only two.

The LeBaron case posed problems. Yocom's key eyewitnesses—Richard Bunker and Melba Allred—could not identify any of the defendants presently in the dock as Rulon Allred's killers. The state had not been able to turn up either of the guns used in the crime. And proving a conspiracy was always difficult, especially when Yocom had to rely primarily on the testimony of a co-conspirator—Jack Strothman.

Under Utah law, a person cannot be convicted on the uncorroborated testimony of a co-conspirator, an antiquated statute which many states have repealed. Strothman's testimony would have to be corroborated by other evidence which "tended to connect" the defendants with the commission of the crime. In the absence of eyewitness confirmation, it was largely up to a judge's discretion what corroborating evidence he would allow a jury to consider. But Yocom feared that evidence such as motel receipts, a car inspection record and testimony from a Deseret Industries clerk that one of the principals (she remembered only Rena) was in the Salt Lake City area the day Allred was killed, would not be adequate.

But if the testimony of a co-conspirator posed legal problems, the difficulties were compounded if that co-conspirator happened to be Jack Strothman.

"I think it's fair to say Jack was not the best witness I've ever seen," recalls Yocom. "It was difficult to get through to him because of his inability to comprehend the question, let alone give an answer. It was frustrating." At the preliminary hearing, Yocom would ask about the conspiratorial meeting in Dallas, and Strothman would ask, "What meeting?" He was hard pressed to remember people's names, as well as places, dates and other details in the plot until Yocom prompted him extensively and sometimes made it appear that he was putting words in the witness' mouth. Defense attorneys naturally reaped considerable mileage from such coaching.

Strothman was also terribly nervous as he confronted the Lambs of God he was now betraying. As he sat on the witness stand, he would shift restlessly and rock back and forth. He cracked his knuckles and stroked rings up and down his fingers.

"It was really pathetic," says Norma Glover, who sat at the prosecution table with Yocom. . . . "Dave had to ask questions on a first-grade level. Jack would try to describe things and mispronounce words. Victor and Mark Chynoweth were laughing"—laughing all the more, one presumes, when Strothman identified Merlin Kingston, not Verlan LeBaron, as the target for the funeral hit.

But according to Glover, the Lambs' demeanor changed abruptly when fifteen-year-old Isaac LeBaron took the witness stand. "Vic turned white. He leaned over to Mark and said, 'That's Isaac. He can tell them everything.' I wasn't sitting far away and I could overhear that comment. Mark just settled back in his chair and watched. Nancy, who was eight months pregnant, began staring Isaac down." Ramona and Lloyd listened intently.

Actually, Isaac was not in a position to do as much implicating as Strothman. But he tesitified about witnessing test firing of guns in the Dallas warehouse and about the Dallas conspiracy meeting itself in considerably more detail than did Strothman. Isaac's performance was a pleasant surprise for the prosecution, which hadn't been expecting much because the teenager was painfully shy, backward and still very scared. But he came across as clear, exact, articulate and purposeful, and he withstood cross-examination well.

Because of his youth and because of who he was—Ervil LeBaron's son—Isaac's appearance in the courtroom was high drama. The courtroom was absolutely still. The spectacle of the prophet's son dutifully answering questions about the workings of his father's cult, condemning his own past and avoiding all eye contact with the defendants was riveting. If Strothman was nervous, Isaac was terrified. And though David Yocom didn't want to put the boy through any unnecessary agony, he thought it relevant to show why he was terrified.

". . . Do you believe that you might be harmed in the future for your testimony here today?" the prosecutor asked.

"Probably," mumbled Isaac, after pondering the question a moment.

". . . In what way, probably?"

". . . If they find me."

"Pardon me? If they find you?"

"Yes."

"And in what way do you believe you'll be harmed?"

Isaac lowered his head and tears began streaming down his cheeks. "Killed," he finally whispered.

"By whom?" continued Yocom, after a pause to milk the moment.

"Whoever my dad sends."

At the end of the five-day hearing, Judge Paul Grant announced he was binding all the defendants over for trial, except one: Nancy Chynoweth. The judge said the state had failed to prove a cause-and-effect relationship between the .38 special Nancy undeniably bought, and the murder. Until the gun was found, police obviously could not prove it was one of the weapons fired insde Allred's office, and in addition, they could not prove that Nancy bought the gun knowing it would be used in a crime, said Grant.*

The prosecution was surprised. Yocom thought he had more evidence on Nancy than on some of the other defendants—notably Victor and Lloyd. The standards of proof vary greatly between a preliminary hearing and a trial. At a preliminary hearing, the state is required to prove only that a crime has been committed and that there is a reasonable likelihood that the defendants are guilty of what they are accused of. In a case of this stature, it was rare to not even be able to get a bind over.

After seven months in an investigative vacuum, this hearing had been the prosecution's first forum to present its evidence, and now one judge had told the state he was not overly impressed with its case. Yocom speculated whether a trial judge would even let a jury retire to deliberate the case—grounded as it was in insiders, or co-conspirators, whose testimony was largely uncorroborated by other evidence. It would be up to the judge's discretion to decide whether this other evidence was related enough to the crime or not.

But Yocom had to make the best of what he had. Hard as it might be to substantiate the testimony of a Strothman, he was, as of the moment, the only witness who could link specific persons to specific crimes.

If judicial discretion was destined to play a major role in the Allred trial, Yocom reasoned that he might as well give a judge as much as possible to use his discretion on. The prosecutor ordered a stepped-up effort to entice Lloyd Sullivan into the state's fold, as a replacement for Strothman. Lloyd was at least reasonably intelligent. He had been an important figure in the Church of the Lamb of God. And having only attended the Dallas conspiracy meeting—and played a marginal role in it at that—Lloyd's role as a state's witness would have less the foul smell of a deal, than if, say, one of the killers were to assume that role. Furthermore, if Lloyd, by virtue of new religious conviction, truly believed Ervil was a false prophet, he would be all the more credible as a witness.

Lloyd returned to Denver and resumed his writing. Apparently Dan Jordan, Victor Chynoweth and the other Lambs in the city were not aware of his defection from the ranks. Lloyd had said or done nothing at the preliminary hearing in Salt Lake that might have aroused suspicions among his co-defendants. But Dick Forbes thought it dangerous, under

---

*In an interview, Judge Grant, a Mormon, called the case the most "scary" he'd ever presided over because it involved a religious group with "an elitist philosophy, a superior attitude that everybody else was below them and unimportant." The FBI told him his life had been threatened, and the judge's wife became greatly concerned.

the circumstances, for Lloyd to remain in Denver. He called regularly to check in on Sullivan and asked that Denver police do the same.

On February 5, 1978, Lloyd sat down to write a letter to Don and John Sullivan, asking that they give themselves up. Despite the flareup in Houston the previous July, Lloyd said he still loved them both. He didn't know where the boys were now, but he hoped the letter would reach them somehow.

"The evidence that came up at the [preliminary] hearing on this matter is indeed overwhelming," Lloyd wrote. ". . . In my mind, as in the minds of all who were present, I'm sure it was convincing beyond all doubt that E.M.L. was the intellectual author of the case at hand.

". . . I feel that if you, or even some of you, were to come forward and testify to the allegation and probable fact that E.M.L. was indeed the bloody culprit, and that your roles were that of victims of coercion and force and that he used the Lord's name in vain in accomplishing this dastardly deed and blatant act of cold-blooded murder, then it would, by a jury, be taken into consideration and acted upon accordingly. I plead with you . . . I led you to this man because I was sincere and was truly deceived by him. Now let me lead you away from him and his bloody tenure! I testify to you in the name of the Lord God of Israel that from all that I can find out through prayer, research and study, this man is Satan!

". . . I realize that if this falls into the wrong hands, I'm in deep trouble, so I must be careful what I write. The enemy never sleeps! They're after you, me, John and all else who even remotely oppose them!"

As part of his desire to repent and become rebaptized into the Church of the Firstborn, Lloyd had also contacted Verlan LeBaron and asked to meet with him, so as to make a full "religious confession." Verlan, knowing how much the Lambs wanted him dead, was wary. He called Dick Forbes and asked for instructions. Forbes said he was convinced of Lloyd's sincerity, and he urged Verlan to go ahead with the meeting, then report back to the police.

Verlan drove to Denver and, on February 13, had a steak dinner at Lloyd's expense, and then returned to his motel room to write notes on what Lloyd had told him. Verlan later gave his notes to Salt Lake authorities.

The Lloyd-Verlan session was a watershed event because for the first time Lloyd supplied information alleging that Ervil was responsible for four murders, over and above those of Joel LeBaron, the two Los Molinos boys and Rulon Allred—which he already was officially considered to have ordered. Lloyd informed Verlan that Vonda White told him she had killed Naomi Zarate and Dean Vest on commands from Ervil. Lloyd admitted that he himself had lured Robert Simons away to his death, though he failed to tell Verlan who had actually killed Simons. And finally, Ervil had ordered his own daughter, Rebecca, killed, Lloyd said, adding that he had personally heard LeBaron issue instructions that the deed be done because Rebecca "was tearing up the whole deal."

Then Lloyd told of sitting with Ervil in Dallas one day when the prophet mused: "I wonder if they did anything to Rebecca last night." When Lloyd said that the trunk of Ervil's Ford LTD was sagging noticeably, Ervil said, "Go look." Lloyd did, and saw the teenager sprawled out dead.

At the Denver meeting, Lloyd also:

• detailed Ervil's failed prophecies;

• said that Ervil had given the Lambs of God standing orders to kill Verlan on sight;

• told of Ervil's constant paranoia that the Church of the Firstborn was out to kill him;

• admitted that he had taken part in an abortive plot to murder Rhea Kunz [Rulon Allred's sister, and Verlan's mother-in-law]. But Lloyd said he abandoned the plan. One of the purposes in killing Rhea, Lloyd added, was to lure Verlan to her funeral, where he then would be killed;

• confirmed that Ervil had the same thing in mind at the Allred funeral. Verlan was to have been hit there, not Merlin Kingston;

• admitted that he had passed out threatening notes directed at Allred in 1975;

• said he briefly attended Dallas conspiratorial meetings prior to Allred's murder, then was sent to Jackson, Mississippi, so as not to be in the way, he thought;

• revealed that Ervil once ordered him to go to Nicaragua and kill Floren LeBaron. But the plan was abandoned;

• warned that Ervil would kill again soon "to save face." Firstborn leaders should be especially wary. There were more than twenty persons on a Lamb of God hit list, including the leadership of the Mormon Church;

• quoted Dan Jordan as saying Ervil was not worried about any of the Lambs currently facing charges in connection with the Allred killing. "If they get any of our men in jail, we will blow the jail apart," Dan reportedly vowed, on Ervil's behalf;

• said Ervil had no desire to appoint his own successor because he felt he would not die.

And finally, Lloyd said he would like to get a grant of immunity from Utah authorities, but that he had every intention of giving police a full confession and statement concerning all Lamb of God crimes, in any event. "The minute I let these men [police] know what I know, Dan Jordan etc. will be after me . . .[But] my moral obligation and civil duty is to expose this thing," Verlan quoted Lloyd as saying.

Dick Forbes was overjoyed after hearing of Lloyd's meeting with Verlan. When this information was officially in hand after a statement from Lloyd, Salt Lake authorities would serve as the focal point for murder investigations in California, central Utah, Texas and perhaps Mexico. Their sphere of responsibility had now expanded far beyond the murder of Rulon Allred. The Allred investigation had prompted the other pieces of the LeBaron puzzle to finally start falling into place.

Lloyd agreed to a preliminary interview with an FBI agent before leaving Denver and coming to Salt Lake with his family. Having made the irrevocable decision to become a state's witness, there was no longer any wisdom in staying in Lamb of God-populated Denver.

Before he sat down with Dick Forbes et al, Lloyd naturally wanted to secure the best possible terms. At the moment he was only charged with conspiring to commit the murder of Rulon Allred—a marginal charge, considering Lloyd's role in Dallas, which the state would not be averse to dropping. But since he had been the wheelman, Lloyd stood to be accused of murder itself in the death of Robert Simons.

Lloyd's court-appointed attorney in Salt Lake, Thomas Vuyk, engaged in a little verbal sparring with prosecutor David Yocom before he allowed anxious detectives to talk with his client.

"I can't promise him anything until I know what he has to say," complained Yocom, knowing, via Verlan, basically what Lloyd had to say, but wanting to preserve his options nonetheless.

"And I can't let him say anything until I know what you have to promise," countered Vuyk. But Vuyk finally gave his permission for Yocom to go ahead and question Lloyd and use him as a state's witness, with the tacit understanding that things would go very easily on him in return.

So Lloyd sat down and talked. He told of the Allred conspiracy, and of the murders of Naomi Zarate, Robert Simons, Dean Vest and Rebecca LeBaron Chynoweth. Dick Forbes listened intently as Sullivan methodically supplied details of other murders the detective had only heard and speculated about.*

With the greening of Lloyd, and the opening up of the other murder investigations, things were going very well for the prosecution and then, all of a sudden, things got even better.

At 1:20 P.M. March 7, Dick Forbes received a call from Kansas City authorities with the news that John Sullivan had been arrested. He had been stopped for an automobile taillight violation, whereupon the policeman who pulled him over ran his name through a computer and found the charges pending in Utah.

Forbes could not contain his delight. "We got him! We got him!" he whooped, knowing that wherever John was, the more important Don

---

*Though there is no reason to doubt his veracity, it should be noted that Lloyd Sullivan did escape prosecution by becoming a state's witness, and some of those he accused of committing crimes would, in turn, accuse him of the same crimes.

Sullivan could not be far away. He boarded a plane that afternoon along with his brother Paul, and Gary Pedersen, and they arrived in Kansas City that night. They were met by FBI agents who reported that Don, too, had been given a traffic citation in December, for which he gave a Kansas City address. But no one had bothered to run his name through a computer at the time.

The Salt Lake trio, FBI agents, and local Kansas City police—including a SWAT team—drove to the address, hoping Don still lived there. It was about 11 P.M. as the squad of some twenty lawmen surrounded the house.

"We'd been told Don, the military leader, had all kinds of weapons," recalls Pedersen, "that he was a crazy sonovabitch and that he wouldn't come out alive. We knew there was someone inside because there were lights on and we could hear voices. The FBI agents knocked on the door and stated their purpose. Then the lights went off inside. We figured there was gonna be a fuckin' shootout at the O.K. Corral."

But then Don appeared at the back door unarmed and nearly undressed. Pedersen, not knowing if Don was still loyal to the group or not, ran up and asked him who else was inside the house, hoping that they'd gotten lucky and Ervil was hiding there too. Don told him he had left the group, and that just his wife and children were inside. He said he'd been running scared from Ervil, and that when he heard the knock on the door, he thought it was LeBaron's Lambs.

He was tired of running and was relieved at finally being caught. Asked why, if he was tired of running and scared of Ervil, he hadn't given himself up, Don replied that he had read all about Gary Gilmore. Utah was a death penalty state. He thought he would die whoever got him, Ervil or the police. Under such circumstances, he wasn't too anxious to give himself up.

Don was taken to jail and booked for murder and conspiring to murder Allred, and conspiring and attempting to murder Verlan LeBaron. John Sullivan was charged with conspiracy in the Allred killing and the attempted murder of Verlan. Don was brought out for a 1:25 A.M. interrogation session March 8 after he agreed to answer questions without a lawyer present. He also waived his extradition rights and said he would go back to Utah with the police.

But having volunteered to answer questions, Don proceeded to stonewall. He denied having a "close relationship" with Ervil; denied that he was LeBaron's military leader or even in the military at all; refused to answer any questions about the rank-and-file Lambs of God, suggesting that they were simply brainwashed; and refused to discuss his own involvement in either the Allred killing or the attempted murder of Verlan. "I'll waive that question," he said repeatedly.

"I have nothing against Allred or anybody else that this thing might be about," Don insisted.

"Well," snapped Dick Forbes, growing increasingly irritated, "every time I ask you a question concerning specific facts regarding that murder, you don't want to answer it, so that would indicate to me that you have some knowledge of it. Is that correct?"

". . . Okay," said Don. "I'll be honest with you. . . . I knew what was going to happen. [But] I don't have any faith in this judicial system and I know what is going to happen to me. I know Salt Lake City has the firing squad. I know what you are going to do. You are going to shoot me. And I'll tell you one thing. You'll be killing an innocent man."

"Why would they kill an innocent man?" countered Forbes. "Do you think it is all a fairy tale? The whole case is a fairy tale. The murder never occurred. You weren't involved. You didn't stay at the Holiday. You didn't stay at the Lone Pine where Rena and Ramona went. You didn't go over to the doctor's office. You didn't test fire weapons. You didn't stay at the Dunmar. Is that a fairy tale? You think it's a fairy tale that we made up, Don?"

Don mumbled something unintelligible, a pause which served only to give Forbes a chance to catch his breath. He wasn't about to stop now. "How about the inspection sticker for Rena Chynoweth's car? Phillips 66 Station at 45 South and State Street. Were you there when she had that inspected or were you across the street in the restaurant eating lunch? Is that a fairy tale? A piece of paper that was signed and dated by the gas station attendants on that date?"

"What are you trying to prove?"

"I want you to tell us the truth, is what I want, Don!" Forbes shouted. "That's all I want, is the truth out of you."

"I've told you the truth," Don insisted. "I didn't have anything to do with Allred's killing. I didn't kill him. I don't know who did."

"You don't have *any* knowledge of who did that?" said Forbes, his voice oozing with sarcasm.

"Would you be willing to take a polygraph?" chimed in brother Paul.

"Polygraph has been known to be wrong." Don hedged. ". . . All I've heard since I've been here is how guilty I am. There is not one thing here where you have said, 'Hey, look pal, it doesn't look like you are guilty here. It looks like such and such happened this way, see.' It has all been everything pointing towards me on this situation, and I'm just trying to tell you—"

"Okay," interrupted Dick Forbes, "here is how it has been. Hey, that's why I'm asking those questions. If you can tell us something different, then lay it on us, because we want the truth and we want the facts, and if you can clarify those for us, or give us a statement that would help you . . . then do it."

"I told you," Don said, shaking his head. "It doesn't make any difference whether I'm innocent or guilty. I know what Salt Lake is."

". . . Don," Forbes said, "there's gonna be a lot of decisions made about your outcome by us—"

"They've been made," Sullivan droned, hopelessly.

"Hey!" Forbes snapped, not taking the interruption kindly, "by a jury, by twelve people who are going to sit and listen to facts, and the facts are going to be presented by us, by witnesses, by people who have been in your group who are no longer with it."

"I'll tell you what," Don said. "I've faced death a thousand times already in my mind, and in my dreams, and I am tired of running, and I'm not running anymore. Here I am . . . I am a man with no hope, is what I am. Now, you tell me what a man without hope is, and I'll tell you what he is too. He is dangerous."

"Let *me* tell *you* what, Don," suggested Forbes.

But Sullivan hadn't finished expressing his thought yet, and so he kept talking, ignoring Forbes' comment. ". . . Because he doesn't give a shit about nothin'. He is in a cage, living, and that is what I am. I am a man without hope. I have got my family torn from me, and my wife, and what else can you do that is worse than that?"

In reply, Forbes launched into a lecture on the virtues of cooperating with law enforcement, changing ways, admitting wrongs and being contrite. Prosecutors, judges and jurors tend to look more kindly on such a man than on one who remained defiant. Forbes noted that Lloyd, Don's father, had cooperated with the law and felt better for it.

Don decided to send out a feeler of his own. "Let me ask you this question," he said to Forbes. "This isn't an admission of guilt. What is the penalty, according to law—I want to know if it varies from state to state—for a person to be under the influence, or brainwashed, to do things that he normally wouldn't do."

"If a person acts under the influence of another person," replied Forbes, "and thoroughly believes that he is doing right, or what he has done is right at the time, if he believes that, that is taken into consideration by a judge and a jury at the time that man is judged. And that's the best I can tell you, Don. That's really where it's at."

"Let me ask you another question. I'm sure you know the records of these people that have been arrested; their past. Any of them been violent?"

"None of them have ever been convicted of a violent crime, Don," Forbes admitted. "I don't know whether they've ever been violent or not. I'll tell you what—I see some innocent people there that were caught up in the Ervil LeBaron thing. Ramona Marston's the best example I can think of. She's one helluva nice girl. And her total life has been affected because that man took advantage of her and used her like he used everyone else. It's brainwashing. It's religious, but it's brainwashing. There's no question about it."

Don searched his questioners' eyes earnestly, as if he now finally had the platform he'd been waiting to spring from. "Don't you think that I [realized this]? Don't you think [I've] thought about it after I left? Don't you think I know I was used, along with everyone else? Don't you think I tried to warn everybody else that I knew . . . would listen? It's not easy to walk up to somebody and say, 'Hey, you're following a false prophet.' "

Forbes decided to cut short the debate and the persuasion, and slip in a little substantive questioning before ending the session and grilling Don further back in Salt Lake. But Sullivan, seemingly having run out of reason not to respond, did so, and proceeded to confirm key elements of the state's case: that he came to Utah under the direction of Ervil with orders to kill Verlan at Allred's funeral; that he went to the funeral but decided to abandon the attempt to murder Verlan; that he and other principals in the plot—including Ervil—rendezvoused in Evanston, Wyoming, before proceeding to Salt Lake; that Ervil gave him money for expenses there; that the hit teams test fired their guns on the outskirts of Salt Lake; that they bought wigs and other clothing at Deseret Industries prior to the murder and dumped it all in a disposal after the murder. But Don still avoided implicating most Lambs of God besides LeBaron.

Satisfied for the present, Forbes turned off his tape recorder and called it a day. It was 3 A.M.

At 1 P.M., after a little sleep, the Utah detectives summoned John Sullivan out of his cell. He impressed them as being only slightly more acute than Jack Strothman in his recollection of detail, and less willing to cooperate. He did say that Rena Chynoweth admitted to him in Dallas that she had killed Allred. Rena showed him a calculator which she had picked up after the struggle, John added.

John said he had gone to El Paso with Mark and Duane Chynoweth on a mission to kill Verlan LeBaron if the Firstborn leader did not appear in Salt Lake City as planned. Sullivan also noted that he unwittingly played a minor role in another murder: that of supplying the shovel which was used to bury Rebecca LeBaron Chynoweth. John alleged that Eddie Marston had strangled her, then buried her with the help of Duane Chynoweth. He said he didn't know where the body was buried.*

Don and John were taken back to Salt Lake where, on March 11, 1978, they again sat down and gave formal, more detailed statements which the detectives billed as "confessions." John added nothing of substance, but Don:

• named names and gave a chronological account of events which occurred between Dallas and Salt Lake. This account conformed to Strothman's in most particulars;

• emphasized that the Allred and Verlan LeBaron missions were related, but separate in terms of planning and responsibility. He said Ervil had instructed Rena and Ramona on the Allred hit, and left the

---

*The only evidence that Rebecca was murdered are the statements of Lloyd, Don and John Sullivan to police. Her body has not been found, and no one has been charged with any crime.

funeral mission to him. Don added he didn't believe the women would
have enough courage to go through with their end of the assignment,
which would then have given him an excuse to cancel his part;

• said that Ervil once considered sending Vonda White and Lillian
Chynoweth to kill Allred, but Lillian was pregnant. Vonda had apparently already paid her dues;

• said Ervil instructed Rena to use the .25 pistol and Ramona the
.38;

• said he thought Mark and Duane Chynoweth disposed of the
guns;

• said Ervil had told him that killing Verlan at the Allred funeral was
a direct command from God, and that if he and his cohorts didn't carry
out the assignment, they "would be destroyed from this earth." Given
the obstacles they would have encountered at the funeral, Don said he
considered it a suicide mission, and that Ervil intended for them to
die.

Lloyd Sullivan visited his son and nephew in the Salt Lake County
jail, and told them how pleased he was to hear that they were cooperating with the state. Then, following Don and John's March 11 statement, Lloyd reassumed the investigative center stage.

Based on Lloyd's statement that Vonda White had confessed to him
in Denver that she had murdered Dean Vest in 1975, detectives in
National City, California, jubilantly reopened their Vest investigation.

Then, in recounting for investigators the chilling tale of how Robert
Simons had been done in, Lloyd said he could find the spot where the
body was buried, even though it had been nearly three years since the
murder.

So, on March 23, Lloyd led a retinue of officials to the town of Price,
in central Utah. They drove to a dirt road twelve miles south of the
Price courthouse and ventured out onto the desert floor. Lloyd said he
remembered the dirt road because it was still marked by a rubber tire
lying near its entrance. He had driven Robert Simons down this road
the night of April 23, 1975, and stopped when he spotted a pile of rocks
which, by prearrangement, served as his marker.

The officials with Lloyd looked around them. The scene was one of
utter desolation, miles from nowhere. Some of them thought they were
on a wild-goose chase, and others, of a more conspiratorial bent, enter-
tained the notion that they were being set up. This mission to the desert
was a secret and no one knew where they were except the searchers
themselves. But Lloyd was out on bail, and chances were he had
probably told his wife, Bonnie, about the trip, and Bonnie was still in
contact with some Lambs. Wouldn't they all be prime bait for a Los
Molinos in the desert? No one would find them until next deer season, if
then.

Near the rock pile, Lloyd told authorities, Eddie Marston and Mark

Chynoweth had lain in ambush for Simons. After Marston had fired one round from a 12-gauge shotgun into the back of Simons' head, killing him instantly, the three men had buried the body in a grave two to three feet deep and about fifty feet away from the actual murder site. Marston had removed Simons' watch and wallet before burying him, Lloyd added, and as they were getting ready to leave, Eddie asked if anyone wanted the watch. When no one did, Marston dug a hole in the ground with the heel of his boot, flipped the watch inside and covered the hole with dirt.

The search party fanned out with shovels to probe for the body and the watch in different areas at Lloyd's direction, but after several hours they had turned up nothing, and returned to Salt Lake City.

Lloyd remained adamant that the body was buried in the area but some officials were openly skeptical. It was a needle-in-a-haystack assignment whose chances of success were dimmed further by the passage of three years. Nevertheless, the search party made plans to return a week later for a final try. In the meantime, the prosecution's Norma Glover thought they should be better prepared. A local pathologist told her that if they did find the body it would have to be carefully packed in a body bag with dry ice. He suggested contacting a University of Utah anthropologist named John McCullough to aid in the excavation work. McCullough was excited by the idea and requested permission to bring along a graduate assistant named Jera Pecotte.

Glover recalls that she obtained this permission "grudgingly" from investigators who were suspicious of the need for any outsiders to intrude on their doings. Meanwhile, Pecotte—who police dubbed "the bone lady"—suggested that Glover call in a "body-sniffer" to aid in the search. A body-sniffer, she explained, was a newly developed machine officially called "Vapor-Tect," which could detect methane gas given off by buried bodies. She said she had seen the machine used while on an archeology dig in Mississippi.

Glover learned that the inventor of this machine was a Californian. When she contacted the man, he told her there were only two Vapor-Tects in existence. One stayed with him and the other he loaned out. He said that the machine had been used in the Juan Corona murder case to sniff out the bodies of farm workers buried in shallow graves, and for other assignments as well. The machine he loaned out had just come back from a job in Saudi Arabia, he said, and was full of sand. It had to be cleaned, but he said he'd be willing for Utah officials to use it in their case free of charge if they paid for shipping and insurance. Glover agreed, and anxiously awaited the delivery of this bit of exotica.

The search party set out again the morning of March 30. Norma and the two anthropologists were to pick up the body-sniffer at the Salt Lake airport and arrive later that afternoon. But the machine failed to arrive on its scheduled flight, so they left without it and made arrangements for the Utah Highway Patrol to pick it up when it arrived and drive it to Price.

Back in the desert, meanwhile, the search was continuing, this time with the aid of metal detectors and a bulldozer. Lloyd was directing the operation while sipping a beer inside a car. It was warm and he didn't want to strain his already weak heart.

Around 1 P.M. Ronald Boutwell, the attorney for Utah's Carbon County, who had been designated to prosecute the Simons case, heard his metal detector make active noises. Murray Detective Byron Vranes began digging beneath the detector and promptly uncovered Simons' watch.

Vranes let out a whoop and held up the watch for all to see. It was clean, and after he shook it a few times, it began ticking—the proverbial advertisement for Timex. Most of the searchers were elated. If they'd found the watch, could the body be far away? But some were suspicious, wondering whether Lloyd might have somehow planted the watch to justify the search effort.

The rest of the afternoon turned up no trace of the body, but the searchers' spirits were buoyed by the finding of the watch and by the arrival, later that evening, of the body-sniffer. They decided to stay in Price overnight and resume their search the next day.

The body-sniffer itself is about the size of a car battery and has gauges on its surface. It is wired to a six-foot-long steel probe that has a sharp point at the end for penetrating into the ground.

Early the morning of March 31, it soon became apparent that the body-sniffer was going to be of virtually no use because the terrain was so rocky that the steel probe could rarely penetrate more than six inches. The machine did show a few positive readings, but they turned out to be only the roots of Juniper trees.

The bulldozer, meanwhile, was ravaging the desert plateau. It would occasionally knock down trees, scrape off three inches of earth at a time, then look to see what had been dug up.

By late morning they still had found nothing, and there was a general consensus that they ought to give up. It was hot. The wind was blowing and it was clouding over. It was supposed to rain later that afternoon. Norma Glover and Jera Pecotte had just put the sniffer away because it wasn't working. The men had their shirts off and were drinking beer. They appeared to have dug up the whole plateau.

Lawrence Hayes, an affable and sunburnt bulldozer operator who had worked for the Carbon County Road Department for years, was still out pawing the earth, kicking over rocks. He stooped absently and picked one up. It had mosslike vegetation growing on one side and pickmarks on the other—not unusual since some of the searchers were using picks. But Hayes thought it odd. He got back in his machine and began scraping over the spot.

Some of the others, having already decided to quit, walked over to see what the old man was up to. He took one six-inch swipe and backed up. Nothing. But when he came in for his second swipe, as Vranes recalls it, "bones and shit started flipping out of there like you wouldn't believe.

Then, all of a sudden, we saw a pant leg coming out of the earth. It was amazing. Everybody was jumping for joy. We'd found him."

Hayes, a smiling hero, backed his dozer away, having beaten the experts and their body-sniffer. The anthropologists moved in and began digging carefully by hand, then using toothbrushes and trowels, dusting and preserving. Slowly, the body was uncovered. The lime his killers had poured over him had helped to preserve rather than erode Simons' body, becuase there wasn't sufficient moisture in the ground to activate the lime's chemicals.

They saw Simons' brown belt. The leather was uncracked and still supple. Then his tan jeans with a Lee's patch, and a button-down blue shirt with red pinstriping. He was wearing black work boots with yellow shoelaces wrapped twice around each boot and still tied in a bow. There were green Adler socks coming out of the boots and bones coming out of the socks. The right leg was intact. The left leg had been severed at the femur by the bulldozer, which had also partially crushed his pelvis.

The left side of Simons' face had deteriorated badly. He had been lying on his side in an S position—left side up. He still had hair on his head. His teeth were intact, including one gold tooth which would serve as a good identifier.

Flies started to gather. There was a smell of decay in the air, though it wasn't overwhelming. The skies began to look more threatening, so the anthropologists hurried to finish their work before it rained. When the whole body was uncovered, they took measurements and described the bones in writing. Police, meanwhile, photographed the body lying in its grave from every conceivable angle.

Norma Glover and Byron Vranes began sifting through the pile of dirt that the bulldozer had left after its two passes. They were looking for bones. Burrowing with her hands, Norma began pulling out what she thought was a root. It kept coming and coming, until there appeared what was obviously a knee joint. She held it up for all to see. John McCullough, the anthropologist, told her with a smile: "You've got the femur!" Everyone laughed, and Glover—feeling "a little squeamish"— quickly handed the bone to somebody.

The remains of the body were taken out of the grave and carefully placed in a plastic bag surrounded by dry ice to preserve tissues. Lest their photos of Simons lying in the grave be somehow deemed suspect, police thought they should have proof that the grave was large enough to hold a man, so Paul Forbes was elected to climb inside and pose for a picture.

That done, the official searching party climbed in their cars and headed back to Salt Lake, some 150 miles to the north. Everyone was delighted with the day's events. New first degree murder charges would soon be filed against Ervil, Eddie Marston and Mark Chynoweth. Lloyd Sullivan would be the state's star witness and would not be charged at all—a necessary trade-off in the enforcement of laws, the prosecution explained.

March 31, 1978, was also a successful day on another front in the
LeBaron investigation: Vonda White was arrested in Denver for the
1975 murder of Dean Vest.

The next day, April 1, Dick Forbes would officially ask Robert
Simons' dentist to compare Simons' dental chart with the teeth of the
corpse found in Price. But this was pro-forma stuff. Forbes, and all the
other searchers who had gone on the Price expedition, were quite sure
whose body they had.

Glen Chynoweth, thirty-six, had never followed Ervil LeBaron. The
cherub-faced, truck-driving Mormon had been an outsider among his
own family, but as far as he was concerned, family was family—people
you never turned your back on, philosophical differences notwithstanding. Glen could not fathom the notion that any of his family could be
involved in murder, and if he could help any of them, he would.

On April 6, Duane Chynoweth called Glen and said he needed his
help immediately. Fearing their phones might be tapped, Duane didn't
say why he needed his brother. He just asked Glen to fly to Dallas right
away.

When Glen appeared at the Salt Lake City airport that night about
10 P.M. on his way to Texas, he was confronted by Dick Forbes. Forbes
had learned of Glen's plans and assumed that he and Duane were going
to Mexico to meet Mark. Glen simply replied that he was going to
Dallas to help Duane on a business deal, then boarded his flight.

In Dallas, the brothers climbed into Duane's 1973 Ford pickup and
began driving straight for Mexico. Glen noted there were two motorcycles in the back. Duane explained that several weeks ago, he and Mark
had contracted with a Mexican acquaintance to deliver two motorcycles
which the Mexican needed in two days for a race. He had sent them the
money and Duane had bought the bikes. But then Mark had to flee the
country. Two people were needed to escort the bikes across the border—
apparently one for each registration—so he had called Glen.

Also in the back of the pickup, Glen noted, were a variety of musical
instruments and amplifiers. Mark was a musician, but Duane said they
merely hoped to sell the equipment in Mexico at a profit. He added that
Mark was aware of the time and place they were to deliver the motorcycles, but Duane said that under the circumstances, he didn't know if
Mark would be there or not.

First, they tried crossing the border at Hidalgo, Texas, but the
Mexicans wouldn't let them in with the new motorcycles. A guard,
however, told them if they came back at 10:30 that night, he would see
what he could do for them. They decided to drive down to Brownsville
and try crossing there. But at Brownsville, the Mexican border guards
told them the motorcycles were okay, but not the musical instruments.
For $30, one guard wavered on the bikes, but then his supervisor
appeared and said that he, too, would have to be remunerated if the
brothers were to cross. Duane and Glen agreed to pay the supervisor if

he could guarantee they could also get through a second checkpoint several miles down the road into Mexico.

But the supervisor refused to provide them any such guarantee, so the brothers decided to go back to Hidalgo that night, April 7, and try to bribe the guard who had extended his hand to them earlier. But on their way back through the U.S. checkpoint at Brownsville, a computer alerted by Dick Forbes spat out the Chynoweth name as dangerous. Guards searched each brother and the pickup thoroughly. Finding nothing suspicious, the immigration authorities permitted Duane and Glen back into the U.S.

But the brothers' troubles continued. At Hidalgo that night, they were surrounded by police as they approached the Mexican border. The U.S. authorities, who obviously had been waiting for the Chynoweths, accused them of running guns and carrying stolen motorcycles. Officers proceeded to ransack the truck, even opening up the amplifiers in an effort to uncover some sort of contraband. Finding nothing, the officials impulsively arrested Glen and Duane on suspicion of possessing stolen property—the motorcycles.

Glen, who had never found himself on the wrong side of the law before, was indignant. He called the cops "pigs" and threatened to sue them all, according to a report from the arresting officers. Allowed one call from jail, Glen called his mother, Thelma Chynoweth, in Oklahoma City and asked her to have the motorcycle dealer where Duane had bought the bikes attest to jail authorities that the vehicles were not stolen.

By morning they were released. They drove back to Brownsville, where motorcycles were allowed over the border, stored the musical instruments on the U.S. side and finally crossed into Mexico. They drove straight through to Villahermosa, some 400 miles east of Mexico City, in the state of Tabasco, arriving at 10:45 A.M., in time for the Chynoweth client's noon race, which he proceeded to win.

Mark was there and Glen asked him why he had fled the United States. Mark replied that he and Ervil had decided it was more important for him to be a missionary for the Church of the Lamb of God than to sit and rot in an American jail.

Not long after Mark's flight, Ramona Marston—the alleged number-two gunwoman in the Allred murder—decided that it was in her best interests if she, too, jumped bail and fled rather than return to Salt Lake for the Allred trial scheduled later that month of April. With Mark and Ramona gone, with a judge having dismissed charges against Nancy Chynoweth and with Lloyd Sullivan now a star state's witness—the prosecution was left with a slim cast of characters with which to go to trial.

Don and John Sullivan had given full confessions, were cooperating fully with authorities and both would probably reach a settlement with the state wherein they would plead guilty to lesser charges. That left just Victor Chynoweth, who was charged only with conspiracy in the murder of Allred. Prosecutor David Yocom deemed Victor a minor player hardly worth staging a trial for as the lone defendant. In any event, he probably couldn't get a conviction. The best way to convict the minor players, Yocom thought, was to lump them in the dock together with the more significant ones like Rena, Ramona, Eddie Marston, or better yet, Ervil himself—and let some of their guilt rub off on the lesser lights.

So Yocom opted to delay the trial, sit back and wait for the fugitives to trickle in.

On April 24, Lloyd Sullivan ventured out for his first court test as a state's witness: the preliminary hearing for Vonda White in San Diego. Worried that Lloyd would be a prime target for an Ervil assassination attempt, the prosecution had tucked Sullivan safely away in remote Twin Falls, Idaho, and given him the alias "Lloyd Jay Burch." Lloyd had established a small appliance business and seemed quite content with his lot.

Authorities wanted him to testify at Vonda's preliminary hearing so that his testimony would be "preserved," or, usable at the trial itself if, for whatever reason, Lloyd could not appear. That possibility was considered real, in view of the danger he faced from LeBaron and because of his history of heart trouble.

Lloyd's appearance at the closed hearing was met with tight security. Five armed guards were posted inside the courtroom and three more stood watch outside. His testimony was flawless. He said Vonda had told him in Denver that she killed Dean Vest "by command of God," and that as a result of doing so, she was to become one of heaven's "elected ladies." The order actually came from Ervil LeBaron. Lloyd explained that Ervil had said at least three times that "judgment had come down" against Dean Vest—the equivalent of an execution order.

Lloyd proceeded to relate in detail what Vonda had told him over the kitchen sink in Denver as to the details of the murder. The judge, allowing the prosecution wide latitude, also permitted Lloyd to testify to Vonda's admission that she had killed Naomi Zarate in Ensenada a few months before the Vest murder.

In explaining the inner workings of the Church of the Lamb of God, Lloyd said that Ervil's authority over the group was absolute. If the Lambs followed all orders, LeBaron promised "that we would be accepted in the universe as gods and goddesses," he testified. If any orders were not followed, ". . . we would receive justice, hot lead and cold steel or a one-way ticket to hell—things of that nature."

"What did the term, 'one-way ticket to hell' mean?" asked prosecutor Gary Rempel.

"That meant you die, unequivocally," said Lloyd.

"Hot lead and cold steel, would that be the same thing?"

"Death."

Lloyd said Ervil also described murders by calling them "dangerous exploits"—an Old Testament phrase—or "Law of the .38." The presiding judge, Kenneth A. Johns, found such testimony so bizarre that he remarked at the conclusion of the hearing: "Incredible case. I don't see how people can interpret the word of God the way it has been done in this case. Just incredible!"

The judge ordered Vonda bound over for trial July 10, and directed that she be held in jail in lieu of $350,000 bond—a fortune compared to the paltry bail sums set in Utah.

On May 25, just one month after his testimony, Lloyd Sullivan died of a heart attack.

The Utah prosecution, stunned, staged a private "wake" for him around David Yocom's backyard swimming pool, where, like the Irish, they drank numerous toasts to Sullivan's memory and mourned the passing of their star witness. "We were upset," recalls one of the participants, "and having a party seemed like the right thing to do. No one knew how else to respond."

19.

SETBACKS

With the death of Lloyd Sullivan, the fortunes of the prosecution began a decline which would not be seriously checked for nearly two years.

Don Sullivan was required to substitute for his father as the prosecution's new key witness. Originally charged with conspiracy to murder Verlan LeBaron, Don pleaded guilty only to conspiring to murder Verlan, in return for dismissal of the other three counts. He would testify for the state in the Allred, Simons and Vest trials—as well as in any Rebecca trial if Texas authorities were able to find her body or otherwise decided to prosecute that case. Sentencing of Don was to be indefinitely postponed pending his performances in the various trials. Privately, however, no one expected Lloyd's son to ever do any time in prison.

Don was given a new identity and he quietly started an appliance business in a western state—determined to carve out a new life for himself, but careful to frequently glance over his shoulder for stray Lambs of God.

His cousin, John, had also been charged with conspiracy in the Allred and Verlan LeBaron cases. The state dropped the Allred count and delayed John's trial indefinitely, in return for John's agreement to testify for the prosecution.

Ervil LeBaron, meanwhile—still a fugitive in the bowels of Mexico—was predictably reaping considerable mileage from the timely death of Lloyd Sullivan. The Lord had chosen to strike the traitor down, Ervil told his followers.

Utah investigators had strong reason to believe that all the Lambs of God they still were looking for were hiding in Mexico. Dick Forbes and his cohorts were frustrated at their inability to influence the course of the investigation south of the border. They were eager to go down and hunt for Ervil themselves—they had the motivation that they doubted Mexican authorities did. But Mexican officials had let it be known through diplomatic channels that any American policeman setting foot on Mexican soil in an official capacity would be liable to arrest.

So Forbes was officially at the mercy of a usually cumbersome FBI liaison with seemingly less than zealous Mexican police. Unofficially, he got the help of an occasional Mormon missionary who might have seen or heard of Ervil while traveling through the country, but this tended to be a passive, hit-or-miss method of obtaining information. Until the summer of 1978, there was no evidence that official Mexico was responding in the slightest to repeated American requests for action in tracking down LeBaron and his Lambs of God. Ervil had foiled the Mexican judicial system twice, and from all reports seemed to be able to roam the country with a certain confident discretion.

But on June 8, 1978, there was an indication that Mexico's attitude toward LeBaron and his group might be changing. At 3 A.M., in the state of Tabasco, nearly a score of federal police burst into a house with machine guns, rifles and pistols—and arrested Eddie Marston. Some three weeks later he was dropped at the U.S. border in Laredo, where waiting FBI agents took him into custody. An official announcement said Eddie was captured while trying to cross into the U.S.

After Marston's arrival in Salt Lake, police arranged a confrontation between him and Don Sullivan in a Murray Police Department office. The two men were left alone with assurances that their conversation would not be taped. The purpose of the meeting was to talk doctrine, and to see if Don could convince Eddie scripturally that Ervil was a false prophet. If he could, the official consensus was that Eddie would confess. Don had prepped for the session extensively, and came armed with the Bible, the Book of Mormon and other scriptures. At the end of their meeting, which lasted several hours, Eddie hadn't changed his mind, but Don thought he'd been able to get a foot slightly in the door.

However, Anna Mae Marston quickly nipped any possible spiritual rapprochement between Don and Eddie in the bud when, visiting her son from Denver, she ordered him to have nothing more to do with the traitorous Don. Anna Mae urged Eddie to keep the faith and brought him a revelation from Ervil that he would be acquitted of all the crimes with which he was charged.

Don, in yet another encounter, challenged Eddie to think for himself and not rely on his mother, but it was no use. Marston said he was "100 percent on Ervil's ball team." The lines between the two were clearly drawn. Eddie knew Don would testify against him in court, but, strangely enough, seemed to bear no animosity toward his former colleague. "We both knew what he had to do," remembers Don.

Seeing they could do nothing else, the Utah police transmitted a detailed summary report on Rebecca's murder to the Dallas District Attorney's Office. The opening statement said: "Everybody that has had contact with [the Lamb of God] group said that Rebecca caused the organization a great deal of trouble and that Ervil [LeBaron] had her killed in approximately April 1977." It continued that statements were obtained alleging that Eddie Marston had strangled the girl, Duane Chynoweth had at least been present and assisted in the burial and Victor Chynoweth bought the tent used to hide the grave.

On the eve of Vonda White's July 10 trial in San Diego, the exile in Mexico decided to speak. Breaking a twenty-month public silence, Ervil fired off an 8,000-word harangue to Vice-President Walter Mondale which bemoaned the deplorable state of the Union and condemned what he called a joint church-state conspiracy to undermine LeBaron's own "administration." It was the first time Ervil had been heard from publicly since he issued the last Society of American Patriots tirade in the fall of 1976, and this letter was similar in tone and rhetoric to many of the SAP documents.

LeBaron took another backhanded slap at Jimmy Carter, whose fervent Baptist beliefs Ervil thought served to condone Mormon-backed efforts to wipe out the Church of the Lamb of God. "Government officers," he wrote, "whose thinking is distorted by religious fanaticism and who are consequently dedicated to protecting the different types and forms of criminality that constitute a part of lawless religions, are readily entangled in church-sponsored persecutions that are designed to suppress true freedom." As an example of such persecution, LeBaron went on to give his own detailed version of the Mexican raid which had resulted in the arrest of Eddie Marston.

Then, after going on to heap praise on his own "worldwide educational government," and accusing the U.S., again, of "lawless" conduct, Ervil called Mondale's attention to the San Diego trial of Vonda White, one of his wives. "At the present time, a Mormon prosecuting attorney [Gary Rempel was Mormon] at San Diego, California, is heading the campaign of false testimony and persecution of an innocent mother of six children for the express purpose of defaming my administration, and to entangle me in a lawless judicial web of church vice and political corruption," LeBaron seethed.

He also accused the State of Utah of "violently kidnapping" his two sons, Isaac and Pablo, from Texas and "criminally brainwashing" them.

And after raking the U.S. government, the Mormons, the FBI and all other police, Ervil had one final word for his archenemies: the leaders of the Church of the Firstborn.

"All charges against me, of which I am aware, have been instigated and motivated by the leaders of a small cult that has almost completely disintegrated as a result of my exposure of its unfounded doctrines and practices.

"I request," LeBaron wrote Mondale, "that all propaganda and vicious slander coming through this class of individuals be discredited and that you intercede with President Carter and all other competent authorities of the federal government to put an end to these terrible crimes and prevent further implication of the present administration in the type of actions that lead to disaster in every respect." The letter was signed, "Yours for truth and justice—Ervil LeBaron."

A copy of the letter was sent to Vonda White in the San Diego jail, and intercepted by authorities, who deemed the reference to Gary Rempel a threat. The prosecutor took to arming himself, wearing sunglasses and going incognito. As the trial got underway, he was assigned two bodyguards amidst tight security and a bomb threat.

The trial was good theater. The witness list featured a virtual Who's Who of past and present members of the Church of the Firstborn and the Church of the Lamb of God—all appearing in one courtroom for the first U.S. trial of one of Ervil's followers.

The witnesses included: Verlan and Alma LeBaron; Conway LeBaron—Ervil's cousin who had fled the Church of the Lamb of God in 1974 after LeBaron ordered him to kill his own wife; Linda Johnson—Ervil's rotund wife who had been Vonda's roommate at the time of the Vest murder; Dan Jordan—LeBaron's right-hand man who had to be arrested in Denver to assure his appearance in San Diego, where he proceeded to take the Fifth Amendment seventeen times before he was ordered released; Isaac LeBaron—Ervil's teenaged son, now a ward of the State of Utah; and finally, Don Sullivan, who testified that in a February 1975 conversation with Ervil in Ogden, LeBaron told him of his revelation that Dean Vest should be killed and that Vonda should carry out the assignment.

It soon became apparent that most of these witnesses had absolutely nothing to do with the issue at hand: whether or not Vonda White had actually killed Dean Vest.

With bizarre testimony about polygamy, murder by command of God, blood atonement and other bits of exotica, Gary Rempel was titillating the jury, packing the courtroom with spectators and getting plenty of newspaper and television coverage. But Rempel was also irritating Judge Earl Maas, who finally warned the prosecutor that he was conducting the trial like a "16th century witchhunt."

Vonda was charged with conspiring to murder Vest, as well as murdering him, and Rempel argued that to establish this conspiracy he had to go into polygamy, the LeBaron family history and Ervil's strange beliefs in order to give the jury a proper context for understanding the murder itself. Vonda, after all, was alleged to have killed Vest on orders from Ervil.

Vonda's counsel, Salt Lake City attorney Steve McCaughey, countered that to prove conspiracy, Rempel had to establish that an agreement existed between Ervil and Vonda. There was testimony that Ervil had told others he would have Vonda kill Vest, but no testimony that he had spoken with Vonda and that she agreed to carry out the assignment.

Judge Maas agreed. He conceded to Rempel out of the presence of the jury that with blood on Vonda's shoes, and her admission to Lloyd Sullivan that she had killed Vest, there was ample evidence to prove that she was guilty of murder, but he said too much of the trial had been devoted to irrelevant and prejudicial information about LeBaron's life-style and philosophy. The judge said he allowed the jury to hear such testimony in anticipation that Rempel would be able to make the conspiracy count stick. But the prosecutor had failed to prove a conspiracy, and Maas granted a motion by McCaughey to dismiss that count. The judge went on to conclude that it would be impossible for the jurors to ignore all the testimony relating to the conspiracy without having it taint their consideration of the murder charge. He was virtually inviting McCaughey to move for a mistrial. After briefly consulting with Vonda, the lawyer did just that.

Maas promptly granted the motion. The case would have to be tried again.

But if the forces of LeBaron had won the first round, the police would soon win the next. On Halloween night, Mexicans in the state of Veracruz mounted another of their mysterious commando-style raids on two adjoining houses. Inside one of the houses was Rena Chynoweth and Dan Jordan. Inside the other was Ervil himself.

Rena—who was several months pregnant with her second child—would later give the following account of her arrest:

Several federal police burst into both adjoining buildings at 3 A.M. while the occupants were sleeping. In her building, the police entered with machine guns drawn and warned them, "You'd better not move or we'll shoot." She was immediately placed under arrest, as was Dan Jordan, who the police thought was Ervil. Rena says Dan produced identification attesting to his real name, but the police rejected it as false. Rena and Dan were then taken outside and placed in a police van for six hours while officials questioned the people in the other building.

Rena insists that Ervil was questioned at length and even displayed identification with his real name on it. But he had had a mild heart attack earlier that year and lost a lot of weight. He didn't look like the picture police had of LeBaron and officials suspected he was merely trying to pass for the real Ervil LeBaron already tucked away in the van outside—Dan Jordan. So Ervil, the proverbial cat with nine lives, was released.

Rena and Dan were driven off to Mexico City. On the way, Rena says she laughed at the police, called them incompetent and insisted that they had let the big fish slip away once again. But finally Dan quieted her down. Better to let them think he was Ervil, at least for the time being.

Not until they reached Mexico City did the *federales* realize their mistake. "They were very embarrassed," Rena recalls, laughing. Dick Forbes couldn't believe it when he heard Ervil had been in the very clutches of lawmen and had beén released. It was the best argument yet for someone like him helping the Mexicans when they went on their forays—someone who knew, and could at least recognize, LeBaron.

Rena was stripped of her official papers, told she was in Mexico illegally, then, after several days, driven to Laredo, where she was picked up by FBI agents. A trio of Utah police waited for her in an interview room of the Texas jail, but she refused to make any statement. "She just got up and walked out of the room without saying a word," one of the officers recalls.

Meanwhile, U.S. authorities had finally persuaded Mexican officials to prosecute Dan Jordan for Joel LeBaron's 1972 murder. Mexico had refused earlier to extradite him on the charge, when Oregon authorities helpfully held him on a Selective Service charge in 1977, which was dropped. But now that he was already in Mexico, authorities agreed to fly him to Ensenada, where his trial—the painfully slow process of gathering witnesses and depositions which can take up to a year—was begun.

While in jail, Jordan agreed to one interview with a San Diego *Tribune* reporter, in which he hinted about a general disaffection with Ervil. He talked nervously for an hour about LeBaron, who "is a very difficult man to find. He has a lot of friends in Mexico, including a strong power base in Veracruz in the PRI [Mexico's ruling Institutional Revolutionary Party]." The reporter described Jordan as a "short but powerfully built man with eyes that frequently rolled to show the whites when the interview was steered toward Ervil LeBaron's beliefs."

Only one man was likely to give enough evidence to hold Jordan— Conway LeBaron, the self-confessed wheelman who was at the scene, and had the murder described for him by Jordan. But Conway felt safely tucked away in Utah, and was not willing to budge an inch. His lawyer and a Utah policeman traveled to Ensenada and won for Conway promises of immunity in return for testifying. "That wasn't good enough for Conway," one of the negotiators commented. "I think he wanted it written in blood and engraved in gold before he was going to go there. I guess you can't blame him." Jordan was eventually released without a trial.

Some Lambs of God had thought it was foolish for Dan to enter Mexico in the first place, but he had crossed the border to arrange for his friend Mark Chynoweth to go back to the U.S. and turn himself in. That mission was aborted by Dan's arrest, but Mark had become tired of running anyway. He was anxious to go back to Utah and try to clear himself. The state's charges against him in the Allred murder and the Verlan LeBaron attempt were tenuous, at best, and with the death of Lloyd Sullivan, they had virtually no evidence implicating him in the Simons murder.

So on December 15, 1978, Mark drove across the border at Laredo with the intention of going back to Utah to turn himself in. But he showed a customs agent identification with his true name on it, which was immediately picked up by the border computer. He was promptly arrested. To his detriment, he proved more talkative than Rena with Utah officers in Laredo.

During a two-hour conversation, he told the officers that Ervil was a great leader, and said he still supported him. He expounded on some LeBaron teachings, including a characterization that he and other "people in the [Lamb of God] church were soldiers in a war—God's soldiers—and as a result, like any war they couldn't be charged with crimes as soldiers in an army," one of the participants, Dick Forbes, recalled. Forbes later testified to the statements in court. He admits admiring Mark, "an intelligent kid—one of the few in the group that had his stuff together—a well-rounded invidivual."

This left only Ramona Marston, Arturo LeBaron and Ervil as fugitive Lambs of God.

While he was in hiding, LeBaron didn't want his primary targets, the leaders of the Church of the Firstborn, to forget him. Nor did they.

Ervil was suspected as the inspiration behind an extortion letter Colonia LeBaron received in January 1978. The missive demanded $6,000 in small bills be delivered on the 16th at the entrance of a neighboring church at midnight. Signed "The Morrelian Group," after Ervil's middle name, the letter threatened: "If you don't do as asked, the LeBaron township will be destroyed along with its people. We warn you not to call the police or else you will be destroyed at once." A postscript carried an almost unnecessary reference to the 1974 Los Molinos raid: "If you don't do as you're told, your destruction will be worse than in Baja California."

After consulting with the police, a Firstborn Church leader personally delivered a paper bag stuffed with newspaper wadding—and a Murray police arrest warrant—to the Catholic church in the village near Colonia LeBaron. But no one ever showed up at the dropoff point.

Now, a year later—January 1979—the community was visited by Lambs of God bearing a new LeBaron writing which, like the many that preceded it, scathingly denounced the Church of the Firstborn as fallen and criminal. Local Mexican police arrested the trio, one of them Nancy Chynoweth, but only held them a short time. The Firstborners, not wanting trouble, took blankets and food to the Lambs during their incarceration.

At about this time, America's "largest circulation paper," the *National Enquirer*, placed Ervil LeBaron's face in practically every grocery store in the country. As if his previous exploits weren't lurid enough, the tabloid, with Ervil's face on the front page, displayed a huge headline that said:

JFK ASSASSINATION
CULT LEADER IS NO. 1 SUSPECT

The article began in the same manner: "The Number One suspect in the JFK assassination is a murderous cult leader known as the 'Avenging Angel.' His name is Ervil LeBaron—and he heads a cruel killing cult that has painted the Southwest red with blood."

It was a nicely timed charge, coming after a House of Representatives select committee determined Kennedy was "probably assassinated as a result of a conspiracy." The *Enquirer* laced its story with the 1963–1964 FBI documents that did note Ervil was one of thousands of suspects in the assassination, and managed to induce a congressman and former Dallas police chief to call Ervil "the prime suspect" and "the major suspect," respectively.

The *Enquirer* did add an intriguing hypothesis—that LeBaron had also had porno publisher Larry Flynt shot on March 6, 1978, in Georgia. The *Enquirer* reasoned that LeBaron feared Flynt's offer of a sizable reward for new information on the JFK assassination would flush Ervil out. In fact, LeBaron was a suspect in the shooting that paralyzed Flynt from the waist down. But it was for a different reason. Flynt's *Hustler* had published a very unflattering article on Ervil's misdeeds, and LeBaron had previously signaled the vengeance of the Lord would come on scribes who twisted his teachings. Also, two weeks after the attempted murder, police informant Lloyd Sullivan called with the tip that one of Jordan's wives "said she wished they had killed the 'son of a bitch' Larry Flynt." It was all armchair detective fun, but far off LeBaron's beaten track.

On January 29, 1979, in Price, Utah, Eddie Marston, Ervil's twenty-three-year-old stepson, went on trial for the murder of Robert Simons.

It was in the desert outside of Price, a desolate coal mining town located about 120 miles southeast of Salt Lake City, that police alleged Marston, abetted by Mark Chynoweth and Lloyd Sullivan, had crept up behind Simons the night of April 23, 1975, and shot him in the head.

Sullivan, the man who had lured Simons to his death, was now dead himself. If the state's key witness had been missed in the first trial of Vonda White in San Diego, his absence would be even more critical in the Price trial of Marston. The prosecution was missing testimony from a participant in the plot against Simons who had told police he watched as Marston carried out the murder.

With Lloyd gone, the only bit of substantive evidence authorities had left against Marston was the testimony of Don Sullivan that Eddie had admitted killing Simons to him.

Compounding these problems was the fact that the state was unaccountably relying on an inexperienced prosecutor whom most viewed as unqualified to present a case of this stature.

There was speculation that Salt Lake City's David Yocom would be called in as a special prosecutor since Yocom was an expert in the background and workings of the LeBaron cult, having worked with investigators on the case since its inception. Yocom was considered to be one of the leading criminal attorneys in Utah besides.

But the Simons murder had taken place within the jurisdiction of Utah's Carbon County, not Salt Lake City, and the Carbon County attorney, Ron Boutwell (in effect the district attorney), was not about to step aside.

Boutwell, an apple-cheeked forty-five, was leaving the county attorney's office, and he may have felt that the publicity of the Marston case could be very helpful to his future private practice in southern Utah. Yocom was reluctant to interfere with a fellow prosecutor, and so confined himself to attending the trial as a legal éminence grise.

As the trial began, Boutwell frequently stopped whatever he was doing to seek advice from Yocom or a bit of information about the complicated LeBaron movement. Boutwell was slow, uninspiring, a poor speaker and an ineffective examiner of witnesses.

He had come to Price in 1975 and was later elected county attorney on a write-in vote.

Marston, for his part, seemed to be approaching his murder trial with equanimity. "It don't matter what happens to me," he had said in one jailhouse interview prior to the trial. "Ervil already told me I got my calling and election assured. What happens in this life don't mean nothin'."

Subsisting on prison food for the past seven months seemed to have done Eddie no harm. He looked as if he had gained about thirty pounds, enough so that his Sunday best, a pale-blue, three-piece denim suit, had to be let out all the way and was still rather tight. No matter, the idea was not to look hard. As he sat down at the defense table, Marston looked more like a chubby Mormon missionary than a killer.

Steve McCaughey, having staved off a conviction of Vonda White in San Diego, was retained as Marston's lawyer as well. McCaughey was amused by press speculation that had him emerging as virtually the house counsel for the Lambs of God.

McCaughey wanted to neutralize the unseen force at the trial, Ervil LeBaron, by having several cult members testify that Ervil was no Manson who ordered dazed followers about at will. McCaughey guessed that like the San Diego prosecutor, Boutwell would not be able to resist straying far afield to rhapsodize about LeBaron's bizarre background and his incantations in the name of God. On hand to testify that they were not Ervil's robots were Victor, Duane and Lillian Chynoweth.

Lillian's husband, Mark Chynoweth, was also in Price as a defense witness. Mark, though also accused in the Simons murder, was not in the dock with Eddie because he had been only recently captured, but his interest in the proceedings was considerable. If Marston were acquitted or otherwise fared well, the state could hardly bring the same charges against him.

Boutwell offered a rambling opening statement in which he seemed quite pleased that his cramming had given him some understanding of LeBaron theology. He said Ervil had set up a timetable for taking over the world in twenty-five years. He also noted that Ervil considered himself the Patriarch of Israel and the administrator of a Law of Liberty. Those who resisted this law were to be killed, added Boutwell gravely.

With Lloyd Sullivan gone, Dick Forbes managed, nonetheless, to slip in as much of what Lloyd had told police as was possible under what the judge ruled was an exception to the hearsay rule. Forbes could not, however, repeat that portion of Lloyd's story that concerned Marston by name. Thus he told of Lloyd luring Simons to the Carbon County desert where "two others" were waiting to kill him.

Unable to produce the smoking gun via the late Lloyd, the state turned to his son, Don Sullivan, who testified that Marston admitted to him that he had killed Simons, and had bragged about being a good shot.

Eddie then took the stand in his own defense, and Steve McCaughey quickly asked him the operative question.

"I did not kill Robert Simons," Marston replied. He said he had never ever heard of Simons until Don Sullivan told him of Simons' murder in a 1976 conversation. Sullivan said then that he and his father, Lloyd, had killed Simons, Eddie told the jury, adding that he could not remember where he was the day Simons was killed.

Boutwell, after failing to shake Marston on cross-examination, produced payroll records proving that Don Sullivan was in Salt Lake City the day of the murder. But this wasn't enough. McCaughey suggested that Don could still have been in Price by 10 P.M. that night when the killing occurred. He called Mark Chynoweth to the stand to deny that he had had anything to do with the plot, then further impugned Sullivan as the proverbial opportunistic state's witness with too much to gain to be believed.

McCaughey laid the blame for Simons' murder at the door of the two Sullivans: Don and Lloyd. Before Lloyd's heart attack, he and Don had cooked up the story they would tell here in court, McCaughey asserted.

Helped by Boutwell's glaring shortcomings, McCaughey succeeded in muddying the waters enough so that the eight-man, four-woman jury saw fit to deliberate only two hours before returning to find Marston not guilty.

At this, Lillian Chynoweth, Ervil's tall and stunning daughter, was heard to mumble: "Thank you, God my father."

Ervil himself must have received news of the Price verdict with delight. He had predicted it all through revelation. Having struck down the turncoat Lloyd Sullivan with a heart attack, won at least a reprieve for Vonda White and now an outright acquittal for Eddie Marston, Ervil watched his mystique grow among the Lambs of God.

The long-awaited Rulon Allred murder trial finally got under way on Tuesday, March 6, 1979, with only four of the seven accused present and accounted for.

It was nearly two years since two women had assassinated the polygamist naturopath. Since then, police believed they had solved eight separate LeBaron murders and considerably reduced the membership of the Lamb of God cult. But the prosecution had also suffered three serious setbacks.

Now four defendants faced trial in the Allred murder, and the attempted murder of Verlan LeBaron at the Allred funeral—Rena, Mark and Victor Chynoweth and Eddie Marston.

Before jury selection, Judge Jay E. Banks granted the motion of prosecutor David Yocom to reduce first-degree murder charges to second-degree against all but Victor, who was only charged with conspiracy. Yocom's reasoning was multifold: he thought no jury was likely to convict the attractive Rena, eight months pregnant, of a capital offense; it would be difficult to prove a first-degree-mandated aggravating circumstance against the defendants, like pecuniary gain; and he stood a better chance of convincing eight jurors, rather than the twelve allowed for capital cases, of his evidence. The last rationale was a gamble. With four separate defendants, and an extra challenge of prospective jurors allowed for each, it weighed the choice of the jury heavily in favor of the defense. A six-woman, two-man jury was selected.

This was the courtroom battle Utah had awaited so long. The court was filled with about seventy-five spectators. Security was tight: guards were posted inside and outside the court, and each observer was subjected to a metal detector search.

Yocom began his opening statement by instructing jurors on points of law. At times he tried to be folksy, disavowing the magic of television barristers. "I remember a TV show called 'Petrocelli' . . . where the lawyers would get up in court, and all of a sudden on the screen would be a flashback of what took place. It would be great if we had that for you." Short of that, Yocom narrated the facts of the murder scene, the chronological events of the police investigation and what each significant Lamb of God defector had related. Yocom knew the case might sound preposterous to jurors, but he couldn't avoid sounding like a carnival barker at times. "You'll be shocked and amazed," he said at one point, "at the distances that were traveled by these people to accomplish these murderous deeds."

Rena's lawyer, John O'Connell, was first up for the defense. A colorful, successful lawyer, O'Connell had, however, lost a significant case to Yocom not long before. His client, convicted sex-killer Ted Bundy, was found guilty of a kidnapping charge. O'Connell was not planning to lose this one.

"Our defense is simple and straightforward. Rena Chynoweth did not kill Rulon Allred. She did not agree to kill [him] . . . all the people who . . . claim to have direct evidence, who accuse this girl of being this cold-blooded assassin are people who themselves were involved in this killing, and who were shifting the blame . . . to others in order to escape punishment themselves. In so doing, they place primary responsibility on Ervil LeBaron who they portray as some sort of super monster with incredible power over his followers, such that he could—that Rena Chynoweth here would unquestionably commit unspeakable crimes just because he tells her to."

O'Connell sarcastically focused on the most noticeably absent person and threw him to the jury as an easy sacrifice. "I am not here to defend Ervil LeBaron. Rena, as one of his followers and one of his wives, loves him and believes in his innocence. But he is not on trial here today, and I'm not going to defend him . . . it doesn't make any difference to our defense whether or not you believe these crimes were instigated by Ervil LeBaron or not. He may have. I know Rena doesn't agree with this, but as far as we're concerned, he very well may have, but our point is that Rena was not involved.

". . . I believe evidence will show that whether he is a prophet of God, or whether he is a devil, that his administrative ability is downright pathetic. He can argue complicated theological points endlessly, in fact he's very good at that, particularly the Old Testament scriptures, jump around among those scriptures and can deliver a fire-and-brimstone sermon quite well, but he can't seem to give simple instructions on anything, let alone teach somebody like Rena Chynoweth how to pull off a commando-type raid with split-second timing.

"The evidence will show that the Church of the Lamb of God was not the well-oiled machine that the state will try to prove to you. Rather, in the spring of 1977, it was a group of confused and frightened people who didn't know what was going on . . ."

He outlined the Lamb of God factions, pitting the Chynoweths versus the Sullivans. O'Connell portrayed Don Sullivan as a heinous Gestapo-type enforcer who kept the group in line through fear. "It was Don Sullivan who came up with . . . ideas that the disobedience of a military order was treason and with the death penalty. . . ." Worse than that, O'Connell said he thought the evidence would indicate that Don Sullivan, dressed as a girl, was the actual murderer.

O'Connell outlined Rena's life in sympathetic detail, and explained away the Lamb of God penchant for secrecy as a common trait of all polygamist groups. "They do not want to leave the evidence of who they are with and that sort of thing. They do not trust the police. To them the police are the enemy of their family. And it's the sort of thing that doesn't go over big in the courtroom, but I hope you would understand that."

O'Connell urged the jury not to be bigoted—"just because it's a religion that probably looks peculiar to you people, let's not think that they are just a bunch of people all alike, all involved in some kind of machine." And he concluded by once again getting to the nub of his defense: "The only evidence that Rena participated in these crimes or entered into a conspiracy by agreeing to commit these crimes comes from people who are guilty themselves, accomplices."

Another able attorney, Robert Van Sciver, was next, appearing for clients Mark and Victor Chynoweth. He correctly identified his clients as supporting actors, with Victor only making a "cameo appearance" in the drama. "My guys are second-stringers," he explained, "and I'm going to have to play that kind of a role in this trial. So, if I don't participate as much as others, it's not because I care less. It's because my clients are more minimally involved."

Eddie Marston's attorney, Stephen McCaughey, chose not to make an opening statement.

The first witnesses recited the same testimony about the murder scene offered at two preliminary hearings. Neither of the two eyewitnesses would identify Rena as one of the two assailants, although Melba indicated that she couldn't rule Rena out. This was a significant loss for the state's case, but it had been expected.

On Thursday, thirteen witnesses trooped to the stand before there was a surprise—Phyllis Rindfleisch, a cashier at the Murray outlet of Deseret Industries, the Mormon equivalent of Goodwill Industries. For the first time, she identified Rena Chynoweth as one of a group of three girls who had come shopping there for clothes on May 10. "I remember the one woman in particular," she testified. "I don't know why . . . she was a beautiful woman and she had such a sweet smile. That's the only thing I can tell you." The defense attorneys were slow to respond and finally cried foul after two more witnesses testified.

After a legal attempt to impugn her testimony, Phyllis Rindfleisch was recalled to the stand Friday in an effort to shake her statement. Though grilling by Van Sciver and O'Connell established she'd seen as many as 100 people a day as cashier, Rindfleisch refused to compromise on her testimony. "I know I saw them [the three women]. . . . I remember waiting on those people, and it was in May . . . it was after lunch. . . . I remember faces. . . . The one person [Rena] I remember very, very clearly, and very distinctly."

The state's chief witness, Donald Sullivan, began an ordeal on the stand Friday afternoon that ended Monday afternoon, with a weekend break.

Under direct examination, Sullivan said that all four defendants had been at the April 20 conspiracy meeting; Rena traveled with Don to Albuquerque to discuss the murder plans with Ervil; Rena and Eddie Marston were among the Evanston group that met just before the murder and worked out its details; Rena and Eddie traveled to Salt Lake, tested guns and drove to the Allred murder scene where Rena killed the doctor, according to her admission afterward; Eddie helped steal trucks and drove in them to attempt to murder Verlan LeBaron at the Allred funeral; Mark and Eddie conducted surveillance in El Paso on a Firstborn Church house, expecting to "hit" Verlan LeBaron there.

His account of the attempted funeral murder was particularly riveting. Don adroitly demonstrated how their guns were converted to fully automatic weapons. "We got in the truck and we drove by the school, and at that time I decided to call the strike off . . . I told Ed and Jack Strothman both that there was no way. I told them if we were to go in and get Verlan, that we didn't even know he was there. And if we did go in, we could never make it in. There was too many policemen there. We'd have a big shoot-out, you know, and we'd never make it inside the building."

Before closing his Friday testimony, Sullivan recounted Victor's speech at the April 20 conspiracy meeting. "He said if we're questioned by the police, not to talk to them. . . . It's better to say nothing than anything at all. . . . Supposing they asked where Ervil was at, and you tell them, well, he went east. And they go ask somebody else, and they say he went west. And they ask yet another person, he went north. Then they know the only place they didn't say was he went south. So, they can get information that way."

On Monday, Sullivan provided an account of Ervil LeBaron's final instructions to the Lamb of God squad in Evanston, that proved chilling to spectators.

"He told [the girls] that the most important thing for them to do was to remain calm, to walk, not run. They should be disguised. Walk into the doctor's office real calm, collected. Take a can of Mace with them. He emphasized that they should use Mace, that they should spray him in the face, first, because he feared [Allred] might be a violent man and might be able to handle them. So, they should spray him with Mace, first, and then shoot him later. . . .

"Ervil told [Jack Strothman and Eddie Marston] that we were called to a high calling, and a very important task, very dangerous task, too. The Lord called on us because he knew that we were worthy to do the job. And that because the risk was so high, the reward was so great, that if we did what we were ordered to do, that we would have our—would receive our Godhoods, or we would have it made. We would go to heaven for what we did regardless of whether we died at that time or not. He told us at that time that chances were high that we would be killed, but, nevertheless, death is sweet to those who die in the favor of the Lord. And he got our courage up by telling us these things."

If that didn't persuade them, Don said, LeBaron added "that it was a standing rule that if somebody got left behind, or if somebody backed out, that it was considered treason, that they would be done away with there on the scene so they couldn't talk about it . . . the other two were to kill him if he turned traitor or didn't go through with it, so he couldn't turn state's evidence against them."

During a clever cross-examination, Van Sciver elicited some facts that helped draw the defense picture of Sullivan as a suspect. For instance, Don admitted owning seven or eight guns, though he said he did not fire them regularly. Van Sciver inferred that Don's wife, Noreen, was in Salt Lake on May 10, and was the other assailant along with Don.

Under Van Sciver's questioning, Don said Victor Chynoweth also talked about the Lamb of God business operations during his antipolice speech.

"Now, he didn't say, and there's going to be a lot of heat brought down on us, or a lot of people are going to be asking questions in May, did he?" Van Sciver pressed.

"Yes, he did," was Don's reply.

"Oh, he did?"

"Yes."

"Okay. And have you told anybody this at any prior time that you've testified?"

"No."

Van Sciver couldn't help the sarcasm: "Just kind of thought you'd save that one for the trial?"

"No. You just brought it up and I remembered. . . . He said that after this there's going to be a lot of police investigating, and we should be on our toes and not talk to them. If they start bothering you, come to your house, close the door in their face, not say anything. . . ."

"Did he say why?" Van Sciver ventured again.

"Because of the questions and so on about the things that were going to take place, the strikes, and so on."

"I thought you said there was no discussion about strikes at that meeting."

"There was. I didn't say that. . . . He said that we were going to go on a military escapade and that the people should prepare themselves for it because it was going to take a lot of diligence on their part, and a lot of finances, and that their part in finances was just as important as the people going in on the strikes."

Van Sciver closed by questioning Don about his reasons for becoming a state's witness.

"Did you or did you not say on prior occasions that the reason you wanted to work a deal was because of fear of the death penalty in Utah?"

"I have a family that I'm very concerned about at this time," Don responded.

"Did you or did you not say that the reason you were here to testify in behalf of the government is because of your concern about the death penalty?"

". . . Yes. I don't want to die. I have a family and a wife I have to look out for."

Defense attorney McCaughey implied Sullivan was testifying because charges in other murder trials hung over his head, and attacked his image as a self-serving state's witness. If he had second thoughts about participating in the Allred hit, why did he?

"Because I was ordered to," Don matter-of-factly replied. "You have to do certain things or you're a traitor, and he deals with traitors by killing them. *If he would kill his own daughter, he wouldn't hesitate on me, and he always had my wife in his custody.*"

McCaughey jumped to ridiculing the man-without-hope speech Sullivan had given when he was captured, eliciting, to his own dismay, Don's compelling response:

"I was very upset. I was ripped away from my wife and children. I had been running for quite some time from Ervil LeBaron. I had got tired of running. . . . I've had dreams a lot of times, nightmares you might call them, about having shoot-outs, him chasing me down thinking I was going to testify. At that time I felt like, 'What the hell!' "

O'Connell was more damaging, by inference, than the previous attorneys in his cross-examination of Sullivan. He accomplished this by asking dozens of leading questions like, "In fact, practically everybody in the church was afraid of you, weren't they?" which placed the thought in jurors' minds, despite Don's denial.

Spectators learned Sullivan had had two wives at one point, but LeBaron had ordered him to let one go. O'Connell also elicited an interesting response when he asked what Don was doing outside the doctor's office.

"Now, you just testified that if somebody backs out they'd be killed right on the spot, isn't that right?"

"That's what Ervil said was a standing order."

Now O'Connell planted his own idea. "Was that your job when you were standing outside the doctor's office in case Ramona or Rena chickened out . . . to kill them?"

"That isn't what I told them I was going to do. . . . I could not— didn't have any authority or jurisdiction to kill them. . . . I believe Ervil told the girls that if they went in and didn't come off right, that it was no big thing, to do the best that they could. He didn't impress them with the idea that they would be killed, because it was their first time out to do anything."

"Oh, I see," O'Connell grunted. "That just had slipped your mind through all these proceedings up until now?"

"We had absolutely nothing to do with that. Besides, Ervil told us to stay completely away from them. Had I judged them and shot them, then the whole objective would have been exploded. We couldn't have got Verlan. So, it was a no-no. There was no way I could have done that to them. So, that did not hang over their heads."

"So, this was the one exception to the rule, that if you got out—"

"Ervil had exceptions to his rules all the time. . . ."

O'Connell tried throwing up more smoke about Don's shaving his beard, probably before the Allred murder, so he could disguise himself as the murderer, and asking him to explain how Ramona Marston's new baby arrived in Salt Lake May 10, and was being taken care of during the actual killing by Eddie Marston—a mystery no one ever solved. Finally, bringing in other murders tied to the Lambs of God, O'Connell asked, "In all these cases you're the star witness, right, or a witness?"

"A witness, yes."

"Whenever there's a—any kind of a killing attributable to the Church of the Lamb of God, it always seems to be you or your father is right there," O'Connell observed.

"That's because we turned state's evidence," Don pointed out. "No one else did."

Yocom used his redirect examination to clean up some fuzzy points.

Ramona's baby? "[Ervil] said he thought it would be a good idea for them to have the baby with them when they left town. That way the police wouldn't suspect them. If they pulled them over and they had a baby with them, it would be hard to suspect that they was involved in any kind of murder."

Any other reasons why he was testifying, other than fear for family? "Yes. I believe Ervil's a false prophet, and I know there's a lot of good people in that group, and I'm afraid under his leadership and his direction he's going to raise them up to kill people or false prophets the same as what has happened, and I'm afraid there's a lot of innocent people that are going to die. And I'm testifying to break his power any way I can, because I know he's that type of man."

Further testimony added that LeBaron had ordered Sullivan to rent a house in Evanston so the "people next door [wouldn't be] able to hear the clank and so on [of the weapons], and the drilling of the serial numbers." On the stand, Sullivan also remembered that Ervil had actually mentioned the word conspiracy at the April 20 meeting. "He said the conspiracy was a serious crime and everyone in this room can be charged with conspiracy just for hearing or mentioning what has been talked about here. You're all involved in it. So be careful what you say."

This brought a snide remark from Van Sciver who, after getting Don to admit this was the first time he'd brought this up, then asked icily if Ervil didn't use "the words 'pecuniary gain' " at the Dallas meeting also?

Sullivan was the heart of the state's case, and neither side was sure who'd won the exchange with him at this point in the trial.

Accomplices Jack Strothman and John Sullivan, testified before the state's second most important witness walked slowly to the stand, sixteen-year-old Isaac LeBaron, Ervil's son. Isaac was crucial to the case because he was more believable than the accomplices, and his testimony did not need corroboration as such.

Isaac was present at the April 20 meeting, and named all four defendants as being there. "Tell us what your dad said at that time as best as you can remember, Isaac," Yocom asked.

"He brought up false prophets and what they should do with them."

"What did he say?"

"They should be put to death. They're not allowed to live. And two—he asked everybody's opinion who they should—he said he needed two women in their twenties to go and kill them, you know."

"Did he say who they were going to kill?"

"He said a false prophet in Salt Lake. He didn't mention his name."

Rena and Ramona's names were discussed, Isaac continued, before his father "said anybody who ever talks to the police against . . . any of their men, they can count theirself as a dead person."

Isaac's memory of Victor Chynoweth's speech paralleled Sullivan's. "He says there was—things are hot, you know," Isaac said. "Things are going to be real hot, you know. Going to be a lot of police. And people coming over and ask questions."

The defense attorneys were lighter on Isaac than they had been on Don. Isaac was young, and he was not involved in any of the murders— a victim of family circumstances. Under cross-examination, Isaac said that while Sullivan was the "military leader" of the group, it was Eddie who "threatened me if I turn to a traitor he'll kill me."

This paranoia of Isaac's chilled the courtroom, the only time, according to observers, when everyone was transfixed by the testimony of a witness, particularly his hushed, frightened closing remarks. They had surprised Van Sciver, who was trying to imply that the police put all the suggestions in Isaac's head.

"Would it be fair to say—you know, the police officers have struggled to solve things. Have they suggested things to you?"

"Go hide," Isaac said quietly.

"That's the only thing they've ever told you?"

"All I remember. And I knew that already . . . I was really scared when I first testified. I went to my room. I stayed in the house for about a month without coming out. . . . And we had some guns in the house just because we were scared."

"Are you hiding because the police tell you to hide?"

"No, because I'm scared, because I have a reason to be scared."

"And the police, apparently, continue to remind you of that?"

"No. I have that perfectly in mind. I know the—if they had a chance they'll kill me. I know they would."

After calling forty-five witnesses, the state rested on Wednesday, March 14.

The defense called nine witnesses, including two of the defendants, who testified in their own behalf. Thelma Chynoweth, mother of three of the defendants, was the first to take the stand on Thursday. She remembered the April 20 meeting well, but it was "basically a business meeting." Daughter Rena played the piano, Mark was not there, Victor spoke about their constitutional rights and Ervil "spoke about the responsibility that the young children had . . . to begin to learn how to assist in the business and be helpful with their families, and then he talked a little scriptures and stuff, which I don't remember."

She said she'd never heard talk of "military missions" in the church, but then acknowledged Sullivan was the "military leader," which she thought had something to do with self-defense for the Lambs of God. Toward that end, she said she owned a "cheap little gun," a .25 caliber weapon, which she planned to put in her purse but had never taken out of the box.

Yocom could not restrain himself from being as mocking with this witness as the defense had been with his witnesses. After Yocom had cut her off on one answer, Mrs. Chynoweth said, "Do you want the truth? I mean, the whole truth, or do you want just a yes or no?"

"I'd love to have the truth, Mrs. Chynoweth," Yocom pertly said.

Once, during her testimony, Mrs. Chynoweth was emphatic about getting a statement on the record. "Do you follow the teachings of Ervil LeBaron?" Yocom asked.

"Yes."

"Do you believe that he has a plan for the salvation of the world?"

"I object, your Honor," O'Connell hopped in. "I think a person's belief—"

"Sustained," Judge Banks promptly said.

But Mrs. Chynoweth wanted to answer. "Yes," she got out.

"You don't have to answer that," Yocom offered.

"Yes, I do."

Nancy Chynoweth was next on the stand. Like her mother-in-law, she was presentable and very sure of herself. She admitted buying the .25 automatic in Denver, with Rena along helping her. But she insisted it was only because Don ordered her to, and instructed her to bring it to Salt Lake City. Because Nancy was busy, she asked Rena to drive it to Salt Lake, which Rena did. Yocom was able to raise some doubts about her simple story, closing with an interesting dialogue about her history for telling lies.

"You've already testified on direct that [Detective Richard Forbes] asked you about that gun [during the arrest in Dallas]?"

"Yes."

"And you lied to him?"

"That's right . . ."

"Well, yeah." Nancy admitted to several more lies under Yocom's questioning. "Have you been taught to lie to the cops?" he asked.

"No."

"This was a spontaneous thing at that point?"

"Yes."

"To protect Rena?"

"Yes."

"And you'd lie here today to protect Rena, too, wouldn't you?"

"No."

Yocom acted incredulous. "What's the difference?"

"I'm under oath."

The next three defense witnesses established that Mark Chynoweth was in Texas about the time of the May 10 murder.

Victor Chynoweth took the stand in his own defense. His attitude was unruffled, almost cavalier.

He freely admitted association with Ervil LeBaron, and estimated that he had contributed about $20,000 to the Lamb of God cause in the last five years. He paid for the plane tickets to the April 20 meeting "because I always paid whenever Ervil doesn't have any money, and I was ordered to pay for it."

Victor said he traveled to Dallas with Ervil to scout locations for a Lincoln Auto branch and give advice to the Lambs on their washing machine business. Lloyd Sullivan met them at the airport, and Don Sullivan pulled him aside before the meeting for a conversation—which Don had already denied under oath.

But, according to Victor, Don told him that "a lot of the CFB . . . and the Secret Service and the FBI and I don't know who all else . . . had been nosing around, that they had been talking to the little kids about, you know, who their dads were and who their moms were. . . . He told me something about—I think the word he used was military rule . . . he was going to get up and tell all the kids that they'd be executed if they talked to the police or anybody. . . . I felt like there'd be a more diplomatic way to go about it than that, and he was kind of hotheaded. So, I asked him if it would be all right, you know, if I could let [them] know they weren't supposed to talk to people."

That's the reason, he continued, that he gave his antipolice talk. Victor said Mark was definitely not there because he had fired him from their business and both had "decided it would be better if we were not in the same state, let alone the same town or house." Also, whenever Mark was at a religious meeting, being a superior musician, he played the piano, not Rena. He (Victor) had offered advice—"stuff like personal appearance, you know, wash yourself once in a while, not smelling too bad when you're meeting the public. How to close a sale."

Though Victor couldn't be shaken on cross-examination, he offered a few deprecatory observations about Ervil. He said LeBaron and the Sullivans were the main reason the Lamb of God businesses were failing. But it was difficult to explain that to Ervil because he wasn't an easy person to talk to "if he doesn't see it [your] way to start with." About Ervil's religious teachings, Victor said he had read few of the pamphlets and didn't recall many of his speeches. "I remember some of the stuff that was said. It's pretty easy to sleep when Ervil's talking. Really is."

For a brief interlude, the defense put eighteen-year-old Alex Chynoweth on the stand. Alex had been reared by Thelma Chynoweth since his mother, Naomi, had disappeared in January 1975; he apparently never knew, or believed, that the Lambs may have been responsible.

Alex said Don Sullivan had been a friend to him "but he usually always punched me around. So I didn't appreciate that." He said "Don was always a military guy. He wanted to be the leader," and was fond of showing Alex self-defense techniques.

Alex's testimony added little, except to reiterate that Mark Chynoweth was not at the April 20 meeting, contrary to state witness testimony. The final question under cross-examination by Yocom: "Do you think [Ervil] was a prophet?"

"Oh, prophet, yeah. I don't know."

"All the little kids think he was a prophet?"

"I never did ask them."

"Were you told that and taught that?" Yocom persisted.

"Well, they told us he was a prophet, but—I don't know."

The final witness of the trial waddled to the stand Friday morning. Rena Chynoweth, twenty, slightly discomfited by her condition, sat down for a siege she was told to expect. "Her pregnancy weighed heavily on that jury," Yocom says. In fact, her attorney, John O'Connell, played it up constantly by patting her on the stomach during the trial and holding hands with her. When the child was born after the trial was over it was named after him, John Chynoweth LeBaron.

O'Connell began lightly, getting a testimonial about her childhood, her marriage to Ervil LeBaron as his youngest wife, and her trials with the chauvinism of the group: Some of the guys that worked there are really down on women," she said. She'd heard talk in the group about military rule, and Don Sullivan, she said, was always talking about suspicious cars and suspicious people who were after them. "Women didn't go out alone," Rena remembered. "You know, they were to be accompanied because there were people lurking around."

Rena couldn't remember what Ervil said at the April 20 meeting, because she was tired. She said she did recall that Victor spoke primarily about their finances, and that her brother Mark was not there, because she didn't play piano whenever he was.

Rena admitted going to Albuquerque about May 6 with Don Sullivan to meet Ervil and his wife Anna Mae Marston, but no military mission was discussed. She went from there to Denver, where she learned Don wanted Nancy to buy a gun. Rena said she did drive it to Salt Lake, where an angry Sullivan told her it was the wrong kind of gun. She didn't need that kind of abuse, so she checked into the Lone Pine Motel under the false name, Patti Sanders.

Rena categorically denied that she killed Rulon Allred, much less went into his office. Further, she denied ever admitting such to anyone in conversation, particularly in Amarillo, as Strothman had testified. She said she never met him in Amarillo. Rena appeared a personable, credible witness, handling Yocom's cross-examination with some finesse.

"Did you become aware of being identified at Deseret Industries [buying clothing and such] through the course of this trial?" Yocom asked at one point.

"I became aware of a woman who seems to have a very strange memory," she countered.

At another point, her misunderstanding broke up the courtroom in the only humorous episode of the two-week trial. Yocom had been asking about Lamb of God finances. "Where were the profits when this business was going?"

"He was back and forth as usual," Rena responded, thinking he meant her exalted husband, the prophet.

"Pardon me?" Yocom asked, as the court burst into laughter.

"He was back and forth."

The judge put an end to it. "If there's any more outbursts in the courtroom from the audience, I'll clear the courtroom," he warned.

Rena seemed to change her testimony once after a courtroom break. She began agreeing that Ervil did give her orders. "You weren't willing to say that a few minutes ago. . . . Has anything changed your opinion in the break about that?" Yocom inquired. "My lawyer told me not to fight with you," a more subdued Rena responded.

She surprised the court once with a headline-making statement about false prophets. Rena agreed Ervil did preach that false prophets should be killed, a belief that came straight from the Bible, she averred.

"Do *you* believe that false prophets should be killed?" Yocom asked. "That they should be put to death?"

"It says that in the Bible," she equivocated.

"Try to be responsive. I'm asking if you believe, not what it says in the Bible."

"Yes." Yocom allowed for a long pause after her response.

For more than an hour, she answered specific questions about her movements, including why she had so willingly delivered a gun to Salt Lake City without, allegedly, knowing what it was to be used for. Rena noted at one point that Don Sullivan once hit her, which made her a little more responsive to his orders. Yocom closed by pressing her once again on her beliefs.

"Do you think there's something higher than the laws of the land?" he asked.

After an objection by her attorney, she said, "The laws of God, yes."

"As taught by Ervil LeBaron?"

"As taught by the Bible," she said.

"And Ervil LeBaron?"

"He teaches it the way it says in the Bible, so, yes."

"And you believe he is a prophet of God?"

"Yes, I do," Rena answered.

On Monday, Yocom methodically offered up his closing argument. "In my opening statement, I . . . told you that otherwise normally appearing individuals were and are followers of Ervil LeBaron, a self-proclaimed prophet, a man that they believe is a prophet of God," Yocom said. A man who has the power and authority to murder other prophets or, as he refers to them, false prophets, in God's name.

"Well, that was pretty shocking to you at first blush—that anyone would in fact kill in the name of the Lord, claiming this authority. I think I have kept my promise to you that we have done that. Otherwise normally appearing people have been proven guilty of doing exactly that."

He covered, once again, all the facts established by the state's witnesses. "The only lies I think you've heard in this trial," he concluded, "came from some of the witnesses for the defense."

On his part, O'Connell appeared supremely confident. "I think we have this one going away," he bragged to the jury. At least, "I'd hope that you people do not believe this girl here is the cold-blooded assassin that the state claims she is."

O'Connell asserted that the Sullivans were being let off simply because they were the first ones caught, and the first ones to make up a story pointing the finger at others in the group. "That's why they go free, because they're the first ones in," he said. O'Connell acted particularly dismayed that Don Sullivan was "being given the red carpet treatment, this hero treatment . . . When you tell a murderer you'll let him go if he blames somebody else you're asking for trouble. You're asking him to lie. You're putting a gun in his hand."

He urged the jury not to convict anyone on abstract religious principles. "It isn't an ordinary murder case. It's cluttered up with all this religion and polygamy junk," he said. "This underworld—underground world does exist, and it's the world that Rena lived in." Because of the illegal aliens they harbored, and other transgressions of the law, they were naturally secretive—"just because people are secretive does not mean that they've killed somebody."

O'Connell reviewed some of the evidence and hit hard on eyewitness testimony. "Not one of them said Rena was there. Not one of them even said she looks like the person who was there. Not one of them picked out her picture as possibly being there. The strongest statement made by the people who were there was by Melba Allred, who said she could not say she was, but could not say she wasn't. That's the strongest evidence. She saw that killer several times face to face under circumstances where you'd think it would be burned in her memory."

His closing appeal was powerful—and personal. "She came here a stranger in a strange land," O'Connell said. "I had to convince her that she could get up here and talk to you people, and you would listen to her. You'd give her a fair trial. That you would give her a chance to tell her version of it. You wouldn't prejudge her. And she did get up there, and she did testify, and she was under cross-examination for two and a half hours. And I was damn proud of her. She never testified before. . . . That was her first time, and she sat up there with confidence. Confidence in you people that you'd treat her fairly, and confidence in herself, and her own innocence.

"The law presumes her to be innocent, and the state has failed to prove otherwise, and I think there's a simple explanation for that, ladies and gentlemen. It's because that is not only a presumption, it's a fact. And all the lying accomplices, and all the fancy charts, and little models, and the rest of this stuff can't do a thing against that!"

Van Sciver was not to be outdone. He told the jurors: "It's a rare experience ever to have been selected to be on a murder jury. It's an even rarer experience to have been selected to be on a murder jury involving people who belong to a church."

Van Sciver confessed that he was "not into prophecies," but he acknowledged that "we have seen some fanaticisms, and we've seen some horrors of people following the dictates of others. We know that Jimmy Jones . . . dispatched the people in Guyana. . . ."

He suggested it was not unusual that the Lambs of God had a military branch. "I believe that all churches have security," Van Sciver said. He talked about his acquaintance with the former Salt Lake City police chief, now head of Mormon Church security, and "the Pope has his own army . . . don't think that the churches don't guard zealously their physical assets, their church buildings, their farms, and so on. So this is not a new wrinkle."

The only person—aside from a confused Isaac LeBaron anxious to please the prosecutor—who really testified against his two clients was Don Sullivan. "You can label Don Sullivan any way you want," Van Sciver said. "In my judgment he's probably the most morally despicable person who has been in this courtroom, and who has certainly acted in a fashion which is more heinous and onerous than any one of those people seated at that [defense] table."

After taking on the evidence against Mark point for point, Van Sciver said that "the most outrageous injustice that can be done in this trial is to convict Mary Chynoweth of murder. It ain't there. Not guilty means not proved." As for Victor, he was equally not guilty. "Vic got used," Van Sciver said. "One of the witnesses testified that all Ervil ever wanted Vic for was his bread. Nancy got used [to buy the gun]."

Once again the odd man out, attorney Stephen McCaughey's closing statement was slower than that of his two more colorful defense associates. McCaughey's oration was dry, painstaking and nearly tedious as he rebutted the state's evidence against Eddie Marston. He took special care to note that "the failure of a defendant to testify is not . . . a circumstance against him."

Yocom was allowed the last word, and he was up to the task. Point for point, he took time to debunk, with equal candor, the arguments raised by the three attorneys:

The first in, first to confess theory: "This is not . . . a case of giving deals to the first guys arrested. Mark and Vic were arrested long before Don and John." Vic was evasive and his wife, Nancy, lied when she talked to police, Yocom said.

Offering immunity to the wrong fellows: "Why didn't we nail them to the wall with their confessions . . . that's what O'Connell thinks we should have done. Stick it to the guy who cooperates. Stuff the voluntary confessions down their throats and put the SOBs away. Put them in prison forever. [These were] difficult, weighty decisions."

Don's hero treatment: "Mr. O'Connell says that Don Sullivan was getting this hero treatment for the confession, to be testifying, to be through what he's been through, a conviction for a felony. No simple matter, facing sentencing up to fifteen years in prison. But that's not the half of it. A life of looking over your shoulder, of wondering when and where Ervil LeBaron or any one of these still loyal Lambs of God are going to be behind him. . . . Don, that despicable person . . . that horrible, immoral individual, that snake that had the audacity to tell the authorities what happened. To subject himself to test after test by cross-examination for the truth. A man that now has to assume a new identity, a new place, and be hidden. Heck of a hero treatment, isn't it?"

O'Connell defending Rena: "O'Connell on evidence. He's emotional, sometimes irrational, but sometimes it sounds good. He likes to take the good parts and leave out the bad parts. . . . Mr. O'Connell in his rhetoric standing before you . . . says [he] tried to deprogram this poor girl and convince her she'd get a fair trial. And she doesn't trust the system because the Mormons are framing her. That's Mr. O'Connell talking."

The prime nonaccomplice: "Isaac, that little boy, little fourteen-year-old boy. He's not little any longer, obviously. He has grown. I've watched him grow. Isaac, that boy, young boy, was the key to this whole case and still is . . . a fourteen-year-old boy so afraid . . . that he locked himself up in his room for a month with a gun after the first time he testified in court."

"All I can close with," Yocom concluded, "is what I started with: truth, ladies and gentlemen. What has been presented. These defendants committed it. And they're guilty. . . . Implausible as it may seem, this wild, bizarre, ridiculous plan to kill. It did take place. Believe it or not. And it took place just the way we have presented it, with what the evidence and exhibits demonstrate beyond a reasonable doubt."

The jury retired to deliberate.

Yocom was not hopeful about the outcome, and said as much to some of his associates. He had been reading juries for years and, while he couldn't be sure, he detected some fear among the six women about Lambs retaliating against them. Too, just before his closing arguments, the court bailiff told Yocom that "one of the jurors mentioned to him that he was spooked. His wife had noticed this strange car watching their house at night and he was really concerned about it." Yocom upbraided the bailiff for not reporting the incident to the judge, and Yocom promptly did so. But the juror was not removed. Instead, he became the foreman of the jury.

Yocom thought the complexity of the trial—four defendants and many different charges—weighed in favor of the defendants. There were over 100 exhibits to review; the two weeks of testimony later was transcribed into 1,487 pages.

The jury was out just four hours before returning its verdict: all four defendants not guilty on all four counts.

Interviews with jurors suggested that, as one put it, many "of us felt they were guilty but [the state] just didn't have enough evidence. For traveling, they had all kinds of that—how they traveled from place to place. For killing them, no." Most significantly, each juror pointed out that not a single eyewitness was able to identify Rena as the murderer, though Melba Allred and Richard Bunker presumably had had a very good look.

Jurors pointed to one fellow juror, a state welfare worker who had been on two previous trial juries, as the person they had allowed to lead their decision-making. "I had very strong feelings that we couldn't convict on the evidence presented," she says. She found it difficult to believe Don Sullivan's testimony and impossible to assimilate the entire tale about Ervil LeBaron. She called Yocom's theory of the case "a little far-fetched," and felt certain people simply don't live the way he and his witnesses described the Lambs of God living.

Besides, she adds, at least two jurors had the wrong reasons for wanting to convict. "One of the ladies was really taken with David Yocom. She just thought he was a real neat guy and whatever he said, that was the way it was. Another lady was prejudiced because they were polygamists—that whole thing."

Today, several of the jurors privately admit they, or others, had been fearful of all they'd heard about LeBaron and the kind of retribution he exacted. Neighbors, friends and family sometimes reminded them of that during the trial. The few holdouts for conviction were won over by the leading juror—though one said a year later she still feels guilty for giving in so fast.

The prosecution and police were stunned. "We were all down and really felt beaten," Dick Forbes recalls about this last in a string of setbacks. "We felt cheated; the state had been cheated; the people had been cheated. A murder had occurred. We felt we had the responsible parties and they were turned loose."

20.

JUSTICE

For Ervil LeBaron the centuries-old town of Atlixco, about 130 miles southeast of Mexico City, was a made-to-order hideout—the kind Butch Cassidy loved during his Bolivia days. Its remoteness is assured by the jostling one-hour ride it takes to get from Puebla to the town, situated between a snow-capped volcano and an Aztec pyramid where archeologists are still uncovering the skulls of human sacrifices.

The town was best described as "at ease," its peace only occasionally broken by a dog barking or a shout from the direction of a door stoop where sat a resident who'd had a little too much pulque. Automobiles, like the green Ford LeBaron drove, were a rarity. Instead, donkey carts filtered through the steep dirt streets, usually headed for the town's only well. In the afternoon, some of the residents gathered around the well, and at the nearby butcher shop, where a pig's head was hung to dry. They talked about many subjects, and one of their favorites was Ervil LeBaron and his *muchas señoras.*

Most townspeople steered clear of LeBaron and his followers, who would stay there with a relative, Aurelio Rios, for periods of time. Atlixco, and other towns like it, offered LeBaron tranquillity and some anonymity. No lawman lived there, and friendly relatives were abundant. Long adobe walls provided complete privacy. Besides, the *campesinos,* who make bricks and raise maize, were masters at minding their own business—particularly when it came to *locos* like LeBaron. One of them whispered to a visitor: *"El hombre LeBaron es mitad diablo."* (The man LeBaron is part devil.)

There were numerous phantom sightings of Ervil, and many people were out hunting him during the two years he evaded the law—the Mexican police, halfheartedly, and the Mormons only occasionally;

Owen Allred and Fundamentalist groups in Mexico; Church of First-born members, particularly Siegfried Widmar; mercenaries after the ever-increasing reward offered on wanted posters; and a few men who simply thought there ought to be an end to Ervil LeBaron.

"Several times I've found myself thinking that Ervil should be taken care of—put out of his misery, you know, like a mad dog," said former associate Chuck Henderson. "And yet I try to tell myself, this isn't your affair. But he's a mad dog, so what do you do? You can't correct the problem; you destroy it."

Ervil kept on the run, and cut his preaching to a minimum—which must have been the hardest thing for him to do. Instead, he was reduced to selling blenders door to door to raise some cash. He'd apparently obtained a large quantity of small appliances, and made a fair salesman, only slowing down after a mild heart attack and subsequent weight loss.

Dick Forbes was the most frustrated hunter, trying to direct often-clumsy and disinterested Mexican police to LeBaron's hideouts. He had given them the address of Marston's hideout, and Rena's, but they had fumbled and let Ervil slip out of the trap. Forbes' best ally was the legal attaché in the Mexico City U.S. Embassy who happened to be a Mormon, and also happened to come from Midvale, Utah, just a few miles down the road from the Murray murder scene.

He had stressed to Forbes that their contact must be low-key—"no press" should know of the extent or nature of the effort to track down the Lambs of God.

At the outset, after the September 1977 warrants had been issued, Forbes had been told by contacts that if LeBaron or any of his followers were captured, there should be no inquiry as to how it was accomplished. Undesirables like LeBaron were never formally extradited from Latin American countries. Instead they were "expelled," shoved across the border where U.S. lawmen just happened to be waiting. Some call it kidnapping, but American courts have traditionally been unconcerned about what happened to a prisoner before he arrived in their jurisdiction, even though these prisoners are quite likely to be roughed up. Some, in South American countries, have been extensively tortured.

LeBaron had already published lurid tales about the abuse of Eddie Marston at the time of his arrest. Marston himself discusses physical abuse only circumstantially. He says that he was sleeping in a private house when the *federales* burst in and began firing their guns. One shot ricocheted off a wall and grazed him in the crotch. One of his Mexican companions, Gamaliel Rios, was shot three times in the leg.

Marston says he was taken to a military stockade, then transported to Mexico City in a light plane. He was taken to a prison and kept blindfolded and handcuffed at all times, he says, and later questioned by Americans who he suspected were FBI agents. Eddie admits they showed no identification, but he says a Mexican guard told him they were from the FBI. When the Mexican officials seemed good and ready, they drove him to Laredo and dropped him off as an undesirable, even though he had a six-month visa.

Eddie had actually been captured for an unrelated reason, according to prosecutor Yocom and detective Forbes. They said Eddie Marston had raped a Mexican girl who apparently had political connections. It wasn't until later that they learned Marston was a fugitive wanted in connection with various LeBaron murders. At that point they brought him to the border and dumped him.

It would ultimately be the same situation with Ervil LeBaron. On May 25, 1979, Dick Forbes was tipped that LeBaron and his wife Lorna Chynoweth had finally been arrested in Mexico, and he was advised to be on the streets of Laredo June 1 for a pickup. The reason for the capture was as bizarre as anything involving LeBaron. As related by Dick Forbes, who was briefed by his Mexican contacts:

Two days before the verdict was given in the Salt Lake City trial for Rena and associates, LeBaron had kidnapped a woman whose father was a Mexican public official. Either she had been the woman responsible for Eddie Marston's arrest, or, Forbes theorizes, "they may have kidnapped her and taken her to hold her hostage should these people up here have been convicted."

She was taken to a shack in the Mexican hills and told that in two days the "One Mighty and Strong" would be there. About 6 A.M. on a Tuesday morning, a woman using the alias Patty removed the victim and drove her in a Volkswagon across country that had no roads, finally releasing her at a highway near Mexico City.

"That stirred up the Mexicans," Forbes says. "I think that their vigor increased to the point where they arrested Ervil and Lorna."

The Mexicans had no compunction about knocking the prophet LeBaron around. He'd caused them enough trouble and publicity. Further, they imagined a Jonestown in their own country with LeBaron at the head of his weird following. "I've heard so many tales about what happened down in Mexico," says one of LeBaron's attorneys. "It appears to me that Ervil was, in fact, kidnapped by some people in Mexico, beat up, kept blindfolded and finally just handed over to somebody."

LeBaron was shoved across the border 12:30 P.M. Friday, June 1. The FBI took him into custody, as a fugitive, and he was incarcerated in the Webb County jail of Laredo. The arrest sheet described him as fifty-four years old, 6 feet 4 inches, weighing 200 pounds and sporting a beard.

At 3:40 P.M., Dick Forbes, Murray detective Gary Pedersen and National City police lieutenant Wayne Fowler (there on the Dean Vest case) stepped into the lockup area of the U.S. marshal's office to conduct an interview with Ervil LeBaron.

He was much as the officers had pictured him, except thinner. Forbes could hardly control his elation at having LeBaron in custody. But he was apprehensive and nervous about this first key conversation. "I talked to so many of his followers that absolutely refused to talk to us," Forbes recalled. "By the same token, I felt that he was a compulsory preacher and he firmly believed that he'd be destroyed by God if he didn't do everything he could to teach everybody; so he had to talk."

Initially, LeBaron was silent. Forbes advised him of his rights and listed the outstanding warrants against him from Salt Lake City, San Diego and Price, Utah. At the end of Forbes' twenty-minute statement, LeBaron was ushered into the U.S. magistrate's chambers to be arraigned on an unlawful flight warrant. Bail was set at $100,000, and he was removed to the lockup room.

At 4:25 P.M. the three officers asked if they could speak with him, cognizant of his rights. He agreed.

Forbes explained his opening strategy later: "I felt that he would at least talk to us on religion. I was willing to listen to it, fully realizing that what he taught was criminal and that in those statements, the religious teachings, were very important elements to the entire case. It was the motive for all his crimes. My main interest was just kind of putting him at ease first. Keep him talking."

Ervil LeBaron remained essentially close-mouthed, answering questions put to him with a "yes" or "no." But the questions were leading, and later damaging to LeBaron.

"Are you still head of the Church of the Lamb of God?"

"Yes."

"Are you prophet of that church?"

"Yes."

Forbes wanted to get Ervil's admission of authorship to the blood-and-thunder statements. "Have you written the church's pamphlets?"

"Yes."

"Did you write *Law of Liberty*, and do you still believe in it?"

"Yes."

"Did you write the other publications, like *Hour of Crisis, Day of Vengeance; Response to an Act of War; Contest at Law; Open Letter to a Former Presiding Bishop; Causes of the Great Conflict* and *The Art and Powers of Deception*?"

"Yes."

"Do you believe the millennium is now being ushered in?"

"Yes." This finally loosened Ervil up. He added, according to the Forbes report, that "he had been anointed to usher in the millennium and lead the Kingdom of God in the latter days in preparation for the second coming of Christ. He stated that that had already occurred, as he had written in many of his teachings.

"At that time, Ervil LeBaron further stated that God, throughout history, had always had to do his work through people on this earth, and that now God's work was being done by himself, Ervil M. LeBaron, as head of the church which he was representing himself as prophet.

"He stated that he was the only man on this earth who had the authority to establish the laws of God on this earth . . . that the leaders of this country are committing criminal acts by not allowing him to establish God's law as part of the constituted laws of the land of the country."

Forbes and the other officers were tiptoeing around the crux of the case, but finally struck it. "He was then asked if a person could be sentenced to death after having knowledge of God's law and not complying with it."

Ervil was not that dumb. He'd had practice at double-talk for years. "He stated only if that man had the proper education . . . and the legal government of God had been established," the report said.

Forbes asked him again about the *Law of Liberty*, and Ervil admitted authorship again. According to that book, Forbes continued, it was "implied or stated in various places that the death penalty would be dealt for persons who were traitors to the Kingdom of God, for persons who were false prophets, for children who failed to obey."

Ervil was evasive. He told Forbes the investigator didn't understand what the *Law of Liberty* said, and diverted the conversation to another subject. The meeting ended at 6 P.M., with the agreement they'd meet again Saturday morning.

The three met Ervil at 8 A.M. in the county jail booking room, and he immediately dashed their hopes about more conversation. "He had decided to let things stand as they were, and he walked toward the door as though he were about to leave," the report says.

Lieutenant Fowler ordered him to stop. He was not excused and, while he might have the right to remain silent, Fowler bluffed, LeBaron didn't have the right to leave the room at that time. LeBaron patiently sat at a table.

The officers told him they had some things to say. Forbes and Fowler then began to tick off in detail their knowledge of LeBaron and all the murders. "He had this idea of a giant conspiracy on the part of the Mormon Church to destroy him," Forbes recalls. "I wanted to tell him very clearly and definitely that that wasn't the case. We were police officers."

The two detectives spoke for ninety minutes, nonstop. They discussed the murders of Dean Vest, Rulon Allred, Robert Simons, Rebecca Chynoweth, Joel LeBaron, and the Los Molinos raid. Ervil sat quietly, his head in his hands, not looking at the officers. Several times they asked if he were listening, and he responded affirmatively.

They finished at 9:45 A.M., and prepared to leave, gathering up their papers into briefcases and walked to the door. Ervil stopped them.

LeBaron said he had listened very intently to all that was said and was impressed. The presentation was brilliant, he offered, well prepared, well thought out, well planned. Forbes said nothing had been prepared formally. Nevertheless, LeBaron continued, it was brilliant. Now that he had sat so quietly for so long, it was his turn. He wanted the officers to listen. "I don't want to talk about certain things," he said, "but I do want to tell you some things that may help you to understand." Ervil was hooked.

"For the next five hours," the report enthused, "Ervil LeBaron described to us at great length and in great detail the teachings of the *Law of Liberty* and many of the other philosophies and beliefs of himself and of the members of his church." The officers took extensive notes for the first three hours, then Fowler taped it, using a surreptitious recorder in the top of his briefcase. LeBaron didn't seem to mind. At one point, Ervil advised Fowler that his microphone was dangling outside the briefcase.

Among the points Ervil made during these five hours, according to the report were:

•"There is no government existing in the world today, nor no other church than this own that has the authority to administer the constitutional laws of the Kingdom of God";

•"A person who is educated [in the true beliefs] and does not honor them . . . has committed a much, much greater offense [and he emphasized that on numerous occasions] than the offense of first-degree murder";

•"Mr. LeBaron referred several times to President Eisenhower as having established the greatest law that had ever been established in this country when he changed the Pledge of Allegiance of the United States to include the words 'under God.' He stated that that absolutely established in this country God's laws. . . .";

•He admitted writing the letter to President Carter about the need to establish God's laws and that anybody who refused to accept them, including those in "government positions . . . were in violation of the Law of Liberty and subject to capital punishment";

•It is an erroneous and "spiritualistic belief of the Roman Catholic Church" that the "punishment for disobeying God's laws would be administered in the hereafter, after death on the judgment day." In fact, "those punishments would be administered on this earth during this lifetime."

Ervil continually harped on the theme that church leaders who didn't conform were perpetrating "the absolute worst criminality." Forbes decided once to interrupt him and cut to the quick. Did Rulon Allred, being a false prophet, die for that reason?

LeBaron looked at Forbes and smiled. "No comment," he said.

The session was adjourned for the evening and began again on Sunday at 1 P.M. By that time, Ervil had contacted an attorney, who told him not to talk to the police. LeBaron said he'd still continue the conversation, but would not discuss specifics of the cases. "I will not be a slave to an attorney," he vowed.

Ervil expounded for another four hours, covering some new points;

•"According to the Constitution," he averred, "I am the present head of the United States of America, as it should presently be correctly interpreted." He said he had been the head ever since President Eisenhower added the words to the Pledge of Allegiance;

•LeBaron said he himself was responsible "for the crimes of this nation and this world," since he was the ordained leader, and he would suffer the consequences during judgment;

•The people of the earth were obligated to pay Ervil tithing and "failure to pay the tithing was subject to the death penalty; the people who did not pay it would die."

Ervil surprisingly boasted about his ability to make written threats and not be caught for them. He said he had begun developing the talent at the age of twenty-two, devising "a system or a means of writing things wherein he could say things that were illegal, but that were not subject to prosecution." It was with this in mind, he acknowledged, that he had written the letter to President Carter that had stymied the Secret Service.

Finally, Forbes broached an issue that greatly concerned him. He had long wondered if Ervil were jailed, would one of the group take over and continue the violence? He asked Ervil if he knew to whom he would pass his own authority.

"If I did know," Ervil responded, "I couldn't tell you."

LeBaron was taken out at 5:15 P.M. for his jail dinner. He asked them to bring along a Bible the next time. The officers borrowed a Gideon Bible from their motel room.

The final session began at 8:45 P.M. that night and lasted an hour, Ervil tracing through the Bible and quoting scriptures to prove his points. He reiterated his teachings about false prophets, his own personal authority, and closed with a quote from the Bible. "If you do not listen to your prophets," LeBaron read, looking at the officers, "you shall be destroyed."

The series of interviews had been an exhausting but unforgettable experience for the officers. They had not, however, been without their lighter moments. Forbes recalls that Lloyd Sullivan had often launched into an unerring imitation of Ervil so "as I sat there listening to Ervil talk, seeing his various motions of tugging at his eyebrow, clearing his throat, using his hand and everything, I remembered seeing it before." LeBaron was also still afflicted with something as unchangeable as his doctrine—his halitosis.

The prosecution had good fortune on another front—Vonda White was finally convicted May 14, 1979, for the 1975 murder of Dean Vest. The San Diego prosecutor, Gary Rempel, removed most of the religious elements he had originally included and which had led the judge to order a mistrial.

Instead, Rempel had focused on telling evidence like the blood spatters on Vonda's shoe and taped testimony from her children that she was the only adult in the house, and was downstairs when the shots were heard, which was contrary to White's own assertion. Don Sullivan identified the gun last seen in the possession of Ervil LeBaron— testimony he was able to offer because he had broken the weapon previously and constructed a new firing pin. Isaac once again proved a formidable witness in establishing the religious motive, adding that his father's church had trained women and children as young as ten to kill in the name of God.

Vonda White was given a life sentence on June 13, after Rempel noted that "under her serene and mild countenance is the heart of an assassin." The Superior Court judge who sentenced her said she was dangerous to society because of her beliefs and loyalty to LeBaron.

Arturo LeBaron, Ervil's son, driver and bodyguard, was captured in Guatemala and deported to Miami, where he was arrested July 1 stepping off the plane. He unsuccessfully fought extradition and was transferred to Utah to await trial with his father.

Ironically, Ervil LeBaron's first choice for his lawyer was John O'Connell, the flashy attorney for Rena who had openly ridiculed LeBaron in court—called him a poor administrator, a coward and a man probably guilty of the criminal acts with which he was charged. The selection had only one drawback. The Lambs of God apparently couldn't afford a first-rate private lawyer for the leader of their church. So Ervil accepted three court-appointed lawyers from the Salt Lake Legal Defenders Association. The association's president, John Hill, would lead the defense and attorneys Bruce Lubeck and Fred Metos would assist.

Lubeck remembers meeting Ervil for the first time. As a public defender, he had encountered all types of people, but was especially curious about the infamous LeBaron. He was taken aback by Ervil's "kindness, his gentlemanly manners, his gentleness. It was like talking to anybody's grandfather—although a little younger than my own grandfather."

The trio of lawyers lacked the familiarity that prosecutor Yocom had with the case. The task of poring through thousands of pages of police reports and trial transcripts caused them to seek a continuance of the preliminary hearing five separate times.

This case was to be far different from the trial of the four followers. All the pieces of evidence fitted around LeBaron, the leader. As the lawyers searched for a defense theory, the massive investigative work of the Murray PD proved an "extraordinary handicap," according to Lubeck. "It was what separated this case from all others. No matter what we tried to do, we felt they had an answer for it. They had anticipated everything we could think of or everything we could do. Too, Yocom knew the people and the players, which was an extreme disadvantage. There was so much that we didn't know that they did know."

Ervil worked hard to help them overcome the handicap. He began writing reams of paper on the case, consulting frequently with Lubeck to uncover testimony that would be effective in the trial. The Lambs scurried to the task, at the call of their prophet. The correspondence included, primarily, three of his wives, the imprisoned Vonda, Lorna and Rena.

An August 1, 1979, letter to Rena is enlightening about LeBaron's frame of mind and his ability to dispense with double-talk when it came to personal matters.

"Darling Rena,

"It was extra good to receive your encouraging letter a few days ago, telling me so many things I wanted to know about. It has been so long since I have seen you and so many things have happened, that everything I hear about what is going on is very interesting. It's terribly hard being separated from those I love most for so long, but I trust this will be over in the near future. I love you very much and hope you will write often in the period of time that's just ahead."

He discussed some minor matters—his conversations with a Mormon chaplain, needing respectable suits for the hearing and his interest in real estate more "than any other business"—before addressing the weighty details of his pending trial. The problem with court-appointed attorneys is that "it can not reasonably be expected that all the work will be done that our case demands on the basis of what public defenders are accustomed to being paid."

Because of that, he needed the Lambs to help. "There are too many transcripts and documents that must be carefully gone through, with more coming up," LeBaron explained. "Thanks to God these liars and conspirators have told their weird tales and are trapped by what they have already asserted," which meant the transcripts could trip them up. "As you know, we are being framed, which means that we must act wisely and firmly at this time. Every time I read through the transcripts I . . . find we are being assailed idiotically."

He asked Rena to "interrogate" other Lambs with an eye to debunking the "wild and woolly tales" of state witnesses, particularly the Dallas conspiracy meetings.

Ervil was primarily disturbed by the testimony of Don Sullivan and his son, Isaac.

"It is a scream how Don's testimony is becoming *enriched* with dogmatic statements about events back in those times [the Dallas days]," Ervil wrote. "You [Rena] are charged with traveling along with that S.O.B. and with staying with him some two or three days in a motel room." He delighted in finding Don Sullivan "contradict[ing] himself by changing vital parts of his story" from trial to trial. "I do want to know if you ever did travel with that bitter, hateful liar," he reiterated.

As for Isaac, Ervil's recollection was that his son "was very retarded in his ability to understand the administrative problems and the judicial procedures of the leaders of the community." He acknowledged, though, that "Isaac's B.S. is the toughest to overcome," and the Lambs should "make precise notes on the facts regarding his testimony and let us know what your findings are."

LeBaron ended with a felicitous apology that belied his fire-and-brimstone image: "I would like you to be understanding about my requesting so many items and putting you guys to extra trouble—but I can not equate the charges with the time setting. . . . I remember some events, but can not for certainty recollect what order they took place in or the respective dates without something to . . . properly nail it down."

Ervil's preliminary hearing began January 15, 1980, and ended the 17th. The regular retinue of state witnesses testified, proving enough to bind him over for trial on four charges—the first-degree murder of Allred, attempted murder of his brother Verlan and a conspiracy count for each act.

Arturo was freed on the 16th. Judge Larry Keller dismissed the four counts against him because, he said, the state could not prove Arturo was a principal co-conspirator in the murder or the planned murder. Before Arturo left the courtroom, his father called over the former bodyguard and gave instructions in Spanish. "Get a hold of your little brother [Isaac] and talk to him," he said, according to a guard who overheard the comment and understood the language. The prosecution immediately ordered extra protection for their key teenage witness.

For the first time in his life, Ervil Morrel LeBaron came to trial in a United States court on Monday, May 12, 1980.

Until this moment, he had been remarkably able to elude the combined efforts of dozens of U.S. legal entities to make him account for violating an array of American laws. According to police, he and his small cult ignored immigration regulations and harbored illegal aliens; broke public schooling rules regarding their children; flaunted some consumer laws with their business; received welfare and Social Security fraudulently; disobeyed Selective Service regulations; trafficked in stolen cars and unregistered weapons; and threatened hundreds of private and public figures, including the president of the United States.

Cult defectors had also identified Ervil as a man who ordered murders with regularity, at least four of which were carried out in the U.S.—two in Utah, one in Texas and another in California.

The first trial was for the Rulon Allred murder, and began just two days after the third anniversary of Allred's death. Police had originally issued warrants for eleven persons. Some had pleaded guilty, some had been acquitted, some had had charges dismissed or had not faced trial at all. By dint of those circumstances, Ervil LeBaron now came in to the dock alone.

His hopes primarily rested on the ability of public defender John Hill, a smooth and methodical attorney who, nonetheless, was no Melvin Belli, and who had neither the emotion nor color O'Connell and Van

Sciver displayed in the first Allred murder trial. Hill did, however, have able help from his assistants, Lubeck and Metos.

David Yocom had been named as the special prosecutor. He had already returned to private practice, but the Salt Lake County Attorney's Office asked him to handle the trial both because of its complexity and Yocom's own personal convictions about the defendant. He had learned a few things since losing the trial of LeBaron's four followers the year before. For one, he was determined not to alarm the jury with the elaborate security precautions and ultradramatic testimony of the first trial. No armed guards were visible, and spectators were limited to a couple dozen in a small courtroom that was closed once the trial began.

Judges in Salt Lake are assigned to criminal cases on a routine, rotating basis, not according to the preference of either judges or attorneys. It was Ernest Baldwin's turn to preside over the murder case. A controversial judge, he had often been unfavorably compared to a Utah federal judge who, before he died, was vilified in newspapers and the halls of Congress as dictatorial, arbitrary and senile. Certainly Baldwin was considered unpredictable—so much so that both the defense and prosecution met in several huddles before the trial to discuss removing Judge Baldwin from the case, but neither side would agree to file an affidavit of prejudice. Baldwin lived up to a portion of his reputation by, unaccountably, giving an hour lecture on crime and punishment at the outset of the trial. His rambling lecture appeared to be directed at the unusual number of press attending the trial.

The jury selection took most of the first day, with sixty prospective candidates from which to choose. Only two said they had never heard of LeBaron before, but the rest said each had not read enough to influence his or her opinion. One said she couldn't be fair because she had a friend who had followed polygamist leader Allred.

Nine men and three women were finally selected. Yocom was pleased. He assumed the six to two ratio of women in the first trial had lost the case for him—partly because he felt they were more frightened about LeBaron's cult and what they might do after a trial to jurors, and partly because he felt they were more likely sympathetic to the LeBaron defendants than men.

Yocom stood up on Tuesday to give his opening statement. Though much of it was a reiteration of his previous opening, he was less impassioned this time, even managing to show some sparks of humor. He also eliminated some believe-it-or-not elements in his speech. For instance, in the first trial he had claimed that the women returned to administer a final ritualistic shot intended to mar the face of Allred, the "false prophet." This time he simply called it an "insurance shot," to make sure the victim was dead.

He pointed out that Ervil LeBaron was charged with first-degree murder because there were two aggravating circumstances—one, creating a great risk of death to others during the murder, and the other, having it committed for pecuniary gain. "We allege that the pecuniary gain for Ervil is his belief that he was commanded by God to kill and take over Allred's church and Verlan's church and their tithing and membership and eventually take over the world," Yocom stated.

After recounting in narrative fashion the chronological events of the Allred murder investigation, Yocom detailed his witnesses and said some of them, who were Lamb of God defectors, "firmly believe they are marked for death by Ervil LeBaron for talking to police." Hill objected to the remark, and was sustained.

Both the prosecution and the jury learned of the defense theory first in Hill's opening statement, which lasted less than an hour.

"At no time did Ervil LeBaron aid, consult, command or encourage any individual to cause the death of Rulon Allred," Hill pronounced. He portrayed the Sullivans as the real perpetrators in the affair—the "violent" Don and his father, Lloyd, who had been trying to wrest the Lambs of God from Ervil, and also have an affair with Ervil's wife Rena.

Meanwhile, Ervil LeBaron, according to Hill, "was not a leader. He was a theologian, a student of the Bible. He was a preacher. There was no structure within that church."

Paul Forbes related details of the murder scene before Melba Allred recounted how her husband's murder occurred, weeping a little as she described it. She admitted never being able to identify Rena Chynoweth as the woman who shot Rulon Allred, but said her features were "very close" to those of the assailant.

The fourth witness, Richard Bunker, provided the first surprise of the trial.

That morning, Dick Forbes had shown him a mug shot taken when Rena was arrested in Laredo in 1978. After Bunker reiterated his basic testimony and had been cross-examined, he made a comment about the picture during Yocom's redirect examination. He was asked about the photograph's likeness to Allred's killer.

"It's very much like her," he maintained. "Of all the pictures I've seen that was the closest. I feel that that's the girl," he said, before again examining the photograph. "I wouldn't have any reservations." After three years of equivocation, he had finally identified Rena Chynoweth, but Rena had already been acquitted. Hill did not challenge the identification since he was defending the Lamb of God leader; it could hardly matter which follower was accused of the actual shooting.

Don Sullivan, hub of the state's case, appeared on Thursday and his testimony spread well into Friday's hearing. Court observers said he was sure of himself for this trial, and "much more presentable," neatly dressed in a three-piece suit.

Yocom led him through the indictable details of the LeBaron-fomented conspiracy to kill Allred and Verlan during the morning session and, after lunch, concentrated on more specifics. There were some subtle additions, tailored to convict Ervil LeBaron as the mastermind of the operation.

At the April 20 meeting, "Ervil LeBaron told us there was going to be a big thing coming down . . . a military emergency," Sullivan said. At a meeting for the men that followed, "he told us he had a revelation to kill Dr. Rulon Allred. He said he wanted two women. He said Rena would be one and asked our opinion on who the other should be. He wanted to make sure none of the men had anything to do with it so that it wouldn't look like our group."

Sullivan and others were to attend the Allred funeral "and kill Verlan LeBaron. . . . He said we were to use automatic weapons and if anybody got in the way we were to shoot them down, even if they were children."

In Evanston, where guns were oiled and the serial numbers filed off, Ervil said "Allred was a doctor and listed in the phone book, instructing Sullivan and others to "make [an] appointment to see him, if not just go see him." Spray Mace in his face so he won't fight. For the third time, Ervil discussed the Allred and funeral hit with Don. This time he added that "if Verlan didn't show up at the funeral, we were to go to El Paso. He would probably show up there" at Siegfried Widmar's home.

LeBaron, according to Sullivan's testimony, "told me [killing] was a good way to expose false prophets. If they could be killed, it would show they were not protected by the Lord and then their people would see they were false and flock to him [LeBaron] and he could take over their churches."

Hill debunked Sullivan's defection and his "I'm a man without hope" speech to police, and Sullivan explained he "was scared to death" and had no faith in the laws of the land, which he was taught were "null and void under the law of Ervil's church. . . . I thought I would be judged under the ax and hammer."

Regarding the murder and planned murder, Ervil had peeled about $200 from a wad of about $1,500 in bills for the mission when he met Don in Albuquerque. Ervil took an additional $400 to $500 out of his pocket in Evanston to help Don perform God's work. "Ervil said [both amounts] were to be used in military escapades," Don testified.

Yocom's final question: "Don, did you kill Rulon Allred?"

"No, I did not," Sullivan said without flinching.

Isaac LeBaron came to the stand next. He was now seventeen, and had been testifying against his father for three years but it was the first time his father had been present.

As Yocom began the examination, it was clear that, though his English was better and he was generally communicative, Isaac was under a great strain. He became circumspect, forgetting facts he had testified to several times before. Finally, a Yocom assistant noticed that a youth in a bright-orange T shirt was giving Isaac head and hand signals from the back of the court. The bailiff and two of the jurors also noticed this cueing of Isaac, to the detriment of the prosecution. Though no one learned why the youth, a cousin of Isaac's, was doing this, he was excluded from the courtroom after a break.

Isaac's memory and cooperation then markedly improved.

Yocom drew out the often-heard details of the April 20 conspiracy meeting from Isaac, his father's talk about false prophets and the LeBaron threat which, considering the source of the testimony and the fact that it was the first time the jurors were hearing it, chilled them. "He [my father] said anybody who speaks to police can count themselves a dead person." As this was said, Ervil showed no emotion.

Under cross-examination, Isaac said he had trouble remembering what he'd said in the past because it was difficult with "so many trials to keep the story exactly the way it happened." Yes, the police had made promises to him—"that I would be away from that group. That I'll go to school and be with my family [sister Alice]." He denied Lloyd was the real leader of the Lambs of God and that he had had an affair with Rena. Isaac said Lloyd and Rena "were really good friends," and sometimes hugged. But they never kissed that he knew about.

Isaac's testimony had a marked impact on the jury. Only one was unmoved by it. "I spotted the head nods [signals from the cousin]," he recalls, "and I didn't know if the testimony was for or against Ervil. So when that happened I more or less disregarded it. I didn't take any more notes." The rest were sympathetic to Isaac's plight, as he portrayed it. Two even called the long seven-days-a-week working hours at the warehouse a classic case of child abuse. "At fifteen years old, Isaac realized his life was going to go by him and he'd have nothing to show for it. The insanity of it all," one juror says, "when he was living with the fact that he couldn't even go to school and learn how to read. If we were up there for parental abuse, this would have been a great case."

On Monday, nine witnesses appeared before the state's next cooperative accomplice, John Sullivan, took the stand. He repeated what he said at the first Allred trial, except for testimony about Lloyd Sullivan, which Hill drew out of him under cross-examination. He said Lloyd was a religious leader in the group, and seemed to act, at times, as a spokesman for LeBaron. "Ervil spoke so high above everybody's head that I have to speak for him," he remembered Lloyd saying. But Lloyd never talked about upcoming trouble with the police or any "military" matters. Lloyd also gave no orders concerning Lamb of God businesses, in fact gave no orders at all that John knew of.

Jack Strothman was next. This time he had a short haircut and wore the uniform of an Army private.

Recalling the Dallas conspiracy, Strothman said that in a smaller meeting April 20 with only the men present, Ervil had asked him, "Are you ready to get into military service?" "I guess, if I had to do something, I'd do it," Jack said he responded. LeBaron added at this meeting that "if anybody said anything about what we was talking about we'd be shot right between the eyes."

When Strothman continued his testimony on Tuesday, he described the events at the funeral in simplistic, stark terms. "We went to the high school. We was going to go in and kill a bunch of people." While Don Sullivan killed Verlan LeBaron, "me and Ed [Marston] was to get anybody that looked at us." The mission had been aborted because there were too many television cameras and police.

Bonnie Sullivan, Lloyd's wife, described Lloyd's evolution in the group, clearly indicating Ervil LeBaron was head of the Church of the Lamb of God. When Hill pressed her on the possibility of a relationship between her husband and Ervil's wife Rena, she broke down and cried. Hill persisted in this line of questioning until Judge Baldwin grew angry and ordered him to stop.

Yocom next called Owen Allred, who testified that the Apostolic United Brethren was organized about thirty-six years before by his brother Rulon. They'd developed a membership on more than 2,000, an annual income of about $125,000 in tithing, and owned more than $1 million in property. With this witness, Yocom wanted to establish the pecuniary gain aspect of the charge against LeBaron.

To counter this, Hill established under cross-examination that the line of succession in the Allred church was known and predetermined. Allred also said the money in the church was controlled by a body of ten men, not one leader. Hill thus implied by his questioning that Ervil had no reason to kill Rulon Allred either for money or for control of the church, if it was well known that Allred would be succeeded by someone within the group—and not Ervil LeBaron, as the state had suggested.

Verlan LeBaron, brother of the defendant and his murder target, took the stand. He appeared good-natured but forceful as he traced the history of the Church of the Firstborn and began to explain why he became leader of the church: "When Joel was killed . . ." Hill jumped up with an objection, and Judge Baldwin advised Verlan he could only say that Joel LeBaron had died. The defense had made a concerted effort to discuss no other LeBaron-related murder during the trial, other than the Allred killing. But Verlan stressed it again, apparently without thinking, "Joel was killed," and Judge Baldwin, this time angrier, ordered him to stop saying that.

Richard Forbes testified about the lengthy interview he'd conducted with LeBaron in the Laredo jail. The interview was admissible because LeBaron had been reminded many times of his rights and had agreed to talk in spite of that. Jurors were informed about LeBaron's own religious claims and views as of June 1979, almost as if Ervil were expounding them himself.

LeBaron sat impassively through this testimony, as he had sat through the testimonies of his son and his brother. He occasionally made some notes or whispered suggestions to his trio of lawyers. He seemed cocky, and unfazed. The only "evil eye" he apparently gave was to members of the press. "He used to stare at us," recalls Deseret *News* reporter Joe Costanzo. "He'd pick out one member of the press, knit his eyebrows and stare. He picked me out one day and [Salt Lake *Tribune* reporter Con Psarras] another day. It was so direct. He'd walk in and turn around and stare for ten or fifteen seconds. I sure noticed when he was looking at me. Con jabbed me."

Conway LeBaron, Ervil's cousin, appeared as the first of five new witnesses in the LeBaron trial. These witnesses, whom one reporter called "the soothsayer five," would testify about LeBaron's long-term teachings and his intent to kill Rulon Allred, Verlan LeBaron and others.

This element of the LeBaron trial made it distinctly different from the earlier trial of his followers—and had wreaked havoc with his attorney's efforts to defend Ervil. "We weren't just dealing with something that was a year or two old," Lubeck explains. "Everything that Ervil had ever done was in that sense opened up to examination over many many states and over many many years."

The defense was poorly prepared for the five witnesses because "we didn't have a semblance of a clue where they were" before the trial, Lubeck adds, and efforts to contact them through police channels were unsuccessful.

Conway detailed Ervil's teachings about false prophets with the fervor of an erstwhile disciple. With a fondness that seemed to come from reliving old proselyting times in the west, he recounted being Ervil's missionary companion on a number of occasions and hearing frequent remarks about Rulon Allred: "He told me about how Rulon and his people went down and lived on a LeBaron ranch in Mexico and how they tried to get the family to join up and give the property to Allred. He said Rulon didn't follow the revelation of the Lord. Had broken the covenants of the Lord. Made a solemn covenant [and was now] a covenant breaker."

Did Ervil LeBaron teach there was a penalty for that? Yocom asked.

"That was death."

During one conversation with Ervil in Ogden, Conway said, "Ervil related a vision he had saying three timbers must fall before the Church of the Firstborn can collapse and said Verlan was the first timber who must fall."

According to Ervil, Verlan accepted the title of Patriarch illegally, and because he "accepted it he was a false prophet." What was the punishment for assuming that position? Yocom asked.

"It was death."

Conway explained later in his testimony that Ervil LeBaron taught he was the only man who could administer God's law in America. Regarding the "administration" of it in Verlan's case, Ervil "said we must be careful so that Verlan wouldn't go deeper into hiding. He said it would be harder to kill him or put him out of circulation."

Before the cross-examination began, Hill turned to his aide, Lubeck, and said: "You do it." Lubeck was dumbfounded, but then realized that as a ranking Mormon with a knowledge of the scriptures, he was expected to pick Conway apart on religious grounds.

But although Lubeck questioned Conway masterfully, he could not get around the confident Conway's assertion that LeBaron was talking about capital punishment of false prophets in this day and age—not at some future time, as Lubeck suggested Ervil taught.

Lawreve Widmar was the next state witness. Usually in the background helping her husband, Siegfried, bring Ervil to justice, she had agreed to testify about conversations in which she had been a participant.

One, which took place between Ervil, herself and Dan Jordan, included a special denouncement of Verlan. "Ervil said Verlan had no business talking to me and if he didn't repent and stop his usurpation of authority he would be put to death." That wasn't all. "Ervil said he was going to Salt Lake to talk to Rulon Allred . . . give him another chance to pay his tithings and change his mind and if he didn't he would be put to death."

At another, earlier time—August 2, 1971—Ervil, in front of Dan Jordan and Lawreve, "explained to me his plan, and told me [if] the Church of the Firstborn . . . didn't help him they would be put to death." Joel LeBaron was still a leader at the time.

Ervil's sister, Esther, now living in Salt Lake and attending college, then testified that she had overheard the August 2 conversation between Lawreve and her brother. She eavesdropped outside as they spoke for more than an hour together. She agreed with Lawreve's account of the conversation, adding that Ervil was "speaking like the execution was about to take place . . . . He said he was going to kill anyone who stood in the way. . . . He had a long list of executions."

Merlin Kingston, leader of the Davis County Co-op, then detailed Ervil's threats to his economic-religious group, particularly the December 17, 1974, meeting. His story of the threat was left undisturbed by cross-examination.

Finally, the fifth new witness, Carol Jensen, took the stand. She testified about her 1975 meetings with the man she long loved, Ervil, in Ogden restaurants at which he said "that sooner or later [Verlan] would have to be annihilated. He had accepted a position that had placed him as a traitor to the kingdom . . . It was an abomination in the sight of the Lord. [He'd be] done away with."

Ervil's remarks about Rulon Allred, she remembered, were generally the same. He said Allred "had been given many years to come forth to deliver his means and congregation. That he would be done away with."

A total of forty-three witnesses had been called by the state before resting its case Thursday, May 22.

* * *

The defense logged several motions at this point, and Judge Baldwin granted one. He said there was insufficient evidence of pecuniary gain and dismissed that as an element of charges.

Yocom was stunned. It left him only one capital aggravating circumstance to bring in a first-degree verdict, and he didn't think it would hold—that the "defendant and/or his accomplices did knowingly create a great risk of death to a person or persons other than the intended victim and the accomplices." Ervil had not been on the murder scene, and had ordered the followers to do it quietly, according to the testimony given. The jurors would never bring back a first-degree verdict, Yocom feared.

When he saw Judge Baldwin later at a local club, he complained, "You knocked the hell out of my case when you did that." After that comment, Judge Baldwin overruled nearly every objection Yocom lodged. The defense quickly picked up on this apparent judicial prejudice, and, according to one of the defense lawyers, made objections "just to see if he would sustain them." The judge did.

The wife who shared a fugitive life and was captured with Ervil in Mexico, Lorna Chynoweth, was the first of only four witnesses called for the defense. Originally eight had been listed, among them Victor Chynoweth. But Chynoweth, living then in Spokane, apparently told Hill he wanted nothing more to do with Ervil.

Lorna began a theme under examination by Hill that was built upon by her mother, Thelma. Many times when they were asked a question by the defense or the prosecution, they would begin the answer, "Well, Lloyd said . . ." For instance, Did Ervil have revelations? "Well, Lloyd had revelations," they'd say. At one point, Yocom angrily interrupted an answer and remarked: "I know you want to keep bringing up Lloyd but just answer the question." One courtroom observer described it as "bizarre. No matter what the question, they'd bring Lloyd up."

Lorna identified herself as one of LeBaron's twelve to fourteen wives and said, during the course of her testimony, that her husband didn't have revelations, couldn't control the Lambs of God and wasn't their prophet—surprising testimony considering LeBaron's own admission on tape from the Laredo jail that he was.

She said that Lloyd and Don Sullivan were the only ones who called meetings. At one spring 1977 meeting, among about ten women, Don "told us that perilous times were coming and before long blood was going to run down the streets of Salt Lake City." According to Lorna's testimony: "He told us that anything they told us no matter what, we was to do it . . . Don said Ervil LeBaron had nothing to do with [the military]. He told us he had a dream. His men [Ed and Jack Strothman] went to a funeral, went around it once, then went around it again, and then attacked it."

Not long after that, Lorna said, Lloyd called a meeting at which "he said he purposely didn't invite Tío [Ervil] because he wanted to say something privately. He said God had called him to be a mouthpiece and spokesman for him because Ervil wasn't qualified." She described Lloyd as emotional, colorful, dramatic and "very hypnotic."

Lorna recalled Lloyd once boasting "if he had enough dollars he could convert all of Jackson, Mississippi," in six months, then telling her "he knew that Verlan was his and he was just waiting for an opportunity to get him. He had a dream of a snake with Verlan's head on it and he heard a voice tell him to kill the snake."

Under cross-examination by Yocom, Lorna admitted an acquaintance with some of Ervil's writings but said he never claimed to be a prophet. "I think he has some inspiration," she offered, but "I've never heard of him having revelation," just "very good ideas." She said he took no money from the Lamb of God till.

In contrast, she portrayed Lloyd Sullivan as having followers, perpetrating paranoia about the Church of the Firstborn, claiming revelations, controlling all the money and being a religious leader. Yocom asked why she didn't tell her husband, Ervil, about Lloyd's criticisms of LeBaron and attempt to take over the church. She said she did, but Ervil "told me he knew Lloyd had a lot of faults and wanted to give him every chance."

Thelma Chynoweth, oozing confidence and a gurulike pacifism, was the next witness to testify about the innocuousness of the April 20 meeting and, in fact, of Ervil himself.

She repeated much of Lorna's testimony about Lloyd, adding that Ervil was so busy with the businesses that, in early 1977, the leader of the church was Lloyd Sullivan. She admitted that she knew Ervil had had some revelations, but added quickly that Lloyd did too.

The defense's last two witnesses appeared Friday—Bill Rios and Alex Chynoweth. Both couldn't remember what LeBaron said at the April 20 meeting. Both, speaking with Spanish accents, said Lloyd and Don Sullivan ordered everybody around in the group, and that Don was particularly hot-tempered.

The defense rested its case—leaving a very noticeable gap, Ervil LeBaron's testimony in his own defense. They had started rumors he would be called, and spectators had been anxiously awaiting the event—as well as jurors. Up until now, Ervil had been mute.

Yocom understood the decision not to put Ervil on the stand. "It was the main reason they were so stymied," he said. "They couldn't use Ervil. They couldn't possibly put him on the stand. He wouldn't have lied. He would have said, 'I'm the chosen one. I'm the guy.' "

Lubeck outlined the defense thinking as this: "We couldn't put Ervil on the stand for the same reason that was the main problem in the whole case. What does it open up? Where do you draw the line on what they can ask him? We could have put him on to hear his name and age, but the jury wouldn't have been interested in that. We could have put him on for a categorical denial—to say he wasn't in Evanston, for instance. But it could have opened up his whole life. It opened up all his doctrines.

We felt we couldn't do much of anything with [the prosecution] theory of the case, the amount of work they'd done on it—it all combined to make it devastating."

Four days passed before the trial was reconvened on Wednesday, May 28. Yocom offered his closing arguments, which seemed to have taken on a deeper significance from the time that had elapsed.

Yocom again touched on the high points of the prosecution's case, adding that it was elevated from a second-degree murder case to first degree because the lives of others were endangered during the Allred murder, and Ervil had created that risk. He rapidly progressed to LeBaron's belief he was God's instrument for exacting the death penalty against false prophets. "The death penalty, not as taught in the Old Testament, ladies and gentlemen," Yocom told the jury, "but as taught now by Ervil LeBaron. He taught it was he who would call on the judgments of God."

He wound up his hour-long argument with a series of questions. "Who had the power and authority to order others to kill? Who taught the killing of false prophets? Who claimed authority from God to determine false prophets and call for the death penalty? There's only one answer. You know it and I know it. Ervil M. LeBaron."

Hill's closing argument centered on the Sullivans once again, accusing them of being the masterminds of the murder and planned murder. They had made up the story about Ervil and other Lambs of God being involved to save their own necks. The logic of the prosecution's case—including the theory that the Allred murder was ordered so Verlan LeBaron could be killed at the funeral—defied comprehension. "An unbelievable proposition," Hill argued. "An absurd proposition."

Finally, borrowing heavily from the successful closing arguments in the trial of LeBaron's four followers, Hill heaped abuse on the chief prosecution witness. "Don Sullivan is not an honest man," Hill said. "Don Sullivan is a violent person. Don Sullivan's testimony is not worthy of credible belief. Don Sullivan is the most despicable person to testify in this courtroom."

When Yocom rose for his final rebuttal, he knew it was all or nothing. The final chance to convict a Lamb of God, this time the major culprit, for the Allred murder was now.

"Not once did John Hill stand before you and deny that Ervil LeBaron claimed to be the leader of the Church of the Lamb of God," Yocom pronounced. "There was only one leader on May 10, 1977. No one usurped that power from him." Nevertheless, Hill had pressed the Sullivan theme to the "point of ridiculousness," having Thelma and Lorna Chynoweth tell almost identical stories with strikingly similar details.

Yocom's voice was rising now, filled with passion. The defense had obviously decided, "We'll hang it on Lloyd, the dead man," Yocom said. He recalled the movie *Oh, God!*, in which the personage was dramatically called to the witness stand to testify. "I'd like to just turn to the door and call Lloyd Sullivan, and have him walk in," Yocom said, grandly gesturing toward the door, the eyes of the jury unconsciously following. "Unfortunately, I can't do that. I can't call a dead man to the stand."

He reminded them of Hill's words, that the murder plan, as related by the prosecution, was unbelievable. Yocom turned to point at LeBaron, seated quietly at the defense table. "He's unbelievable. He's got a mind that's unbelievable. The plan is unbelievable because the man is unbelievable. He's got a theory and a plot for the salvation of man that is unbelievable. He believes he talks to God. He believes he is God's prophet. If this case is unbelievable, it's because Ervil Morrel LeBaron is unbelievable!"

Yocom defended his witness, Don Sullivan, then Isaac: "Do you think we put those words in his mouth to testify against his own father? Impossible!" He then pulled his trump exhibit out of the hat—the curious document he had introduced by authenticating Arturo LeBaron's signature. It was a border-crossing paper, showing Ervil LeBaron had fled to Mexico on May 12, 1977. Yocom waved the paper around as proof of Ervil's guilt.* "Where did Ervil go [after the Allred murder]?" he asked the jury. "Into Mexico, into hiding and remained there years."

Finally, he made his last plea. "I think the state," he paused, "the men who made this case deserve a compliment for solving this crime, and the only compliment you can give them is a guilty verdict."

The jury retired to deliberate. It was Wednesday, May 28, 1980.

The jury could give a variety of possible verdicts, but could not legally find LeBaron guilty of all four counts. Either he was guilty of ordering Allred's murder or conspiracy; they could not find for both. The same was true with the Verlan LeBaron charges—either he was guilty of attempted murder or the conspiracy to attempt that murder. The jury could also decide that Ervil had committed the Allred murder as a second-degree, not a first-degree offense.

When the jury retired to its room, foreman Andrew Smith shortly called for a vote on the most serious count—that Ervil LeBaron "on or about the 10th day of May 1977 . . . did solicit, request, command,

---

*The introduction of this document had been a calculated risk. Yocom had been given the border-crossing paper by Mexican contacts, unofficially. Had he introduced it during the testimony phase for what he now claimed it was, the defense would have forced him to prove it was authentic. That would have required testimony from Mexican border guards, which Yocom could not obtain. Instead, he authenticated Arturo's signature earlier and claimed more than could be substantiated for it during his rebuttal, after which the defense had no opportunity to challenge it.

encourage or intentionally aid others to intentionally or knowingly cause the death of Rulon Clark Allred" in the first degree.

The vote stunned everyone: it was eleven to one for conviction.

The eleven had no hesitation about their vote. One of the elder jurors said, "I was completely satisfied that LeBaron was the leader of this group, that he was masterminding the things that they were doing. It was almost ridiculous trying to make us believe that he was just an old man who failed to interest people enough that they forgot what he said."

None of the jurors had any great sympathy for Don Sullivan; but believed him.

Most discounted the testimony of Lorna and Thelma Chynoweth. They used words like "rehearsed" or "unbelievable"; one of them, reacting more harshly, said: "They were lying through their teeth." Most of them were impressed by Isaac's testimony—"his sincerity and his beauty," as one of the female jurors put it. They thought him immensely brave to have stood up to his father. Some immediately pored over the LeBaron writings that had been introduced into evidence, and that swayed them quickly.

Since the jury conviction had to be unanimous, Smith called for another vote. After one more, the lone holdout identified himself, John Green [not his real name].

Green spent the next hour detailing his objections and listening to juror response. "What I did was took on eleven people at one time," Green remembers. "It was pretty difficult. They'd back off and then they'd come on again." Eight out of the twelve jurors had taken extensive notes; one was even a professional stenographer who taught shorthand, was a good friend of both the court reporter on the case and the judge, and naturally put her talent to use as a juror.

These were some of Green's qualms, as he recalls offering them in the jury room:

•"Let's face it," he acknowledged, "Ervil's got a few marbles loose. I don't disagree with that. But you have the right in this country to be as nutty as a fruitcake. Now, if somebody picks up the gauntlet and decides to act on it, that's not your fault. Okay?"

•He was convinced Don Sullivan "ran the scam. When it came right down to doing the actual pulling of the trigger, he got cold feet. He was great for playing the leader; he was great for flashing it around." He felt Sullivan did all the threatening, including the coercion of the girls.

•He accepted the defense line about convicting Lloyd Sullivan. "If Lloyd Sullivan was alive, and he'd of been in that courtroom, I'd send him to jail." In Green's mind, Lloyd was the instigator, Don was the doer and Ervil just picked up on the plan.

•He said there was no evidence from Evanston that "Ervil ever touched a weapon, ever fired a weapon, ever showed anybody how to fire a weapon, ever converted anything to automatic weaponry, ever scratched off a serial number. . . ." Green concluded that "you're coming down to one thing. He handed Don Sullivan a roll of cash." He told his fellow jurors they'd be convicting a man of first-degree murder "for handing over a roll of dough."

Green urged the jurors to reconsider. "If it'd been seven to five, I think I would have had it made. I would have had some of the argument taken off of me—some of the pressure."

As it was, he thought it was important for everybody "to realize, hey, we're talking the heavy heat here. We're not talking about two to five in the slammer and time off for good behavior. We're talking about the heat here. We're going to come right back here and decide this man's fate [death penalty or no]. I think everybody realized that. I hope, for their sake, that they did."

Green eventually gave in, by conceding a number of points. Primarily, he and other jurors thought the testimony of Jack Strothman was pivotal. "He was the man that convicted Ervil LeBaron in my eye because he had no family ties to this mess. He was an innocent human being. Yocom did a great job of qualifying Jack Strothman. He was just too slow to lie."

Generally, Green said he and others had been influenced by the fact that the defense witnesses "didn't even stop and think. I mean Sullivan took some time sitting there, and Strothman would sit there and give you a couple of 'duhs' before he'd answer. The man was trying to recollect; so was Isaac. They worked hard on the stand. But the [Chynoweth] women, holy cripes, I was wondering if they had shorthand on the back of their hands or something."

One thing disturbed all the jurors, which was discussed in the room: that four of those they felt participated in the murder had been acquitted. The jurors were not supposed to have knowledge of this fact, but they did. And with the identification by Richard Bunker of Rena Chynoweth during their trial, most felt, as one put it, "that we would have hung her right there in court."

The next phase of deliberation concentrated on whether the attempt to murder Verlan at the Allred funeral was an actual attempted murder or whether Ervil should be convicted only of conspiracy. Green came down on the side of the conspiracy, since the three-man hit team had never gotten out of the truck. Others supported him this time, and he finally won on this count.

The jury returned to the courtroom. They had been out a total of three hours, and Yocom was concerned. In a murder trial, short deliberations often mean a verdict of not guilty.

Foreman Smith read the verdict: guilty of the first-degree capital homicide of Rulon Allred and guilty of conspiring to commit the murder of Verlan LeBaron.

Ervil was expressionless; his wife Lorna rose and stood with tears in her eyes. Prosecutor Yocom and investigator Dick Forbes were ecstatic, hugging and patting each other before holding an impromptu press conference. LeBaron looked at them and smiled. When Dick met his brother, Paul Forbes, coming up the stairs to learn about the verdict shortly afterward, he leaped right on to his shoulders. "We were thrilled to death and couldn't stop shaking," Dick said.

Admittedly, there had been some losses. Ramona Marston was still at large and had never been brought to trial—though her husband, Dan Jordan, and his Denver lawyer had hinted as they watched the LeBaron trial that she might give herself up if Ervil were acquitted. Jordan himself had slipped away from Mexican justice thanks to the recalcitrant Conway LeBaron. And of course there were the four followers who had won not-guilty verdicts.

But all that seemed of little consequence now. They had convicted the man they had stalked for three years, the Patriarch, LeBaron. Now, he would either be executed or spend the rest of his life in prison. And with that, his Lambs of God would surely wither away and die.

Thursday, May 29, was the date set for hearing defense motions before the penalty phase of the trial, during which witnesses could testify to demonstrate "mitigating" or "aggravating" circumstances that would affect whether or not LeBaron was given the death penalty.

The defense offered several motions aimed at reducing or throwing out the first-degree verdict rendered by the jury. Hill and associate Metos argued that no corroborative evidence was introduced to show that LeBaron knew that someone other than Allred could be killed during the crime. They asked the court to stop the penalty phase and impose a life sentence or at least enter a judgment for murder in the second degree.

"That was a jury question," Yocom countered, "and it has been resolved. If the evidence wasn't there, then it shouldn't have gone to the jury."

In fact, the jury had considered the degree, and decided that the risk of death to others in the Allred waiting office had been great—and assumed Ervil would have known that too. The jurors had even discussed the specifics of the threat to Richard Bunker, the man who had briefly struggled with the two assailants.

One juror, with knowledge of weaponry, said, "If there had been a bullet left in that .25 automatic, Bunker would be a dead man today. When she raised that .25 automatic to his head, it didn't click. He didn't think she pulled the trigger, because an automatic, when it's empty, doesn't click. She converted to the .38 [after the scuffle] because she had only one intention in mind, and that was to blow Bunker's head off. And I am firm in my belief that that was first-degree murder right there."

Pressed on the specifics of Ervil's actual knowledge, one of the jurors responded: "My point is, I don't see how you could send anyone into a doctor's office who's practicing and not figure there's going to be someone there, if only his nurse. I've never been to a doctor's office yet that there weren't at least a couple people there in the office, plus the nurse and the doctor.''

Judge Baldwin dismissed the defense motions without prejudice, which meant they could be reconsidered until Hill offered a motion to have a new jury hear the penalty testimony. He cited a television interview Wednesday night, following the conviction, during which Firstborn Church leader Siegfried Widmar said on the air that LeBaron had ordered eight other murders.

Baldwin was advised of the interview out of hearing of spectators and reporters. When he returned, he launched a full-scale attack on the news media. He threatened to subpoena a tape of the TV news program and "haul the station manager in here by the scruff of his neck." Judge Baldwin called the news agencies who covered the LeBaron trial "scandalmongers who will do anything to sell advertising and get people to watch." He added:

"I have nothing but total contempt for those arrogant members of the media who have this misconception that they are the guardians of the public's rights but are really just scandalmongers. It is a small portion of the media, a small majority, who have no common sense, no public sense, no sense of discretion."

The courtroom was cleared.

The jurors had been instructed not to watch TV news accounts of the trial or read newspaper stories about it. But one was asked by her fourteen-year-old grandson if it was true that LeBaron ordered eight murders. Another juror had heard a radio report on Baldwin's comments while driving his van to work.

All the principals in the case met on Monday, June 2.

The jurors had four days to think about imposing the death penalty, depending on what additional evidence was presented.

Fear was no longer a factor. A few had been nervous; some neighbors had joked, "Hey, you're on his list now." One of them said, however, that he dropped his "concern about recriminations" toward the end of the trial.

Another, during the trial, had woken up in the middle of the night, after a weird dream "and had the hair stand up on the back of my neck like somebody was looking at me and you don't know where they're at but you know they're there." He got up then, about 3 A.M. and "walked around the bed in a cold sweat." He passed a gun cabinet in one room, but he didn't have the key. "I was sitting there thinking somebody was walking around my house," he said, before he remembered where a key was. With a loaded gun in hand, he searched the grounds—"walked clear around my place and inspected everything." The incident troubled him for a time in the courtroom, where he "had a feeling there were a lot of people out there eyeing me, checking me over," but he eventually dismissed his fears.

Most of the jurors later said they would have given LeBaron the death penalty, though they did not expect it would ever be carried out. The strong holdout, John Green, however, said "no way would [Ervil] have gotten the death penalty." Green opposed it, and "we'd still be there if they were trying to get it."

Actually, the defense attorneys had already decided to waive the jury and ask the judge to pass sentence. It was the only logical thing to do when a jury returns a first-degree murder verdict within three hours.

Judge Baldwin must have surmised that and, no doubt, also realized the position in which that placed him—deciding whether or not to give Ervil LeBaron the death penalty in a state that three years before had carried it out against Gary Gilmore.

Instead of deciding the issue on his own, Baldwin called in the jurors one by one to determine if they had heard the news reports linking LeBaron to eight other murders. Two jurors had learned of them by accident. Although they claimed that this would not affect their ruling on LeBaron's sentencing, the judge decided to dismiss the jury. This meant that, by law, he could then impose only a life sentence, which he did—adding a term of between five years and life in Utah State Prison for the conspiracy count.

Yocom was furious. Judge Baldwin had refused both a defense and prosecution motion to sequester the jury, at least between the verdict and the penalty hearing. This would have prevented his having to dismiss the jury, an incident laced with irony in that Ervil's most indefatigable pursuer, Siegfried Widmar, might very well have inadvertently saved him from the firing squad.

That morning, as required by law, Ervil had attended the questioning of the jurors by Judge Baldwin. He sat impassively as each of them was questioned, except for one woman juror. After she had answered Judge Baldwin's questions, she expressed some concern that a mistrial might be declared. Turning to Ervil, she said, "I expect to go to the Man Upstairs and be judged on what I did and said—my God is also Ervil LeBaron's God." Turning back to the judge, she commented that "nowhere in the world could you get a jury where half of them do not at least get on their knees every night and pray to God that they'll bring in a fair and honest verdict." At that, she saw the True Prophet smile.

EPILOGUE

During the year following his conviction, Ervil LeBaron languished impenitent in the maximum security wing of Utah State Prison, the appeal of his conviction pending.

He had mixed freely with the rest of the prison population, even condescending to work for a time as a plumber's aide. But then, according to authorities, he wrote an apocalyptic letter warning that another inmate would be killed for snitching on him, and that within a year, the prison walls, Jericho-like, would come tumbling down and all the inmates freed. So he was placed in solitary.

But this had not diminished his writing output. LeBaron, who had steadfastly refused all requests for interviews, still cranked out fire-and-brimstone tracts reaffirming himself as God's chosen one and threatening doom to those who did not recognize him as such.

In the harsh and nitty-gritty world of state prison, LeBaron was regarded as something of a lunatic. His celebrity did not translate to an ability to gain any converts, and since his incarceration prevented him from ministering to the needs of his own flock, LeBaron had been given to severe bouts of depression and mood swings. At low ebbs, he had refused to eat, bathe or otherwise take care of himself. "He just [sat] around and [looked] like an old man," said one person who saw him in such states.

Adding to LeBaron's woes, no doubt, was the fact that since his conviction, some of his key followers had deserted him. According to police, the four Lamb of God stalwarts charged in connection with the Allred murder—Eddie Marston, and Mark, Victor and Rena Chynoweth—all left the cult. Rena, once the apple of Ervil's eye, divorced him, and for a time considered marrying Marston.

Dan Jordan, once Ervil's doctrinal high priest and longtime right-hand man, also defected.

Though the former Lambs of God have consistently made themselves unavailable for interviews to explain the reasons for their actions, Utah investigators interpret the defections as a case of "finally seeing the light." Officials speculate that while Marston et al. were never convicted of any crime, they nevertheless spent considerable time either in jail or on the lam in furtherance of Ervil's gospel, and that continuing to dance to LeBaron's tune finally reached the point of diminishing returns—economically and spiritually.

Without Ervil personally on hand to perpetuate cultic tension and foster a we-they mentality of Lamb of God vs. the outside world, the process of breaking away must have seemed easier.

Just as it was LeBaron's hypnotic presence which created the tissues that bound, his absence could create an atmosphere conducive to weakening the totalitarian model around which the Church of the Lamb of God was constructed.

The more time the four lambs spent away from Ervil and with their attorneys and others, the more difficult it became for them to swallow the undiluted LeBaron gospel. Black-and-white absolutes began taking on shades of gray as the lambs' circle of contacts grew to persons outside the cult and it became increasingly possible to free-associate.

Even before the split, those that knew the Lambs of God thought they weren't as hard or single-minded as police made them out to be.

"Everyone in the church thought Ervil personally was a jerk," says John O'Connell, Rena's lawyer. "They objected to having to turn over all their money to him and, contrary to popular opinion, would often challenge this as a foolish business practice. As Victor Chynoweth said during the Allred trial: 'Ervil never understood the concept of working capital.' It was his ideas which held them all."

But with time and Ervil's capture, apparently even his ideas grew less compelling.

For his part, O'Connell made a great impression on Rena, not merely because he saved her life in the courtroom, but because he helped her to transcend the cult and become more self-reliant. He keeps in close contact with her, and, today reports that she is emerging from her shell and has taken an avid interest in photography—under the off-duty tutelage of a Houston homicide detective, no less.

Despite the signs of maturation, it may also have been that the lambs were simply getting out while the getting was good; that is, with Ervil locked up and presumably out of harm's way. Recent history has shown that the cult committed no crimes or exacted any revenge on traitors while Ervil was in jail.

But at least Dan Jordan and Mark Chynoweth seemed to be taking no chances. According to authorities, both have come to Salt Lake City inquiring about police protection after they received threatening LeBaron missives penned from prison.

Jordan and several wives are still in Denver, where Dan presides over his fledgling appliance repair business. Reached by phone, Dan still insists that he "would prefer not to give any statement at this time," but his attorney, Floyd Marks, reports that Jordan and family are "just trying to make an honest living and shed the [LeBaron] stigma."

One of Jordan's wives home in Denver is Ramona Marston, originally charged with being the second trigger-woman in the Allred slaying along with Rena Chynoweth. Having been on the run in Mexico for nearly three years, Ramona, after learning of Ervil's conviction, let it be known through her attorney, Marks, that she would consider giving herself up. The State of Utah, not hopeful of getting far with Ramona since her cohorts had been acquitted, agreed to a plea bargain: if Ramona turned herself in, she would be charged only with bail jumping. She agreed, surrendered in January of 1981, and was sentenced in May to two years' probation and a $1,000 fine.

For their part, Mark, Rena and Eddie are reportedly living in Houston, also still plying appliances. Victor, ever independent, is said to be in Seattle, selling and repairing used cars.

Dick Forbes says that LeBaron retains a hard-core dozen followers, scattered between Arizona and California, who would kill for him or otherwise do his bidding. The leader of this group is son Arturo LeBaron, to whom Ervil, according to prison writings police intercepted, has already passed on his mantle. At Ervil's death, Arturo becomes the One Mighty and Strong.

Thus, for Forbes, the work is never done. He worries that there is little he or society can do to prevent an Arturo from rising up with the help of Ervil's halo to infect his own bank of followers with his own brand of fringe delusion, and that the LeBaron threat, though currently dormant, could again rise up and begin playing itself out as a Biblical Western written in fear and in blood.

* * *

On August 16, 1981, the central conflict of the LeBaron saga was mysteriously resolved.

At 5:30 A.M., Ervil Morrel LeBaron was found dead in his Utah State Prison cell. The evidence indicated he had suffered a massive heart seizure.

Verlan LeBaron, whom Ervil tried to have murdered at least twice before, was killed two days later in an automobile accident outside Mexico City. Police said Verlan's car was struck head-on by another vehicle that had veered out of its lane.

Verlan, who was on his way home to Colonia LeBaron, had recently told friends he still feared Ervil's followers were stalking him. He only felt safe when on the move.